现代英文选评注

增订第二版

夏济安 著

北京联合出版公司
Beijing United Publishing Co.,Ltd.

出版说明

《现代英文选评注》是夏济安的名作。此书原为《学生英语文摘》杂志 Grammar Road and Rhetoric Street 专栏连载稿。所谓的选，是现代英语作家的佳作选篇；所谓的评，是对文章做的简要介绍和语言文字风格的评述；而所谓的注，则是对于文字意义、词句结构、语法细节、语言特征等的解析。这本书有非常强大的实用性和功能性，书稿问世以来，曾多次重印，海内外好评如潮。《现代英文选评注》是中国人高阶英语学习、写作进阶的必备读物，是大学和研究生英语学习的重要参考书。

然而从另一方面讲，这部书稿也存在一些问题。因为是连载稿，所以全书体例并不统一。它是教材，也可以被看做是"讲义"。当年的连载因为整理时间有限，夏济安没来及仔细校对，文稿中留下了一些错误。夏济安去世较早，这部书稿曾经由朱乃长和夏志清分别做过修订。朱乃长的修订非常少，夏志清的修订内容更少，很多明显瑕误都一仍其旧。这些错误，在以前的出版版本中，一直被简单因袭。瑕不能掩瑜，然而作为教材，勘校修改是有其必要性的。

本次出版的文稿修订工作，我们聘请 Dr. Stevens Powell 和陈雨博士共同主持。夏济安所使用的语法术语，跟现今标准说法有相当的歧异，作为教材来说，当然应该做出相应的调整统一。涉及英语高级语法的某些细节，由于人言人殊，夏济安的说法自有他的道理，修订过程中则尽量少做改动。有几个英文单词，英美原作者就拼写错误，校订过程中径改。有些错误解释，如 lap、mules、motar 等，已直接订正。有些解释不对或者不通的地方，比如 Two Buttes 的笑话，比如莎剧语言特征的段落，做了大幅度修改。还有些滞涩的语句，做了调整。

读者如果在修订版本中发现有问题，欢迎联系我们，我们将在再版时订正，争取让此书做到尽善尽美。

目 录

001	The Bear 熊	118	Rosie 露西姑娘
007	The Whistle 寒笛	123	The Treasure Game 觅宝
021	The Life and Work of Professor Roy Millen 米伦教授的生活与工作	140	At Gallipoli 大军出征
034	The Ballet Dancer 芭蕾舞者	145	The Duck 鸭
042	Herb Gathering 采药	149	A Special Occasion 两小
048	Two Mutes 两个哑巴	158	Bookshops in Paris 巴黎的书店
062	The Last Puritan 最后一个清教徒	163	A World of Glass 玻璃世界
069	The Great Fire of 1945 一九四五年大火记	169	A Hemingway Sample 海明威的写作技巧
082	The Jersey Heifer 泽西牛	174	Kant the Man 康德的日常生活
097	A Visit to the Grandfather's Grave 扫墓	184	In Dreams Begin Responsibilities 君子好逑
102	Natives Don't Cry 亨利小姐的信	198	A Mountain Adventure 登山遇险记

217	Father and Daughter 父与女	365	University Days 大学生活
222	Merry Christmas 圣诞快乐	374	British Bicycles in Spain 英国自行车在西班牙
229	D-Day 诺曼底登陆	379	The Reigning Royalty of Europe 欧洲之王室
237	A Student in Economics 勤工俭学生	385	A Professor in Retirement 退休教授
264	Prescott 史学家普雷斯科特	399	A Writer's Life 作家甘苦
281	Man and Woman 男与女	417	We Need Humor 我们需要幽默
295	A Pretty Girl 美丽的姑娘	423	Skeffington's Decision to Run for Re-election 市长决心竞选
301	Her Graduation Day 毕业的那一天	433	Moon Shell 月形螺壳
308	Emergency Landing 紧急着陆	443	Invite 邀舞
313	Romeo 情圣	451	Captain Carlsen 卡尔逊船长
337	Dialogues of A. N. Whitehead 怀特海对话录	455	Moscow, 1918 一九一八年的莫斯科
348	Michael and Mary 金船		

The Bear
熊

William Faulkner（1897—1962）

　　福克纳是一个难读的作家，《熊》又是一篇难读的中篇小说。福克纳的艰涩，同近代诗的艰涩是同一种性质：都是用不平常的词，再用词和词之间不平常的结构来表现一个对于作者有特殊意义的世界。福克纳所描写的范围很狭窄，通常只是美国南部密西西比州的一个角落，但是这也就是他所认识的整个人生。他的世界是污秽而充满罪恶的，但仍不失其壮丽和光怪陆离的诱惑性。他特别敏锐的感觉，和他对于这个世界强烈的爱好和憎恶，使他不得不创造一种特别的风格，作为他的工具。流利晓畅不是他的特点，他的作风是曲折的、沉郁的、粗犷的。他总是着力地描写，因此往往使人有浓得化不开之感。但是他又好细腻：他的粗野的句法里，载满了精细的观察和令人耳目一新的譬喻。福克纳是值得仔细研究的。下面所选的几句，在原文还不到一段。这几句所讲的，是人们如何地"谈熊色变"，拿这只怪物没有办法。这几句是比较笼统的描写，并不包含强烈的感觉上的反应，福克纳的长处还不能充分表现，但是读者从这里已经可以觉得一种可怕的野性的力量了。本篇选自《福克纳选集》(*The Portable Faulkner*)。

[1]

　　He realized later that it had begun long before that. It had already begun on that day when he first wrote his age in two ciphers and his cousin McCaslin brought him for the first time to the camp, the big woods, to earn for himself from the wilderness the name and state of hunter provided he in his turn were humble and enduring enough.

[注]

He 是小说的主角 Isaac McCaslin，整篇小说是从他的视角来写的，熊的可怕只是从这个少年的所闻所见里表现出来。

it：猎熊这件事情。**before that**：that 指那天早晨。当地的人每年冬天要去猎这一头熊，小说开始是 Isaac 十六岁时十二月的一个早晨。以下是倒叙以前的事。

on that day when he first wrote his age in two ciphers：他刚满十岁的时候。**two ciphers** 意为"两位数"，一百以上就是 in three ciphers 了。他满了十岁人家才让他去参加猎熊大会，但是事实上，大熊在这孩子出世以前就已经猖獗。when 所引起的从句有两个，中间由 and 连接。

his cousin：照小说上看来，这个人（McCaslin Edmonds）年纪虽然比 Isaac 大，辈分却比 Isaac 小，大约是表侄之类，反正英文里，凡是远亲都可以算是 cousin 的。

woods 是 camp 的同位语。他的表侄把他带到猎人的营帐里去，带到大森林里去。

earn 的宾语是 name and state。"好让他（infinitive phrase used as an adverb）替他自己从这原野里挣来一个猎人的名声（name）和地位（state）"。从小去实习，大了可以成为一个猎人。

provided 是连词 = if。他假如是相当地"虚心"（humble）和肯吃苦（enduring），那么他也可以成为一个猎人。这本来是他表侄的打算。**were** 表示 subjunctive mood，他的表侄还不知道这个孩子是不是虚心，肯不肯吃苦。

in his turn：别的猎人，都是从小被大人带到森林里去实习，虚心吃苦学出来的。现在"轮到"这位 Isaac 了。

[2]

He had already inherited then, without ever having seen it, the big old bear with one trap-ruined foot that in an area almost a hundred miles square had earned for himself a name, a definite designation like a living man — the long legend of corn-cribs broken down and rifled, of shoats and grown pigs and even calves carried bodily into the woods and devoured, and traps and deadfalls overthrown and dogs mangled and slain, and shotgun and even rifle shots delivered at point-blank range with no more effect than so many peas blown through a tube by a child — a corridor of wreckage and destruction beginning back before the boy was born, through which sped, not fast but rather with the ruthless and irresistible deliberation of a locomotive, the shaggy tremendous shape.

【注】

句子很长，但是本篇里还有一句长达一千六百词，比这一句要长十倍。那种长达一千六百词的、创纪录的句子，是要从感觉印象和回忆所交织的心理状态里反映出几十年的事情，那是不容易分析的。这里的一句实在并不难，很明显的可分成三节，节和节之间，有一破折号（dash）分隔开来（或联系起来）。

第一节：then 还是讲他十岁的时候；那时候他虽然从来没有（without ever having）看见过这头熊，却早已听惯了关于这头熊的事。中文的代词总放在它所代的名词的后面，但是在英文里，代词可以先见，名词可以后见，如这里的 it 和 bear。

inherited 是及物动词，它的宾语是 bear。动词和它的宾语之间，不管插多少 phrases 或 clauses，读者应该要注意的还是把它们的关系找出来。

inherited 原意是"继承"，但是这里这个解释要稍加更动，才安得上去。关于这头熊的事，已经成为一种传说（legend：此词见于第二节）。传说是世代相传的，成人们传给小孩，小孩子好像继承祖业似地把这种传说好好保存。这里假如不说 had inherited，改用较普通的 had come to know of，那么就显不出这件事的严重性了。

trap：捕兽机关。trap 同 ruined 这两个词这样一连接，可以省很多词：这头熊的一只脚是曾经给机关压伤的（从此它成了跛脚，很容易辨别它的足迹）。

that 是关系代词(代 bear)，引起一个 adjective clause。在这个从句里 that 是主语，had earned 是动词，name 是宾语。

designation 和 name 是同位语，意思也是一样的，不过第二个词用以加强第一个词。山林里的野兽同猫和狗不同，人们不认识它们，不会给它们起名字的。但是这头熊却已经有了一个"固定的名称"(definite designation)，同一个人一样。这头熊的名字叫 Old Ben。

前面讲这个孩子，刚刚用过 to earn for himself，这里讲这头熊，又来了 had earned for himself，这种重复是作者故意的。当然作者要换几个词，未尝不可，但他故意让这几个平凡的词重复一次，衬托出下面的精彩文章。

第二节：legend 是"传说"，同本句 inherited 的宾语 bear 同位。（但我们也可以说：The bear had become a legend.）

legend 下面是大熊历年的所作所为，都是用"of + 名词 + 过去分词"的形式构成的。可以下表示之：

	名　词	过去分词
①	corn-cribs（玉米仓）	broken down（被撞毁），rifled（被搜劫）
②	shoats（小猪），grown pigs（大猪），calves（小牛）	carried（被衔走），devoured（被吞吃）bodily（全身拖走，不是衔去一条腿就够了）
③	traps, deadfalls（千斤闸之类的机关）	overthrown（被推翻）
④	dogs（猎狗）	mangled（被打得遍体鳞伤），slain（被杀）
⑤	shotgun（shots）（鸟枪弹），rifle shots（步枪弹）	delivered（被发射）

最后一项的意思："在直接瞄准（point-blank）的距离（range）里所发出的这些枪弹，效果（effect）同小孩子从管子里吹出来的豆打在它身上一样。"大熊不为枪弹所伤。

第三节：corridor 和上节 legend 同位，原意是"走廊"，这里约相当于 career（生命的过程）。这许多年来大熊破坏了很多的东西（此处 wreckage 和 destruction 的意义可不分）。这种过程是在这小孩出世以前就开始的。

但是作者不要读者想象一个抽象的"过程"，他要读者想象一个具体的"走廊"。而且这走廊又并不存在于空间里，而是存在于时间里；就是说走廊并不从某个地方连到另一个地方，而是从某一年连到另一年的。这许多年连成一个走廊，在里面闯过了这一头大熊。读者假如能体会到这一层意思，已经尝到一些近代诗的滋味了。

corridor 有一个以 through which 开头的 adjective clause 来形容它。这个从句的主语 shape 放在最后，动词是 sped（speed "急行"的过去式）。

那个急行的东西，当然就是那头熊，但是作者偏偏说是"毛茸茸的巨大的形体"（shaggy tremendous shape）。走得太快了，看不清楚，只好说是某种形状的形体了。

但是作者又不承认这头熊是走得快的（not fast），他说它走得像火车头（locomotive），火车头不是很快吗？作者偏偏不注意它的"快"，而要注意火车头的"不顾一切，往前直进"（**ruthless**：无动于衷的；**irresistible**：不可抵抗的）。他用火车头比喻熊，可是又假定火车头是活的，火车头是"蓄意"要前进的（**deliberation**：经过考虑后的行动）。这样一比，熊的走路姿态我们可以想象得出来了。但是作者并不说熊在森林里是这样走的，而说它是在"时间"里走路——这许多年它是这样闯过去的。

[3]

It ran in his knowledge before he ever saw it. It loomed and towered in his dreams before he even saw the unaxed woods where it left its crooked print, shaggy, tremendous, red-eyed, not malevolent but just big, too big for the dogs which tried to bay it, for the horses which tried to ride it down, for the men and the bullets they fired into it; too big for the very country which was its constricting scope.

[注]

大熊不但在时间里行走，也在我们小说的主人公的思想里占着很重要的地位。它在他的脑筋里（knowledge 姑且译成"脑筋"吧）奔跑。

before he ever saw it 使我们想起上一句里的 without ever having seen it。这好像是歌词里的反复句（refrain），作者有时是模仿音乐技巧的。前面的 to earn for himself 和 had earned for himself，再前面的 it had begun 和 it had already begun 都有同样的作用。

loomed：浮现着。大抵指模糊的可是大而可怕的东西。**towered** 的意义在这里同 loomed 差不多，但是这个词有两层特殊意义：一，像塔一样高；二，所指的东西比较具体。

unaxed：未经斧斫的。森林还没有经过砍伐。

print：脚印。**crooked**：歪曲的，因为大熊的一只脚是受伤的。where clause 的主语 it 有五个形容词形容它。五个之中，前两个 shaggy 和 tremendous 在上一句已经见过，三个是新添的：red-eyed，not malevolent（并没有恶意，并不存心害人），big（只是"大"而已）。

下面跟着几个平行的 too big for ... 的 phrase。

（1）对于那些想阻挡它的猎狗，它是太大了。bay 的意思不单是 bark at，也有 bring it to bay（使陷入困境）之意。

（2）ride it down：赶上它（指骑马的人）。

（3）对于人和他们所放射的枪弹，它也太大了。

（4）对于这个区域(country)，它也太大了。constricting：限制它的。scope：范围。very 当 adjective 用，指"就是"这一个区域。

四层意思，一层比一层紧，在修辞学称为 climax（渐进法）。最后说出那个地方根本容纳不了它。前面讲 legend 的地方，也是用的渐进法。

The Whistle

寒笛

Eudora Welty (1909—2001)

本文是尤多拉·韦尔蒂所著短篇小说集《绿幕》(*A Curtain of Green*) 里的一篇。韦尔蒂女士是美国南部密西西比州人,少年时即开始写作。她的短篇小说剪裁经济,勾画生动,笔触轻灵,含意丰富,堪入世界名作之列。

[1]

Night fell. The darkness was thin, like some sleazy dress that has been worn and worn for many winters and always lets the cold through to the bones. Then the moon rose. A farm lay quite visible, like a white stone in water, among the stretches of deep woods in their colorless dead leaf. By a closer and more searching eye than the moon's, everything belonging to the Mortons' might have been seen — even to the tiny tomato plants in their neat rows closest to the house, gray and featherlike, appalling in their exposed fragility. The moonlight covered everything, and lay upon the darkest shape of all, the farmhouse where the lamp had just been blown out.

[注]

sleazy:稀薄的。将黑夜比作一件不能御寒的敝衣。lets 的主语是关系代词 that, the cold 是它的宾语。through 是副词,作用和 pass through 相同,"让它穿过",

to 是介词。

visible（清楚可辨）是 complement，形容主语 farm（田庄）。田庄在月色之中，犹如水中白石，这样比说"月色如水"要高明一筹。

stretch 原意是一长条，stretches 并不是几条，而是绵延不断的一块或一片，一片深林。**leaf** 在这里是 collective noun，即等于 leaves。**colorless**：黑、白、灰，皆非彩色。

the Mortons' 在文法上称为 absolute genitive，把后面应该跟的名词 house（莫顿夫妇的家）省掉了。这一句是被动语态，又是虚拟式。我们不知道有没有一只眼睛，可以比月亮看得更仔细，更能洞察一切，假如有的话，莫顿家每一样东西都可"被"（即句首之 By）它看见了。这只眼睛应该是小说家的眼睛。

然而作者并没有列举她家里的东西，在横线之后只举了一件东西：番茄田。替番茄防冻是本篇的主题，别的东西自可以不提，写短篇小说不得不注意描写上的经济。

even to 的 to = as far as：每样东西都可以看见，小小的番茄秧，也可以看见。后面跟着几个形容 tomato plants 的词。**featherlike**：像羽毛似的,指番茄的茎叶而言。**fragility**：脆弱。**exposed**：暴露(在寒夜中)的,番茄这样暴露着,使人惊心(appalling)。the farmhouse 是 the shape 的同位语。

[2]

Inside, Jason and Sara Morton were lying between the quilts of a pallet which had been made up close to the fireplace. A fire still fluttered in the grate, making a drowsy sound now and then, and its exhausted light beat up and down the wall, across the rafters, and over the dark pallet where the old people lay, like a bird trying to find its way out of the room.

[注]

pallet：稻草所铺成的床，铺（made up）在火炉附近（close）。

grate：火炉里的铁格子。**drowsy**：催眠的。**exhausted**：无力的。把火炉里的光比作一只寻出路的鸟，可称妙绝。动词用 beat 也妙，譬喻还没有点明以前，单凭这个动词，已经显出有一样东西在东碰西撞了。**fluttered**：跳动，可以用于火，也可以用于鸟。**rafters**：屋椽。

[3]

The long-spaced, tired breathing of Jason was the only noise besides the flutter of the fire. He lay under the quilt in a long shape like a bean, turned on his side to face the door. His lips opened in the dark, and in and out he breathed, in and out, slowly and with a rise and fall, over and over, like a conversation or a tale — a question and a sigh.

[注]

long-spaced：两声鼾声之间停顿得很长。**bean**：以豆荚中的豆子比喻被子下睡着的人。**turn on his side**：侧着身。turned 是过去分词。

in and out he breathed = he breathed in and out。**rise and fall**：起伏。最后一句的节奏，也模仿鼾声的起伏。

[4]

Sara lay on her back with her mouth agape, silent, but not asleep. She was staring at the dark and indistinguishable places among the rafters. Her eyes seemed opened too wide, the lids strained and limp, like openings which have been stretched shapeless and made of no more use. Once a hissing yellow flame stood erect in the old log, and her small face and pale hair, and one hand holding to the edge of the cover, were illuminated for a moment, with shadows bright blue. Then she pulled the quilt clear over her head.

[注]

lay on her back：仰天而卧。**agape**：张着（嘴）。**indistinguishable**：分辨不清楚的。**the lids strained and limp** 是 nominative absolute phrase，"眼皮是绷紧的又是软软的（limp）"。她的眼睛就"像两个窟窿，张大得已经不成形状，而且给弄得不再有什么用处了"。在"which" clause 里，有两个动词 have been stretched 和（have been）made；shapeless 和 of no more use 都形容主语 which。

第四句又是描写火光：一下子她的脸、头发和捏住被单边缘的一只手都给照亮了。火是嘶嘶作响（hissing）的黄色火焰，笔直地（erect）立在（炉子里的）陈旧的木柴（log）上。

hold 作不及物动词用，有 cling（紧附）的意义，所以 holding to 比 holding（及

物动词）可能捏得更紧。末一句的 clear 是副词，解作 completely，把被单拉上，把头全盖没了。

[5]

Every night they lay trembling with cold, but no more communicative in their misery than a pair of window shutters beaten by a storm. Sometimes many days, weeks went by without words. They were not really old — they were only fifty; still, their lives were filled with tiredness, with a great lack of necessity to speak, with poverty which may have bound them like a disaster too great for discussion but left them still separated and undesirous of sympathy. Perhaps, years ago, the long habit of silence may have been started in anger or passion. Who could tell now?

[注]

communicative：喜与人交谈的，形容主语 they。受暴风雨打击的两扇百叶窗，即使有个别的反应，也不会交谈。这一对老夫妇生活困苦，而且并不交谈，两个活人的话并不比两扇窗的话更多一些（no more than）。**went by** = passed。

他们的生命充满了三件东西：第一是"疲倦"；第二是"没有说话的需要"（**filled with a lack**：充满了一种缺乏——好像是不通的；这样把两个意义相反的词连在一起，修辞学上称为"矛盾修饰法"oxymoron，中文也有这种说法，例如"公开的秘密"）；第三是"贫穷"。

poverty 后跟着一个 adjective clause。在这个从句里，作者就她写作的时候（故用现在时的助动词 may），去猜想当时的情形（故用完成时不定式 have bound 和 have left）。贫穷把他们老夫妻俩联系（bound 是 bind 的过去分词）在一起，可能如同一个灾祸一样（同受灾者命运相同）；灾祸太大了，用不着再去讨论它。但是贫穷使得他们俩仍旧是彼此分离的，而且是不希望别人来同情的。(separate 和 undesirous 两个形容词都是 objective complements。)

末一句，作者猜想他们什么时候开始互相不交谈的。这个沉默的习惯可能很多年（years 前面不必加 many 也可表示很多年）前就开始了。怎样开始的呢？可能有一次在生气的时候，两人不说话，以后就一直不说话了（**passion** = violent anger）。但是现在谁知道呢？

[6]

She was so tired of cold! That was all it could do any more — make her tired. Year after year, she felt sure that she would die before the cold was over. Now, according to the Almanac, it was spring … But year after year it was always the same. The plants would be set out in their frames, transplanted always too soon, and there was a freeze … When was the last time they had grown tall and full, that the cold had held off and there was a crop?

[注]

第二句的 it 代 the cold。make 是省去了 to 的不定式。

Almanac：历书。虽然交了春，天还是很冷。交了春，番茄苗要从苗圃里移植到田里去。但是年年总是如此，移植（transplant）得太早了，一夜春寒，可能把番茄全冻死，助动词用 would 表示过去屡次发生的事。**set out** = planted（此解根据 Thorndike-Barnhart: *Comprehensive Desk Dictionary*）。**frames**：番茄太重，番茄枝支持不起，需搭架子来扶助。

年年种的番茄，都在春天冻死，她已记不起哪一年的番茄是种活的。末一句是 Sara 自己问自己，上一回是什么时候，番茄苗（they）长得又高，结得又满；寒冷不来侵犯（**hold off** = keep at a distance）而有收获呢？

[7]

Like a vain dream, Sara began to have thoughts of the spring and summer. At first she thought only simply, of the colors of green and red, the smell of the sun on the ground, the touch of leaves and warm ripening tomatoes. Then, all hidden as she was under the quilt, she began to imagine and remember the town of Dexter in the shipping season. There is in her mind, dusty little Dexter became a theatre of almost legendary festivity, a place of pleasure. On every road leading in, smiling farmers were bringing in wagonloads of the most beautiful tomatoes. The packing sheds at Dexter Station were all decorated — no, it was simply that the May sun was shining. Mr. Perkins, the tall, gesturing figure, stood in the very centre of everything, buying, directing, waving yellow papers that must be telegrams, shouting with great impatience. And it was he, after all, that owned their farm now. Train after train of empty freight cars stretched away, waiting and then being filled. Was it possible to have saved out of the threat of the cold so many tomatoes in the world?

[注]

这一段是回忆五月间收购番茄时的盛况（就是番茄有收成的那一年），运用视觉（colors）、嗅觉（smell）、触觉（touch）的描写，正同上文凄凉寒夜作一对照。

all hidden as she was under the quilt = though she was all hidden under the quilt。

Dexter 在密苏里州。**shipping season**：装运的季节。注意，shipping 是"装运"，水路旱路均可，这里是指装火车。

theatre：场合。**legendary festivity**：如传说般的盛大庆祝。

leading in：通到 Dexter 城去的。a wagonload 是装满一辆马车那么多，这里用的是复数。**bring in** 的 in 是副词。

packing：（给番茄）装箱或装篓子。**sheds**：专作此用的帐篷。**decorated**：装饰起来。但是作者（或者可以说是 Sara）又修正自己的话：并没有装饰，只是阳光照耀得灿烂夺目而已。

下面接着描写 Mr. Perkins：一个高大而装腔作势的人（**figure**：人的形状，Sara 所记得的是这个人的形状）；**directing**：在指挥别人；**waving yellow papers that must be telegrams**：手里拿着一叠黄纸挥舞。这叠黄纸，据 Sara 猜想起来，一定是电报。四个现在分词 buying, directing, waving 和 shouting（叫喊），都是形容主语 Mr. Perkins (with great impatience：很不耐烦的)。

after all = all things considered：总而言之。

freight cars：货车。**stretched away**：长长地延伸出去。

末一句 Sara 还是很奇怪：怎么可能从寒冷的威胁下救出这许多番茄来？ saved 的宾语是 tomatoes。

[8]

Sara, weightless under the quilt, could think of the celebrations of Dexter and see the vision of ripe tomatoes only in brief snatches, like the flare-up of the little fire. The rest of the time she thought only of cold, of cold going on before and after. She could not help but feel the chill of the here and now, which was not to think at all but was for her only a trembling in the dark.

[注]

weightless：觉得自己很轻（因此更冷）。**vision**：景象。**in brief snatches** 短短的片刻之中。**flare-up**：突然发光。这一个譬喻，把过去同现在（或者说，把回忆同当前的感觉）联结了起来。

could not help but feel：不能不感觉到。**the here and now**：此地此时。这种寒冷对于她不是头脑里的思想（to think），而是黑暗中的一阵战栗（trembling）。

[9]

She coughed patiently and turned her head to one side. She peered over the quilt just a little and saw that the fire had at last gone out. There was left only a hulk of red log, a still, red, bent shape, like one of Jason's socks thrown down to be darned somehow. With only this to comfort her, Sara closed her eyes and fell asleep.

[注]

peered：窥视。**at last**：最后总算灭了——Sara 当然早就预期到炉火会熄灭。

a hulk of red log：木柴烧红成为炭。log 这个词上文已经见过，我们可以猜想，炉子里就只有这么一块柴。这块柴烧完了，火也灭了。**hulk**：原意是废船的空壳子。**shape** 是 hulk 的同位语。那块木柴成了一个静止的、红色的、弯曲的形体，就像她丈夫的一只袜子（sock），掷给她叫她织补（darn）的。**somehow**：用某种方式（随便她怎样织补）。

从火炉里的余烬联想到家政。Sara 心平气和，心理描写至此可以告一段落，Sara 也入睡了。

[10]

Every hour it was getting colder and colder. The moon, intense and white as the snow that does not fall here, drew higher in the sky, in the long night, and more distant from the earth. The farm looked as tiny and still as a seashell, with the little knob of a house surrounded by its curved furrows of tomato plants. Cold like a white pressing hand reached down and lay over the shell.

[注]

getting（系动词）= becoming。

intense：强烈的。"月色皎洁如雪",但是那个地方是从来不下雪的。全篇叙事均用过去时,此处忽然出现现在时 does not fall,这是表示常理,并不限于故事发生的那一段时间里。

drew（不及物动词）= moved。后随 higher 与 distant 两个 subjective complements,形容主语 moon。

still（形容词）：静止的。**seashell**：贝壳。请参阅本文第一段把田庄比作水中白石的描写。**the little knob of a house**：房子看上去就是圆圆的一小块。of 在这里的用法是很特别的,这种用法很像 appositive genitive,但这里 of 前后两名词的关系不是"相等",而是"相像"。所谓 appositive genitive 的例子,如 the city of Rome (Rome is the city), the habit of smoking (smoking is the habit);但是这个 phrase 的意思是:The house seemed like a little knob。同样的用法如 an angel of a woman（天使般的女人）, a mountain of a man（魁伟如山的人）。**furrow**：畦,即犁在田中所挖成之浅沟。

末句之 cold 是名词,为全句主语。**pressing hand**：用力按的手。**reached**：伸。**reached down**：往下伸。

[11]

In Dexter there is a great whistle which is blown when a freeze threatens. It is known everywhere as Mr. Perkins' whistle. Now it sounded out in the clear night, blast after blast. Over the countryside lights appeared in the windows of the farms. Men and women ran out into the fields and covered up their plants with whatever they had, while Mr. Perkins' whistle blew and blew.

[注]

题意至本段才点明。whistle 指工厂、火车、轮船上所用之汽笛,这里的汽笛是作"防冻警报"之用。**blown**：汽笛呜呜作响。**threatens**：来袭。

Mr. Perkins 上文已介绍,是番茄田的主人。首两句用现在时,表示这是每年经常之事。

blast：一阵汽笛声响。**lights appeared ...**：听到汽笛声，农民纷纷起床为番茄防冻。屋内种种忙乱，小说家让我们看见的，只是窗上露出光来而已，描写何等经济。

whatever they had：有什么（他们就用什么盖上去），包括衣服被褥等。

[12]

Sara felt herself waking. She knew that Mr. Perkins' whistle was blowing, what it meant — and that it now remained for her to get Jason and go out to the field. A soft laxity, an illusion of warmth, flowed stubbornly down her body, and for a few moments she continued to lie still.

[注]

waking：将醒未醒。她觉得自己在醒过来，又尚未全醒。神智在瘩寐之间，最难描写，作者本段着墨不多，而慵倦疏懒之状，已跃然纸上。

第二句 knew 的宾语是 that ..., what ..., that ... 三个 noun clauses。

a soft laxity（懒洋洋的感觉），**an illusion of warmth**（钻在被窝中睡，似乎温暖，其实并不真温暖）：这种感觉都是朦胧恍惚，若有若无。动词 flowed（如水之流，贯注全身）显得不用力量，顺应自然；可是副词 stubbornly 之意为坚决地、用力地。懒洋洋的感觉虽懒虽软，却真有力量叫人起不了床，stubbornly 一词安得妙。

[13]

Then she was sitting up and seizing her husband by the shoulders, without saying a word, rocking him back and forth. It took all her strength to wake him. He coughed, his roaring was over, and he sat up. He said nothing either, and they both sat with bent heads and listened for the whistle. After a silence it blew again, a long, rising blast.

[注]

without saying a word：上文已说过，老夫妻俩是很少交谈的，此处再提一句。

rock（动词）：摇。**roaring**：鼾声。**listened for ...**：谛听，而声音尚未来。

rising：声音由低升高。

[14]

Promptly Sara and Jason got out of bed. They were both fully dressed, because of the cold, and only needed to put on their shoes. Jason lighted the lantern, and Sara gathered the bedclothes over her arm and followed him out.

[注]

they were both fully dressed：这句话的 predicate 并不表示一个动作，只是一种状态：他们是穿好衣服的（和衣而卧）。

over her arm：挽在臂上。**bedclothes**：被褥，包括枕头。

[15]

Everything was white, and everything looked vast and extensive to them as they walked over to the frozen field. Stooping over the little plants, Jason and Sara touched them and touched the earth. For their own knowledge, by their hands, they found everything to be true — the cold, the rightness of the warning, the need to act. Over the sticks set in among the plants they laid the quilts one by one, spreading them with a slow ingenuity. Jason took off his coat and laid it over the small tender plants by the side of the house. Then he glanced at Sara, and she reached down and pulled her dress off over her head. Her hair fell down out of its pins, and she began at once to tremble violently. The skirt was luckily long and full, and all the rest of the plants were covered by it.

[注]

stooping：俯身。**For their own knowledge** = for all they knew，据他们所知。for = regarding 或 so far as concerns，意思是"就……而言"（据《简明牛津词典》）。破折号后三个名词，都是 everything 的同位语，found 的宾语。"他们发现这些都是真的：冷是真的，发警报真有理由，他们也真该行动。"警报的"正当性"(rightness) 和行动的需要（need）都是真的，抽象名词在中国语法习惯里用得较少。中文常用形容词或动词的地方，英文可以用抽象名词来表达，这是学英文的人应该注意的。

set 是过去分词。**over the sticks** 形容 laid。他们把被单一层一层地铺在插在番茄秧间的小竿上。**ingenuity**：灵巧。

Jason 把自己的外套（可能是大衣）脱下了，铺在番茄上，再对 Sara 一望（glance），这一望使得 Sara 也非脱不可。她的女式衣服（dress），像运动背心一样，穿上要从头上套进去，脱下也得要过头。脱衣服的时候，把发针（pins）弄松了，头发披了下来。

末句 luckily 一词用得最为沉痛。上面刚说到：衣服脱掉，冷得发抖；这里接着说，亏得（或幸喜）衣服的下摆（skirt）长而肥大，把没有盖到的番茄秧统统盖上了。真是 luckily 吗？这里用这样一个反语（irony），胜过许多慷慨激昂的牢骚。

[16]

Then Sara and Jason stood for a moment and stared almost idly at the field and up at the sky.

There was no wind. There was only the intense whiteness of moonlight. Why did this calm cold sink into them like the teeth of a trap? They bent their shoulders and walked silently back into the house.

The room was not much warmer. They had forgotten to shut the door behind them when the whistle was blowing so hard. They sat down to wait for morning.

[注]

teeth of a trap：捕鼠（兽）机的刀齿。

had forgotten：刚才他们出去抢救番茄的时候，忘了关门了，寒气进了屋，屋里一样地冷。

[17]

Then Jason did a rare, strange thing. There long before morning he poured kerosene over some kindling and struck a light to it. Squatting, they got near it, quite gradually they drew together, and sat motionless until it all burned down. Still Sara did not move. Then Jason, in his underwear and long blue trousers, went out and brought in another load, and the big cherry log which of course was meant to be saved for the very last of winter.

[注]

这时候这对老夫妻的情形是，火炉里的火灭了（见前文），被褥衣服都给番茄秧盖上了，自己身上反而没有盖的了，天还不亮，屋子里同外面一样冷，该怎么办呢？

kerosene：煤油。**kindling**：引火柴。**squatting**：蹲着。

underwear：内衣。**another load**：又是一堆（小木片，引火柴）。**cherry log**：樱桃树木柴。**saved**：节省；"这是预备省下来，度过整个冬天的"。**last** = end。

[18]

The extravagant warmth of the room had sent some kind of agitation over Sara, like her memories of Dexter in the shipping season. She sat huddled in a long brown cotton petticoat, holding onto the string which went around the waist. Her mouse-colored hair, paler at the temples, was hanging loose down to her shoulders, like a child's unbound for a party. She held her knees against her numb, pendulant breasts and stared into the fire, her eyes widening.

[注]

把最后一块大木柴烧掉了，该怎么办呢？作者所描写的这对老夫妇，差不多是没有思考能力的。他们像动物一样，只有感觉和简单的反应。对于这种可怜的人来说，冷应该更加可怕。

agitation：（心理上的）激动。注意：这里的 sent 的意义和平常不同。**her memories …**：请参阅上文。

huddled：蜷缩，过去分词，形容主语。**petticoat**：衬裙，不连上身的。holding，现在分词，仍是形容主语。**onto** = on to，手捏牢这根绕腰而过的带子（string）。

temples：太阳穴。**a child's** = a child's hair。**party**：宴会。小（女）孩子参加宴会时，有时把头发解松了，披在肩上，算是一种打扮。

numb：麻木的。**pendulant**：下垂的。

[19]

At last every bit of the wood was gone. Now the cherry log was burned to ashes.

And all of a sudden Jason was on his feet again. Of all things, he was bringing the split-bottomed chair over to the hearth. He knocked it to pieces … It burned well and brightly. Sara never said a word. She did not move.

Then the kitchen table. To think that a solid, steady four-legged table like that, that had stood thirty years in one place, should be consumed in such a little while! Sara stared almost greedily at the waving flames.

[注]

on his feet：站起来。**of all things**：有"什么都不搬，偏把椅子搬来"之意。**bottom**：椅子之座位部。**split**：裂开的。**over**（副词）：解作"从那边搬来"之意。

to think = It is hard to think。下面的 noun clause 的动词 should be consumed 是虚拟式："竟然会这样快就烧掉！"

a table like that 之 that 是指示代词，"像那样一张桌子"。第二个 that 是关系代词，引起一个 adjective clause，也是形容 table。

greedily：贪婪地，想占有这个火。用中文说是"想把这个火吃下去"。

[20]

Then when that was over, Jason and Sara sat in darkness where their bed had been, and it was colder than ever. The fire the kitchen table had made seemed wonderful to them. ... But Sara trembled, again pressing her hard knees against her breast. All at once, without turning her head, she spoke.

[注]

that was over：那张厨房桌子也烧完了。**where their bed had been**：一度是他们铺床的地方。他们的床是铺在火炉旁的地上的，现在被褥已经都搬了出去盖番茄秧了，床已不再存在。

the kitchen table had made：adjective clause 形容 fire，关系代词省略。had made 的时态，也是表示"不再存在"。

[21]

"Jason ..."

A silence. But only for a moment.

"Listen," said her husband's uncertain voice.

They held very still, as before, with bent heads.

Outside, as though it would exact something further from their lives, the whistle continued to blow.

[注]

老夫妻俩从来没有开过口，现在忽然交谈起来了。是什么东西打破了他们沉默的习惯呢？Sara 在一阵寒战之后，有什么话是非说不可的呢？

they held very still 之 held 是 linking verb，相当于 continued。still（安静）是 predicate adjective。 exact：问（他们）要。汽笛声已经把他们的衣服家具都要了去，现在又在吹了，好像再要向他们要什么似的。汽笛在吹，天气还要冷下去。番茄秧或许可以救活了，但是人呢？寒夜笛声，境界至为明净，然人世痛苦，似亦尽在几声长鸣之中。小说家之剪裁，至此已告结束，然文虽终局，意似尚有未尽焉。

The Life and Work of Professor Roy Millen
米伦教授的生活与工作

Robert Penn Warren（1905—1989）

　　作者罗伯特·潘·沃伦就像这篇小说的主人公一样，是一位英文教授。他是美国肯塔基州人，写过小说、诗、传记和文学评论，最著名的作品是长篇小说《国王的人马》(*All the King's Men*)（曾改编为电影）。他的辈分比海明威、福克纳等稍晚（海明威等是二十世纪二十年代成名的，他是三十年代成名的）。他是美国一个很重要的写实主义作家。本篇选自他的短篇小说集 *The Circus in the Attic*。

[1]

　　Professor Roy Millen had loved his wife devotedly, and now she was dead ... He made his plans to go abroad, to England, to work in the libraries there, as he and his wife had planned. It was what she should have him do, he told himself. And the book would be a kind of monument to her. He would dedicate the book to her. As he walked slowly back from the campus to his house in the late afternoons or early evenings of spring, he would try to compose the dedication, saying the words aloud to himself as he looked up at the paling, peach-colored sky beyond the newly leafed branches. He had decided to sail in June, as soon as he could leave after commencement.

[注]

第一句和第二句之间,原文还有好几段(约有一千五百词),是他过去生活的回忆,主要讲他的妻子。作者口口声声地说他们的婚姻是如何美满,但给我们的暗示是,这位教授的婚姻生活并不快乐,恐怕也没有什么爱情。他的妻子是系主任的女儿,本是一位三十岁出头的老小姐,他在初教大学一年级英文的时候认识的。婚后很"恩爱",她支配着他的生活。二十多年后,她死了,他更感觉到空虚,唯有继续写他的那部书。

第一句 had loved 的时态表示是在他的妻子故世之前。

第三句 should have him do 之间的 have = cause to (使得),后随不定式 do,should 表示虚拟式(假如她活着的话,"她该会要他这样做的"——到英国图书馆去研究)。

monument:纪念碑。他的书将用以纪念他的太太,好像是纪念碑,但并非真的是纪念碑,故云 a kind of monument。**dedicate**:献。西方作家每将其书献给一个他所亲爱或尊敬的人,作为纪念。

campus:是个美国词,指大学范围内全部的场地。

the book would be ..., **he would dedicate** ... 两句的 would 表示将来。**he would try** ... 的 would 表示他的习惯:那年夏天,每当黄昏薄暮,他慢慢步行回家的时候,"他总要……"。

compose:打腹稿。**dedication**:(预备刊在卷首的)献词。**paling**:pale 的现在分词,"颜色在暗淡下去",形容 sky。**newly leafed**:新长树叶的。嫩芽初绽,树着新绿,是状"春"也;露艳似桃,薄暝徐合,是状"夕"也;用介词 beyond,则天在树外,红绿相映,夕阳春光,各得其所。如易 beyond 为 and,则立刻化立体为平面,化图画为剪贴,文趣索然矣。

commencement:毕业典礼。**sail**:坐船去(英国)。

[2]

"I hear you're going away for a year, Professor Millen," Tom Howell said, standing respectfully before Professor Millen's office desk. Then he added, in a dutiful tone, "To work on your book."

"Yes," Professor Millen said, "to work on my book." Then, as though recollecting himself, he made a little gesture toward the chair in front of the desk, and said, "Won't you have a seat, Howell?"

"Are you going to finish it in a year?" Howell asked, and sat down.

[注]

in a dutiful tone：用恭恭敬敬的语调。**dutiful**：尽（学生对老师之）本分的。to work on your book 补充第一句的 going away，表示出国的目的。

recollecting himself：恢复镇定。突然有学生来访，米伦教授忘了该请来客先坐下，然后再同他说话。

[3]

"I still have a little research to do. I have to settle a few points ... points which can't be settled in libraries in this country. I have to do some work yet in one of the great English libraries." Professor Millen paused, looking over the green lawn outside his office window. "But I'll get it written within the year. Practically everything is in order. Though, of course," he paused, again looking at Tom Howell, who listened respectfully and with what seemed interest, "I'll have to do a good deal of retouching ... style and so on, you know ..." he waved his hand modestly in the air, "when I get back."

[注]

research：研究。**settle**：解决。

yet：还有。在美国已经做了不少工作，还有些工作，一定（have to）要到英国图书馆去做。

practically = almost。**in order**：有秩序的，安排好了。

with interest：有兴趣地。**with what seemed interest**：听者有一种似乎是有兴趣的表情。米伦教授不敢断定那位学生对于他的写作计划真发生兴趣。

retouching：小小的修改，润饰。到英国去还不能完稿，回国以后，对于文字及其他方面，还要有很多（a good deal of）的修饰。

[4]

"I'm hoping ..." the boy hesitated, fumbling in his pocket to draw out a folded paper, "I'm hoping to be able to go abroad next year. If I can make it. That's what I wanted to see you about, Professor Millen."

"Anything I can do, I'll be glad to do."

"It's a scholarship. A French scholarship, and I was hoping you'd recommend me. I have had a lot of work with you, and all. The French Department will recommend me, but I have done my minor in English, you know. What you'd say would count a lot."

[注]

hesitated：吞吞吐吐地说。**fumbling**：摸索。**next year**：下学年，可能就是同年秋天。**if I can make it**：假如能走得成的话。这句话没有说完全，意思是跟着上面那一句来的。

scholarship：奖学金。**I was hoping you'd**（= you would）**recommend me** 意思比 I am hoping you'll recommend me 委婉。用现在时显得太迫切，用过去时只是表示"我在来看你之前"或是"知道有这个奖学金的机会的时候，我是这样希望"。现在是不是也这样希望，没有明言，对方如加拒绝，两方都不致太难堪。**recommend**：推荐。

and all = and everything else：我曾跟着你学习过，还有别的种种（关系）。这两个词有点含糊，但说话的人恐怕也不想指明什么，含糊一点好。

the French Department：法语系，法语是此君的主修（major），英文是他的辅修（minor）。

最后一句用虚拟式，也显得很客气。"我不知道你会不会推荐我，假如你推荐我的话，那么你所说的（what you would say）将很起作用。"

[5]

"Howell," Professor Millen said, judicially putting the tips of his fingers together and inspecting the boy, "I've never had a better student than you are. Possibly never one as good. I'll say that in my recommendation. I'll write a strong one." He felt his enthusiasm mounting as he spoke, and a warmth suffused him as though at the prospect of some piece of happiness, some success for himself.

[注]

judicially：像法官似的（把两手手指对顶起来）。**inspecting**：仔细地看。

possibly never one as good = possibly I've never had a student as good as you are。

that：那件事实，即"你是个杰出的学生"。

a strong one = a strong recommendation：一封强有力的推荐信。

enthusiasm：热忱。**mounting**：往上升。**suffused**：遍布。**prospect**：所期望的东西。

他觉得说话的时候很兴奋，心头热了起来，好像自己将要有什么得意的事一般。

[6]

"I certainly appreciate it," the boy said. "This is about the only thing I've got in sight for next year, and I'm graduating. Oh, I reckon I could get a little teaching job or something for a year or two to save up some money to go on. I don't think I ought to ask my family for any more ... they've been swell, putting me through college and giving me that trip to France two years back ..."

[注]

appreciate = I am thankful for。**about** = almost。

in sight：现在可以看得到的出路（thing）。**I'm graduating**：快要毕业，大学四年级下学期。**I reckon** = I suppose。I could ... 的实现可能性比 I can ... 小，could 是 can 的虚拟式。**to save up**：储蓄。**to go on**：继续下去，指进研究所攻读。**any more** = any more money。**swell** 是俚语（slang）"很好"的意思，这个词很常用，大约同北京话的"棒"或上海话的"赞"相仿。末一句讲：他的家庭供给他读四年大学，两年前还送他到法国去游历一次，待他很好，他不应该再问家里要钱了。

[7]

"Yes, yes," Professor Millen said abstractedly, "oh, yes, you did go over one summer, didn't you?"

"Oh, that was just for fun," Howell said, "but this time it would be for work. And when I get back I ought to be able to get a pretty good job so I could save enough to get my Ph. D. quick. Up East."

"A year of study in France will be a fine opportunity," Professor Millen said. That enthusiasm and warmth which had filled him like a promise of happiness was waning now, he did not know why. He wished the boy would get up and go and leave him alone.

这个学生的头发是金色的（blond），硬而细（crisp），从方正的前额往后梳；他的眼睛是蓝色的，看人的时候，显得很有自信；外套穿在身上，也显得潇洒自得。**saw** 的宾语是 hair, gaze 和 way；the coat ... shoulders 是 adjective clause，形容 way，从句前面省了 in which 两词。中国旧小说的习惯，人物一出场，就描写他的状貌服装，现在这位学生早已出场，他的状貌服装，到这里才描写。中国旧小说的写法，用的是一个超然的、局外的观点。小说这里用的是主角的观点：起初，米伦教授不注意他，所以不描写；现在米伦教授注意他了，所以才开始描写。人物描写同小说中主角的心理活动相配合，较旧法似胜一筹。

[11]

The boy stood up. "I've stayed too long. I know you've got a lot of work to do."

"No," Professor Millen said.

"And I certainly appreciate your recommendation. The address of the scholarship committee is on here," he said, and laid a printed sheet on the desk. "That's the circular, and all the information."

"I'll attend to it right away," Professor Millen said. "Thank you," the boy said, and was gone.

[注]

you've got = you have，got 在这里并没有"得到"的意义。**circular**：散发的通知书。即上文中所述该学生从口袋里掏出来的纸，上载一切有关奖学金的事项。

attend to = pay attention to。**right away** = at once。

[12]

For a few minutes Professor Millen sat there, his eyes on the bare wall opposite his desk. Then he read the circular. He laid it back on the desk and pressed a button. When the secretary came in, he handed her the printed sheet. "The address is on that," he said, and waited while she copied it. Then he said, "I'll give you the letter." He studied the wall for a moment, then began:

[注]

bare：墙上不挂照片图画，也无糊墙花纸，或其他装饰。

button：电铃的按钮。**I'll give you the letter**：他读信稿，由秘书速记下来。

studied：细细地看。

[13]

"Gentlemen. I can truthfully say that I take the most sincere pleasure in recommending to you Mr. Thomas Howell. In my long career as a teacher I have never had a better student. He has an acute and penetrating intelligence, and, as is so often not the case with young men of his capacity, the patience and honesty of a true scholar. I am sure that if he is appointed to..." He hesitated, looking at the wall. "I am sure that..." he said at last, then stopped.

[注]

引号内为米伦教授所读之信稿。照写信格式，gentlemen 后面该用冒号，今用句号者，只表示教授读此词后，语气一顿而已。

in my long career as a teacher：自我任教以来。

intelligence：智力。**penetrating** 意思比 acute 进一层。acute 敏锐而已，并不一定深入，penetrating 则能发幽探微，洞察根本矣。

此句 and 以后，意思又进一层：聪明人每无恒，巧慧者鲜笃实，唯此君则"智者"、"仁者"兼于一身。patience 和 honesty，仍为 has 之宾语。as 为关系代词 = which fact，所代者即为从句 (he has) the patience and honesty of a true scholar。**case**：情形。**capacity**：才力。**so** = very。

I am sure 之后似应跟着"如能出国深造，必能百尺竿头，更进一步"这一类的话。他用了 appointed（勉强可解作"获选"）一词之后，句子很难往下做，故而停顿。学生的名字，前面是 Tom，这里是 Thomas，Tom 是 Thomas 的较亲密的叫法，犹中国人的学名与小名之别。

[14]

The secretary, her pencil poised above her pad, waited while Professor Millen seemed to withdraw, to sink within himself. Her foot made a slight reproachful scraping sound as she changed her position in the chair. She, too, began to look out the window, where Professor Millen's gaze now was fixed.

"That's all ... all for the present," Professor Millen said, suddenly. "Just hold that and I'll finish later. I've just thought ..." he managed to look directly at her, "of something else I've got to do. There's something else."

[注]

her pencil poised above her pad：是 nominative absolute。**poised**（过去分词）：悬空握在手里。above 所表示的关系，笔不靠在纸上（否则要用 on）；笔是悬空的，但也并不正在纸的上面（否则要用 over）。**pad**：记速记用的拍纸簿。withdraw 原意是"退出"，这里只是指"出神"。**to sink within himself**：陷入深思。

scraping sound：皮鞋底与地板的摩擦声。**reproachful**：声音中似带"责备"，不耐久候也。**managed to look**：似乎不愿或不敢看她，结果还是提起精神，对她直视。

[15]

After the secretary had left the office, closing the door softly behind her, he did not move some time. Then he again looked out the window. The shadows were lengthening over the smooth lawn. The faintest premonitory flush was touching the puffs of white cloud visible toward the top of his window. Before long now he would be going home. He picked up the circular. He read it again, very carefully, dwelling on it almost painfully, as though he were an illiterate trying to extort some secret from the words. He lifted his eyes from the sheet to look at the chair where the boy had sat leaning forward, the pleasure shining on his clear, handsome face, the good coat riding easy on his shoulders, saying, "…you know how Paris is, it sort of knocks you off your feet. You've been there?"

[注]

the shadows were lengthening：影子拉长，时间更晚。**flush**：霞光。**faintest**：极淡的。**premonitory**：预示的（预示黑夜来临）。

puffs of white cloud：朵朵白云。霞光自地平线上发出，照到在天空中的白云。**toward** = near。

he would be going home 比 he would go home 更强调 go 的动作。

dwelling on it：长时间地想它。**painfully**：痛苦地。这词前面加了副词 almost，份量已大为减轻。但是作者为什么要用"痛苦地"这样一个词呢？本段末一句中，隐约说明。**illiterate**：文盲。他并非文盲，故动词用虚拟式的 were。**extort**：用力逼出来或找出来。

the pleasure shining on his ... face 和 the good coat riding ... on his shoulders 都是 nominative absolute phrase。**riding on** = hanging from，但用 riding 更见活泼。

最后他想起学生问他的那句话。为了这句话，他撒了一次谎，他想起这件事，心里不免难过。据作者所描写，这个学生只是一个天真活泼的大孩子。但是他的天真活泼，似乎反惹教授之厌。他的活力与自信（前面本文里连用两次 confidence），似乎是给教授的一种威胁。他的不假思索地假定教授青年时期的生活，是同他自己的一样逍遥快乐，是给苦读出身的教授的一种讽刺。教授不愿向学生示弱，至少也不愿使学生失望，就随随便便地答应一声。等到他发现自己已经撒了一回谎的时候，他当然恨自己，而且很难避免地、连带地更讨厌那个不知不觉中逼他说谎的人。Tom 无意中已经得罪了教授，而且很伤教授的心，这是 Tom 所绝对想象不到的，作者描写的精微（subtlety）也在此。人和人之间真是这样难处吗？人的心理真是这样变幻莫测吗？所谓写实主义作者 Warren 恐怕相信真是这样的。浪漫主义作家笔下的人生就比较单纯，好人坏人也判然易分。这篇小说的主人公，快要自食其言，非但不去帮助那学生，而且要去破坏他了。我们看完后觉得他是不是个坏人呢？（或者，凭了那几句话，教授对于学生的个性真有新认识了吗？）

[16]

Professor Millen let the circular slip from his lap to the floor. Then, decisively, he reached into the drawer of his desk and took out a sheet of paper. He wrote rapidly in his large, firm script:

Gentlemen:

I have been asked to recommend Mr. Thomas Howell to you for a scholarship for study in France. As you will observe from a transcript of his academic record, with which no doubt you have been provided, he has made the grade of A in all of his work in the English department of this institution, and I understand that his grades in French (his major subject) have been very high. This achievement, of course, deserves consideration, but candor compels me to say that a superficial facility and cleverness seem to characterize his mind. I do not wish to prejudice the committee against his case, and I may be wrong in my estimate; certainly, I hope that the committee will consider him very carefully. But I do feel that he lacks solidity of character, the spirit of patient inquiry, and what might be termed the philosophical bent.

Very respectfully yours,
Roy Millen,
Professor of English.

[注]

slip：滑下去。**lap**：衣兜。

decisively：已经有了决定了。**drawer**：抽屉。

firm：笔力坚挺。**script**：字体。

have been asked：被动语气，可不必明言是谁托他写这封信的。**academic record**：成绩单。**transcript**：重抄的副本，正本留校。**with which no doubt you have been provided**：成绩单谅必业已达览。with which 应该连到 provided 后面去，"无疑人家已经把那个东西给你们了"。**institution**：指该大学。

this achievement：这种成就，指成绩全优。**deserves consideration**：值得考虑。**candor** = honesty in giving one's opinion，相当于中文的"良心"。**compels me**：迫使我。**superficial**：肤浅的。**facility**：做事太容易，不肯认真。**cleverness**：此词本来有坏的意义，指"小聪明"。**characterize his mind** = are the characteristics（特征）of his mind。

prejudice（动词）：使（人）发生偏见。**case**：他来申请奖学金的这件事。**estimate**：判断。

solidity of character：性格上的稳重。**the spirit of patient inquiry**：耐心探求的精神。最后一个 noun clause 的意思是：他还缺一种素质。这种素质，无以名之，姑名之曰 **philosophical bent**：研究哲理的倾向（或兴趣）。

[17]

Without looking up, he addressed an envelope hurriedly, the pen making a dry, scratching sound. Then he blotted and stamped the envelope, inserted the sheet, put the letter into his pocket, picked up his hat, and left the office. He would, he remembered, pass a postbox on his way home.

[注]

addressed：写地址。**dry**：墨水不足，故干。**scratching sound**：笔尖抓纸的声音。**blotted**：用吸水纸（blotting-paper）来吸。**stamped**：贴上邮票。**inserted**：将（信纸）放入信封。

postbox：邮箱。对于 Tom 很不利的一封"推荐信"就此要寄给奖学金委员会了。

The Ballet Dancer
芭蕾舞者

Jane Mayhall（1921—2009）

本篇选自《一九四九年美国最佳短篇小说集》（*The Best American Short Stories 1949*, edited by Martha Foley）。作者珍·梅霍是一位女作家，曾有多种作品问世。原题 *The Men*，记作者记忆中印象最深刻的三位男性，第一位就是这里所要转载介绍的舞蹈家，第二位是她中学时代的一个图书馆管理员，第三位是大学时代的一位教授。就严格的体例言之，全文似乎不像是一篇短篇小说，而像是三则速写（sketches）。但是作者对于感觉印象，把握得准而稳；尤其可贵的是她对于瞬息间感觉印象的变化，都能很正确生动地记录下来。本文不但可以当一件艺术品来欣赏，作者这种认真的写作态度，也是值得有志文学创作之士效法的。

[1]

I remember when I was eleven years old and attended a ballet for the first time. It was held at the Memorial Auditorium, a large building in the town where I lived.

During the first group of dances, I sat up very high in the balcony with my family and the stage seemed too far away. It was a pretty show at such a distance, but the dancers with their bright dots of costumes appeared as small and no more alive than marionettes.

[注]

ballet：通常译作"芭蕾舞"。按，ballet 以舞蹈表示故事的进展和人物感情的起伏，似可译作"舞剧"。

Memorial Auditorium：纪念堂。

first group of dances：头几个舞。**balcony**：剧院包厢，一般设于剧院二楼之上。这里末一句开始显出作者的功夫：从远远的、高高的包厢往下望，舞台上的演出该是怎么回事。戏是很美丽的戏，但是舞者显得太小，动作也不活泼，同木偶戏（marionettes）差不多。**costumes**：演员的服装，大多为丝绢所制，本有光彩，经灯光照耀，更显明亮；但是观察者坐得远，一身衣服看上去只成一小点（dot），故云 bright dots of costumes。**as small** 之后，照一般语法书规定，还应跟 as。

[2]

When intermission came some friends of the family suggested that I sit down in the second row orchestra with them. This was probably because they considered me a "nice little girl," a point of view to which I had no objection.

[注]

intermission：休息时间，观众可以离座出去谈话。

sit down 之 sit 是 subjunctive mood 现在时。作者家里长辈的朋友在楼下正有空座，提议把她接到那边去看。先不过是一种提议，并非是事实，故用 subjunctive mood。

second row orchestra：池座第二排。orchestra 这里不解释作"乐队"，而是"池座"。

他们认为她是一个"乖女孩"（nice little girl），所以要她坐在一起。他们这种看法，她并不反对。**a point of view** 综括地代表前面所说的这种"看法"，是一种同位语的说明法。

[3]

The world of second row orchestra was an immensely different one. The seats were softer and had slightly reclining backs. Here the members of the audience sat with much dignity, as if each had been appointed to a separate throne, I thought. A sweet flowery scent came from the ladies. As they settled into their places, one heard a faint sound of silk and fur.

[注]

她的长辈如何地让她下去，她如何地被搀着走……这些与题旨无关，作者都略而不记。

world：指环境而言，从楼上搬到楼下来坐，好像进了另外一个"世界"。
immensely different：大大地不同。
backs：椅子的靠背。**slightly reclining**：微向后倾。
audience 作"听众"解是集合名词。"听众中的一位"便是 a member of the audience。**with much dignity**：很庄严地。前排观众多半是社会上有身份人士，**as if** …从句中的动词是 subjunctive mood。**throne**：王座。他们的座位并非王座，故用虚拟式。**separate**：个别的，每人分到一座。
scent：香味。**flowery**：花似的（可能是香水的香）。
as they settled into their places：休息时间将满，观众进场就座。作者鼻觉芬芳之香，耳闻丝裘悉索之声，虽未用眼睛，而女士们服饰的豪华，已如在目前。

[4]

Then the music began. Everyone leaned forward. The high arc of the curtain lifted as if moved by a hundred tiny unseen hands. The stage before us was a forest, bathed in willowy green light. The backdrop was splotched with painted leaves and gawk-headed birds whose artificiality seemed, for some reason, particularly exciting.

[注]

音乐声作，戏又将开场。观众的上身往前倾——这是很自然的反应，但写文章的人能有几个会注意到这种"小节"？

arc of the curtain：幕布呈弧状升上去。未升之前，不见其成弧状（arc），故 high 与 arc 不能分。幕升上去，很整齐，很灵巧，很利落（坐在远处就注意不到了，所以一定要在作者座位更动后才描写）。一个十一岁的女孩子看幕布升起觉得很奇怪，所以说"好像是一百只看不见的小手把它提起来的"。
bathed：舞台"浴"于灯光之中。**willowy green**：杨柳似地绿（请注意作者此处选词的功夫)。

backdrop：作为布景的一块幕。**splotched**：斑斑点点地涂上去。**gawk-headed**：头的姿态很笨拙的。**artificiality**：人为性。树叶和小鸟都是画上去的，故云 artificial（人为的）；小孩子看舞台布景，明知是假的，但是看上去更有劲。要问什么理由，自己也说不上来。**for some reason**：为了某种理由。

[5]

The dancers stepped forward, the make-up sharp on their faces.

But how near, how human they were! Their eyes moved, their lips smiled. Rising together and beginning to twirl on the tips of their toes, they were much more admirable from here than from afar!

[注]

make-up：脸上化的妆，脂粉油彩。**sharp**：很明显的。make-up 和 sharp 之间，照一般语法书说来，该有一个现在分词 "being"。作者坐近了，看得清楚了，大为兴奋。**how human ...**：多么像人。请不要忘记，刚才只像木偶。

twirl：旋转。注意介词用 on。

[6]

It was a warm spring night. The sky appeared to reflect a pleasant tropical heat. Men wearing sky blue jackets leapt to girls whose dresses ruffled like swans. Their smiles mingled, their arms embroidered the air with wonderful patterns. Several more dancers came forward, carrying garlands of green and yellow flowers into which they wove themselves. And all with such remarkable enjoyment! Surely something marvelous was going to happen.

[注]

warm spring night：不可能指演戏的那天晚上，而是指舞台上所表现的情景。作者已经把全副精神放到台上去了。

reflect：反射出来。**tropical**：热带的。

jacket：短上衣。**leapt to** = leapt to meet：跳过去迎接，to 是介词。**ruffled**：起

皱纹像天鹅（swans）的毛一样地蓬松起来。男性舞者们穿的是天蓝色上衣，女性舞者们的衣服可能是白色的。

mingled：混合。（男女舞者的笑容怎么会混合起来的呢？）**patterns**：图案。**embroidered**：刺绣。手臂舞动，在空中绣出种种奇妙的图案。

garlands：花环。**into which they wove themselves**：把自己也编进花环里去。使人看得眼花缭乱，"人""花"不分。wove 是 weave（编织）的过去式。

enjoyment：舞者做种种动作，精神显得很是愉快。舞蹈如此，似乎已尽美矣，然而不然，这一切似乎不过都是准备，好戏还在后头。

[7]

And then it did.

Suddenly the music stopped. The only sound to be heard was a thin, somewhat unsteady tone of a violin. The gaily costumed characters moved back silently and made way for someone.

A little flap in the backdrop pulled open. And a young man stepped forth.

[注]

and then it did = And then something marvelous did happen。奇妙的事果然发生了。

unsteady：不稳定的，似断似续的，两个词都形容小提琴的声音。**gaily costumed**：衣服色彩鲜艳的。**characters**：剧中人物。**made way for**：让开路，好让别人走。

flap：幕上可启闭的小门。

[8]

The rest of the dancers departed and left him alone. The lights took on a white hue and one saw that the young man was very pale with dark-penciled eyes. He was dressed in a light blousing shirt and tight breeches of cream-colored satin.

Stepping forward, with casual grace, he began to dance.

[注]

the lights took on a white hue：灯光本来绿如春日之柳，现在绿得稍微淡一点了（hue：颜色的浓淡层次）。淡淡的绿光照着，青年舞蹈家的脸色显得苍白，相形之下，很明显可以看出他的眼睛用黑笔画了眼线。

light：轻飘飘的，形容 shirt。blouse 本意是"宽松的上衣"，因此可作动词（= to assume a blouse-like form，宽宽松松，作 blouse 状。见《韦氏新国际词典》）。blousing 是动词 blouse 的现在分词。裤子（breeches）很紧。全身衣服，都是乳黄色缎子所做成。

他向前走来，漫不经心（casual），而姿势优雅（grace），举起双臂，舞将起来了。

[9]

At first, all I could realize of him was the delicate-footed motion, the coolness and lightness of the figure. He wore soft close-fitting slippers and the insteps of his feet were so beautiful and alive that I fell in love with them at once. He was small and perfectly formed, slender-hipped and probably quite typical of the ballet dancer. And perhaps there was something too mannered and too self-conscious in the face. His eyes were drawn to appear elongated, Oriental. The head was finely shaped, dark-haired. But the very self-conscious style of him seemed to add to the charm. What could equal the stance, the quick lightning movements of the body, or the severe control of its quietness?

[注]

all I could realize of him：我所能看出来的（realize = be fully aware of），**figure**：身段。**coolness**：冷静，不露出狂热。**lightness**：轻灵。

close-fitting slippers：贴肉的软底舞鞋。**insteps**：脚背。这个小女孩最先爱上的不是那个舞蹈家的脸，也不是他的身段，更不是他的不可捉摸的精神，而是他的脚背！一个芭蕾舞蹈家最迷人的地方恐怕该是他的灵活的脚背吧。

perfectly formed：身材合度。**slender-hipped**：臀部瘦细。**typical of the ballet dancer**：是个典型的芭蕾舞蹈家。

下一句讲脸上的表情。**mannered**：做作的。**self-conscious**：自觉的（自觉在表演，未能忘我，艺术恐尚未臻化境）。

drawn：勾画（可能作"吊起"解）。**elongated, Oriental**：细长的,像是东方人的。西洋人以为东方人的眼睛大多是斜而细长的。

the very self-conscious style of him …：他的表演虽未能忘我,似乎却益显其为人之可爱。very 是形容词,加重语气之用。

stance：站的姿势。**its quietness** 的 its 指 the body。

[10]

But none of these features by themselves gave the full effect. The complete harmonious accord of the moment — there was no way to explain it.

When the ballet was over and the dancers were bowing outside the curtain, I felt a terrible childish sadness, the kind that is felt only after the accidental pleasure. It is a puzzling sensation, the regret for the loss of that which one had not — no, never — even hoped for in the first place!

[注]

features：特色。**harmonious accord**：和谐一致。作者所感觉到的效果,并不是由于上述特色中的任何一种,而是由于这些特色的和谐的配合。她以为这是没法说明的。

accidental pleasure：无意中得来的乐事。起初本来不准备有这样的快乐的经验,失掉了不应该觉得可惜,可是现在却另有一种怅惘之感。**puzzling sensation**：令人难以了解的感觉。

[11]

The young man stood a little in front of the others, bowing. I noticed that his ears were beautifully pointed and his hair was sleek.

[注]

青年舞蹈家出来谢幕,她看得更清楚了,她注意到他的耳朵的形状和头发的光滑。(鞠躬的时候不是头发和耳朵尖在最前头吗?)

[12]

The lights in the Auditorium went up. The orchestra began to play. People put on their wraps and began to talk in matter-of-fact voices. But I was gravely occupied with the memory of the young man. Moving slowly in the large arena of the Auditorium, I felt that I would never forget him. I listened dreamily to the music and watched the audience make its dignified parade to the rear exit. It seemed, to my impressionable mind, that everything existed only for the contemplation of him.

［注］

went up：灯亮起来了。**wraps**：大衣外套之类。**matter-of-fact**：枯燥无味的，家常的，他们已经脱离舞蹈的幻境了。

large arena of the Auditorium：在这纪念堂的大屋子里。**make its dignified parade**：很堂皇地排班而出。make 是省掉 to 的 infinitive。its 代替 of the audience。**rear exit**：后面的出口。

contemplation of him：想念他，好像一切事物都是为了想念他才存在的。小妮子痴矣。

Herb Gathering
采药

Truman Capote（1924—1984）

  杜鲁门·卡波特是美国作家，本篇选自其所著长篇小说《草琴》(*The Grass Harp*)。美国旷野，印第安草（Indian grass）繁生，高可逾顶，一望无际，风吹其间，声如筝簧，故"草琴"者，亦"天籁"之意也。

  小说的主人公 Collin Fenwick 是一个孤儿，依两表姑居。两表姑皆老处女，行为怪僻，然各有其可爱处。书中故事简单而含意深远，人物描写非常生动，写景亦多佳句。卡波特之风格，精致细腻，轻描淡写中，颇多晕润含蓄之妙。于现实世界之外，似另暗示一理想世界。其小说虽以美国南部为背景，然读来犹如童话：亦真亦幻，文字之妙用尽矣。

[1]

  Once a week, Saturdays mostly, we went to River Woods. For these trips, which lasted the whole day, Catherine fried a chicken and deviled a dozen eggs, and Dolly took along a chocolate layer cake and a supply of divinity fudge. Thus armed, and carrying three empty grain sacks, we walked out the church road past the cemetery and through the field of Indian grass.

[注]

River Woods 是当地一座森林的名称。**lasted**：（时间之）持续。每星期去一次，一去就一整天。Catherine 为一黑人老妪，年约六十。**deviled**：用醋、辣椒、酱油、色拉油等调味品炮制（蛋先煮熟切开，蛋黄泡制后，再放入蛋白之内）。Dolly 为书中主角之大表姑，年六十，天性十分纯朴善良。渠有秘方，依法配制，能治水肿。所谓"采药"，即为配制该单方之用。**layer cake**：分层之蛋糕。**fudge**：普通软质美式糖果。divinity fudge 是 fudge 之一种，原料以 cream、蔗糖、胡桃仁为主。**a supply of** = a quantity of，相当多。

armed：原意是武装配备，转作一切配备。这里所配备的是供野餐用的食品和糖果。**grain sacks**：盛谷类的麻袋或布袋。空的布袋，可以装药草。**church road**：通至教堂的路。**cemetery**：公墓，在教堂附近。

[2]

Just entering the woods there was a double-trunked China tree, really two trees, but their branches were so embraced that you could step from one into the other; in fact, they were bridged by a tree-house; spacious, sturdy, a model of a tree-house, it was like a raft floating in the sea of leaves. The boys who built it, provided they are still alive, must by now be very old men; certainly the tree-house was fifteen or twenty years old when Dolly first found it and that was a quarter of a century before she showed it to me.

[注]

过了草地，便是森林。在森林进口处是两棵楝树。楝树高丈余，叶繁密如槐，初夏开淡紫色花，结实似枣而小，色黄，俗名金铃子，入药。楝树在美国称为 China tree（或 chinaberry tree）。

trunk：树干。**double-trunked**：两根树干的。本来是两棵树，因为上面的枝叶纠缠难分，好像是一棵树有两根树干似的。**embraced**：拥抱。**step from one into the other**：从一棵树跨到另外一棵。树可 step into（"走进"），其繁茂可想。**bridge**：树上架有木屋，犹如两树之间的桥梁。**spacious**：宽敞的。**sturdy**：坚固的。**a model of a tree-house**：树上房屋的模范。同前面的 a tree house，在语法上是同位语。**raft**：木筏。屋居树巅，如筏浮水上。

provided = if。造这座木屋的孩子们假如现在还活着的话，也该是很老的老头儿了。Dolly 起初发现这座木屋的时候，它已经有十五年到二十年的历史；事到如今，又过了二十五年了。

[3]

To reach it was easy as climbing stairs; there were footholds of gnarled bark and tough vines to grip; even Catherine, who was heavy around the hips and complained of rheumatism, had no trouble. But Catherine felt no love for the tree house; she did not know, as Dolly knew and made me know, that it was a ship, that to sit up there was to sail along the cloudy coastline of every dream. Mark my word, said Catherine, them boards are too old, them nails are slippery as worms, gonna crack in two, gonna fall and bust our heads don't I know it.

[注]

gnarled bark：多结节的树皮，可供踏脚（foothold）。**grip**：握；硬藤可攀援。**rheumatism**：风湿病。**complain of**：自称害（什么病）。

to sail along the cloudy coastline of every dream：上文把树巅木屋比作木筏，同时又把树叶比作海，尚不过是就形象而言。这里把木屋比作船，船居然能行，文思至此，乃更进一层。船往那里开呢？"沿着梦境的云雾茫茫的海岸航行。"什么样的梦全有，故云 every dream。

she did not know 之宾语是两个"that" clauses。

末一句照语法惯例，应加引号。Mark my word 之 my 是 Catherine 自道。them boards ... 和 them nails ... 之 them 并非宾格，而等于指示形容词 these。**boards**：木板。年代过久，铁钉已松，触之似能出入自如，犹如小虫，故 Catherine 担忧木屋将垮。**gonna** = going to：将要。**bust** = burst：打破。皆为美国土话。**don't I know it**：我岂不知之哉？我知道得很清楚。don't 之前，标点原文缺。

[4]

Storing our provisions in the tree-house, we separated into the woods, each carrying a grain sack to be filled with herbs, leaves, strange roots. No one, not even Catherine, knew altogether what went into the medicine, for it was a secret Dolly kept to herself, and we were never allowed to look at the gatherings in her own sack: she held tight to it, as though inside she had captive a blue-haired child, a bewitched prince.

[注]

provisions：食品，即上文所述之煎鸡等等。**separated**：分头出发。

what went into the medicine：Dolly 的药是什么东西配成的。go 这一类常见的动词，用法颇多，学者宜随时留意。Dolly kept to herself 是定语从句，关系代词 which 省掉。**gatherings**：搜集所得，**tight**（副词）= firmly。**captive**（形容词）= held as a prisoner，此处作 objective complement。

blue-haired child：蓝发童子，指不常见的怪物。**bewitched prince**：中了魔法的王子。西洋童话中，常有王子因为魔法作祟变形易体，化作怪物。Dolly 的袋里的东西总不让别人看，好像捉住什么怪物似的。

[5]

This was her story: "Once, back yonder when we were children there were gipsies thick as birds in a blackberry patch ... not like now, maybe you see a few straggling through each year. They came with spring: sudden, like the dogwood pink, there they were — up and down the road and in the woods around. Then one evening, it was April and falling rain, I went out to the cowshed where Fairybell had a new little calf; and there in the cowshed were three gipsy women, two of them old and one of them young, and the young one was lying naked and twisting on the corn-shucks. When they saw that I was not afraid, one of the old women asked would I bring a light. So I went to the house for a candle, and when I came back the woman who had sent me was holding a red hollering baby upside down by its feet, and the other woman was milking Fairybell. I helped them wash the baby in the warm milk and wrap it in a scarf. Then one of the old women took my hand and said:

[注]

本段乃 Dolly 自叙秘方之由来。

back yonder：很多年前。yonder 本代表空间之"远"，此处代表时间之"远"。**thick**：因人数多，密集而成"厚"。**patch**：一块地。种黑莓之地上，鸟雀常群集，当年吉普赛人（gipsies）人数众多，亦复类彼。**straggling**：三三两两地走过。maybe 是副词，may 与 be 之间不分。

pink：石竹（花名）。dogwood pink 恐为 pink 之一种，入春怒放；而吉普赛人于春季亦突然大群出现，如石竹花焉。

it was April and falling rain：此从句插入以说明时间，与全句结构无关。**cowshed**：牛棚。**Fairybell**：母牛名。**had a new little calf**：新添一犊。**corn-shucks**：玉米外面的包壳，是牛的饲料。**twisting**：辗转反侧，临盆前阵痛之相。

would I bring a light：照语法书上规定，应作 whether I would bring a light。

who had sent me：定语从句,刚才差我去的(那小女人)。**hollering**：大声叫喊的。**red**：初生婴儿的颜色。**holding upside down by its feet**：握着脚，倒提着。**milking**：挤奶。

wash 和 wrap 都是 infinitives，前面的 to 省略。在 help 之后，infinitive 的 to 常常省略。**warm milk**：才挤出来的奶，故温暖。

[6]

"Now I am going to give you a gift by teaching you a rhyme. It was a rhyme about evergreen bark, dragonfly fern — and all the other things we come here in the woods to find: *Boil till dark and pure if you want a dropsy cure*. In the morning they were gone; I looked for them in the fields and on the road; there was nothing left of them but the rhyme in my head."

[注]

rhyme：韵文，口诀。吉普赛老妪为谢其照料之恩，乃授以药方口诀。第一句是吉普赛人语，用现在时；第二句又是 Dolly 本人的口气了，用过去时。

fern：蕨类植物。dragonfly fern 为蕨类植物之一种。**we come here … to find** 是定语从句。草药的其他成分，Dolly 秘而不宣，即以 all the other things 概括。

斜体字为口诀之一部分，注意 pure 与 cure 押韵。采得各种药草之后，加热煮沸，煎到色呈乌黑，杂质去尽为止。**dropsy**：水肿病。**cure**：特效药。

[7]

Calling to each other, hooting like owls loose in the daytime, we worked all morning in opposite parts of the woods. Towards afternoon, our sack fat with skinned bark, tender, torn roots, we climbed back into the green web of the China tree and spread the food. There was good creek water in a mason jar, or if the weather was cold a thermos of hot coffee, and we wadded leaves to wipe our chicken-stained, fudge-sticky fingers. Afterwards, telling fortunes with flowers, speaking of sleepy things, it was as though we floated through the afternoon on the raft in the tree; we belonged there, as the sunsilvered leaves belonged, the dwelling whippoorwills.

[注]

owls：猫头鹰。它们的叫声英文称为 hoot。**loose**（形容词）：飞出来的。

skin（动词）：剥皮。**skinned bark**：剥下的树皮。tender（鲜嫩的）和 torn（撕断的）都是形容 roots。**green web**：楝树枝叶繁茂，如绿色之网。

jar：缸。mason jar 是玻璃所制，本为贮藏蔬菜鲜果之用，这里盛水（mason 是纪念发明人的名字）。**creek**：溪涧。**thermos**：热水瓶。a thermos 跟句首 there was 而来。**if the weather was cold** 是状语从句。**wadded**：捏成小块。**sticky**：黏性的。**wipe**：抹拭。

telling fortunes with flowers：用花算命（通常是数花的花瓣，是种消遣）。**speaking of sleepy things**：讲些叫人打瞌睡的事情。可能话没有说完,就会睡着了的。

floated through the afternoon：一下午就这么飘荡过去了。假如就时间言, through 不过是"整个下午这么过去"的意思。但是细看文义,作者似乎要把时间化成空间, afternoon 是一个海,他们是在乘桴泛海, through 简直就是"渡过"的意思。

sunsilvered：因阳光照耀色如镀银。**as the sunsilvered leaves belonged** = as the sunsilvered leaves belonged there：树叶和树不可分,彼此是一家,他们三人同树叶一样,也是属于这棵树的。**dwelling**：住在那边的。**whippoorwills**：三声夜鹰,和主语 we 同位。他们三人,高踞树巅,食于斯,寝于斯,就像三只怪鸟。

Two Mutes

两个哑巴

Carson McCullers（1917—1967）

本文节录自长篇小说《心是孤独的猎手》（*The Heart Is a Lonely Hunter*）的第一章。全书以聋哑人 John Singer 为主角，充满怜悯与同情心。作者卡森·麦卡勒斯是美国佐治亚州人，其文章之朴素率直与同情心之深厚，论者比之于英国的 D. H. Lawrence 与十九世纪俄国作家 Dostoyevsky。本文句法均甚简单平稳，值得学者效法。

[1]

In the town there were two mutes, and they were always together. Early every morning they would come out from the house where they lived and walk arm in arm down the street to work. The two friends were very different. The one who always steered the way was an obese and dreamy Greek. In the summer he would come out wearing a yellow or green polo shirt stuffed sloppily into his trousers in front and hanging loose behind. When it was colder he wore over this a shapeless gray sweater. His face was round and oily, with half-closed eyelids and lips that curved in a gentle, stupid smile. The other was tall. His eyes had a quick, intelligent expression. He was always immaculate and very soberly dressed.

[注]

第二句的动词 would come ... and walk ... 中的 would 表示过去的习惯。
steered the way：领路。两个哑巴之中，一人个性较强，已于此句点明。
obese：肥硕的。**Greek**：美国各国移民都有，此人乃希腊人。
polo：马球。**polo shirt**：带领短袖衫。
sloppily = carelessly。**stuffed**：塞。短袖衫前摆潦草地塞在裤腰里，后摆松松地挂在外面。
sweater：（羊）毛衫。此词是 wore 的宾语。**over this** 之 this 代表 polo shirt。
immaculate：洁净无垢。**soberly**：朴素地。

[2]

Every morning the two friends walked silently together until they reached the main street of the town. Then when they came to a certain fruit and candy store they paused for a moment on the sidewalk outside. The Greek, Spiros Antonapoulos, worked for his cousin, who owned the fruit store. His job was to make candies and sweets, uncrate the fruits, and to keep the place clean. The thin mute, John Singer, nearly always put his hand on his friend's arm and looked for a second into his face before leaving him. Then after this good-bye Singer crossed the street and walked on alone to the jewelry store where he worked as a silverware engraver.

[注]

paused：稍停。每天早晨,两人一同上班。到了肥哑巴所服务的糖果鲜果店门前,他们必定停一下。停住了,瘦哑巴要同他告别。第五句说 Singer 如何依依不舍,拉着朋友的臂膊,眼睛细细地对他看。天天见面的,尚且如此难分难舍,哑巴心里如何寂寞,不言自明。
crate（名词）：篓子。**uncrate**（动词）：从篓中取出。同样地,打开包裹是 unpack,解开绳子是 unstring。**silverware**：银器。**engraver**：刻花匠。

[3]

In the late afternoon the friends would meet again. Singer came back to the fruit store and waited until Antonapoulos was ready to go home. In the dusk the two mutes walked slowly home together. At home Singer was always talking to Antonapoulos. His hands shaped the words in a swift series of designs. His face was eager and his gray-green eyes sparkled brightly. With his thin, strong hands he told Antonapoulos all that had happened during the day.

[注]

第四句 **was always talking** 表示"停了又说",总是在那里说。哑巴怎么能说话呢?他是用手势代替语言的。**series of designs**:一连串的手势图样。

eager:迫不及待的神气。眼睛里还发着光。心中有话,即使是很不重要的话,也非吐不可。

[4]

Antonapoulos sat back lazily and looked at Singer. It was seldom that he ever moved his hands to speak at all — and then it was to say that he wanted to eat or sleep or to drink. These three things he always said with the same vague, fumbling signs. At night, if he were not too drunk, he would kneel down before his bed and pray awhile. Then his plump hands shaped the words "Holy Jesus," or "God," or "Darling Mary." These were the only words Antonapoulos ever said. Singer never knew just how much his friend understood of all the things he told him. But it did not matter.

[注]

那希腊人只是懒洋洋地坐着,对他的朋友看着,他除了本能的要求之外,似乎没有什么理智活动,也没有什么话要说的。

at all = in any way:用任何方式,总是用在否定或疑问的句子里。**vague**:模糊的。**fumbling**:笨拙的(动词 fumble:乱摸)。**plump**:肥厚的。**it did not matter**:也没有什么关系。Singer 只管自己把话"说"出来,不管对方"听"不"听"。

[5]

They shared the upstairs of a small house near the business section of the town. There were two rooms. On the oil stove in the kitchen Antonapoulos cooked all of their meals. There were straight, plain kitchen chairs for Singer and an over-stuffed sofa for Antonapoulos. The bedroom was furnished mainly with a large double bed covered with an eiderdown comfort for the big Greek and a narrow iron cot for Singer.

[注]

shared：共同使用。**business section**：商业区。**stove**：炉子。胖子好吃，菜是他煮的。但是在别的事情上，他总是占便宜。Singer 坐的是硬板厨房椅子（**straight**：直挺挺的。**plain**：没有垫子椅套等装饰的），胖子坐的是软厚沙发（**over-stuffed**：垫得满满的），胖子睡大双人床，Singer 睡小铁床。

comfort：床上的被子，通常拼作 comforter。**eiderdown**：鸭绒（eider 是一种野鸭，down 是鸟的软毛）。**cot**：小床，如帆布行军床，可折叠的铁床之类。

[6]

Dinner always took a long time, because Antonapoulos loved food and he was very slow. After they had eaten, the big Greek would lie back on his sofa and slowly lick over each one of his teeth with his tongue — while Singer washed the dishes.

[注]

lick：舔。牙齿一只一只舔过，足见吃得津津有味。胖子非但好吃贪舒服，而且行动迟缓。本段内两见 slow。

[7]

Sometimes in the evening the mutes would play chess. Singer had always greatly enjoyed this game, and years before he had tried to teach it to Antonapoulos. At first his friend could not be interested in the reasons for moving the various pieces about on the board. Then Singer began to keep a bottle of something good under the table to be taken out after each lesson. The Greek never got on to the erratic movements of the knights and sweeping mobility of the queens, but he learned to make a few set, opening moves. He preferred the white pieces and would not play if the black men were given him.

After the first moves Singer worked out the game by himself while his friend looked on drowsily. If Singer made brilliant attacks on his own men so that in the end the black king was killed, Antonapoulos was always very proud and pleased.

[注]

哑巴以下棋为消遣，chess 大致与中国象棋相类。棋子叫 pieces 或 men，棋盘叫 board。**moving the various pieces about**：把不同的棋子（兵、马、后等）各处搬动。about（副词）= here and there。那希腊人对于各种棋子走法（如马可走"日"字，而兵只可前进一格）的理由不感兴趣。

a bottle of something good：一瓶好东西，指好酒。棋教完以后，Singer 拿酒出来给希腊人喝。要把希腊人训练成他的棋友，Singer 不惜用酒来引诱。

got on to：学会。**erratic**：不规则的。**knights**：chess 中的一种棋子，相当于中国象棋里的"马"，走法也是一步一拐，并非不规则，但是在一个没有弄懂的人看来，好像是不规则的。**queen**：地位相当于中国象棋里的"士"，但是威力强大得多，可以像"车"那样横走直走，又可以像"象"那样斜飞（不限格数）。**mobility**：机动性。**sweeping**：一扫而过的，横冲直撞的。**set, opening moves**：固定的开局法，如"当头炮，马来跳"之类（按，chess 中没有"炮"）。set 是过去分词。

preferred：挑选，喜欢使用。**Singer worked out the game by himself**：他一个人来下完这盘棋。他的对手只会开头几下，以后便应付不了，Singer 就代他走，把黑子白子一手包办下来。**drowsily**：打瞌睡似地。胖子本来爱打瞌睡，对下棋又没有兴趣，只是迷迷糊糊地看着而已。可是胖子的好胜心还是很强。Singer 代他下白子，把自己的黑子"将"死了，胖子还很得意呢。**brilliant**：精彩的。

[8]

The two mutes had no other friends, and except when they worked they were alone together. Each day was very much like any other day, because they were alone so much that nothing ever disturbed them. Once a week they would go to the library for Singer to withdraw a mystery book and on Friday night they attended a movie. Then on payday they always went to the ten-cent photograph shop above the Army and Navy Store so that Antonapoulos could have his picture taken. These were the only places where they made customary visits. There were many parts in the town that they had never even seen.

[注]

alone together：只有两个人在一起。**disturbed**：扰乱。**withdraw**：抽出，即借出。**mystery book**：侦探小说。**payday**：发薪水的那一天。**ten-cent photograph shop**：一角钱照一次的照相馆。**above**：在楼上。**customary**：经常的。

[9]

But the two mutes were not lonely at all. At home they were content to eat and drink, and Singer would talk with his hands eagerly to his friend about all that was in his mind. So the years passed in the quiet way until Singer reached the age of thirty-two and had been in the town with Antonapoulos for ten years.

Then one day the Greek became ill. He sat up in bed with his hands on his fat stomach and big, oily tears rolled down his cheeks. Singer went to see his friend's cousin who owned the fruit store, and also he arranged for leave from his own work. The doctor made out a diet for Antonapoulos and said that he could drink no more wine. Singer rapidly enforced the doctor's orders. All day he sat by his friend's bed and did what he could to make the time pass quickly, but Antonapoulos only looked at him angrily from the corners of his eyes and would not be amused.

[注]

他们在那城里一共住了十年。忽然有一天那希腊人害病了。

big, oily tears：那胖子本来脸上有油汗（见第一段），眼泪滚下来也像油了。

arranged for leave：办请假手续。他要整天地陪伴病人。**diet**：规定的食品和食量。

enforced the doctor's orders：强制执行医生的命令（他们同医生可以笔谈的）。

to make the time pass quickly：消磨光阴，解除病人的寂寞。

[10]

The Greek was very fretful, and kept finding fault with the fruit drinks and food that Singer prepared for him. Constantly he made his friend help him out of bed so that he could pray. He fumbled with his hands to say "Darling Mary" and then held to the small brass cross tied to his neck with a dirty string. His big eyes would wall up to the ceiling with a look of fear in them, and afterwards he was very sulky and would not let his friend speak to him.

[注]

fretful：容易发脾气的。**finding fault with**：找错，挑眼。kept 是不及物动词，表示"继续地做"。finding 是现在分词做 subjective complement。

fruit drinks：果汁，用以代酒。

held to：紧握。

wall：眼睛（戏剧性地）转动。**sulky**：闹别扭的样子。

[11]

Singer was patient and did all that he could. He drew little pictures, and once he made a sketch of his friend to amuse him. The picture hurt the big Greek's feelings, and he refused to be reconciled until Singer had made his face very young and handsome and colored his hair bright yellow and his eyes china blue. And then he tried not to show his pleasure.

[注]

patient：有耐心的。**sketch**：速写。Singer 可能把他画得很胖，因此他不高兴了。

reconciled：言归于好。"until" clause 中有两动词，had made 和（had）colored。**china blue**：青瓷色。young、handsome、bright yellow、china blue 都是 objective complements。Singer 把他的脸画漂亮了，那胖子该高兴了。可是他心里高兴，脸上还不肯表示出来。Singer 想尽办法，无非要使朋友高兴，朋友偏不让他称心如愿。

[12]

Singer nursed his friend so carefully that after a week Antonapoulos was able to return to his work. But from that time on there was a difference in their way of life. Trouble came to the two friends.

[注]

nurse 作名词是"护士",作动词便是"看护"。病是好了,却有别的麻烦来了。

[13]

Antonapoulos was not ill any more, but a change had come in him. He was irritable and no longer content to spend the evenings quietly in their home. When he would wish to go out Singer followed along close behind him. Antonapoulos would go into a restaurant, and while they sat at the table he slyly put lumps of sugar, or a peppershaker, or pieces of silverware in his pocket. Singer always paid for what he took and there was no disturbance. At home he scolded Antonapoulos, but the Greek only looked at him with a bland smile.

[注]

irritable:容易发脾气的。**close**(副词):贴近地。**slyly**,偷偷摸摸地,鬼鬼祟祟地。
peppershaker:内盛胡椒粉,盖上有细孔的小瓶。
disturbance:纷扰。偷走的东西有人给付账,不会有什么吵闹了。
bland:温文的(按:此词带一点"油腔滑调"的意思)。

[14]

The months went on and these habits of Antonapoulos grew worse. One day at noon he walked calmly out of the fruit store of his cousin and urinated in public against the wall of the First National Bank Building across the street. At times he would meet people on the sidewalk whose faces did not please him, and he would bump into these persons and push at them with his elbows and stomach. He walked into a store one day and hauled out a floor lamp without paying for it, and another time he tried to take an electric train he had seen in a showcase.

[注]

in public:当众。**urinated**(动词):小便。**urine**(名词):尿。**bump**:撞(上去)。
stomach:肚皮。肥人腹大,亦可用以撞人。**hauled out**:拖出来。不是偷偷摸摸地拿,而是明目张胆地拖了。**electric train**：电动火车（玩具）。**he had seen in a showcase** 是定语从句。**showcase**：商店陈列货物之玻璃柜。

[15]

For Singer this was a time of great distress. He was in a constant state of agitation. The money he had saved in the bank was spent for bail and fines. All of his efforts and money were used to keep his friend out of jail because of such charges as theft, committing public indecencies, and assault and battery.

[注]

distress：痛苦。**agitation**：激动。**bail**：保释。**fines**：罚款。**charges**：罪名。**committing public indecencies**：在公共场所做不体面的事，指上段的当众便溺。**assault and battery**：（法律名词）殴打罪，指街头撞人。

[16]

The Greek cousin for whom Antonapoulos worked did not enter into these troubles at all. Charles Parker (for that was the name this cousin had taken) let Antonapoulos stay on at the store, but he watched him always with his pale, tight face and he made no effort to help him. Singer had a strange feeling about Charles Parker. He began to dislike him.

[注]

上文讲 Antonapoulos 是在他的一个亲戚所开的糖果铺里做事的，亲戚也是希腊人，名字拼起来大约也很长，Charles Parker 是他到美国后新起的名字。那亲戚坐视 Antonapoulos 屡蹈法网，而不加援手。Singer 渐表不满。

[17]

Singer lived in continual turmoil and worry. But Antonapoulos was always bland, and no matter what happened the gentle, flaccid smile was still on his face.

[注]

turmoil：（心里的）动乱，意义同前面的 agitation 差不多。**no matter what happened**：不论出了什么事。**flaccid**：（肌肉）松松的。

[18]

And then the final trouble came to Singer.

One afternoon he had come to meet Antonapoulos at the fruit store when Charles Parker handed him a letter. The letter explained that Charles Parker had made arrangements for his cousin to be taken to the state insane asylum two hundred miles away. Charles Parker had used his influence in the town and the details were already settled. Antonapoulos was to leave and to be admitted into the asylum the next week.

[注]

made arrangements：办手续。**state**：州立的。**insane asylum**：疯人院（第一个词的意思是"疯人的"，第二个词的意思是"收容所"）。

influence：势力（面子，朋友交情等）。随随便便送一个人进疯人院，恐怕不容易。Charles Parker 利用了他在镇上的一点势力，才办妥。**details were settled**：各项手续都已办妥。

[19]

Singer read the letter several times, and for a while he could not think. Charles Parker was talking to him across the counter, but he did not even try to read his lips and understand. At last Singer wrote on the little pad he always carried in his pocket:

You cannot do this, Antonapoulos must stay with me.

[注]

read：仔细地看，端详。普通人如用英语说话，Singer 看嘴唇动作，亦能会意。**pad**：拍纸簿。

[20]

Charles Parker shook his head excitedly. He did not know much American. "None of your business," he kept saying over and over.

Singer knew that everything was finished. The Greek was afraid that some day he might be responsible for his cousin. Charles Parker did not know much about the American language — but he understood the American dollar very well, and he had used his money and influence to admit his cousin to the asylum without delay.

[注]

none of your business：不用你管。Parker 不大会说美国话（American），就拿这四个词重复地说。

responsible for his cousin：替他负责，受他的累。怕受累，因此赶快把 Antonapoulos 送走。

[21]

There was nothing Singer could do.

Then came the day when Antonapoulos must leave. Singer brought out his own suitcase and very carefully packed the best of their joint possessions. Antonapoulos made himself a lunch to eat during the journey. In the late afternoon they walked arm in arm down the street for the last time together. It was a chilly afternoon in late November, and little huffs of breath showed in the air before them.

[注]

suitcase：轻便衣箱。**joint possessions**：（两人）共有的物品。

huff = puff（一口一口的气）。空气寒冷，吐气成雾。

[22]

Charles Parker was to travel with his cousin, but he stood apart from them at the station. Antonapoulos crowded into the bus and settled himself with elaborate preparations on one of the front seats. Singer watched him from the window and his hands began desperately to talk for the last time with his friend. But Antonapoulos was so busy checking over the various items in his lunch box that for a while he paid no attention. Just before the bus pulled away from the curb he turned to Singer and his smile was very bland and remote — as though they were many miles apart.

[注]

Singer 送他们表兄弟二人到长途汽车站。Charles Parker 冷酷如旧，Antonapoulos 还是只顾他个人的舒服，只有 Singer 真感到痛苦。

crowded into：挤进去（不一定表示车子里人多，可能只表示门小人肥，走进去很费力）。**settled himself**：坐下。**with elaborate preparations**：做些细心的准备工作（如掸掸灰尘，提提裤子，检点一下手里的包裹等）。

lunch box：午餐盒。**items**：项目（面包、肉、蔬菜等）。那希腊人坐下来，先检点盒子里的食物，哪管得 Singer 在窗外对他"说话"？

pulled away：开走。**curb**：人行道的边，汽车常停在它的旁边。**remote**：遥远的。

[23]

The weeks that followed did not seem real at all. All day Singer worked over his bench in the back of the jewelry store, and then at night he returned to the house alone. More than anything he wanted to sleep. As soon as he came home from work he would lie on his cot and try to doze awhile. Dreams came to him when he lay there half asleep. And in all of them Antonapoulos was there. His hands would jerk nervously, for in his dreams he was talking to his friend and Antonapoulos was watching him.

[注]

did not seem real：不像是真的，不知道怎么过去的。**bench**：这里不作"长凳"解，而是"工作台"（Singer 是个银器刻花匠，已见前文）。

more than anything：比什么都要紧。照一般语法书规定，anything 后应跟 else。**jerk**：抽动。**nervously**：神经失常地。在梦中"说话"，手不知不觉动起来了。

[24]

　　Singer tried to think of the time before he had ever known his friend. He tried to recount to himself certain things that had happened when he was young. But none of these things he tried to remember seemed real.

　　Singer recalled that, although he had been deaf since he was an infant, he had not always been a real mute. At the school he was thought very intelligent. He learned the lessons, before the rest of the pupils. But he could never become used to speaking with his lips. When he was twenty-two he had come South to this town from Chicago and he met Antonapoulos immediately. Since that time he had never spoken with his mouth again, because with his friend there was no need for this.

[注]

recount：详细地说一遍。这里有"回忆"的意思。

intelligent：聪明，尤其指"读书、学习"方面的聪明。

before：指学得比别人快。used 在这里是过去分词，不是 finite verb。to 后接动名词 speaking。他不习惯用嘴唇说话，还是做手势方便。有了这位哑巴朋友之后，他就用不着再开口了。

[25]

　　Nothing seemed real except the ten years with Antonapoulos. In his half-dreams he saw his friend very vividly, and when he awakened a great aching loneliness would be in him. Occasionally he would pack up a box for Antonapoulos, but he never received any reply. And so the months passed in this empty, dreaming way.

[注]

vividly：生动地，活生生地。

aching 是动词 ache 的现在分词，作"疼痛"解。**loneliness**（寂寞）本来只是一种空泛的感觉，今以 aching 来形容，则心头烦恼，化为身上疼痛，虽仍未着形象，然而隐者显，虚者实，触之宛然如在矣。

pack up a box：包好一盒（礼物送去）。

empty：空虚的。**dreaming**：梦幻似的。此两词应本段开首 Nothing seemed real 一句。未认识 Antonapoulos 之前，所经所历，似无一实在之事；今 Antonapoulos 已走，触目空虚，如梦似幻，生命又复虚度。

前文有句曰：The *weeks* that followed did not seem real at all，本段又曰：the *months* passed in this empty, dreaming way。生活空虚如旧，而 weeks 已延长为 months 矣。

[26]

Each evening the mute walked alone for hours in the street. Sometimes the nights were cold with the sharp, wet winds of March and it would be raining heavily. But to him this did not matter. His gait was agitated and he always kept his hands stuffed tight into the pockets of his trousers. Then as the weeks passed the days grew warm and languorous. His agitation gave way gradually to exhaustion and there was a look about him of deep calm. In his face there came to be a brooding peace that is seen most often in the faces of the very sorrowful or the very wise. But still he wandered through the streets of the town, always silent and alone.

[注]

gait：走路的姿态。哑巴的手，本来就是他的嘴。听他说话人既然已经不在了，手是可以塞起来了。

languorous：闷人的（天气）。**gave way ... to**：原意是"让开路，让别人走"，或是"撤退了，让别人前进"。**his agitation gradually gave way to exhaustion**：他的激动渐渐地消失而疲惫之感继起。**there was a look about him of deep calm** = there was a look of deep calm about him。

brooding：沉思的。**peace**：平和的气象。the very sorrowful 和 the very wise 中的两个形容词，都当名词用——有大悲哀的人和有大智慧的人。望之穆然深思者，大抵其人非为哀伤已极，即已参透人生。今 Singer 脸上之表情即此类也。

The Last Puritan
最后一个清教徒

George Santayana（1863—1952）

美国早期的移民，很多是英国来的清教徒，因此清教徒主义（Puritanism）也是美国立国基本精神之一。清教徒所过的是一种严肃的生活，以天理制人欲，培养独立自尊的人格，除了相信上帝这一点以外，他们的理想，大致和宋儒传统下的中国士大夫相仿。桑塔耶那在《最后一个清教徒》（1935）里描写一个典型的清教徒 Oliver Alden，下面几段讲的是那位"清教徒"幼年时候所受的教育，由此我们知道：一个严肃的（可是也是拘谨狭仄的）生活是怎么开始的。

下面所选的几段（见原书第二编第三章）都比较浅近容易，并不能充分代表原作英文"构思精妙"、"辞藻华丽"的好处。但是这几段已经把"Puritanism"说明得相当清楚了。

[1]

The advent of Fräulein Schlote was a blessing all round. Mrs. Alden, on whom everything depended, smiled on the newcomer from the beginning. As for the child himself, neither the disappearance of his old nurse nor the appearance of the new Fräulein seemed to impress his young mind. He was accustomed to strangers, and not afraid of them; they all behaved in much the same way. Gradually, however, he became aware of something else in her: there was sympathy in her movements, there was playfulness: Irma was *affectionate*. Discipline was relaxed: it was no longer imperative to play only with clean gravel especially poured out for him: he might now run and dig up his own gravel from the path. The routine of life might have become more plastic, making a little room for caprice. But was caprice less tiresome than law?

[注]

本书主人翁 Oliver Alden 原有一老保姆（nurse），后从德国请来 Irma Schlote 小姐任看护管教之职，即英文所谓 governess。

Fräulein 德文，意即"小姐"。**advent**：来到，义同 arrival，但用于较庄重重要之场合。**blessing**：（天赐）恩典。**all round**：对全家的人说来。

Mrs. Alden 书中主人翁之母亲。**on whom everything depended**：什么东西都得靠她。她是主妇，家庭教师是好是坏，就凭她一句话。

impress：给予印象。

aware of：觉得。**something else**：有些别的东西。就这小孩子看来，到家里来的陌生人似乎都差不多，可是这位家庭教师他渐渐地发现有些与众不同。

sympathy：同情。**playfulness**：活泼好弄。**affectionate**：温馨慈爱。他的母亲待他是冷冰冰的，家庭教师的慈爱给他的印象特别深，故此词用斜体字排，以示重要。

discipline：纪律。**relaxed**：放宽。接着就有例子说明：小孩子喜欢玩沙，本来家里管束得严，沙是先淘好了给他的，现在他可以自己到地上去挖了。**gravel**：较 sand 为粗。中文应作"沙砾"。

routine of life：日常旧规、刻板生活。**plastic**：便于塑造的、可以任意变化其形状的。**caprice**：中文成语"忽发奇想"里的"奇想"、"怪主意"。**making room for** 里的 room 原意是"地位"，"让出地位来给（别人）"；这个小孩子的生活本来只是循规蹈矩的刻板文章，现在新家庭教师来了，生活可以多点变化，"可以让出些地位来给出乎常规的思想行动了"——可以偶然"随兴之所至，自由行动了"。

虽然有这种可能性，可是事实上却并未实现，动词 might have become 隐含 did not become 之意。为什么呢？末一句"反问"（rhetorical question）即说明其原委。**but was caprice less tiresome than law?** = But caprice was not less tiresome than law。

循规蹈矩的生活（law）固然无聊（tiresome），然而就兴之所至，率性行事（caprice），亦复无聊，所以仍旧是规规矩矩地过日子。

[2]

It was a distinct relief to discard the perambulator and to trudge along with Fräulein for a country walk. And sometimes Fräulein lengthened these rambles more than was pleasant for him. He was no baby, to say he was tired, or hot, or wished to be carried; the old perambulator, even if thought of at such a moment, was not to be mentioned.

[注]

perambulator：小孩坐车。**discard**：废弃不用；小孩渐大，能蹒跚而行，用不到坐车了。**relief**：(束缚的) 解除；坐车拘束而累赘，一旦下车步行，自有轻松之感。**distinct**：很明显的。**trudge**：吃力地走路。

rambles：漫游。**lengthened**：放长，（走远）。than 在这里的用法很像是一个 relative pronoun，丹麦籍语法学家 Jespersen 称之为 relative conjunction。(见其所著 *Essentials of English Grammar* §34.41，与 *A Modern English Grammar*, II.§9.11)

to say…：infinitive phrase 当形容词用，形容 baby。"他不再是一个可以说是他疲倦了的婴孩了"。他已经自认是一个大孩子，即使是走累了，或是走热了，或是想抱（carried）了，都不愿意讲出来。

thought of：两个词连起来当"及物动词"用。他即使想到要坐"坐车"，也不愿意对家庭教师提起。真是一个有骨气的小孩子。

[3]

If a pebble got into his shoe, it might be unpleasant, but he said nothing. Pebbles were insignificant accidents, like certain needs of the body: and if Fräulein said they *must* get to the top of the hill, the view would be so *wunderschön*, the hill must be stoically climbed.

[注]

pebble：石子。

insignificant：无足轻重的。**accidents**：偶然的事件。like 以下，作者语带讥讽：石子进了鞋子，那个刚会走路的小孩子还是往前走，认为这是一件不足道的小事，"就像身体上某些需要一样"。身体上某些需要是些什么？是不是指饿了想吃、渴了想喝、痒了想搔？清教徒是可以不理会这些需要的，桑塔耶那似乎并不以为然。

　　must 和 wunderschön 都是引用那位德国小姐的原词，故用斜体字排。must 表示非去不可，*wunderschön*（德文）= very beautiful。the view would be so *wunderschön* 是 noun clause，做 said 的宾语。

　　stoically：坚毅地。Stoics 本来是希腊一派哲学家，译作"斯多噶学派"，其教人以"克己忍苦"为主。这个小孩子不管气力够不够（鞋子里还有石子呢！），一往直前地跟了家庭教师爬山，这种精神就够得上称是 stoical。

[4]

The view was nothing to him: but by the time he had plodded bravely to the top, he had forgotten the pebble; and when later, after running down the hill, he felt it again in a different place, he knew that they were going home and that it didn't matter. Such was the nature of country walks; and when he changed his shoes and stockings before dinner, he would shake the pebble out. The next time he would remember to lace both his shoes equally tight, so that pebbles shouldn't get into either of them.

[注]

　　德国小姐为了要欣赏风景才爬到山顶上去，可是这位清教徒小孩对于风景的美，并不觉得什么，他只是"为了爬山而爬山"，忽略美育的陶冶，偏重意志的锻炼，这也是清教徒主义的特征之一。桑塔耶那对于这一点，亦颇有微辞。

　　plod 意义同前面的 trudge 差不多：吃力地走路。

　　到了山顶，就忘了鞋子里的石子：回家的路上，脚底下又感觉到有石子了（虽然石子能滚，已经挪了地方了），可是反正要回家了，这点不舒服也就可以不理了。

　　nature：性质。乡间散步的性质就是如此，有点不舒服也在意料之中。

　　lace：系鞋带。**tight**：紧。**either**：两者之一；两只鞋子系得一样紧，没有一只进得了石子了。

[5]

One day without any reason, he climbed up from her knee and put both arms round her neck, holding on very softly and very tight for what seemed to her a long time.

"But darling," he said, smothering her emotions, "why do you do that?"

[注]

for a long time：过了一段长时间；**for what seemed to her a long time**：过了一段在她看来是很长的时间。

smothering：抑制。**emotions**：感情。学生对她忽然如此亲热，这位家庭教师可能惊喜交集。但是她还是抑制住了感情问他。

[6]

His German, and even his English, was inadequate to frame an answer, and he merely held on.

"But do you ever hug your mother like that? And of course it would be very wrong not to love her ever so much more than you love me, because she is your mother."

[注]

他同家庭教师之间是说惯德文的，但是当时的感情，他非但用德文说不出来，就是用英文也说不出来。"and even his English"前后两逗点（,）的功用好像括号一般不影响主语 German 的 number，所以动词还是用单数的 "was"。

inadequate：不够。**frame**：形成。

hug：拥抱。**not to love her** = if you did not love her。**ever** = very（此解根据《简明牛津词典》），**so** 也是用以加强 much。比较级的形容词（或副词），如 more 等，前面加 ever so much 三个词来加强语气，是很普通的用法。

[7]

Somewhat slowly and absent-mindedly Oliver let go: he certainly never hugged his mother like that. It was all rather discouraging. Irma felt this too, and gradually ceased to take him on her lap. "You are such a big boy now," she would say. "You must sit up in your high chair."

[注]

absent-mindedly：心不在焉地。**let go**：松手。

discouraging：扫兴的。小孩子喜欢他的家庭教师，而且把这种感情天真自然地流露出来，本来也很正常。可是清教徒认为感情的流露是可耻的，Oliver 从来没有向他的母亲亲热过，以后也不会再同家庭教师亲热了。家庭教师渐渐地也不去抱他了。**lap**：膝上。

[8]

One day Fräulein unsuspectingly mentioned at table the urgent need of a cushion for Oliver's chair. Mrs. Alden let her talk on; but after a little pause pursed her lips and said: "I don't think little boys ought to be brought up to sit on *cushions*. It is effeminate. The chair comes from the very best makers in Great Falls. I paid a particularly high price for it, and I'm sure it must be quite right as it is — much cooler and healthier in summer than sitting on a stuffy cushion, which is always slipping about and getting tumbled and making one restless. If only Oliver wouldn't fidget, but keep his clothes properly pulled down under him, he would be perfectly comfortable, and wouldn't need to find fault with what is provided for him."

[注]

unsuspectingly：没有猜想到会产生什么后果的，脱口而出的。（德国小姐以为座椅质地太粗，有伤小孩的嫩皮肤，所以主张要用垫子，想不到她这种主张竟大受女主人的反对）。**at table**：用膳之时。**urgent**：迫切的。

pursed her lips：把嘴唇缩起来，大不以为然的样子。女主人也是清教徒，涵养功夫到家，虽然话听不入耳，可是还是等人家说完了，再停一停之后（after a pause），然后发表她的高见。

brought up：教养成人。（cushions 一词应重读。）

effeminate：太娘儿们气了。

Great Falls：地名，在康涅狄格州，为女主人娘家所在地。

makers：制家具的。

as it is：照它现在这样子（就很好）。**stuffy**：不透气的。**slipping about**：滑来滑去（about = here and there）。**getting tumbled**：坐瘪了，压皱了或是翻过来了。**restless**：神志不安。

fidget：乱摸乱动。**under him**：坐在他身体下面。

find fault with：找错。**what is provided for him**：（家里）替他准备好的东西。注意：他们家里资财百万，并不是为了省钱才不给小孩子买（或做）一个垫子的。照清教徒的想法，任何不舒服的事情都该忍受，何况大人替小孩子所设想的，绝不会有错。所以垫子就用不着了。

The Great Fire of 1945
一九四五年大火记

Margaret Shedd（1900—1986）

本文选自《一九四七年欧·亨利奖得奖小说集》(*Prize Stories of 1947, The O. Henry Awards*)。作者玛格丽特·谢德为美国女作家，有长短篇小说多种问世。

原题"一九四五年大火记"，文中叙一巨宅被焚之时，宅中女主人仓皇逃出。女主人已与其夫别居，其子战死，生活本甚孤寂，今身处火场之外，目睹火势蔓延，巨屋被毁，勾起种种回忆。本文于火景描写之中，掺以心理活动，勾勒深刻，描写生动。此处所录，因篇幅所限，略加节删，但大体俱在，仍不失为一短篇杰作也。

[1]

Standing on the high ground behind the house, she saw that one small flame had separated itself from the matrix of fire within the house and was gliding up the wall. It licked the shingles nimbly and delicately, and, still only a golden tongue, found the window of her room. She herself had left that window open and leaned out of it helplessly calling help before she ran from the room down the hot stairs out of the house to the earth never more friendly than then.

[注]

女主人公于小说开场时，已站立在屋后高地，全篇小说描写，即由此视点出发。

[4]

When, shortly before, the housekeeper had come pounding on her door, screaming, beating on the wood, "Wake up, wake up quick, Mrs. James! The furnace has burst, the house is afire, get up quick!" She had had time to get the bracelet and bring it out. She had, half consciously, gone to the window and called for help. Then she had wrapped herself in a heavy gray dressing gown and had looked around the room deciding whether to take out her fur coats and some letters. In her mind's eye she had seen the bracelet lying in the top drawer of her green French Provençal dressing table along with the other trinkets. She had had time to think, No, I won't take it; leave it where it is. So, remembering now the bracelet's earlier associations, which for many years she had forgotten, she was more glad than ever that it was gone. She was honest enough to admit that life had failed her. And as between apathy and pain she had made her choice.

[注]

女主人公面对大火，回首前尘，想起了丈夫于某年圣诞节所送给她的一只手镯（bracelet）。手镯象征了他们婚姻生活的幸福。现在他们的婚姻既已破裂，她不愿意再想起这只手镯，也不愿意把它从火里救出来。本段之前，原文有三段回忆描写，今已节去。

本段开始，她想起了火起之时，她于睡梦中惊醒，仓皇呼救逃生这一段情景。

pounding：用力地打。**beating on the wood**：打门。管家婆来报讯的时候，她还有工夫把手镯抢救出来。

第二、三句叙述她惊醒后所做的事：迷迷糊糊地跑到窗口去叫救命，披起一件灰色的厚睡衣，把全身裹住，再检点一下什么东西该抢救出去。

in her mind's eye：脑子里很清楚地想到，好像看见一般。**dressing table**：梳妆台。**Provençal**：法国普罗旺斯式的（家具的一种形式）。**trinkets**：小件珠宝玩物。she had had time to think 之后跟的是"直接引语"，可是把引号省去了。

So, remembering now 之 now 又跳到她在火场前的那时候了。读英美新派的心理小说，一定要把书中主角所处的时间、空间，时时留心辨明，才有线索可循。因为近代心理小说的特点，就是描写"回忆"，而且是把"回忆"同"眼前情景"

夹杂着写。看惯十八、十九世纪那种条理清楚、层次井然的小说的读者，乍读新派小说，往往有"茫无头绪，不知所云"之感。

associations：联想。想起了当初和手镯有关的种种，她想把它丢了也好。**admit**：承认。**life had failed her**：生命没有给她什么好处。

apathy：麻木，尤其指对于痛苦的麻木。**pain**：痛苦。痛苦与麻木之间，她挑选了一样。把手镯带出去，过去的一切悲喜哀乐，又要在她心头重演，这是所谓"痛苦"。让火把手镯给烧了，把过去都毁灭了，这是所谓"麻木"。两者之间，她早已决定了选择其一。**as between** 这一 phrase，是从 as for "至于"化出来的。这里的 as 不可省。

[5]

As if to test that decision, the fire peeled off one wall of the house, and the room she had just left opened up before her. There was no distortion; the fire illumined and had not begun to destroy the room which she suddenly realized was dear to her. There was the Provençal dressing table, bought for a white-plastered bedroom they had had in a house in the Berkeley hills.

[注]

peeled off：剥去。屋子有一面的墙已经烧掉，但是烧得很快，干净利落，好像剥去一层皮似的。

墙剥去以后，她的卧室赫然在目，好像要考验（test）她所下的决心似的：到底她真是麻木呢，还是痛苦。**she had just left** 是定语从句。她的卧室还没有烧坏，还没有走样（distortion）。**illumined**：照亮。火还没有把房间毁了，只是把它照亮了，使她看得更清楚。盛手镯的梳妆台就在眼前。她想起了这只梳妆台还是以前住在其他房子的时候买的，后来搬来了。**white-plastered**：四周墙壁和天花板涂白灰的。

[6]

Now she saw the fire whirl up in a rotating gesture to snatch the clock and the vase with its white flowers, and, as if that were the signal for holocaust, the room was blotted out in a dance of up-prancing, laughing, clapping flames and the dressing table writhed in their grip. I never saw the bed, she thought, nor the curtains, the fabrics I loved. Now they were gone and, again to her surprise, she was grieved; she had thought she was immune to simple emotions like nostalgia or the faint sadness of having old friends depart who forget to say good-by.

[注]

whirl up：回旋而上。**in a rotating gesture**：以旋转之势。**snatch**：抢走，攫取。形容火势之迅速。**holocaust**：原意为"燔祭"，烧全牛全羊以祭神，转为"彻底毁灭"，尤其是用火来烧毁的。**signal**：信号。火把台钟和花瓶一烧去，好像是一声信号似的，立刻火势大作。**blotted out**：涂没。满室是火，房间都看不见了。

形容 flames 的三个形容词都很有力量：prancing 原意为马用后脚站起来跳，借作"跳跃"。**up-prancing**：往上跳的。**laughing, clapping**：火焰会笑，会鼓掌吗？这三个形容词都和前面的名词 dance 呼应。

writhe：辗转反侧，受煎熬之状。**in their grip**：在火焰的魔掌之中。盛手镯的梳妆台终于不保了。

she thought 的前后是没有加引号的直接引语。从墙壁被剥去，到卧室被毁，只有很短的时间，她来不及周览全室，很多东西已经不可复见了。床没有见到，帐子窗帘等也没有见到，而这些纺织品（fabrics）是她所喜欢的。fabrics 是 curtains 的同位语。

again to her surprise：又是使她惊奇的。她历经沧桑，自以为已经磨炼得心如铁石，冷酷无情。不料今晚大火一起，所见所思，无不触目惊心，甚至悲从中来，她自己也觉得惊奇起来了。

immune（形容词）：有免疫力、抵抗力，不受支配或伤害。"支配"或"伤害"她的东西放在介词 to（或 from 或 against）之后。她本来以为（had thought）她可以不受简单情感的支配。简单的情感有两个例子，一是思乡病（nostalgia），一是当老朋友远行忘了来辞行时所感觉到的那种"淡淡的轻愁"（faint sadness）。这一类的情感，她自以为是不能支配她的了。现在床和帐子被焚，其最后一瞥，她竟亦未能见到，直如老友之不辞而别，心中难免怅然耳。

按：good-by 是美国拼法。

[7]

Someone was walking that way, hailing her. "They've got here at last, Mrs. James. They may be able to save some of the things downstairs."

"It's all right." She did not try to compete with fire and hose roar and the bells of rescuers arriving.

"What?" the voice shouted to her. "What did you say?"

"Never mind."

[注]

hailing：高声招呼。

they 指来救火的人。**rescuers**：救援人员。**compete**：竞争。**hose**：（救火车上的）水管。火声、水声、警钟声，一片喧哗，讲话很费力。她没有提起嗓子说话，"她不想同那些声音竞争"。

来人没听清楚她说什么，所以嚷着问：What？她根本没有注意来人是谁，她只听见有个声音同她说话而已，故曰 the *voice* shouted to her，而不说 the *man* shouted to her。

[8]

"They've already got out some of the papers from Mr. James' study, and they've started on the furniture. That brocade settee." The shouting voice was triumphant, an achievement boasted. It was an achievement, men risking their lives to extract furniture from a burning house. She tried to remember if they had ever used that settee. Yes, there had been a time, and she was forgetting it on purpose ... The last time she had seen of Mr. James; she was sitting on the brocade settee ...

[注]

papers：文件。**study**：书房。**brocade**：锦缎。**settee**：沙发似的长椅子。**boasted**（过去分词）：夸耀。**achievement**：（救火的）成绩。**extract**：取出。

if 用来引起一个名词从句时 = whether。

on purpose：故意地。过去的事情想起来太痛苦，她故意地要忘了它。

the last time 三个词连起来当 conjunction 用。这一类表示时间的所谓 group

conjunction 常用的有 the moment、every time、by the time 等等。为什么这把椅子所引起的回忆是痛苦的呢？因为最后一次她同她丈夫吵架的时候，她就是坐在这把椅子上。

[9]

The fire had blown to statuesque grandeur. It had taken hold of the house trees, which were now dying. The three tall sentinel firs made their pyre apart, but the others, among them the maple outside her window, were meeting common death with the house they shaded. This was a great fire, the biggest in these parts for twenty years. The firemen drew back to safer distances. The rescued settee, which had not been carried out far enough, began to smolder, and no one would brave the heat to rescue it again.

[注]

blown：膨胀。**statuesque**：像雕像似的。**grandeur**：雄伟。

sentinel：哨兵。**firs**：枞树。枞树三棵，本耸立守卫，犹如哨兵，今均焚去。**pyre**：火葬堆。**apart** 与 **common death** 相对照：三棵枞树分三处烧，别的树同屋子一起烧去。**maple**：枫树。they shaded 是定语从句。**they** = the trees：屋本居树荫之下。

drew back：向后撤退。火势太大，救火人员都不敢再走上前去了。

smolder：焚化（火不冒出来的）。长椅本已着火，抢救出来后，没有搬多远，现在它自己烧起来了。**brave**（动词）：冒，犯，敢去碰。

[10]

The fire chief, village druggist disguised in a helmet, came up to comfort her and apologize, "It's a pity, Mrs. James, we couldn't save anything to speak of. The way the draft carried the flame you'd have thought that house was built to be burned. Excuse me, ma'am, I guess you're feeling bad enough."

[注]

druggist：卖药的，药剂师。乡间守望相助，救火会亦为村民所组成。**disguised**：化装。**helmet**：（铜）盔。

to speak of：值得一提的（东西）。**draft**：气流，风。**the way**：也是一个 group conjunction，这里的意思好像是 from。从火随风走这种情势看来，你会以为那屋子是造来专给火烧的。

[11]

She had no idea what words he expected from her, so she pointed toward the fire, as much as to say, What is there to say? But he thought she was indicating the settee, now smoking like a Christmas pudding, and he felt guilty about it.

"I know," he said humbly. "I thought we sure had it out far enough."

[注]

idea 后有一介词 of 省去：她不知道他期待她怎样答复。

What is there to say？前后引号省去：还有什么可说的？这句话并没有说出来，可是从她的姿势看来，效果上是等于说了（as much as to say）。

Christmas pudding：圣诞布丁。面粉、鸡蛋、黄油、葡萄干、梅干等调制而成，食时热气蒸腾。**guilty**：自责内疚（自觉救火不力）。

sure 当副词用。I thought we had ... 用过去式：我起初还以为……（现在才知道那张长椅子搬出来得还不够远）。

[12]

"Throw it back into the fire." She heard her own harsh, unkempt voice and she hadn't meant to offend the druggist-fireman, who backed off hurriedly, disconcerted by her ferocity; it was just that she could not help voicing exactly what was in her mind ... because she had decided to throw into the fiery furnace every shred of her life that she could lay hands on.

[注]

harsh：粗声粗气的。**unkempt**：随便的，不检点的。**offend**：得罪。**backed off**：向后走开。**disconcerted**：弄得很窘。**ferocity**：凶狠之状。

it was that：句子这样开头往往用来说明上文"事实是这样"。**could not help**：

不得不。**voice**：当动词用时，解作"表达出来，形诸语言"；这里是动名词。

furnace：炉。此处是暗喻（metaphor），指焚烧中的房子。shred 原意是极细的布条。生命里的"一丝一缕"，她都要掷到火里去，那张长椅子也不必说了。**that she could lay hands on**：定语从句，"凡是她的手所拿得到的"。

[13]

But the house burned brightly enough, as fine a fire as hell.

It was hell, nor more nor less. It tore at her eye-balls, and looking at it was more than looking because it had already begun to devour her.

[注]

照基督教传说，地狱里不断地烧着火。一个在基督教传统里长大的人，看见大火，很容易联想起地狱（hell）。

nor more nor less：不多也不少，正是（地狱）。

tore at：本意为"使劲地拉"。屋子大火，刺激她的眼睛，好像要抓破她的眼球似的。**looking at it**：对它看。**more than looking**：不只是"看"而已。大火不单对她的"视觉"发生作用，她的整个身心都受到影响，它已经开始把她吞下去。

[14]

The clawing flame fingers began to encircle her heart. What did they want? Could they release the dream that had been walled up in her? A dream as soft-feathered and surely molded as a thrush, but lifeless now, head battered and wings shredded from beating against the walls of defeat. This dream of life, giving and taking and of loving — poor love — was dead. She had failed; and the heart was a tomb and the flame fingers could probe and claw to no purpose — forever. That was it. She had forgotten. Hell was a flame forever; that was the whole point. Eternal fire.

[注]

clawing：用爪来抓的。女主人面对大火，火光刺目，热浪袭人，加以思潮起伏，百感交集，此身似已为大火吞去。本段又云：烈焰嚣张，伸指欲抓，开始向其方寸之间围攻。是则非但身外火势逼近，而且中心焦灼如焚，亦不堪熬炼矣。

这些火焰的手指要些什么东西呢？它们能不能将"砌"（walled up）在她心头的一个梦"释放"（release）出来呢？a dream 之下并无 finite verb，句子不完全，只是用以说明上一句的 the dream。她的梦像一只小鸟（thrush：画眉鸟），羽毛柔软，形体宛然（surely molded：她的梦不是空虚的，而有确定的塑造成的形体的）。现在这只小鸟是死了，因为想破壁而出，自己撞死的。battered 和 shredded 都是过去分词"头破翅裂"。围着那只小鸟的墙是什么墙呢？是"失败之墙"。她一生多故，累遭挫折，好梦难圆，情思郁结——梦想之鸟，难破失败之墙，终于梦碎鸟死，生机奄然矣。

次句说明"梦"之内容："生命之梦——施与受"。照语法结构，taking 后最好接 comma，可是接了 comma 之后，dream of life 和 dream of loving 硬是成对立之局。作者之意不然，of loving 既似与 of life 对立，又似附属于 of life 之下，而和 giving and taking 相平行。此时小说中主角心头本不甚清楚，此种句法似更能代表当时之心境。

she had failed：她的生命是失败了。**probe**：探察（尤其指用尖锐的外科仪器以探察伤口）。**to no purpose**：没有结果。"她的心已经像一座坟，探察它撕抓它也得不到什么结果了。"

she had forgotten：她已经把过去都忘记了。她还是自以为她的过去已经毁灭，她的心已经死去，看下文乃知事实并不如此。

that was the whole point：就是如此而已，只剩下大火，地狱，永久的（eternal）火。

[15]

And she sighed. For the first time she took her eyes away from the fire. That was all that happened. She paused and looked around.

She saw that oddly enough the woods behind the house had had nothing to do with the fire. Under her feet there were buds of bleeding heart and violets. In the valley, beyond the fire engines, a living thrush twittered. Could it be that the sky was reddening not with blood but with dawn?

[注]

sighed：叹气。

that was all that happened：所发生的就是这么一件事。叹了一口气，眼光转了一下。可是这么一来,她在心理上就大有转变了。

had had nothing to do with the fire:跟火不发生什么关系。第一个 had 表示过去完成时,第二个 had 表示"有"。

bleeding heart:花名,中国俗名"荷包牡丹"或"倒挂金钟"。**twittered**:啾唧而鸣。

reddening:(天色)转红。不是为血所染红的吧?或者可能是天亮了吧?

[16]

Spring dawn became something faintly more than the shadow smell of ground flowers under the leaves; and when she breathed she had to unclench her hands, because it was impossible to inhale the violet-tinged, dogwood-tipped air without also moving her neck and shoulders to relax them, then relaxing her arms, and at last her hands, which she held upward waist high and opened into palms.

[注]

shadow:名词当形容词用,指"依稀恍惚,不可捉摸"——草花之香是如此。花香虽轻淡如影,然对于小说中主人公之心理,已起作用;今晨光熹微,春日之黎明已可隐约觉得,在其人心理上亦起作用,其作用略甚(faintly more)于花香。

unclench:松开。她因为神经紧张过度,双手一直是紧握着拳的,现在透了一口气,手也松开了。impossible 跟 without 意义相连:不那么做,这个也不可能了。要做这个也得连那个一起做。

inhale:吸入。所吸入的空气有两个"复合词"(compound words)形容:**violet-tinged**(微微地带一点紫罗兰味儿的),**dogwood-tipped**(尖头上抹着山茱萸香味的)。空气怎么会有尖头(tip)的呢?中文也有"香味钻进鼻孔里面去"的说法,既能"钻",就可以有尖头了。

relax:放松。闻了那种空气,脖子和肩膀就得动一下,以求松弛;然后臂也松了,手也松了。她的手抬得同腰一般高,现在张开来了。

[17]

In one of them, of course, lay the golden bracelet. She had saved it without knowing it, and exactly when she thought she had made up her mind not to save it; and she had taken it because it was all she had worth saving.

[注]

of course：当然如此，不用说的。她手心里本来就捏着那只金手镯，手张开来，当然还在那里。

had saved 有一个 adverbial phrase（without ...）和一个 adverbial clause（exactly when ...）形容，两者之间有 and 连接。她把手镯带了出来，自己还不知道；那时候她正还下了决心不把它带出来呢！手镯是她丈夫所送的，她是不愿意再想起这一段姻缘了，决心让那手镯付之一炬。可是人生的神秘就在这里（心理小说的妙处也在这里），意识里想做的是一件事，下意识支配人所做的是另一件事。而迷迷茫茫仓皇逃生的一刹那，亦正是下意识发挥作用之时。手镯还是给带出来了，因为她所有的东西里面值得抢救的，就只是那只手镯而已。

The Jersey Heifer
泽西牛

Peggy Harding Love（1920—　）

本文选自《一九五一年欧·亨利奖得奖小说集》。该集共收短篇小说二十四篇，颇多名家作品，如福克纳，如韦尔蒂。（据该书编者 Herschel Brickell 于序文中云："It seems to the editor that Miss Welty and Mr. Faulkner are incomparably the present American masters of the short story."）本文作者潘琪·洛芙为一新晋女作家，作品不多。本文借一头小牛的故事，道出人生真谛，文笔清新，含意深远，的是佳作，入选并非偶然。

[1]

In October the cows went apple-crazy. The sweet, sun-warmed apple smell drifted from the orchard, tempting them unbearably; and by afternoon one or the other — the heifer usually, she was the mischief-maker — would have nudged down a rail from the old fence around the pasture. Once, only once, young Phoebe Matthews looked out the kitchen window and caught them in the act, but the picture stayed forever in her mind, an image of transcendent innocence and freedom. Leaping negligently, her hoofs tucked up delicately, the Jersey heifer went over the lower rails like a deer, and close behind, clumsy but with drooling haste, Daisy, the three-year-old Guernsey stepped clumsily out.

[注]

apple-crazy：此词乃作者杜撰，意为"苹果狂"，想苹果想痴了。**went** = became。

drifted：飘（来）。**orchard**：果园。**tempting**：引诱。**unbearably**：（引诱力极大）无法忍受。

one or the other：不是这头，就是那头。这就表示只有两头牛。两头牛中，一头是泽西种（Jersey）的小牛（heifer：尚未生育之小母牛，本文中之 heifer，跳踉活泼，顽皮好弄，尚不失幼犊本色），一头是根西种（Guernsey）的母牛，名叫"雏菊"（Daisy）。泽西、根西均为英伦海峡中英属岛屿。两地所产牛，以乳汁丰富著称于世。

she was the mischief-maker：祸都是她惹的，捣蛋鬼是她。

nudged：拱（以鼻部轻推）。**rail**：杠（栏杆上的横条）。**fence**：栅栏。**pasture**：牧场放牛之地。本句之 would 表示"习惯"；have nudged 表示"已经"：到了下午，她们常常已经推倒了栅栏上的一根横条（逃了出去）。

caught them in the act：当场查获。不是真的去把它们捉住，只是"发现"而已。act 指它们逃出这件事。

picture 和 **image** 指的是一件事：即书中主角 Phoebe 在厨房窗口所看见的景象。**transcendent**：超越一切的。**innocence**：天真。苹果甘香诱人，两牛越藩篱，弃牧场，奔走前往。她们这一个举动，有一次给女主人看见了。这是一幅图画，一幅洒落超脱、天真自由的图画。看见一次之后，Phoebe 再也不会忘了。

末句就是这幅"图画"具体的描写。小牛把蹄（hoofs）缩起（tucked up），姿态轻盈（delicately），随随便便（negligently），一跃而过，犹如小鹿一般。栅栏上每段本有横木数条，今某一段顶上一条已被推落，高度已减，小牛自可跃过。大牛行动颠顿（clumsy），紧随小牛之后，举步跨出，然而迫不及待，唾液满口（drooling）矣。

[2]

They trotted eagerly along the quiet dirt lane, turning their heads from side to side; and later, near milking time, Phoebe and Joe, her husband, had come upon them drunk with bliss in the long grass of the orchard. Each time they were discovered there, the cows stood perfectly still, their red and tawny coats bright against the blue sky, their soft, wide eyes looking out innocently among the apple branches. Long threads of saliva trailed from their velvety muzzles and glistened in the late sunlight, and under their hoofs the crushed and rotting apples gave off a heady fragrance.

[注]

trotted：急走。**lane**：乡间小路。**dirt**：灰土，路面未经铺修者。

come upon：发现，撞上。**drunk**：陶醉。**bliss** = great happiness。

tawny：褐黄色。Their ... coats (being) bright against the blue sky 和 their ... eyes looking ... 都是 nominative absolute phrases。

saliva：唾液。**threads**：细线。**muzzles**：（兽之）口鼻突出部分。**velvety**：色泽光洁如丝绒者。**heady**：醉人的。树上苹果，甘香四播，苹果成熟而落地者，香更浓郁，中人欲醉。双牛呆立林际，蹄践芳香，口水直流，如醉如痴。

crushed：踏碎的。**rotting**：溃烂的。

[3]

Always at the sight of them there Phoebe's heart leaped in delight. But Joe would drive them back to the pasture with a slow-moving, gentle stubbornness that matched their own. "Apples cut down Daisy's milk," he told Phoebe firmly. "I've got to wire that fence."

[注]

双牛陶醉于苹果香味之中，女主人见了，如有同感，心里也喜欢得跳起来了。

第二句之 would 强调"意志"，有"坚欲"之意。**stubbornness**：倔强精神。双牛坚不肯走，是为倔强；男主人非驱其归不可，亦是倔强。可是倔强而不暴烈，双方的倔强，都是和（gentle）缓（slow-moving）的一种。男主人这种"牛劲"，可与双牛的相比（matched）。

cut down：减少（产量）。**wire**：当名词是"铁丝"（或别种金属线）。此处是动词，解作"张以铁丝"。

I've got to = I have to：我非这么做不可。

[4]

"Let them go," Phoebe pleaded, begging as earnestly as for herself, "let them have a little freedom."

"Well," Joe said, musing, "well," and looked off over the fields that were so newly theirs. "The apples will be picked pretty soon now anyway," he said.

[注]

as for herself：好像替她自己恳求，她对那两头牛十分同情。
musing：沉思着。**newly**：他们新买下来的。
anyway：不管怎样，"反正现在苹果也快摘了"，让两头牛快乐几天吧。

[5]

By the end of October they had picked all the apples on the trees. They knelt carefully in the long grass, collecting even the windfalls and hauling them up the wagon ramp into the upper story of the old barn for cider-making.

[注]

windfall：给风吹下来的果子。他们非但把树上的苹果全摘了，连地下的也都捡回去。**hauling**：拖。**wagon ramp**：梯道，功用如梯，然面平，无梯级，故大筐水果可以拖上；坡缓而道宽，牛也会走得上的。大车也拉得上，故用 wagon 一词。**barn**：仓。普通 barn 的结构，底层养牲口，上层作储藏干草谷实等之用。**cider**：苹果汁。

[6]

They were pressing cider the afternoon the county agent stopped by for his first visit, and the first thing he told them was that the orchard should be cut down. Those old trees would never show a profit, he said. The orchard should go, the horses should be replaced by a tractor and modern equipment, new fences should be built, the chickens not allowed to run.

[注]

pressing：挤压（苹果作汁）。the afternoon 两词作 conjunction。**county**：郡（比"州"小的行政单位）。**county agent**：本郡的巡回调查员，协助农民解决各种困难者。

第一句中的 **the orchard** = the trees in the orchard。

［7］

After a minute Joe said: "I guess you better not put us down as farmers. We are grateful for your advice and we sure need a lot of it, but I guess we'd rather live peaceful than make money."

［注］

put down 本意是 write down（记下来），这里只是"当作"、"认为"的意思。

I guess = I think（通常是美国用法）。

we'd rather = we would rather：我们宁可这样；下面常跟着 than，表示"不愿那样"。

［8］

"No, son, I'll put you down as two romantic dreamers and come around again next spring." The agent got in his car and was starting out the dirt lane when he leaned out the window again, pointing to where the pasture fence rail was down again. "Your cows are out," he called. "Who's boss around here, you or bossy?" and, laughing slyly, he jounced away in his dusty sedan.

［注］

romantic dreamers：浪漫的梦想家。所谓"浪漫"约相当于中文成语"不务实际"。照那调查员看来，务农当以牟利为目的，可是那对小夫妻自认所要求者只是一种美丽宁静的田园生活而已。

leaned out the window：探首窗外。where ... down again 是名词性从句。**boss**：主人。**bossy**：牛。（两词皆美国俗语。）**slyly**：狡猾地。不一定有什么恶意，只是明知其可笑而笑之。**jounced**：颠荡（车行不稳）。**sedan**：轿车。

［9］

For a little while Phoebe and Joe stood where he left them, quiet and abstracted in the pale, slanting sunlight. Phoebe's hands were cold and sticky from the apple juice, and she held them up in the sun to warm them. At last she said, "I'd better get the cows." The orchard was stripped now, completely appleless, so she wouldn't find them there; but the scent of apples still hung everywhere in the air, filling the cows with yearning, and searching restlessly for fulfillment they still broke out of the pasture. Joe looked at Phoebe as if he hadn't heard her. "What if he's right?" he said broodingly. "Maybe it's all an impossible dream." But when Phoebe protested, "No, he's wrong! We've never been so happy," Joe smiled and touched her reassuringly, because of course it was true.

[注]

quiet 和 abstracted（出神的）两词都形容主语 Phoebe and Joe，其时夕阳斜照（slanting），日光淡弱（pale），盖已近黄昏。Phoebe 的手上苹果汁未除，现在觉得冷，也觉得粘。本文以 Phoebe 为主角，心理活动（感觉和思想）只描写她一个人的。牛的快乐是从她眼里看出来的，她丈夫的态度也是从她的观点来写的。

I'd better get the cows：我还是把牛找回来吧。'd 是 had 的缩写。

stripped：果子已摘光。she wouldn't find them there 中之 would 表示将来：到果园去是找不到它们的了。

hung 一词用得很有力量，苹果已经摘尽，然而香味仍遍"悬"空中，诱力不减。

yearning（名词）：恋慕之念。

searching 是分词，形容后面的主词 they。**restlessly**：坐立不安地，寝食难安地。

fulfillment：（欲望的）满足。

broodingly：若有所思地。What if he's right 中的 he 指调查员：假如他的话是对的，该怎么办呢？（Joe 的想法多少还切实一点。）

We've never been so happy = We have never been so happy as now。

reassuringly：安慰地（使她放心）。他们结婚以来，的确是以这段田园生活为最快乐了。

[10]

In a minute Joe went back to the barn to finish pressing the last batch of cider, and Phoebe started down the lane. "Co' ba, co' ba," she sang out dreamily, taking comfort from the sound of her voice in the quiet air. It was a call for cows she had read in a book, but of course they never came.

[注]

他们同调查员谈过话以后，Joe 再回到仓房楼上去榨苹果汁，Phoebe 出去把牛找回来。

batch：（货物之）一批。**Co' ba, co' ba**：Phoebe 叫牛的声音，这种叫法她是从书上学来的。叫了它们，它们总是不来，可是她还是叫，她的叫多半还是让自己听来好听而已。**taking comfort from**：从那里面得到安慰。

[11]

Up the lane two sets of hoofprints lay in the dust — one set large and clumsy, moving ponderously after the smaller, dancing crescents that led the way. "They can't have been out long," Phoebe said out loud to herself. "That minx, that little devil," and, smiling ruefully, looking all around, she walked on after them.

[注]

小路前面，有两组（sets）蹄印：后面一组是大牛的，行动笨重（**ponderously**）。前面领路的是小牛：蹄印较小，呈新月状（**crescents**），步法如同舞蹈。

they can't have been out long：它们出去了还不会很久。can 在这里表示"可能性"。

minx：轻佻的女子。这里骂的是那只小牛，骂虽骂，嘴上说它淘气，心里还是疼它，所以骂过之后，脸上苦笑了（ruefully）一下，然后循着蹄印，跟踪前去。

[12]

Up in the road Phoebe found the cows. They were off on the edge of the woods, nosing around in the faded goldenrod and wild asters under two ancient, half-dead crabapple trees. There was nothing there but a few dried-up, worm-hollowed crabapples, and the cows seemed apathetic, sunk in depression. "Don't look at me like that," Phoebe said, "it isn't my fault." The Jersey stared at her with great accusing eyes. She held her head low, petulantly. When Phoebe touched her muzzle, she tossed her head and leaped sharply back.

[注]

nose（动词）：用鼻子推、擦或掘。

goldenrod 与 **wild asters** 都是紫菀科一类的野草。**faded**：凋谢的；秋深之像。

crabapple：山楂。**worm-hollowed**：给虫蛀空的。**there was nothing there**：什么都找不到了。苹果已全搬回家，然香味犹留林际，经久不退，两牛在山楂树下草丛里去找，再也找不到了。两牛状甚淡漠（**apathetic**：看见了主人并不高兴），没精打采（sunk in depression；sunk 是 sink 的过去分词；sink 不一定作"沉"解，凡是由高转低，由强转弱，由活泼转呆滞，这一类的场合常常可用 sink 一词，请读者随时留意）。

Phoebe 晓得它们不高兴，可是也无能为力。她对它们说："请你们别这样看我，这可不能怪我"。**accusing**：控诉的。**great accusing eyes**：大眼睛里，一副埋怨的神气。**petulantly**：发脾气，撒娇之状。泽西小牛找不到苹果，跟主人怄气，头也不肯抬起来了。主人要摸摸它的嘴，它把头一摆，猛地往后一跳。

[13]

"All right, if that's the way you feel," Phoebe said. "Come on, Daisy, we'll let her sulk." And obediently Daisy lumbered back to the dusty road. She plodded slowly back toward the farm.

[注]

Phoebe 的话第一句是对小牛说的："好吧，假如你的感觉真是这样的话"（假如你真是这样感到不痛快，那就算了）。

第二句是叫大牛回家，"小牛让它去怄气吧"。**sulk**：犯脾气。**lumbered**：颠顶笨重地行动。**plodded**：很费力地走路。没有腿的东西（如卡车）的行动，也可以说是 lumber。plod 一定要用在有腿的东西上的。lumber 是从旁观者着眼，行动看来笨重不轻快，plod 是着重走路的人（或物）所费的力气。

[14]

Before they had gone far, Phoebe heard the quick, light thud of the Jersey's hoofs coming after them. All the way back to the barn the Jersey followed a hairbreadth behind.

[注]

小牛从后面追来了,它的行动是轻快的。轻快从其蹄声知之。**thud** 这里相当于"蹄声得得"。

[15]

When she got back, the sun was nearly gone. She was shivering in a sweater when she went up the steep, crude stairs from the stable to the upper story, through the narrow trapdoor where they threw down the hay. Joe had finished the last batch of cider and was lining up the clear amber jugs beside the door, ready for loading on the truck to take to town. Discarded apples and the pressed-out apple cakes lay in a heap below the haymow, and in the cavernous gloom the autumn smell of apple, sweet and sour, mingled with the summer smell, dusty and sweet, of tender-cut green timothy and clover.

[注]

仓分两层,上层供贮藏之用,有大梯道(wagon ramp)通外边;下层为马厩牛栏,另有一小梯通上层。Phoebe 把牛领返牛栏,自己走小梯上去。时已入暮,她穿了一件长袖套头衫(sweater),身上冷得发抖(shivering)。

小梯险峻(steep)粗陋(crude),顶上是一扇活板门。楼上的干草,就是从活门里掷下来喂牲口的。

Joe 还在楼上,但是苹果汁已经榨完(过去完成时),此时他正在把(过去进行时)装苹果汁的罐子排在门口,以便次日装车送进城去。clear(明净的)和 amber(琥珀色的)都形容苹果汁的色泽。

楼上本堆干草,今又苹果满屋,末句就是描写这两种气味。本文以牛的苹果狂为故事主干,而所以致此"狂"者,乃苹果之香味,故于苹果之香味,不惮再三描写焉。

discarded:舍弃不用的(烂蛀之苹果,不合榨汁者)。**apple cakes**:榨后的苹果渣,呈饼状。**haymow**:干草堆。傍晚时分,屋内已幽暗如洞穴,在这"洞穴状(cavernous)的幽暗(gloom)"之中,有两种气味:一种是苹果的,苹果秋天所摘,故曰"秋天的香味"(autumn smell);一种是干草的,干草夏天所割,故曰"夏天的香味"。秋天之香甜而酸,夏天之香泥土气(dusty)然亦带甜味。timothy 与

clover，两种草名，皆用作饲料。**Tender-cut**：嫩的时候割下来的。最后一从句中，**autumn smell** 是主语，**mingled** 是动词。**sweet and sour** 和 **dusty and sweet** 似乎成排比对偶，然而前者不与 smell 相接而跟在 apples 之后，后者则紧接 smell，句法于对仗中仍有变化，与中文之骈俪不同也。

[16]

"That heifer thinks she's pretty cute," Joe said, pulling on his leather jacket, getting ready to go. "I'll keep Daisy in tonight after milking. Maybe the Jersey won't wander without her." Leaving the wide wagon doors open to the last rays of the sun, they went out of the barn together and up the path to the house.

[注]

pretty（副词）：相当地。**cute**：调皮。泽西小牛自以为很调皮。**keep Daisy in**：把它关在牛栏里；in 是副词。今天晚上挤牛奶过后要把它关起来，由这句话看来，足见平日是常常不关的。关了大牛，小牛还不关，他以为没有大牛做伴，小牛就不会出去游荡了。

wagon doors：顶层连接 wagon ramp 的大门，他们走大路下去，大门没有关，为下文伏笔。**the last rays of the sun**：落日余晖。

[17]

It was late that night that Phoebe woke up suddenly with her heart pounding heavily. She heard a terrible bawling cry from somewhere.

"Joe, Joe," she cried, shaking him frantically, "somebody's crying terribly."

"It's the heifer," Joe said, leaping out of bed and searching in the dark for his clothes. "Please light the lamp first so I can get down there first."

[注]

pounding：（心）怦怦地跳。**bawling**：高声大叫。**frantically**：狂乱地（拿他乱摇）。

[18]

Dressing as fast as she could, shivering with cold and fear, she heard Joe rush out into the night. In a minute she was dressed herself and running for the barn, a lantern in her hand, through the clear, chill blackness.

【注】

第二句的 herself 用以加强主语 she。她的丈夫穿好衣服，她也穿好了。

她的丈夫是往外冲进黑夜里去（rush out into the night），她自己也在黑夜里奔跑，夜清明（clear）而冷（chill），正是秋夜也。

[19]

The bellowing grew closer, more localized, and she headed up the wagon ramp and through the wide door of the barn's upper story, Joe was kneeling beside the open trapdoor, the trapdoor for forking hay down, to the stable. Phoebe saw the opening filled with a grotesque, meaningless shape, and then she saw it was the heifer, hanging head down in the narrow stairwell. From below, the gasping came up in rhythmic agony, hushed a little but not stopped by Joe's quiet voice talking and talking to her as he crouched at the opening, trying to see how she was caught.

【注】

bellowing：牛鸣。**localized**：方位可以确定的，可以确定声音出自何方。**headed up** = moved up。**forking**：以叉来挑或拨。

小牛从梯道上楼，一失足身陷活门。它现在前半身跌在活门下面，后半身还搁在上面，已经身受重伤。**stairwell** = well-hole：楼梯口，即 trapdoor，亦即 opening 或 aperture（缺口）。

a grotesque, meaningless shape：一个四不像的、不成形状的东西。楼梯口里塞了一个奇形怪状的东西，那东西就是小牛的后半身。

小牛的头在下面，还在连吁带喘地叫（gasping cries），叫声抑扬有致（**rhythmic**：有节奏的），然而痛苦极矣（agony）。

cries 有两个过去分词形容：一是 hushed（使寂静），一是 stopped。Joe 蹲伏

(crouched) 在楼梯口，轻轻抚慰，然小牛不能就此忍痛不叫，惨号只是稍歇而已。
caught：卡住，挂住，绊住，牵住。

[20]

"The apples," Phoebe moaned, flinging herself down beside him, "she smelled the apples and came to find them." But Joe had jumped up, taking the flashlight, and was running out and around to the stable door below. Phoebe ran after, her heart hammering, the lantern swinging insanely from her hand.

[注]

moaned：呜咽地说。**flinging herself down**：扑倒地上。

Phoebe 的话说明小牛是怎么上来的：它嗅到了香味，从梯道大门进来找苹果。**flashlight**：手电筒。**hammering**：原意是"锤击"，此处亦作"怦怦地跳"。**insanely**：（似乎是）疯狂地。**swinging**：摆动。

[21]

The low, oak-beamed ceiling and thick stone walls of the stable made a warm, cozy cave, and in it the heifer hung crazily upside down, her head and one foreleg wedged between two treads of the heavy, ladderlike stairs. The wedged foreleg was broken, bone thrusting through the skin. In the lantern light her eyes rolled whitely, blindly, and the helpless, rasping cries grew steadily fainter.

[注]

第一句描写楼下马厩中所见。马厩不高，顶上橡木作梁（oak-beam），周围石砌厚墙，处身其间，温暖舒适（cozy），犹如洞穴。

hazily：荒唐地。牛头倒悬空中，为反常之事，犹如疯人所为。

wedged foreleg：卡住。前腿。**treads**：梯级。**ladderlike stairs**：ladder 是可搬动之梯，stairs 是楼梯。但马厩里的 stairs 比之 ladder 亦相差无几。

在灯光之中，可以看见牛的眼睛在转，然而白多黑少（whitely），眼珠失神（blindly），已是奄奄待毙之状。其鸣声粗沙（rasping）凄婉（helpless），亦渐趋微弱矣。

[22]

"If we could saw the stair!" Phoebe cried in anguish. "Wouldn't that free her?"

"It's no use," Joe said. "The weight of her fall would snap her back, "Phoebe, you'd better get the gun."

[注]

saw：锯断。**anguish**：极端痛苦，然而深度尚不如 agony。牛之将死用 agony（见前文），哀怜同情之人，其心虽十分痛苦，然到底比身受者还差一等，故用 anguish。受 anguish 之苦者，表面上可能很少反应，受 agony 之苦者，必定辗转挣扎也。

snap：折断。梯子锯断了，牛摔下来要把背脊摔断的。

[23]

The heifer bawled again, a hopeless choking cry, and in the lantern light her free leg kicked futilely in the air. "She's suffering, Phoebe. Get the gun."

[注]

牛鸣本趋微弱，现忽又吼叫，然而气息壅塞（choking），临终绝望之哀鸣也。

free leg：未被卡住之腿。

[24]

Phoebe had turned blindly, and was rushing out the door when Joe called, "Phoebe, bring a knife, too, the sharp knife in the kitchen." For a moment she didn't understand, and then she turned back whimpering in horror. "No, no, we can't, I won't!" Across the shadowy stable Joe's voice rose in furious torment. "Get the knife! You know we can't waste food." He stared at her relentlessly. "We wanted a farm, didn't we? To make our own life, our own food? We've eaten meat all our lives, now we've got to earn it."

[注]

Phoebe 奔出去拿枪，要结束这头牛的痛苦了。Joe 叫她把厨房里的刀拿来。

她起初还不懂，后来想起来了——Joe 要先流其血然后宰而食之！

whimper 亦是一种呜咽，与前文 moan 相比，则 whimper 之声断续而 moan 之声细长，whimper 可能含愠抱怨，而 moan 则纯是忧伤凄楚也。

她已跑到门口，Joe 在里面发脾气，内外之间，有一段距离，所以说：他的声音"越过了幽暗的马厩"（across the shadowy stable）。

Joe's voice rose：提起了嗓子说话。**furious**：盛怒的。torment 较 anguish 略轻，Joe 决定忍心杀牛，心里也必非常痛苦，然而比之 Phoebe 的 anguish 究竟还差一等。此词带一点"烦躁"的意思。

stared：瞪目而视。**relentlessly**：残酷无情地。

earn：凭本事去赚。最后两句问话的意义，我们买下这座农场来，本来是靠着它吃的。

[25]

Phoebe laid the knife, the gun and cartridges beside Joe and turned away. She was well away from the stable when she heard the shot. She stopped then, and for a long moment she stood quiet, shaking in the cold.

After her tears Phoebe slept, but she woke early. She lay quietly in bed, her body aching, her mind calm but filled with a clear despair.

[注]

cartridges：子弹。**clear despair**：清明的绝望。她觉得人生没有意义了，可是心头还是清清楚楚的，并不昏沉。

[26]

She went out for fire wood and kindling, and coming back from the woodpile with her arms full she stopped above the pasture, shivering in the still, gray light of the morning. Below the pin oak Daisy lay placidly on the drying grass, untouched by tragedy, and for a long time Phoebe stood watching her from another world. Of course they can't care, she thought; it's part of their innocence. She thought of all the innocent ones — the cow and the dog, the horses and chickens — and she knew at last that she was hopelessly excluded, forever responsible. She turned away, lonely and chilled, but with her armful of firewood she went on into the kitchen, to kindle once more the comforting fire for breakfast.

[注]

kindling：引火之小木片。**woodpile**：木柴堆。

pin oak：橡树之一种。**placidly**：平静地。**untouched by tragedy**：（心）不为悲剧所拂扰。**from another world** = as if from another world：小牛死了，大牛本为其游伴，今竟若无其事，而女主人则心中悲苦，无复乐趣，如处在另一世界。

she thought 的前后都是不加引号的直接叙述法，述其思想之内容："当然它们（那些动物）是不在乎的，这就是它们天真里面的一部分。"既然天真，当然无挂无牵。

下面接一句是全文主旨所在。她想起了那些动物都是无挂无牵的，可是她偏不然，她是"绝对没有希望归入它们那一类里去的"（hopelessly excluded）。她是人就得负起做人的责任，责任永远在她身上，无法推脱（forever responsible）。

这一种想法是幻想的破灭，也可以说是智慧（wisdom）的开始。鸢飞鱼跃，生机活泼，啸傲园林，逍遥自在，素为人生理想所寄，叵奈现实世界不容此种理想乎？Phoebe 初居农村时，未尝不想过一种无挂无牵顺乎自然的生活，对于遨游田野追逐苹果香味的小牛，未尝不心向往之。曾几何时，小牛身陷绝境，丧生枪下，当初放纵之者、歆羡之者，今竟束手不能救，而且可能要割其皮而食其肉，"分尝一脔"矣。现实世界果如是之残酷乎？无论如何，Phoebe 经此事变，心灵上可以说是成熟了。浪漫之梦既破，提起勇气，正视现实，负起做人的责任，其人生之正途乎？就文学流派而言，追求理想，无拘无束，是浪漫主义之文学也；知理想之终归幻灭，拘束之不可避免，此写实主义之文学也。写实主义在二十世纪文学为一大潮流，本文不过一个小小的例子而已。

最后 Phoebe 夹了木柴，进厨房去生火煮饭，又是一天枯燥的主妇生活要开始了，然而人生的意义是不是就在这枯燥平凡之中呢？

A Visit to the Grandfather's Grave
扫墓

James Turner Jackson

本文选自 Mentor Books 出的 *New World Writing* 第一辑，原题 *The Visit*，叙述一个老祖母拖了她的小孙儿上坟的故事。文中描写着重之处，在那个行将就木的老祖母对于坟墓的变态的恋念，和小孙儿对于这个"苦差事"的厌恶和恐惧，以及老少二人之间心理关系的紧张。全文颇不易读，这里所选几段，约当原文篇幅的十分之一，虽然深刻不如原来那篇小说，但仍不失为一篇很好的叙事文章。作者杰克逊是美国密歇根州人，曾在华盛顿州立大学执教，有短篇小说和论文多篇问世。

[1]

In the winter, three years ago, his grandfather died. For almost a year, then, his grandmother never left town. She kept up her garden, and tended the ceremonial plants growing in the bay windows of her house.

[注]

keep up = keep in proper state：使园中花木茂盛。**tended**：照料，整修灌溉。**ceremonial**：礼节上应用的，预备供在坟前的（植物）。**bay windows**：凸窗。窗往外凸出，窗内因此可多吸收阳光。

[2]

In the late afternoon, most often, the car was filled with flowers, and together they drove out to a nearby cemetery where his grandfather was. They were going to see (so she told him each time they went) how his grandfather's grave was getting on. After the car was unloaded, and the flowers and shears and transplanting pots arranged in orderly rows beside the grave, she would send him down to the standpipe with a pail for water. In this manner, his work began. And when he finished the wiring, she would set him to picking up fallen leaves and twigs. Not a moment was wasted.

[注]

drove out：驾车出去。**cemetery**：公墓。

how ... was getting on：情形怎么样了。第二句的括弧中语，他们每次出去扫墓，祖母都要对他这样说。

unloaded：把车上的东西搬下来。**shears**：（刈花草之用）剪刀。**pots**：花盆。**transplanting**：移植用的，有些花得先种在盆里，然后再移植到地上去。**arranged in orderly rows**：整整齐齐地排列成行。arranged 前面省去 were 一词。**standpipe**：竖管（直立于地上的自来水管）。

pail：水桶。祖母差他下去打水，打了水来浇花（watering），浇完了花，再去捡地上的枯枝败叶。

set him to ...：使他去做某一件工作。注意，to 的后面跟动名词（或名词）。

[3]

It was the year when his grandmother was still very clear, and very rigid about what she wanted. By her reckoning, every plot in the cemetery, save hers alone, was poorly tended. Each time a flower was cut or trimmed by her hand, she counted off the number of its blossoms. And pointing to an adjoining grave, she would often shake her head, and wonder how it was that people were so shiftless and lazy-minded and ignorant. She herself would be painstaking unto the last detail; and for this, if for no other reason, always brought with her a mail-order catalogue, to which she might have immediate recourse for pictures

— together with complete descriptions — of monuments fashioned of enduring granite, perpetual marble.

[注]

clear：神志清明。那年她的神志还好，以后就差了。**rigid**：严格的。她所要办的，一定得办到。

by her reckoning：由她看来。**plot**：地段。墓园里的墓地，一家一块。她认为别家的地都照料得不好。**save** = except：除了她家的一块以外。

a flower：本来可解释作"一朵花"，但这里应作"一株花"，与 its blossoms（它上面的花朵）相对。她每次亲手修（trimmed）剪（cut）一株花，一定要把上面的花朵数清楚（counted off）。

an adjoining grave：邻近的一座坟。她常常指着边上的一座坟，摇头叹息，奇怪别人怎么这样地想不出主意（shiftless），不肯动脑筋（lazy-minded），而且没有知识（ignorant）。 **how it was**... 中之 it 代表 that 所引起之名词性从句"这到底是怎么一回事。"

painstaking：非常仔细，决不马虎。**unto** 是 to 的较古的形式。

for this, if for no other reason：为了这个，假如不是为了别的理由。理由可能还有别的，可是我们就拿这点理由来说吧：因为她绝不马虎，所以扫墓的时候她还要来研究坟前应该配什么样的一块墓碑（monuments 也可能包括雕像、牌坊、墓亭等的意思，但这里只是墓碑而已）。

mail-order catalogue：（商店之）函购目录。美国有些大商店，印了很讲究的函购目录，附有详细图文说明。照本文看来，似乎连墓碑都可以函购的。

to which 之 to 照语法结构应连在后面 recourse 之后。**have recourse to**：用来帮忙，用来参考。**immediate**：立刻（就用得着）。

从语义上讲，**pictures** 和 **of monuments** 相连：她要打开目录来，看墓碑的图画。**fashioned**：制造。**granite**：花岗石。**marble**：大理石。enduring 和 perpetual 在这里意义相仿，可以永垂不朽的。

descriptions：说明文字。图画之外，另有详细说明。

[4]

When the flowers had been placed to her exact liking, she stepped back a few paces, customarily, and with the catalogue open in her hand sought to envision which of the pictured memorials would be most seemly at her husband's grave. She walked back and forth, glancing at the catalogue, weighing her decision. Soon, at her call, he stopped whatever he was doing, and came to help her read the fine print beneath the glossy pictures.

[注]

to her exact liking：恰如她所喜欢那样的。**placed**：摆设，供奉。
customarily：成了习惯的了。**sought** = tried。**envision**：从心目中看来。
pictured：绘成图画的（也可能是摄成相片的）。**memorials** = monuments。**seemly**：合适的。她退后数步，打开目录，拿在手里，心里在设想，目录里所画的墓碑，哪一座配在她丈夫的坟上才算最合适。**weighing**：权衡优劣，考虑。**her decision**：她所看中的（那座墓碑）。

at her call：听她一叫。**whatever he was doing**：不论他在做什么（浇花或是收拾地上），他都得住了手，走过去帮老祖母读目录。

fine print：印得很小的字体。老祖母眼睛有病，视力不济，小字看不出，非请帮手不可。**glossy**：明亮光滑的。形容好的铜版纸上所印的图片。

[5]

But each time it seemed that no final decision could be rendered. They would study the catalogue at length, and then his grandmother would send him back to the car. He would load the back seat, and then, while his grandmother remained at the grave alone, he would watch the long arcs of the water sprinklers shining in the last sunlight of the day. In such a light, the cemetery looked very plain to him: the trees simple and lofty in height, and all the tombstones austere in their carving. He tried to keep his head turned decently away, but sometimes, glancing back despite himself, he would see his grandmother above the mounded earth of the grave, her arms rising up in dark weaving shapes of despair and worship. In the coming dusk he would hear the sharp whispering outcries of her lament, above even the humming sound of the water-sprinklers. And though her eye bothered and afflicted her more month by month, that year when they started for home she still drove with lumbering and powerful speed.

[注]

第一句的 rendered，可以用 made 代替。前面的 fashioned，也可以用 made 来代替，但是这只可以表示 make 一词用法之多。render 和 fashion 两词是不可以互易的。

at length：很详细的。

load the back seat：带来的东西用过后，搬回到车子后座上去。

water-sprinklers：喷水机（这里指的是给草地自动浇水的设备）。**arc**：弧状曲线。

tombstones：（别家坟上的）墓碑。**austere in their carving**：碑上的雕刻看来很严肃。

keep his head turned away：故意把头转过去，不朝某一个方向看。**decently**：很有规矩地。祖母在墓前哭，他自以为他是不该看的。**despite himself**：想控制自己而控制不住；他的眼睛偶尔还要朝后看。**mounded earth**：坟堆。

her arms... 以下为 nominative absolute phrase。天色已晚，她的双臂在黑暗中举起，所作（**weaving**：纺织成）种种姿势，礼拜（**worship**）死者之外，亦正显示生者内心悲苦，因此颓然不支（**despair**）也。

coming dusk：暮色四合。**lament**：哀悼。**the humming sound of the sprinklers**：喷水机马达的轰鸣之声。马达虽轰鸣作响，可是老祖母的尖细的哭声他还听得见。

bothered and afflicted her：给她麻烦，也给她罪受。**lumbering and powerful speed**：车子开得很猛，可是笨重不稳。老祖母目疾虽与月俱增，那一年她精神还不减少壮，观其开车之"冲"，便知其内心激动，不能自己：仿佛有力量，从身后驱策着她。其悲痛亦不言自喻矣。

Natives Don't Cry
亨利小姐的信

Kay Boyle（1902—1992）

作者凯·博伊尔为美国现代女作家，明尼苏达州人，曾在欧洲各处寄居多年，著书有长篇及短篇小说集数十种。

博伊尔的文字很简单，故事亦不离奇曲折，然而轻描淡写之中，言似未尽而意亦未尽，颇耐人寻味。其描绘人生，悽怆处有含蓄，挖苦处存忠厚，哀而不怨，谑而不虐，皆深得"简约"之妙者。本文原题直译应为"本地人是不哭的"，与全文有何关系，我们将在后文注解中探讨，今姑且译为"亨利小姐的信"。原文见其短篇小说集《维也纳之白马》(*The White Horses of Vienna*)，1937年出版，1949年收入英国"企鹅丛书"。

[1]

We went to Austria that summer, and Miss Henley came to us the night before we left. She was not very pleased to come, but it was only for the month, so she came as a gift to us. She did not believe she would like us because of the hotel, where we were in London and because of the colour of mother's hair. She did not say these things to us in the same words, but she said them in other ways so that we knew.

[注]

we：从下文看来，指的是一家到欧洲去旅行的美国人：父亲、母亲、两个小女孩、一个小男孩。全篇叙事都是用一个小女孩的第一人称的口气。**that summer**：某年夏天。年代可能隔得很远。

Miss Henley 的职位是保姆兼家庭教师，即所谓 governess。她是英国人，临时在英国受那美国家庭之聘，随赴奥地利，照料孩子。

第二句说她不大高兴来，可是因为好歹只有一个月，勉强答应的。由此可见亨利小姐是个架子相当大的人。

gift 本意是"礼物"，自己没有出钱、别人好意送来的东西谓之"礼物"。我们不好算是出钱雇她的，只好算是她来帮我们的忙的。

第三句还是说明这位小姐架子之大，而且夹着一点脾气怪癖在里面。她以为她不会喜欢我们这一家人的，第一因为是我们在伦敦所住的旅馆（不中她的意）；第二因为是母亲头发的颜色（也不中她的意）。

她的话并不是这样说的。措辞虽然不同，话里的意思是一样的，所以我们听得出来（so that we knew）。

[2]

We thought she was fifty because she had no colour in her face, and her hair was pinned back in a knot in her neck, and it was grey near the ears. Father took her passport on the French side, and when he came back to the car he said:

"I think you're much too young to be leaving home, Miss Henley."

[注]

colour：肤色之红润。**knot**：发髻。**pinned back**：梳到后面去，用发针扣住的。头发在脑后扣成一个髻，打扮不像少女。**near the ears**：耳旁之头发，约相当于中文的"鬓"。

passport：护照。一行人到了法国，护照统归父亲拿去办理过境手续。父亲从她的护照里看见了她的年龄。

to be leaving home 在 to leave home 之外更多一层"正在路上"的意思。假如说 you're too young to leave home，这可能表示根本还没有动身。much 加强 too 的

意思。

[3]

"Miss Henley's almost as young as you girls," said father, and we saw the colour run into her cheeks. "She's only twenty-five!"

"How old did you think I was?" she said, and Francis said: "A hundred."

But he was so young there was nothing to say to him. It was just a number he had heard somewhere.

[注]

Miss Henley's = Miss Henley is。

How old did you think I was？你们现在是知道我的年纪了，你们本来以为我是多大了？动词用过去时。

Francis 是小弟弟的名字。他脱口而出地说是"一百岁"。

so young 的后面省去了一个 that。他年纪太小了，跟他没有什么好说的。他说"一百"并不是真懂什么意思，不知道他哪里听来这样一个数目字而已。

[4]

She had been born in Burma, she was a civil servant's daughter, and she had no patience for the ways of any children except the children she and her brothers had been. In the hotels at night she took their pictures from her bag and set them on the bureau. She spoke of them all, and of the places they had lived. And she spoke of them only a little at a time, and not too often, as if they were too good to be given quite away.

[注]

Burma：缅甸。**civil servant**：公务员。

she had no patience for the ways of children：她对于小孩子们的那一套，是没有耐心的。可是她自己有一度也是一个小孩子，她还有哥哥弟弟，他们小时候也该跟别的小孩子一样顽皮，一样难待候，可是她对于她自己小时候和她哥哥弟弟小时候的那一套，她就"受得了"了。she and her brothers had been 是定语从句，前面省一关系代词 that。

in the hotels：他们已经走了好几处地方，住过不同的旅馆，故 hotels 用多数。bureau 照英国人的用法是"书桌"，照美国人的用法是"衣柜"（五斗柜）。本文作者是美国人，当以后者为是。

她常讲起她的哥哥弟弟，可是每次只讲一点儿的事情，而且所讲的次数也并不十分多，好像他们的事情是件宝贝，不可以全部送人（一次说完）的。

[5]

Her family was dead, even the brothers, so there was no one left to write to, but there was Rudolpho. He was a name written out very big across an envelope.

She did not say these things or anything like them to mother. She never told her about Rudolpho although she wrote to him every day. She said to mother:

[注]

Ruddpho 照下文看来该是她的男朋友的名字。这是怎么样的一个人，叙事的小孩子当然并不知道，作者也不要让读者晓得。作者所要读者注意的只是她的信，而信封上大大地写着的是一个男人的名字。这个男人，她是每天写信给他的。

[6]

"Where would be a safe place to have mail sent to? I have to know about my letters."

And mother would say: "Oh, I'm sure the American Express or Thomas Cook would do."

But mother never said which city because she scarcely ever knew which country she was travelling in. She could not remember the capitals of Europe even.

[注]

第一句用虚拟式的 would：假如有邮件，该寄到哪里才妥当呢？

第二句的 would 只是 will 的过去时：老师那样问，母亲总是这样答的。同句中的另一个 would 也是虚拟式。

American Express 即 American Express Co. 通用译名为"美国运通银行"。该行之旅行支票，信用极好。Thomas Cook 为著名英商旅行社，通用译名为"通济隆"。那两家商号一向办理旅客服务，所以母亲提议托他们代转信件。

never：一路之上老师与母亲之间，常常有这样的一问一答。可是母亲从来不说明是什么城市，因此人家仍旧不知道信该寄到哪里。母亲连自己在哪一国都不大知道，她也记不清楚欧洲各国的首都。

[7]

But she knew from father that we were going to Salzburg.

Father said: "If your young man likes to read so much, Miss Henley, I think he must be quite literary."

"Oh, he's not exactly like that!" said Miss Henley, laughing. "He's foreign, of course, but so many people are these days that one gets accustomed to it. He's been ten years in London, too, so you'd scarcely know. I don't know what he's doing to cheer himself up, poor thing. He must feel like a duck out of water. He wanted me to go, of course, and he told me not to hurry back, but I know perfectly well what's going on inside him!"

"You'll probably have mail waiting in Salzburg," said father.

[注]

Salzburg：萨尔茨堡，奥地利西部的一个城市，为大音乐家莫扎特出生地。

literary：有文学修养的。like that 即指 literary；说他有文学修养，还没有完全说对。

foreign：Rudolpho 不像是一个英国人的名字，所以她说"他当然（of course）是个外国人"。名字以"o"收尾的人，可能是意大利、西班牙、葡萄牙等国的人。

so many people are 的后面省去 foreign 一词：这个年头，很多人都是外国人，所以不足为奇。**accustomed to it**：此处的 it = his being foreign。accustomed，习以为常。

so you'd ... 之 'd 为 would 的省写：假如你看见了他，你也看不大出他是个外国人（因为他在伦敦住过十年）。know 的后面省去 that he is foreign。

cheer himself up：解闷消愁。**poor thing**：可怜的人儿（因为不跟她在一起了）。那个男人似乎非但多情，而且还很识大体：他当然要我到欧洲去的，他还叫我别忙着回去呢。**inside him**：他心里面的事。

[8]

Father went to the post office the first thing in Salzburg. He took the passports in his hand, and when he came back he was carrying a great many things. There were letters from America, and there was mother's picture playing golf in *The Tatler*, but there wasn't anything, there wasn't even a postcard for Miss Henley. She did not say anything. She sat quite still on the terrace of the coffee-house on the Mozart Place, and the sun was shining for a change. She looked straight into the sun, past father, smiling at what he said. He had said:

"There wasn't anything for you today, Miss Henley. Better luck tomorrow."

[注]

就第一句看来，他们的信没有托旅行社转，而是由邮局代收，他们凭了护照去领回的。

The Tatler：英国著名画报。那位母亲恐怕是交际场中有名人物，在英国住了没有多久，她玩高尔夫球的照片就在画报上登出来了。

terrace：（咖啡店前之）露台。**Mozart Place**：莫扎特广场。**for a change**：阴雨多日之后，天气变晴了。

past father：视线越过了父亲，直向太阳望去。past 是介词。**smiling at what he said**：对于父亲所说的话，她只报之以微笑。父亲说些什么话呢？下面接一句补充说明。但是话先说，她后微笑的，所以用过去完成时 had said。

这许多人中间，老师似乎是最急着要看信的人，偏偏没有她的信。可是没有信，她又是这样地镇定。就此人物的性格更值得玩味，而故事也更引人入胜了。

[9]

Mother opened her letters, and father opened his, and we did not look at Miss Henley. No one lifted their eyes, and no one felt easy in the silence at the table: Miss Henley sat with her cup of coffee and cream in front of her, and because she did not speak there was nothing for anyone to say. But Francis said :

"Maybe nobody likes you," and mother said quickly:

"Would you like to wander a bit by yourself this afternoon, Miss Henley? There's quite a lot to see here. You might go and see Mozart's skull."

"Mozart's skull!" cried Miss Henley. "How disgusting!"

[注]

easy：轻松。到底窘不窘我们不知道，但是大家都替她觉得很窘。小弟弟"童言无忌"，说他那位老师"也许没有人喜欢"，母亲赶快出来解围。

Mozart's skull：莫扎特的头骨。莫扎特在 Salzburg 的故居，已改建为"莫扎特博物院"，陈莫氏遗物颇多。其头骨恐亦在彼处陈列。

How disgusting! "该是多恶心呀！"一个有教养、感觉敏锐的女子，是不会喜欢去看死人的头骨的。可是连莫扎特的都不愿意去看（尤其是从英国远道跑来的人），未免太"独立独行"了。大家正在替这位小姐觉得很窘，她的刚强的个性又表现出来了。

[10]

In the evening she was in the room still, she was sitting there in the half-darkness when we came home. She had been writing a letter by the window and she was putting the name on the envelope when we came in the door. Father came with us, and Miss Henley said:

"Where would the best place to change English money be?"

[注]

上段母亲叫亨利小姐下午自己出去逛逛，本段是黄昏时分他们游毕返家（其实是旅馆，但仍可用 home 一词），发现亨利小姐坐在屋子里没有出去。

had been writing 是过去完成进行时，接着又用一个过去进行时 was writing。两种时态用在同一个句子里，更容易体味它们的用法：我们回来之前，她就在写信；我们回来的时候，信是写完了，但是信封还没有写好；那时候她恰巧正在信封上写名字。问话用虚拟式，并没有说她一定要去换钱。

[11]

Miss Henley stood, very small and thin, with her hand holding to the back of the chair. She wore high black shoes, and a blouse, and a skirt that had no year and season, wide at the knees, and dark. She had never worn anything else but this, no matter how the weather changed.

[注]

本段描写亨利小姐问话时的情形。我们出去玩了一个下午，她躲在家里写信，已经够可怜的了；现在看看她的模样，更觉得可怜。

blouse：女装的上身短衫。**no year or season**：看不出是哪一年的式样，或者是该哪一季穿的。裙子的颜色很深，上半截是紧的，到了膝盖下面才张开来。

[12]

"Look here," said father. "If you'd like your salary in advance, you just tell us. I can pay it now or whenever you want it, just as you like."

"Not at all," said Miss Henley. "I had no intention of asking for anything in advance. I just happened to find a few shillings in my pocket and thought I would change them here. I only want to buy a stamp."

[注]

父亲因为她提起要换钱的事，以为她要钱花了。**in advance**：预支（薪水）。可是她说她决不要预支什么。had 用过去时，表示她刚才问话的时候，并没有预支什么的意思（intention）。**happened to find**：碰巧找到（几个先令）。

前面刚刚说她很可怜，可是她傲骨非常，不要预支薪水。足见她不是一个求人哀怜的人物。可是她所要买的只是一张邮票，她收不到信，偏偏还把信看得这样的重要，似乎又值得可怜了。若是亨利小姐只是一味的可怜，非但文章难有波澜，而且将流入"感伤主义"（sentimentalism）的魔道。作者处处要把这个主角写成一个个性极强的人，个性这样的强，而其不知不觉中的言行又复如此可怜（有时抑且可笑），这才是真的可怜了。

[13]

At the end of the week we went away, we went up the valley into the mountains, and Miss Henley rode in the back with us. She held Francis on her lap, and she closed her eyes and told us of the places she had been. There were eight natives struck by lightning in the hills in Burma one night in summer, and she had seen them in the morning when the others carried them down. Their bodies were burned as black as logs in the fire.

[注]

went up the valley：城在山谷里，今离城往高处走，进入山里。**in the back**：汽车之后座。**with us** 之 us 恐指三个小孩子。父母在前座。

lap：膝上。**held Francis on her lap**：把 Francis 抱到她腿上。**the places she had been**：在 she 前省去 relative adverb "where" 一词。

she closed her eyes：闭起眼睛，足见想得出神，而且对于沿路风景，似乎毫无兴趣。亨利小姐对于眼前的东西，似乎都没有什么兴趣；从她的言谈看来，她念念不忘的是她的过去；关于将来，她只有一个期待，那就是男朋友的信。

struck by lightning：遭雷击。**burned**：烧焦。**logs**：木柴。

[14]

"What did you give them to make them stop crying?" Francis said. "Natives don't cry," said Miss Henley. "They don't feel things the way other people do."

[注]

小弟弟问道："你给了他们些什么东西，他们才不哭的呢？"小弟弟以为，天下的人同他自己一样，哭的时候，只要有一块糖来骗骗他们，就会不哭的。小弟弟话里的"他们"，不一定指什么人，可就是那些遭雷击的人，可能是他们的亲属。

亨利小姐的答复："本地人是不哭的。"他们对于一件事情，觉得是喜还是怒，或者是哀还是乐，都同别人不一样（他们的感觉方式同别人的感觉方式不一样）。the way 在这里当 relative adverb 用，引起下面一状语从句：other people do。说完全了应该是 in the same way as，但普通口语用 the way 两个词已够。

雷击土人一段穿插，似和主要故事无关，可是"本地人是不哭的"一句话，作者竟用作全文标题，其意隐晦，颇难索解。可能只是因为这句话在小孩子脑筋里所留下的印象特别深？可能这一句话表示人和人之间的感觉方式不都一样，不哭之人也许正有可哭之由？可能这三个词只是代表一种刚毅坚忍的精神，恰如亨利小姐的为人？也许这几种意思只有这三个词才能充分表达，不说明反而比说明好？

[15]

It was cold climbing and father stopped the car for a glass of wine in a country tavern. We all went in and sat down by the stove, and mother and father and Miss Henley drank a pitcher of red, hot wine.

"How do you like Austria, Miss Henley?" mother said. "This is Austria, isn't it?"

[注]

cold climbing：寒冷的登山之旅，山愈高愈寒。**tavern**：小酒店。**pitcher**：酒壶。

母亲常常弄不清楚欧洲那些国家（见前文），这里问了人家喜欢不喜欢奥地利之后，再添问一句，"这是奥地利不是？"

[16]

"Oh, it's very like the country in Burma, you know," said Miss Henley. "I was telling the children, I've a friend who has a little car of his own. He drives it all over England. I told him we would be driving around Salzburg. It would be a joke, wouldn't it, if he suddenly turned up on the road?"

[注]

the country in Burma：缅甸的乡村。

I was telling the children：我刚才还在对孩子们说呢。这里用过去进行时，接着三个动词都是现在时，讲三件并不限定在某一个时间的事情：我有一个朋友，他有一辆汽车，他常在英国各处开来开去——她又讲起她的男朋友来了。

we would be driving 是 we will be driving 的过去时。这里的 will 只表示将来，不表示意愿；第一人称用 will 代替 shall 以表示将来，在口语里面是很常见的。

turned up：出现（虚拟式）。假如忽然他驾了汽车在我们的公路上出现了，你说这是不是一个很大的玩笑呢？

[17]

"Perhaps he's going to surprise you by coming right over," said father. Miss Henley's face squeezed up with laughter.

"It would be just like him to!" she said. "I'll never forget the time we were asked to a fancy-dress party. He dressed up the same as two friends of his did, and I never knew until the party was over and everybody unmasked that I'd been dancing with somebody else all evening. He had got tired," said Miss Henley, "and gone home early."

[注]

surprise you：吓你一跳。**coming right over**：从英国径自赶来。

squeezed up：皱缩。

it… like him to：他就是这样子的（爱弄玄虚）。to 之后省略 surprise me 等字样。

fancy-dress party：化妆舞会。**as two of his friends did** 之 did = dressed up：他的服装打扮跟他的两个朋友一模一样。

unmasked：除去面具。她发现她一晚上一直是跟别人在跳舞。发现在后，用过去时，跳舞在先，当用过去完成时，可是又是一直地在跳，故用过去完成进行时。

她的男朋友爱捉弄人，化妆舞会上把她交给别人陪着跳舞，自己因为疲倦，早回去了。

[18]

"That was a good joke," said mother. Father said: "Have a little more wine."

"Oh, I never take much," said Miss Henley, watching him fill her glass up. "If this friend I was speaking of did happen along the children would have a wonderful time with him. He's like a child himself," she said, and she began to gasp with laughter. "He'd be down on his hands and knees all the time playing with Francis if he were here."

[注]

I never take much：我酒喝得不多。**fill her glass up**：把她的杯子斟满。

I was speaking of 是定语从句，前面省一关系代词 whom。

did happen along：假如真的碰巧来了的话。did 用以加重语气，所以用 did 而不用 does 者，是要表示"不合事实的假定"。请参照本段末一句 if he were here。

gasp with laughter：笑得透不过气来。

down on his hands and knees：双手双膝爬在地上。

[19]

Day after day Miss Henley walked us slowly over the hillsides. Mother and father went up mountains together. Whenever we went back to the hotel, there would be letters on the table, but there would never be anything for Miss Henley.

"Nobody writes to you, Mrs. Hen," Francis said.

"My dear child," said Miss Henley, "As a matter of fact, Francis, if I wanted my letters sent here I could easily tell people to write to me here, couldn't I? So you see how silly you are."

[注]

walk 当及物动词用是"带着走"。

Mrs. Hen 是小弟弟替 Miss Henley 乱起的一个名字，而且不用 Miss 而用 Mrs.：小弟弟称她是"老母鸡"。**if I wanted my letters sent here**：又是一句不合事实的假定。假如我要把信寄到这儿来的话，我随便一句话就可以通知人家寄到这儿来了，是不是？话中自承不是没有信，而是故意让人家寄到别处去了。

[20]

But we never saw her writing any more letters. She did not even speak of Rudolpho. She would sit reading books that mother gave her, and she never found any of them very good, as the books she had read somewhere else at some other time.

"Always the same old thing," she said, and she gave them back to mother. "Always love, love, love! It's just a bit tiresome I think, you know."

[注]

亨利小姐看得入眼的东西很少，母亲的书她没有一本爱读的，她说它们总没有她以前在别的地方所看的书那么好。

我们不再看见她写信了，她也不再提起男朋友的名字了。她也讨厌小说里老是讲什么爱情爱情的。

[21]

Mother and father put their feet out by the fire and mother said Miss Henley wasn't a good thing for the children even if she was leaving so soon. She said it was the worst thing to have this for every meal with you, this pall, this bitterness, this dead, unspoken sorrow. What could we give her to take away her silence, and her sharpness, and her grieving face?

[注]

父亲母亲伸直了腿在烤火，母亲说，即使亨利小姐快要走了（她只来帮一个月的忙），她做孩子们的老师，总是不大好。thing 可以解作 person，这里的 a good thing 应该就是 a good teacher。最糟的是：每顿饭都要看见她棺材罩子（pall）那样的神气，她那股子怨气（bitterness），那种半死不活（dead），闷在肚子里的（unspoken）忧愁。我们有什么办法可以把她的沉默、她的尖刻、她的愁容消除掉呢？

这里用了好几个抽象字眼。在本段之前，全文所记都是具体事实。作者用了很经济的手法，记录了很多件小事，不评不议，一切留待读者自寻结论。但是这里母亲要用两三句话把她对这位家庭教师讨厌的态度，概括地讲出来，那就非藉抽象名词之助不可。

就作文一般原则而言，如作者目的为求生动、求含蓄，自宜多具体描写；如为求扼要、求明辨，则非用抽象名词不可。初学作文者，大抵喜具体，而不惯抽象；但抽象名词如不能熟用，则散漫之印象，难以统一，思想之精微处，更无由表达。凡善文者，必定具体抽象，左右逢源，得心应手者也。

[22]

Then one morning, father and mother took us up a mountain. We left very early, while it was dark still. When we got to the hotel it was six o'clock and

Miss Henley was giving Francis his bath. There was a look of something else in her face, and whatever she said to us she couldn't keep from smiling.

[注]

父亲母亲带我们去爬山（"我们"是"我"同妹妹，老师和小弟弟没有去）。我们回来的时候，她正在替小弟弟洗澡。她的脸上有一种特别的表情，随便讲什么，都忍不住要笑。笑容刚好和上段所说的愁容成对比。

[23]

"Did we get any mail?" said mother.

"Oh, all the mail was for me for a change today," said Miss Henley.

"Oh, how nice," said mother.

"It was quite a joke," said Miss Henley, her face squeezed up with laughter. "The porter came staggering up — three telegrams and seven letters! They'd never heard of such a thing here! You can imagine!"

[注]

for a change：来信一向都是你们的，今天换过来了，都是我的了。

staggering：踉跄。手里的信多得路都不会走了！夸张正显其得意。**such a thing**：一个人一天有这么多信。

[24]

"I hope your young man's well?" said father.

"Oh, he's awfully well, thank you," said Miss Henley. "He'd put the wrong address on all the letters and they were all returned to him. So that explains how it was, you see. He's awfully excited about the Lindberghs being in England. He's working on a newspaper now and he's been trying to find out where they are so as to get a peep at them and perhaps a word or two for a story."

[注]

awfully = very。

he'd put = he had put。前面她不是说故意不让人家把信往这里寄吗？怎么现在又说是人家写错了地址（address）呢？作者虽未加按语，但亨利小姐的话显然自相矛盾。

how it was：为什么老没有信。

Lindberghs：林德伯格夫妇。**Charles Lindbergh**：美国飞行家，为不着陆飞越大西洋第一人（时在1927年）。

get a peep at them：看到他们一眼。a peep 和下面的 a word 在修辞学上都是"谦辞"（understatement），事实上当然不止希望看到一眼或听到一两句话而已。**a story**：新闻特稿，这里不作"小说"解。

[25]

"Well, we'll get a good bottle of wine tonight," said father, "and we'll all drink to Rudolpho!"

"Oh, that's so nice of you," said Miss Henley, "but you know how little I drink."

[注]

drink to Rudolpho：为他干杯。

how little I drink：我多么地不会喝酒。亨利小姐得意之余，犹不失其小姐架子。但是她是真的得意吗？

[26]

It wasn't until after the bottle of wine had been drunk and Miss Henley had taken Francis up to bed that father said anything about it. Then he said to mother at the table:

"There wasn't any mail at all today. The bus broke down on the road and nothing ever came through. The porter told me when we came back this evening. The mailbag was still hanging there waiting in the hall."

"I think the girls had better go up to bed," said mother. "They've been up a mountain and they're awfully tired."

[注]

until 是介词。**after the bottle ... to bed** 是名词性从句。

at the table：在餐桌上。

broke down：机件损坏，无法行走，俗称"抛锚"。**mailbag**：邮件袋（相当于邮箱）。

亨利小姐的高兴，原来并无根据。做老师的撒谎，孩子们的母亲也许不会原谅的，但是读者会不会原谅她呢？我们细读全文，看不出有什么迹象可以证实她确有一位名叫 Rudolpho 的男朋友。她说收到了信固然是谎话，她的那些关于男朋友的话（虽然说得那么活龙活现），可能也都是向壁虚构。她撒了那许多谎，有什么动机呢？当然她不想害什么人，她假如存心想骗人，也无非想维持自己的尊严（她的自尊心非常之强，文章中屡次提到这一点），免得因为没有男朋友，因为没有亲人和她写信，而遭人看轻，受人怜悯。假如她是在自己骗自己，想从幻想里面得到感情的满足，那么亨利小姐是个很可怜的人了。但是请记住，亨利小姐是不要别人可怜的。

Rosie
露西姑娘

William van Buskirk（1922—2000）

本文选自《新声：美国新作选》（*New Voices: American Writing Today*）。《新声》收美国新作家约六十人，大多皆无藉藉名，然就其一般成绩观之，实可代表美国文坛之新作风。此数十作家皆态度谨严，刻意求精，其忠于艺术、敢于尝试之精神，大致盖秉承 Flaubert、Henry James、Conrad 诸大师之遗教规范。书中所收，虽未必篇篇呕心沥血，要皆务陈辞滥调之是去，语语自出机杼而已。正视人生，取材现实，故事自不落窠臼；慧心妙悟，无遮无隔，描写亦必多奇句。全书文字，大多可读，其运思之精，功力之深，比之世界名作，亦无愧色。虽曰后生可畏，实亦文章正宗也。

"露西姑娘"一文，寥寥数段（此处未加节删），而意味深长，精心之作也。作者范·勃斯柯克生于美国纽约，为会计师之子，第二次大战时，随美国陆军航空队所辖第十三航空军转战所罗门群岛及菲律宾一带，战后执业广告设计。写作虽非其专业，然其文字造诣之深，读本文便知。

[1]

I am remembering now my small Filipina, Rosie, in the far away, long ago islands of wartime. Perhaps it was only because she had few English words, and I had no Tagalog, that we spoke so little together. Certainly she chattered freely enough with her sisters. But because I could not understand their lilting, exotic jargon, the sound was more of music than of talk, their gentle voices rising and falling, tinkling yet sibilant, like the sound of distant bells borne on a rushing wind. The gossiping sisters were as restful and as little distracting as the playful splashings in a park.

[注]

Filipina：菲律宾人（阴性；阳性为 Filipino）。**far away, long ago**：此四词当形容词来形容 islands，用法颇特别。作者大致但求表达方式的简单经济，顾不得习惯的用法了。

Tagalog：他加禄语（菲律宾的一种方言）。

chattered：喋喋而谈，但闻其声，不明其义。

lilting：轻快含糊而多起伏的。**exotic**：异国（情调）的。**jargon**：（令人难懂的）语言。

the sound was more of music than of talk：她们的声音与其说是像说话，不如说是像音乐。**rising and falling**：起伏。**tinkling**：轻脆叮当。**sibilant**：咝咝作响。两词形容，恐犹有未足，接着又用一譬喻，"如疾风飘来远处铃声"。铃声叮当，即为 tinkling；疾风之声嘘嘘然，亦为一种 hissing sound，正好衬托前面的 sibilant。**borne**（bear 之过去分词）：（风把声音）带来。

她们姊妹间的闲谈，并不（little 有否定的意义）乱人心意（distracting），反而有使人安静的作用（restful），犹如公园里（喷泉？）的水珠溅落之声（splashings）。playful 原义"嬉戏的"，这里作"忽快忽慢，时东时西"解。

[2]

The last time I saw Rosie (we knew it was the last), she wore her pale Mestiza gown, with its sheer high-shouldered sleeves like wings of butterflies. Among the boles of a grove of palms — a tranquil, timeless colonnade in the moonlight — we built a diminutive fire. Then through long night hours we watched its embers blacken, die, and fall to ash. My memory of those hours is sharply clear, and only a little sweetened by time, but I can remember no spoken words.

[注]

Mestiza 为 Mestizo（菲律宾人之杂有华人血统者）之阴性形式。Mestiza gown 指的是菲律宾混血女性所惯穿的女式长衣，是土装而非"美式"服装。**sheer**：绝薄的（衣料）。**high-shouldered**：衣袖在肩部耸起的。

grove of palms：一片棕林。棕树干直无枝，叶生干端，人居林中，但见有干 (boles)，不见枝叶。群树矗立拱卫，犹如柱廊 (colonnade)。**tranquil**：安静的。**timeless**：终古常存的。**diminutive**：很小的。**fire**：堆木柴而生之火。

embers：火烬。接着用三个不加 to 的不定式动词：blacken（由红变黑），die（火熄成炭），fall to ash（炭碎为死灰）。

sweetened by time 约相当于中文"愈陈愈香"之意。当时情境，犹历历如在目前，所不同者，唯因岁月推移，回忆益觉甜蜜耳。

I can remember no spoken words：两人言语本不通，今别离在即，相对黯然，更没有话可说。自然也记不起说过什么话了。

[3]

I remember well the yellow and mellow Manila cigar that I gently puffed and rolled between my fingers. I recall how I stretched on the dark, springy earth as the night's gauzy warmth caressed me. I can see the ivory of Rosie's cheek and Rosie's arms that glowed here and there orange-red in the firelight. Her eyes were black and sad like a spaniel's eyes. Her soft lips smiled and smiled.

[注]

mellow：烟味醇和的。**puffed**：以口喷烟。**rolled**：搓卷。

stretched：伸臂舒腿地躺下。**springy**：有弹性如弹簧的。**gauzy**：轻薄如纱的。夜间暖气，轻如薄纱，来抚我身。

ivory：象牙。彼女脸颊双臂之色本如象牙，今火光照处，其肌肤乃发橘色红光。**here and there**：东一处西一处的。火焰跳跃无定，火光有及有不及，明暗亦不一致。**orange-red** 乃形容词，用作 subjective complement。

spaniel：西班牙狗，其眼乌黑而有忧郁之表情。**her soft lips smiled and smiled**：连用两 smiled，而妙在仍不说话。

[4]

She sang me a song whose words I did not understand, and she danced a little round the fire, a lonely slow Lindy with empty arms, hopping barefoot and awkward in the dust.

[注]

whose words = the words of which。**song**：为无生命之物，照有些语法书规定，这里应该用 of which，但有时为求句法紧凑起见，常有用 whose 来代替 of which 的。**Lindy**：即 Lindy Loo，是一种黑人舞蹈。**hopping**：跳跃，为现在分词，形容主语 she。barefoot（赤脚的）可作形容词或副词，但 awkward（拙劣的）只可作形容词，如为形容词，当系形容主语 she。露西姑娘的舞姿并不美妙，作者照实写来，似亦无伤其人之可爱。一个菲律宾姑娘，连英文都不会说的，想必非摩登人物，作者描写，亦在其朴质处着眼。她的歌喉似乎也没有什么了不起。初学作文者描写美人，往往美得"过火"，结果赞叹多而描写少，读此当可悟作文之道。

[5]

Then she came to my side and was quiet. She faintly smelled of unscented soap, and her hair was full of wood-smoke. So quaint and small was this odd brown girl, my throat congealed, and had there been anything to say, I could not have said it. But there was nothing to say, and in this deepening night we were happy and sad together.

[注]

smelled of = had the smell of。**unscented soap**：未加香料之素净肥皂。美人身上，何必一定要发什么"兰麝之香"？这里据实写来，不加夸张，而彼女之朴素洁净，不言自明。**wood-smoke**：木柴烟味，想是生火时所沾上。

quaint：别致，别具风味。**congealed** 原意"冻结"转作"僵化"。这位古怪的棕肤女郎，如此别有风味，又如此娇小玲珑，以致我的喉咙僵住，说不出话来了。她的娇小，她的风味，和他的说不出话有何相干？还不是因为别离在即，愈觉其美，便愈不忍离之耶？

had there been... 为 conditional clause，义同 if there had been...。本来就无话可说，

要是有话可说，此情此境，我也说不出口来的。

  deepening night：夜色渐深。用一现在分词 deepening，表示时间进行，便觉长夜漫漫，缠绵无穷。第二段已说：Then through long night hours we watched its embers blacken, die, and fall to ashes。看烟消火灭，相对无语，竟夕相共，黯然神伤，尽在不言中矣。

The Treasure Game

觅宝

H. E. Bates（1905—1974）

本文选自《大西洋月刊》（*The Atlantic Monthly*）1953 年 7 月号。作者贝茨生于英国之 Rushden，所著长短篇小说甚多。贝茨以观察精微，笔触轻灵见称于世。本文叙一母亲与其盈盈长成之女儿间的微妙关系，故事甚平淡，然描写女性心理，丝丝入扣，简洁细腻，玲珑透剔，不愧名家之作也。

[1]

From the calm of her place under the acacia tree, on the swinging canopy seat, Mrs. Fairfax listened with growing impatience to the loud chock of croquet balls cracking the silence of afternoon, each stroke like the chime of a wooden clock setting off peals of senseless and exhausting laughter. She did not know how anyone, even the young, could be so energetic or so furiously amused in the three o'clock heat of July.

"Children — please! Couldn't you please? Melanie! — Fay! — couldn't you please *shout* a little less? It sounds like a madhouse — *please*!"

[注]

calm 当名词用，英文中颇常见，但似和中国人思想习惯不合。我们常常只把它当形容词用，"安静的环境"或"安静的地方"，很少会说"从那个地方的安静里面听来"这一类的话。

acacia：树名，译名金合欢。**swinging canopy seat**：上有天幕遮阳的悬空摇椅。这篇小说的背景甚简单，一开头点明了大树和摇椅，全文的活动范围即不离此大树之下与摇椅之上。

with growing impatience：愈听愈难受。**croquet balls**：槌球。chock 似为槌击球之声音，普通词典上并无此义，但按上下文语气，似应作此解。**cracking the silence**：打破沉寂。cracking 之意义，除"打破"之外，在修辞上同 chock 一样另有"拟声作用"（onomatopoeia），即模仿实际的"噼啪"之声。

chime：（钟之）鸣声。**wooden clock**：木钟（槌球之槌与球皆为木制）。**setting off**：引起（笑声）。**peals**：轰然之声。**exhausting**：伤人精神的。这里恐怕并不指使笑的人伤精神，而是使听的人伤精神；因为一切心理活动，皆由这位太太出发也。

how anyone could be so energetic or so furiously amused：竟然有人（在这种大热天气）会如此精神焕发，如此狂欢高兴。即使年轻人有这种精神，她也无法理解。heat 与第一句 calm 相类似，中国人惯说 the hot month 或 hot afternoon 的。

Couldn't you please? 加重前面的 please（请）。Melanie 和 Fay 当是她的 children 的名字。用斜体字排印的两个词应重读。**shout**：瞎叫。**madhouse**：疯人院。

[2]

She supposed that if they could hear her they were taking no notice. Or if they were taking no notice it was because of that old habit of hers of calling them children when they were nineteen and twenty.

"Fay — don't *shriek* like that! I won't have that shrieking, Melanie — stop her!"

[注]

母亲要安静，厉声告诫之后，孩子们还在闹。这可能是她们没有听见她的话，也许是她们听见了，故意不作理会（taking no notice）。她也知道她们为什么不理会。女儿已经一个十九，一个二十（至于哪一个十九，哪一个是二十，下文自有分晓），做母亲的习惯（habit）不改，还是叫她们孩子们。她们自己不承认是孩子了，无怪她们只当没听见。

shriek：尖声怪叫。stop her 之 her 指 Fay，母亲命令 Melanie 去制止 Fay 的怪叫。

[3]

She was cut off from the main lawn of the house by a semicircular bank of azaleas and guelder-rose, so that she could not see the figures of her daughters and the three young men. She did not think she had ever been allowed to shriek like that as a girl. It irritated her exactly as if someone had started to fire off rockets in midafternoon.

[注]

main lawn：(园里的)大草坪。**azalea**：杜鹃花。**guelder-rose**：绣球花。花树密集，种在半圆形的土堆（bank）之上，她视线被阻，因此看不见草地上是什么情形了。**figures**：身形。daughters 就是上段的 Melanie 和 Fay，笑声无疑也是这群青年男女所发出来的。

had been allowed（过去完成时，被动语态）：她做小姑娘的时候，大人不许她这样尖声怪叫的。

rockets：火箭（一种焰火）。下午三点钟左右（midafternoon）放焰火，使人难受，今他们的笑声恼人，亦复如此。

[4]

"I shall have to stop it. I shall go and speak to them. I won't have that sort of thing."

Then she remembered that going to speak to them would be awkward because she had suggested croquet herself. She had remembered, after lunch, the old croquet box in the stable loft. It struck her as being just the sort of quiet and companionable game that did not require energy on hot afternoons and she thought that perhaps it would keep them out of mischief.

[注]

I shall have to stop it 中之 have to 解作"非……不可"。

going to speak 中之 going 为动名词，作从句的主语。**awkward**：怪不好意思的；因为打槌球，还是她自己建议的。

croquet box：盛槌球用具的盒子。**stable loft**：马厩的阁楼。连用两个过去完成时的动词 had suggested 和 had remembered，把时间推了两三个钟头。这一段都是倒叙午饭甫罢以后的事，不是她在摇椅里的所见所闻了。

it 代表 croquet。**struck**：忽然使她觉得。这个动作的发生也在午饭方罢之时，动词似乎也应该用过去完成时，为什么这里用简单过去时呢？过去完成时本是用来同过去时比先后的，表示过去的前面还有过去，当这种对比的需要已经不复存在，事情又是顺着次序讲下去了，就不必再用这种念起来很别扭的时态了。这里用了两个过去完成时动词之后，时间已经表示明白，接着再用简单过去时，也不致引起误会。以下几段大多倒叙，时态过去完成与简单过去杂用，请注意。

她那时忽然想起了槌球这种游戏很安静，可以使大家一起来玩（companionable），热天下午玩起来，也不大需要多少精神；她还这样想，她们有了这个玩也免得去淘气（out of mischief）了。她怕她们淘气，无形中还当她们是小孩子。

[5]

For the same reason she had invited three young men to lunch instead of two. That was also companionable. She wanted her daughters to have companions. She was not after all so very old herself, not so very far removed from the time when those things filled your head. But children grew up so quickly. They flashed through childhood. They whisked through adolescence into young womanhood and you did not know where you were. You felt you did not know at times what was best for them.

[注]

for the same reason 之 reason 即本段第二句：**that was also companionable**（人多了更宜于社交）。

after all：此一成语作为"话得说回来"或"说来说去"。"话得说回来了，她自己也不好算很老。"

removed（过去分词）：离开得远。**those things**：男女社交之事。your head 之 your 泛指一般人。人在青春时期，脑筋里所想的总是这些事情，她自己的年龄距青春也还不远。

下面几句是母亲的感慨：孩子们的童年过得太快了，青春发育时期

(adolescence) 很快过去（whisked），转瞬便成少妇；做母亲的真有点摸不着头脑之感（you did not know where you were）。她也不知道该怎么办才算是对她们最合适的。

[6]

Before lunch Melanie, for instance, had made a great fuss about wearing a dress from last summer. Mrs. Fairfax thought it an enchanting dress; she thought it made her daughter look like a young fresh flower. There was something budlike and tender about it, but the child had suddenly thrown an exhausting tantrum up in her bedroom and said she wouldn't be seen dead in it for her or anybody.

"You will wear it and like it," Mrs. Fairfax said. "Don't be so tiresome. It fits just as well as ever. You haven't grown a scrap."

"Fay had a new one on. You bought it for her. If Fay can, why can't I?"

"Fay's that much older than you. She's grown out of hers. That's why."

[注]

for instance：孩子们已经长大，举个例吧。**before lunch**：这两个词提得也很妙，上面才说过有男朋友来共进午膳，那两位小姐在进餐之前，难免要打扮一番。**made a great fuss**：小题大做，空发脾气。**a dress from last summer**：去年夏天穿过的那件衣服。

enchanting：迷人的。**something**：某种性质或情调，后随两个形容词，**budlike**（含苞未放的）和 **tender**（温柔的）。母亲以为女儿穿了很好看，可是这孩子（在母亲心目中，她总是个孩子）在卧室里大发脾气。**tantrum**：一阵脾气。这阵脾气是掀起来（thrown up）的。**exhausting**：此词第二次出现，大约并不是作者爱用这个词，他只是描写 Mrs. Fairfax 的心理，这位太太的脑筋里恐怕常出现这个词。

she wouldn't be seen dead in it for her or anybody 是间接陈述法，直接陈述法当是：I wouldn't be seen dead in it for you or anybody（不论是为她母亲或是为别人，她死了也不愿意让人看见穿这身衣服）。

you haven't grown a scrap：你一点也没有长大。

Fay had a new one on 之 on 表示"穿着"。

Fay's that much older than you：姐姐就比你大那么一点。that 为副词，形容 much。谁是姐姐，谁是妹妹，到这里才完全说明。

she's grown out of hers = She has grown out of her dress：她人长大，衣服穿不下了。

[7]

It ended in a strange thing happening, and she supposed it was that which had begun her irritation. Melanie had not come down to lunch in the fresh, flowerlike dress that Mrs. Fairfax liked so much and thought was right for her. She had put on the last thing for a scorching summer day. It was a shining bottle-green dress of Fay's that was too severe at the neck and far too drawn-in at the waist, and until she saw it Mrs. Fairfax had not realized how alarmingly and fully her child had grown. The girl had done her hair differently too, in a high, severe style that made her look, Mrs. Fairfax thought, old and false and sophisticated.

[注]

女儿发脾气的结果是发生了一件奇怪的事情。她想她自己心里的不痛快，就是从那时候开始的。二女儿下来吃饭的时候，没有穿那身母亲所喜欢，而认为对她合适的衣服（that Mrs. Fairfax... thought was right for her 此一从句中，主语为 that，动词为 was，Mrs. Fairfax thought 相当于括弧中语）。

the last thing = the least suitable thing。在炎热炙人（scorching）的夏天，穿这样一件衣服是最不合适了。

bottle-green：玻璃瓶似的深绿色（按，此词并非作者杜撰，英文中颇常见）。

severe：（领子）贴紧。**drawn-in**：（腰部）扣紧。母亲看见了这身衣服，才明白她的孩子的发育，已经成熟到什么程度，而且是多么地使大人心惊。

done her hair：修饰头发。**high severe style**：头发往上梳，高高束成一团。头发这样一梳，使得她看来年纪大了很多，也显得虚伪（false）、造作（sophisticated）。Mrs. Fairfax thought 三词是插入语。

[8]

Then Fay appeared in a dress that, at first, Mrs. Fairfax did not recognize. She became aware only slowly of its uneasy familiarity. It was not until she was actually sitting at the lunch table that she grasped that this was the new dress: the white summer organdy that had been so fresh and youthful with its wide crinkled collar and cuffs to match. Now it had a broad black velvet waistband and the collar had been taken away, leaving all the soft wide shoulders bare.

[注]

did not recognize：本该认识的，可是不认识了。上面妹妹说母亲替姐姐买过一件新衣服，今天姐姐穿了下来，母亲可认不得了。

aware of：注意到。**familiarity**：本是相识。**uneasy**：发觉了是相识的反而使人难受。

grasped：领悟。**organdy**：一种细薄坚挺纱布，这里指用这种料子所做成的衣服。**crinkled**：皱成波纹状的。**match**：配称。

买来的时候，这件衣服本来（had been）显得青春朝气，但是现在给那位小姐改得老气横秋了。腰部添了一条黑丝绒（velvet）的阔腰带（waistband），领子拆掉，双肩全部暴露在外！

[9]

She was so upset that she looked severely at Fay and said, "Don't go out into the sun without putting something on your shoulders, child. You'll suffer for it if you don't. You burn so easily."

"I never burn. I've never burned in my life," Fay said.

"There's always a first time. You don't want to be sick, child, do you? It's terribly hot today."

[注]

upset：不愉快而又不知所措。**burn**：晒伤。

there's always a first time：以前虽然没有晒伤过，如果不注意防护，迟早有一天会被晒伤。

[10]

After lunch she said to Mr. Fairfax, who was kicking off his shoes in the bedroom with relief before lying on the bed, "Did you notice Fay's dress?"

"What about it?" he said. "Isn't it the one she always wears?"

"She's taken the collar off."

"Well, I can hardly blame her," he said, and began laughing. "I wanted to take mine off. And would have done for two pins."

"You never notice anything," she said. "I don't believe you'd notice if they turned black, would you?"

"I did notice," Mr. Fairfax said. "I thought they both looked stunning and I don't wonder the boys are after them."

"I suppose that's all you ever think about," she said.

[注]

blame：责备。**and would have done for two pins** = and I would have taken my collar off for a trifle。two pins 喻代价之低：即使为了两个小钉之微我也愿意把我的领子拆去的。

if they turned black：假如女儿给晒黑了。

stunning：美极了，美得使人目眩神移。

[11]

That was why she had taken her book and her spectacles and gone off alone to sit under the reclusive calm of the acacia tree, irritated about things and not realizing, until the wooden chock of croquet balls began to scrape more and more harshly on her nerves, how vulgar the sound of shrieking could be in the hot still afternoon.

"You really must stop it!" she said. She lifted her voice at last in a spurt of anger. "Can't you play quietly for a change?"

[注]

上文几段都是倒叙过去，讲到这里，才回到开头出发点。

reclusive：隐遁的。not realizing 的宾语是 "how vulgar..." 这一从句。**scrape**

on her nerves：扰乱（擦伤）她的神经。**harshly**：刺耳的。**vulgar**：恶俗的。等到她感到槌球之声愈来愈聒耳烦心，她才明白这种尖声怪叫，在平静（still）的热天下午听来，是多么地恶俗可厌。

a spurt of anger：怒气突发。从今天下午开始，Mrs. Fairfax 是百般地不痛快，女儿丈夫都在惹她生气，饭后想求片刻宁静，偏偏木球声、笑声、叫声扰得她心情更为不安，现在忍无可忍，怒火直冒矣。

[12]

Then she realized, slowly, and at first with unbelief, that there was not a sound in the afternoon. The air above the tall acacia tree was not strong enough to quiver the smallest leaves. Coming down so suddenly, after the shrieking and the laughter, the silence had a creepiness about it. She actually heard a bird scratching at dry earth, among summer-burned leaves, under the bushes of guelder-rose, a small obsessional sound of tiny claws searching in shadow that awoke in her, almost before she was aware of it, new sources of irritation.

[注]

slowly, and at first with unbelief：她慢慢地才听出来（园里已经寂然无声），起初她还不信呢。照语法结构，realized 应直跟 that；可是作者插进了一个副词(slowly)和一个副词短语，加上了三个逗号，念的时候就得多停三次。本来可以一气直下的，现在便多顿挫。浩浩荡荡，一鼓作气，固然痛快；然而吞吐盘旋，一波三折，文章便多妩媚。初学作文者，往往直叙无文，如欲更进一层，稍事修饰增益，宜在此等地方用功夫。

air 名曰气，实即风也。风弱，虽至细之叶亦不为吹动。**quiver**：使之震颤。

coming 为现在分词，形容主语 silence。**creepiness**：身上如有物爬行之感。怪叫大笑之后，沉寂如此突然地来临，令人起某种悚然之感（a creepiness）。

scratching：扒抓。**obsessional**：萦绕心头的；盘旋耳边的。**an obsessional sound** 是同位语，说明前面的 a bird scratching。**claws**：爪。**searching**：搜寻。**that** 是关系代词，代替 sound。**awoke**：唤醒，引起，其宾语为 new sources（根由）of irritation。细微的扒抓之声，在她耳边萦绕不去，在她心头造成了新的烦恼因素。

almost before she was aware of it：几乎在她自觉烦恼之前，烦恼已经上了身了。她的新烦恼是不知不觉中来的。

[13]

Now what had happened? Now where had everyone disappeared to? Now what were they up to?

In uneasiness she tried to peer first over, then half under, the canopy seat, searching for the movement of figures through the lower branches of the shrubbery of acacia and guelder-rose. But it was no use; there was nothing there to see.

[注]

up to = doing；about to do。她们在搞些什么名堂呢？

uneasiness：不安，不自在。**peer**：窥视。over 是介词，其宾语为 the canopy seat，她先从椅子上面探望，继而半俯身子，向下窥视。**figures**：人的身形。**branches**：树枝。**shrubbery**：灌木。

[14]

It was in a final effort towards calmness, towards being rational, that she lay full length on the seat. The toes of her shoes clung to her feet by the tips and presently one of them fell off, dropping down on the lawn, as she moved on the canopy.

[注]

她力求镇静，力求合理（rational，自寻烦恼便是无理取闹）。东张西望，既然看不出一个结果，她索性全身伸直（full length）了，躺在摇椅之上，这是她使自己心平气和的最后一次努力（final effort），以后孩子们不管多么吵闹，或是再偷偷摸摸地顽皮，她都不去理会了。

toes：鞋的前端。**clung**：附着。**by the tips**：只有鞋子的脚趾部位，还附着在脚尖上。人躺好了，神经宽舒，鞋自然松下；所以她在椅上（canopy 是 canopy seat 的简写）挪动一下，鞋就落在草地之上。她当然也懒得去捡了。

[15]

A moment or two later she was aware that the creeping sound of the bird in its obsessional scratching among leaves seemed to be growing louder. It seemed also to be coming nearer. And suddenly she was aware of it under the very corner of the canopy. She saw that it belonged to the tousled dark head of a young man who was crawling almost underneath her on his hands and knees.

[注]

tousled（过去分词）：头发蓬松的。

crawling on his hands and knees：两手两膝着地地爬。地上悉悉索索在爬的、扰得她心神不宁的，原来并不是鸟。

[16]

"Oh! my God," he said.

He was already holding her shoe in his hand.

"I'm terribly sorry, Mrs. Fairfax," he was saying, and as he opened his mouth, she noticed quickly how handsome the level lines of his teeth were.

"What on earth are you supposed to be doing?" she said.

"I thought you were Fay," he said.

"What ever made you think I was Fay?"

"You're such a lot like her," he said, "and I thought she came this way."

[注]

来者当是三个青年男客中的一个。此人生得一口齐整漂亮的牙齿，给她的印象该是不错。这位太太今天下午事事不顺心，以致烦躁不安，可是现在并不生气。

on earth 用以加强疑问代名词 what，相当中文的"到底"。are you supposed 是被动语态，可能解释作"人家以为你是在干什么的"，但此处似应为反身动词（reflexive verb）的被动语态：What on earth do you think you are doing? 你到底自以为在干些什么呢？

I thought you were Fay 此句的动词是过去时：我刚才把你看错了，以为你是 Fay（大小姐之名），所以才把你的鞋子捡起来的。

such a lot：多么地。对母亲说她像她的妙龄女儿，该是一句很巧妙的谀辞。

这位青年并不存心恭维，但是大约无意中已经博得这位太太的欢心了。

[17]

He began to try to put the shoe on the canopy seat without her noticing it and she said, "What were you going to do if I were Fay?"

"Oh! we're having a game," he said. "It's a sort of treasure game. You have to find so many things in a given time."

[注]

noticing：注意。趁她不注意时，把鞋放在椅上。捡鞋子原来为的是游戏。参加"觅宝"游戏的人（即末句的 you），一定要在指定时间（given time）之内，找到某些东西。

[18]

"Such as shoes?" she said.

"A shoe was one."

"And what else?"

Perhaps because he was still kneeling on the grass, perhaps because both her feet were now shoeless, he seemed more embarrassed than ever. "Oh! a clothespin," he said, and he hesitated so much before the next of his things that she had suddenly an idea he was making things up. "Then a collar stud. That was for the girls."

[注]

both her feet：另外一只鞋也掉下来了。**embarrassed**：窘迫。

clothespin：晾晒衣服时用的木夹子。**before the next of his things**：说了木夹子，再说下一样东西之前，他吞吞吐吐（hesitated）了好久，才说得出来，以致她忽然有了一个印象：她以为他在编造（making up）了话来骗她。其实他是因为不好意思，才难于启齿的。

collar stud：衬衫领子上的活动纽扣（这种衬衫的领子大多不是缝在一起，而是临时装上的。女孩子要觅的宝是男人衬衫上的纽扣，这种事情说出来不大雅观，无怪那人要格格不吐。

[19]

"Oh! it was different for girls then, was it?"

"It has to be," he said. "It's more fun."

"You look terribly hot," she said. "It would do you much good to rest. How far had you got? What had you found?"

[注]

different：男女双方所觅的宝不同。**it has to be**：非这么不可。

had got, had found（过去完成时）：他来到这里以前，找到了些什么了？

[20]

"I'd got the clothespin and the shoe... well, I thought I had," he said, and again she saw the smile, perfect and handsome in the startling whiteness of its expanse between dark lips.

Suddenly she drew her feet up towards her and said, "Wouldn't you like to sit down on the canopy? You look so hot and uncomfortable down there."

"Oh! I don't want to disturb you..."

[注]

I thought I had：我那时还以为找到了。那男子的牙齿洁白整齐，笑时尤为明显。此处不提牙齿，只说他的笑占地甚大（**expanse**：嘴咧得很开），在两片暗红色嘴唇之间，露出一片耀目的白色。

drew up：把脚缩进，好让那人来坐。

[21]

"Not disturbing. Sit down and cool off a bit."

He sat down and began almost at once, unconsciously, with regular motions of one foot, to swing the canopy up and down.

After some moments of that sensation, so delicious and soothing that she wanted to shut her eyes, she said, "You didn't finish telling me what the girls had to find."

[注]

began 应该直连 to swing（摇荡）的，作者又插了好几个形容的字眼进去。**unconsciously**：不知不觉中。**regular motions of one foot**：一只脚有规律地动，一推一撑之间，摇椅就上下摆动起来了。

that sensation：摇荡的感觉。**delicious**：引起醅美的快感的。**soothing**：使神经平静舒适的。摇椅轻轻摆动，她周身快慰舒适，把眼睛闭上了，好好地享受一下。她方才何等暴躁，现在变得如此平易近人，读者请注意其心理变迁过程。

[22]

The swinging of the canopy made the top of the acacia tree rock with heady gentleness against the sky. The sensation it woke in her body reminded her of a swing on which she had played, under a big tree. as a child.
"Oh! it was a bit silly."
"Tell me."

[注]

rock 也是摇动，但并不悬空，其动亦较着实而缓慢。婴孩摇篮之摇为 rock，秋千之动则为 swing。swing 作名词用，即为秋千。摇椅摆动，牵动树梢，动势虽和缓（gentle），但望之亦使人头眩（heady）。**against the sky**：以天空为陪衬。她想把眼闭上，事实上恐怕没有闭，因此看天际树梢摇动而微觉头眩也。

it woke in her body 是定语从句：在她身上引起的这种（快）感。**reminded her of**：使她想起（一架幼时曾荡过的秋千）。

silly：无聊；没有意思。女孩子还得找寻些什么，那男孩子不肯说。

[23]

In a new spasm of nervousness he swung the canopy higher and said, "Well, if you must know, it was a hair off my chest…"
"Oh! what a thing to think of! " she began laughing in spite of herself, partly because under the sensation of that swinging canopy she could not control it, partly as a small protection against being shocked. She supposed she really ought to have been shocked at something like that, but in an odd way the

swinging of the canopy lifted the sensation of shock and bore it far away.

［注］

spasm：一阵发作。**nervousness**：慌乱。**chest**：胸口。

what a thing to think of：惊叹句，相当于"这事亏你们想得出来"。**in spite of herself**：自己按捺不住。她的笑有两个原因：一是摇摇摆摆得自己不能控制了（后文中的 it 就是指 laughing）；二是拿笑来作为小小的掩护，免得自己受惊 (shocked)。男孩子胸口的毛，拔下来藏起，叫女孩子找，这事多么骇人听闻！这位太太爱护女儿，无微不至，更应该不能忍受了。

something like that：像这一类的事。**in an odd way**：不知怎么地。**lifted**：举起，移除。**bore away**：带走。

[24]

"And what about the rest of the things you had to find?"

"Most of them sound stupid too."

"Tell me."

"A shoe was one. Then there were one or two silly things — the clothespin, then a stocking. Then —"

Under the small, thrilling sensation of the swinging canopy she was laughing quite openly now, not so much amused as in sheer exhilaration. Higher and higher, she thought, all the time higher and higher, as she had done when a child, until you were one, as it were, with the sky, until...

［注］

thrilling：钻到汗毛孔里去似的（不一定指恐惧，快乐也可以使人起一种震栗之感）。

not so much... as...：与其说是前者，不如说是后者。与其说她看见了那人神里神经觉得好笑（**amused**：引以为乐），不如说她是完完全全（**sheer**）心里高兴（**exhilaration**）才开口大笑的。

higher and higher：高呀，高呀，愈荡愈高。**one with the sky**：与天空合而为一。**as it were**：似乎；可以这么说。人与天空并不能合一，不过不妨如此夸张而已。

when a child = when she was a child。

[25]

"Oh! you must win," she said. "Take my shoe. Here, you can take this too —"

He turned in time to see her rolling down her stocking, slipping it swiftly over her foot.

"Oh! no, Mrs. Fairfax. I don't really —"

"Go on!" she said. "Take it. Start running. Get there —"

The sudden motion of his reluctant body as he got up, taking shoe and stocking with him, gave the canopy its final swing.

[注]

win：玩觅宝游戏的，当然觅得多的那一方获胜。

take this 之 this 何所指，看下段自明。

turned：转过头去。**in time**：恰当其时。**rolling**：卷。**slipping**：滑过。此两现在分词形容脱袜情形很贴切。

get there：跑到他们那边去。**reluctant**：于心不愿的。那男孩子不好意思把她的鞋袜拿走，所以不大愿意走开。后来突然站了起来，摇椅又被推动：这种突然的动作，使得摇椅得到了最后一次的推动。

[26]

"What a nice boy," she said to herself. "How silly to be playing that game," and then, as the canopy swung less, "Dying, dying, dying down," in the same blissful way she remembered as a child.

It was only when the canopy was nearly motionless that she remembered to put out her foot and start it swinging again. The grass was cool on the naked sole of her foot. The boughs of the acacia tree seemed to sway in exact time with her body. The shade of the tree embalmed her exquisitely, alone but no longer deserted, and out in the hot still sunlight there was now a new sound of voices, hunting for their treasure.

[注]

dying：渐渐停歇。她记起了从前荡秋千每逢停下时，嘴里常这么唱，"停了，停了，停下来了"。唱的时候，心里感到一种极大的快乐（bliss）。

put out her foot：摇椅快停的时候，她才想起了伸脚出去，再把它推动。**sole**：脚底。脚底着了地，就有一种凉快的感觉。作者于此等感觉描写，决不肯放过。

boughs：树之大枝。**swayed**：摇摆，此词含义大致与 swing 相似，所不同者，sway 之摇摆较笨重而不稳定，swing 则专指较轻快之摇摆，rock 着实，swing 悬空，sway 则悬空着实，兼可适用。**exact**：恰巧，适合。**in time with**：动作的节拍相合。

embalmed：使她觉得像涂了香油（balm）一样地舒服。**exquisitely**：很精巧，很细腻的。**deserted**：为人所遗弃，她现在还是一人在树下独坐（alone），但是她觉得她同孩子们已经有了默契，她不再寂寞了。**out**：在她那地方的外面。**still**：静寂的。

综观全文，故事平淡无奇，叙事似亦多琐碎，然而贯串全文的，乃是 Mrs. Fairfax 的心理发展，如何从暴躁化为和易，从严厉化为慈爱。人与人相知本来不易，任何人的同情心假如能增加一点，他的生活内容即多充实了一点。Mrs. Fairfax 午饭之后在树下小息，正满怀气愤，偏偏巧遇"觅宝"青年，交谈片刻，共坐摇椅，态度即判然大变，对青年男女的"胡闹"，非但不再那么憎厌，而且同情之心油然而生，自己在心理上也随着年轻了不少。这一种内心生活的转变，是一个人生命里的大事；可是人生逢到这种转变的时候，可能在外表上很少动静，甚至和他最密切的人，也可能一无所知；写小说的凭了他的同情心和想象力，是不会把这种场合轻易放过的。本文作者选取了短篇小说最理想的题材，以轻松经济的文字，写入情入理的故事，结果才完成了这一篇杰作。

At Gallipoli
大军出征

John Masefield（1878—1967）

  1915 年英法为求打通地中海黑海交通，援助帝俄，曾在土耳其达达尼尔海峡上方 Gallipoli 登陆。苦战累月，终于无功而退。约翰·梅斯菲尔德时随红十字会在军中服务，目击忠勇事迹，随笔著录，成 *Gallipoli* 一书。书已绝版，1959 年 5 月 31 日《纽约时报书评周刊》（*New York Times Book Review*）为纪念英国桂冠诗人梅斯菲尔德七十五岁寿辰，转载数段，誉为英文散文中之杰作，兹介绍如下。按梅斯菲尔德此文写开阔的场面，激昂的情绪，想象丰富，节拍雄健，读之自令人起慷慨悲壮、大气磅礴之感，中文所谓"惊天地，泣鬼神"者，想即指此类文章也。

[1]

  On Friday, the 23rd of April, the weather cleared so that the work could be begun. In fine weather in Mudros a haze of beauty comes upon the hills and water till their loveliness is unearthly it is so rare. Then the bay is like a blue jewel, and the hills lose their savagery, and glow, and are gentle, and the sun comes up from Troy, and the peaks of Samothrace change color, and all the marvelous ships in the harbor are transfigured. The land of Lemnos was beautiful with flowers at that season, in the brief Aegean spring, and to seaward always, in the bay, were the ships, more ships, perhaps, than any port of modem times has known; they seemed like half the ships of the world. In the crowd of shipping, strange beautiful Greek vessels passed, under rigs of old time, and the tugs of the Thames and Mersey met again the ships they had towed of old, bearing a new freight, of human courage.

[注]

第一句很简单，只是说天气晴朗了，工作可以开始了。工作就是大军登舰出发，攻葛利波里。这是何等繁复而又意义重大的工作，而作者不加任何形容词，只是轻轻地称之为"the work"。但是前面保留得愈多，后面便愈容易开展；"作势欲张"有时比真的"铺张扬厉"还要引人入胜；简单的字眼往往有丰富的含蓄，便是这个道理。

Mudros 是爱琴（Aegean）海中 Lemnos 岛上的一个海港，英大军在此集中，为进攻葛利波里之基地。

haze：雾气。**their loveliness is unearthly**：山水为雾气所罩，其美妙疑非人间所有。**it is so rare**：稀有。这部分句子在文法上与前面没有连接，但读来语气极顺，如排印本无误，则似为说明上文：所以 unearthly 者，即为其稀有之故也。

第三句内共有 6 个 and。句法故意松弛，不求紧凑，读者因此可以少用脑筋去想，只要睁开眼睛，东一处西一处的去看，自然海也、山也、日出也、船只也，重重叠叠，纷然杂陈，令人有目不暇接之感。

the hills lose their savagery：雾气笼罩，山色略显朦胧，无复犷悍之状。**glow**：发光，遍体通亮。**gentle**：文静；重复 lose their savagery。

Troy：在 Lemnos 之东，今小亚细亚之西北角，相传古希腊联军围攻 Troy 达十年之久，荷马史诗 *Iliad* 即取材于此。

Samothrace 爱琴海中一岛，在 Lemnos 之北。**peaks**：群峰。此乃远景，当较 Lemnos 本岛上近景 hills 为高。**transfigured**：形状变易。港内船舶亦因景色之诡异，而变得 unearthly 了。

第二第三两句的时态用的是现在时，指的大约是好天气时候的经常情形。第四句起用过去时，以点明大军出征的那一天。

brief：简短的。爱琴海中气候，夏天紧跟着冬天，春天没有几天。**to seaward**：开出海去。它是 adverbial phrase，形容动词 were，主词为 the ship, more ships 用

以加强 ships。"比之近代任何港口（port）所见到（known）的船只还要多，好像全世界船只的半数都在这里。"

　　shipping 是集合名词，一国或一港船只之总称。**rigs**：船上帆、索等配备。这里希腊船的配备是旧式的。

　　tugs：马力极大，用以拖曳大船之小汽船。Thames 和 Mersey 是英国两条河名。那里的拖船现在调到爱琴海上来了，当年被它们拖曳（towed）过的大船也来了，两种船在这里重新见面。(they had towed of old 是定语从句，省去关系代词 which。**of old**：从前。) **freight**：船上所载之货物。当年所载的是一种货物，现在所载的又是一种货物。现在满船是出征的大军，所载者乃人类的勇气耳。

[2]

Ship after ship, crammed with soldiers, moved slowly out of harbor, in the lovely day, and felt again the heave of the sea. These men had come from all parts of the British world, from Africa, Australia, Canada, India, the Mother Country, New Zealand and remote islands in the sea. In a few hours at most, as they well knew, perhaps a tenth of them would have looked their last on the sun, and be a part of foreign earth or dumb things that the tides push. And perhaps a third of them would be mangled, blinded or broken, made imbecile or disfigured, with the color and the taste of life taken from them, so that they would never move with comrades nor exult in the sun. All that they felt now was a gladness of exultation that their young courage was to be used. They went like kings in a pageant to the imminent death.

[注]

　　crammed：挤满。**heave**：海的起伏。船进港之前，本跨海而来，曾经颠簸；现在出港远征，又将感觉到了。

　　第二句用过去完成时，追叙过去。健儿们本是从英帝国各处来的，在此地集中训练编组之后，现在又开发出去。**the British world**：英国统治所及之地。**the Mother Country**：英国本部。按，出击葛利波里，共有军队五师，计英军两师，澳洲新西兰军两师，法国殖民地军一师。

　　达达尼尔海峡素称天险，德土联军防务坚固，今冒险进攻，伤亡必大，下面几句，都是描写健儿们视死如归的精神。

他们都知道，至多几小时之内，他们之中的十分之一可能已经战死了。但是作者避免用"战死"的说法，而说："那时他们将已经（would have）看过了太阳最后的一眼，那时他们将消失在异乡的泥土里面（化为外国泥土的一部分），或则身体化为与木石相等（**dumb things**：不会说话的东西），受到潮水的拍击而已。"

mangled：周身受割裂之伤。**broken**：不健全。**made imbecile**：化为痴呆（脑受伤或神经受震）。**disfigured**：化为丑恶（面目受伤）。**with the color and the taste of life taken from them**：人生的色和味都被剥夺；受了伤，很多东西就不能享受了。**so that**：从句表示"结果"：以致他们不再能和同伴们一起行动，也不再能够在太阳底下踊跃欢喜了。

受伤之后是喜欢不起来了，可是他们现在是满心欢喜，喜的是他们年轻人的勇气快要得其所用了。

pageant：盛大辉煌之行列。**imminent**：即将发生的。君王临死犹不失其庄严，虽明知死在眼前，犹全副仪仗，声威甚盛地从容赴难。

[3]

As they passed from moorings to the man-of-war anchorage on their way to the sea, their feeling that they had done with life and were going out to something new, welled up in those battalions; they cheered and cheered till the harbor rang with cheering.

[注]

moorings：泊船所。**man-of-war anchorage**：兵舰下锚处。moorings 想是在港内，而兵舰则在近出口处下锚碇泊。**to have done with**：了结，结束（注意：do 一定要用完成时态，才可作这个解释）。**well**（动词）喷出、涌出。**battalions**：单数原作"营"解，复数即指军队。他们感觉到他们的生命已经了结，现在正走向一个新的天地（something new 此两词甚难译，是不是指"死"呢？）。这种去旧就新的感觉在出征军队里面，沛然而兴。于是欢呼声大作矣。

[4]

They left the harbor very, very slowly; this tumult of cheering lasted a long time; no one who heard it will ever forget it, or think of it unshaken. Presently all were out, and the fleet stood across for Tenedos, and the sun went down with marvelous color, lighting island after island and the Asian peaks, and those left behind in Mudros trimmed their lamps knowing that they had been for a little brought near to the heart of things.

[注]

tumult：骚嚷，鼓噪。**unshaken**：没有震栗之感。没有一个人想起了这种欢呼之声，会不大受感动的。

Tenedos 为在 Lemnos 以东的一个岛屿，舰队朝这个方向开去。**stood** 并非"站住不动"，而指船照固定方向航行。

载运五师军队当需大量船只，一一出海想必很费时间。如今夕阳西垂，霞光奇艳，反照爱琴海诸岛，并亚洲诸峰，而 Mudfos 市上已是上灯时分。

those left behind：没有随军队出发的人。**trimmed their lamps**：修剪灯芯此三词见马太福音二十五章七节，按"修拾灯"喻指迎接天国或真理而言。**for a little** = for a little while。**had been brought near to the heart of things**："更进一步地认识了宇宙间的奥妙。"刚才壮士出征，那种欢呼鼓舞，视死如归的精神，真够得上说是"正气浩然"。说到"正气"，不免牵涉到宇宙的神秘，"正气"可以说是宇宙秩序之所以赖以维持者，或者说是"万物的中心"（heart of things）。看了刚才那种景象，谁都有几分钟的感动，若问为什么感动？"感动"本身又是个什么东西？我们只好说：受感动的人是接近了正气，他们亲证了万物的中心，至少在这短时间内他们被推送（brought）得和宇宙的神秘更近一步了。

The Duck
鸭

J. B. Priestley（1894—1984）

本文作者普里斯特莱为现代英国作家，生于英国约克郡之 Bradford，第一次世界大战时从军，曾作战受伤，欧战结束后就读剑桥大学。普氏从军时即常有作品发表，在剑桥时写作更勤，毕业以后即以写作为生。三十余年来作品极多，最著名者为长篇小说 *The Good Companions*（1929）、*Angel Pavement*（1930）和 *Festival at Farbridge*（1951）。

普里斯特莱文章明快健朗，小说中充满人情温暖与生命活力，实为继承英国 Fielding、Dickens 等"阳刚"作风的一大作家。本文选自《普里斯特莱自选集》(*The Priestley Companion*)，原为作者于第二次大战时的一篇广播文稿。全文极短（此处未加节删）。二战时，普氏应英国广播公司之邀，曾长期主持广播节目，所谈虽大多身边琐事，然因其取材精当，含意深远，据说对于鼓励英人抗敌士气，贡献颇大。本文尤宜朗诵。

[1]

It was rather late the other night, and we were coming home to Highgate Village by way of High Street, Hampstead, and the Spaniards Road, which run, you might say, on the roof of London. We had to pass the Whitestone Pond. Now I like the Whitestone Pond. On fine afternoons, boys sail their toy boats on it, and when there's a wind blowing across the Heath the toy boats have to battle with enormous waves — about three inches high. At night, this pond is like a little hand-mirror that the vast, sprawling, yawning London still holds negligently; and you see the stars glimmering in it. Well, the other night was one of those mysterious nights we've had lately when there seems to be a pale light coming from nowhere, and the sky has a pure washed look. The dim lights of a few cars could be seen in the dusk round the pond, and some people, late as it was, were standing and staring.

[注]

the other day：最近某一天。**the other night**：最近某天的晚上。日落以后，即可算是 night；那天是黄昏以后，时间已经很晚（rather late）。

we 没有指明是什么人，应该是作者自己和另外一些人。**Highgate Village**：伦敦附近的一个村子。**Hampstead**：伦敦西北郊区的一个镇，属伦敦市。High Street 即大街之意。英国小市镇主要的街道都以此名，美国普通称为 Main Street。此处是 Hampstead 镇的大街。**the Spaniards Road**：公路之名，我们是走（by way of）某某街和某某路回家的。伦敦西北区地势较高，那条街和公路好像是（you might say）在伦敦屋顶上走过。（注意：run 是多数形式，表示 which 代表 street 和 road 两样东西。）

Heath：荒原；伦敦西北的荒原即名 Hampstead Heath。**enormous**：巨大的；池狭船小，浪高三英寸已经可以算是巨大的了。

hand-mirror：有柄可握的小镜子。把水池比作镜子，诗文中已屡见不鲜，本文作者的幻想，更进一步把伦敦比作一个庞然（vast）巨人，伸臂舒腿地躺在那里（sprawling），打着呵欠（**yawning**："夜伦敦"是不是该打呵欠呢？），疏疏懒懒地（negligently），手里还握着这面镜子，镜子里面隐约可见点点繁星。**glimmering**：发朦胧微光。

Well 为转换语气之词，正式文章中避用，本文原系供广播之用，当可尽量模仿家常闲谈口吻。第三句的 Now 意义相仿。

平常日子池畔景色，已经约略描写，接着就描写那天晚上。那是我们最近（lately）所常有的一个神秘的晚上：四周似乎有一层不知是哪里来的淡淡的光辉，天空是洁净得好像有一种洗涤过了的神气。"长空如洗"这样的说法在中文里已经用得滥俗了，放在英文里还是很新鲜的。

lights：车头灯。**late as it was**：天虽然很晚了，还有人站在池边凝目而视。

[2]

We stopped, and heard a solicitous quacking and a great deal of faint squeaking. Then we saw on the pond, like a tiny feathered flotilla, a duck accompanied by her minute ducklings, just squeaking specks of yellow fluff. We joined the fascinated spectators; we forgot the war, the imminence of invasion, the doubts about the French Fleet, the melancholy antics of the Bordeaux Government.

[注]

solicitous：表示关切的（父母对于子女的关切）。**quacking**：鸭鸣声。**squeaking**：啾啾声。

flotilla：小型船只之队伍。母鸭与小小雏鸭，列阵浮于水面，犹如小小船队，唯船身均披有羽毛（feathered）耳。**minute** 义同 tiny，唯 tiny 较通俗，近于白话；minute 较正式，近于文言。

ducklings 后有一同位语说明之：雏鸭形体尚未长成，从岸上望去，只是啾啾会叫的点点粒粒（specks）黄色绒毛（fluff）而已。

fascinated spectators：入了迷的看客；看得出神的人。

the war：时为 1940 年 6 月，法国西线崩溃，法国政府迁至西南部的 Bordeaux 后再迁至 Vichy，希特勒陈兵英伦海峡，入侵英国（invasion）之举，迫在眉睫（imminence），法国舰队（the French Fleet）谁属，于战局影响极大，英人疑虑（doubts）自深；而 Bordeaux 政府倡议求和，行动颇多乖谬，殊为昔日盟友所痛心，故作者称之为"令人伤心的反常行为"（melancholy antics）。时局严重若此，而作者看见池中群鸭之后，竟然将国家大事浑然忘却。

[3]

Our eyes and ears, and our imagination were caught and held by those triumphant little parcels of life. This duck hadn't hatched her brood here; she'd hatched them in some hidden corner — nobody knows where — and had then conveyed them — and nobody knows how — to swim happily in the dusk on the summit of the city. She hadn't asked anybody's advice or permission; she hadn't told herself it was too late or too difficult; nobody had told her to "go to it" and that "it all depended on her." She had gone to it, a triumphant little servant of that life, mysterious, fruitful, beautiful, which expresses itself as a man writes a poem — now in vast galaxies of flaming suns, now in a tiny brood of ducklings squeaking in the dusk.

[注]

imagination：想象力，比耳目更进一步，不限于当前的所见所闻。**caught**：一把抓住。**held**：抓住不放。那时我们的全副注意力都为群鸭所摄，非但目不转瞬，耳不他闻，而且心中杂念顿息，如有所思，亦无非受此奇观之启发而已。

parcel：此处不解作"包裹"，而解作"部分"（此词与 part 同源）。**life**：宇宙全体之生命。任何生物都只是"一条生命"，只可以算是"大生命"里的一部分。鸭子虽小，亦足表示天地间的生机流行，我们看见了群鸭嬉水得意（triumphant）之状，似乎看见了宇宙生物的神秘，无怪看得目定神往，把国事都忘了。（其实作者所忘的只是暂时战局的进退，他对于宇宙人生的信念，由于那天晚上的经验当更形增强。这样一个人将成为一个更坚定、更有决心的斗士。）**hatched**：孵化（用过去完成时，表示时间在前）。**brood**：一次所孵出之雏鸭（或其他鸟类）。**conveyed**：搬运。母鸭在哪里孵的蛋，没有人知道；孵出以后，如何把小鸭带到这里来游水，也没人知道。**summit**：最高点；那地方居于伦敦最高处。**advice**：劝告。**permission**：准许。她把小鸭带到这里来，既未向人求教，亦未得人准许，只是凭了生物的本能，把小鸭孵了出来，再带它们来教它们游水（池边可能并无养鸭人家，此鸭恐是野鸭）。

it was too late 之 it 恐是代表孵小鸭等等的事情。母鸭决不自馁，不怕时间太晚，或者是困难太多，她要做的事情还是要做好。她并不自馁，可是也没有人给她鼓励怂恿，没有人对她说："你去做吧"（go to it）或是"事情全靠着你呢"。

她所以这样做，因为她是受宇宙间生命力的支配；她是那个大生命（that life）属下的一个兴高采烈的小仆人。**triumphant** 表示任务完成以后的得意。

that life 后跟着三个形容词：神秘、美丽、孕育丰富（fruitful）。那个大生命随时表现自己，就同诗人之写诗以表现自己一样，表现的方式大小不一，有时如星河（galaxies）横空，一颗星就是一颗太阳似的火球（flaming：火焰炽盛的）；有时则如今夕所见的池中啾啾雏鸭也。

A Special Occasion
两小

Joyce Cary（1888—1957）

　　本文作者乔伊斯·卡里生于爱尔兰，祖先原为英人，牛津大学出身，第一次世界大战时曾在非洲从军作战。卡里写作兴趣发生甚早，苦练不辍，然难有得意之作，其第一本书易稿多次，于1930年始出版。迄今成书十余种，以 *Mister Johnson*（1939）及三部曲 *Herself Surprised*（1941），*To Be a Pilgrim*（1942），*The Horse's Mouth*（1944）为最著名。卡里在今日已被举世公认为英国大小说家。

　　卡里观察深刻，对人生有强烈的爱好，故最善描写人物。其文字洗炼有力，要言不烦，奇思妙想，络绎而来，生动活泼，逸趣横生，然而不夸张，不以辞害意，层次井然，语语恰到好处。苟非曾经苦功锻炼，实不克臻此。

　　本文原刊 *Harper's Magazine* 1951年10月号，现从《哈珀杂志佳作选》(*Harper's Magazine Reader*) 录出，全文故事甚简单，且可说并无深意，然而其摹状人物，生动有致，若文学本为人生写照，则作者亦可谓善尽其使命矣。

[1]

　　The nursery doors opened and Nurse's voice said in the sugary tone which she used to little girl guests, "Here you are, darling, and Tommy will show you all his toys." A little brown-haired girl in a silk party frock, sticking out all around her legs like a lampshade, came in at the door, stopped, and stared at her host. Tom, a dark little boy, aged five, also in a party suit, blue linen knickers, and a silk shirt, stared back at the girl. Nurse had gone into the night nursery, next door, on her private affairs.

[注]

故事的开头是一个小女孩去拜访一个小男孩，但作者笔下多描写，少说明，他的目的不仅是讲故事，而且要使读者"如见其人，如闻其声"。

Nurse 是那男孩子的保姆。**nursery**：育儿室；供小孩与保姆应用的房间。本段末句另有 night nursery 两词，可见那家人家有两间育儿室，一间供儿童游息之用，一间是儿童的卧室。

第一句"育儿室的门打开了"，谁打开的呢？该是保姆开了门，把那小女孩子送进来的。保姆对小女客们说话，总是用（used）一种甜蜜的音调（sugary tone）。**party frock**：赴宴时所穿的外衣。外衣下幅是裙子，想必浆得很挺，向四外张(sticking out)，如同灯罩一般。把裙子比作灯罩，是作者巧思，亦是文章情趣所在。

knickers（或作 **knickerbockers**）：一种小裤脚的肥大短裤，短灯笼裤。**on her private affairs**：料理自己的私事去了。

[2]

Tom, having stared at the girl for a long time as one would study a curiosity, rare and valuable, but extremely surprising, put his feet together, made three jumps forward and said, "Hullo."

The little girl turned her head over one shoulder and slowly revolved on one heel, as if trying to examine the back of her own frock. She then stooped suddenly, brushed the hem with her hand, and said, "Hullo."

[注]

study：端详，仔细地看。前有 would，表示虚拟语气（好像是一个人看一件宝贝似的）。**curiosity**：奇珍异宝。后随三个形容词：rare，valuable 和 surprising，普通学生作文总把形容词放在名词之前，然有时形容词放在名词之后，句法更易开展。请参阅前篇 *The Duck* 一文末句中 ...that life, mysterious, fruitful, beautiful... 中的形容词的位置。

Tom 是主语，它的动词是 put（把双脚并起），made，said 三词。

双方瞪目而视者良久，小男孩子跳了三步，上前迎候，小女孩子羞答答地回礼。作者不用 bashful 这一类的词，而女孩娇羞之状可掬。她头向后转，以一只脚跟为支点，全身慢慢地转（revolved），好像要转身过去，仔细看看她身后的衣服似的。然后她突然俯下身去，手擦着衣服的边（hem），说声：哈罗。

[3]

Tom made another jump, turned round, pointed out of the window, and said in a loud voice something like "twanky tweedle." Both knew that neither the gesture nor the phrase was meant to convey a meaning. They simply expressed the fact that for Tom this was an important and exciting, a very special occasion.

[注]

twanky tweedle 两词没有意义，是小孩嘴里随便发出的声音。**gesture**：姿势，即指手指窗外这一姿势。**convey**：表达，他做出这种姿势，说出这两个词来，其用意（was meant）并不要表达什么意义。

they = the gesture and the phrase。**occasion**：时机，场合，事件。小客人来拜会，是一桩重要的，动人的，很特殊的事件（点明题意），前面说句法如求便于开展，可将形容词放在名词之后；这里为求结束稳当，收煞有力，还是把名词放在形容词之后。

[4]

The little girl took a step forward, caught her frock in both hands as if about to make a curtsy, rose upon her toes, and said in a prim voice, "I beg your pardon."

They both gazed at each other for some minutes with sparkling eyes. Neither smiled, but it seemed that both were about to smile.

[注]

curtsy：妇人欠身屈膝之礼。**rose upon her toes**：踮了脚尖身体伸直起来。

prim：矜持的，拘谨的。

　　gaze 亦是"凝视"。stare 只是"瞪目"和"瞠目"而视，表情比较呆板；gaze 则显得更用心，或更有意，更露出欣羡赞赏之情。对人 stare 容易引起人家见怪，gaze 则不致引起礼貌问题。**sparkling eyes**：光亮的眼睛。

[5]

　　Tom then gave another incomprehensible shout, ran round the table, sat down on the floor and began to play with a clockwork engine on a circular track. The little girl climbed on a tricycle and pedaled round the floor. "I can ride your bike," she said.

　　Tom paid no attention. He was trying how fast the engine could go without falling off the track.

[注]

　　incomprehensible：大家听不懂的，不可思议的。**shout**：乱嚷。another 和前面的 twanky tweedle 相呼应。**clockwork**：发条（用发条开动的）。**engine**：火车头。**circular track**：环形轨道。

　　tricycle：三轮脚踏车。**pedaled**：脚踏，蹬。bike 原是 bicycle 的俗称，就本文看来，tricycle 因为形状像 bicycle，亦可简称作 bike 的。

　　女孩子踏脚踏车玩儿，男孩子不去理她，只顾玩他的小火车（这种不理睬人独行其是的态度，自是男孩儿的本色）。他在试验：火车头能快到什么程度，同时不至于跌出轨道外面去。

[6]

　　The little girl took a picture book, sat down under the table with her back to Tom, and slowly, carefully, examined each page. "It's got a crooked wheel," Tom said, "that's what." The little girl made no answer. She was staring at the book with round eyes and a small pursed mouth — the expression of a nervous child at the zoo when the lions are just going to roar. Slowly and carefully she turned the next page. As it opened, her eyes became larger, her mouth more tightly pursed, as if she expected some creature to jump out at her.

[注]

女孩子拿起图画书来看，男孩子还在玩他的小火车。**crooked wheel**：轮子扭曲了，所以车子老是跌出来。

pursed mouth：小嘴收缩起来。**expression**：表情。同位语，用以说明前面的 round eyes and a small pursed mouth。这种瞪眼撅嘴的样子就像是一个胆怯的（nervous）小孩子，在动物园（zoo）里，看见狮子快要张口吼叫的时候，那种既兴奋又恐惧的表情。

[7]

"Tom." Nurse, having completed her private business, came bustling in. "Tom, you naughty boy, is this the way you entertain your guests? Poor little Jenny, all by herself under the table." The nurse was plump and middle-aged, an old-fashioned nanny.

"She's not by herself," Tom said.

[注]

bustling：匆匆忙忙的。**entertain**：招待。"你是这样子招待客人的吗？"you entertain your guests 是定语从句，其连接词（该是 in which 两词）通常都是省略的。

all by herself：独自一个，没人陪伴。

plump：肥胖。**nanny** = nurse。

故事进入此段，另开一局面。若无保姆的一句话，不会惹起下面的一场风波。又请注意：女孩子名叫 Jenny，到此段始点出。

[8]

"Oh, Tom, that really is naughty of you. Where are all your nice manners? Get up, my dear, and play with her like a good boy."

"I am playing with her," Tom said, in a surly tone, and he gave Nurse a sidelong glance of anger.

[注]

that is really naughty of you：你真太淘气了。注意"形容词（naughty）+ of +

A Special Occasion | 153

人（you）"这一类结构的用法。**manners**：礼貌。**good boy**：乖孩子。**surly**：悻恨粗鲁之状。**a sidelong glance**：斜视一下。

[9]

"Now Tom, get up when I ask you." She stooped, took Tom by the arm, and lifted him up. "Come now, you must be polite, after you've asked her yourself and pestered for her all the week."

At this public disclosure, Tom instantly lost his temper and yelled, "I didn't—I didn't—I won't—I won't."

[注]

took Tom by the arm：搀他的胳膊。注意介词 by 的用法。

pestered for her：无理取闹地要她来。pester 普通词典认为是及物动词，但这里用作不及物动词。

public disclosure：当众揭发。他闹了一个星期要那小女孩子来玩，这件事情给保姆揭发（disclose）了，使得他大失面子。女孩子为什么来的，这里补叙说明。

I didn't = I didn't ask her。**I won't** = I won't get up，或 I won't ask her。

[10]

"Then I'll have to take poor little Jenny downstairs again to her mummy."
"No—no—no."
"Will you play with her then?"
"No. I hate her—I never wanted her."

At this the little girl rose and said, in precise indignant tones, "He is naughty, isn't he?"

[注]

I'll have to：我将不得不这么做。**mummy** = mama。又按，此处用 downstairs 一词，足见育儿室是在楼上。

precise：咬音准确，口齿清楚的。**indignant**：愤慨的。

客人总应该比主人多守一点规矩，女孩子自然也比男孩子生得文雅些，所以那个小女孩子的言语举止处处故作老成，和男孩子的粗野不文正成一对比。

[11]

Tom flew at her, and seized her by the hair; the little girl at once uttered a loud scream, kicked him on the leg, and bit his arms. She was carried screaming to the door by Nurse, who, from there, issued sentence on Tom, "I'm going straight to your father, as soon as he comes in." Then she went out, banging the door.

[注]

flew（fly 的过去时）：猛扑（后随介词 at 或 upon）。**seized her by the hair**：抓住她的头发。

kicked him on the leg：踢他的腿。介词又该用 on 了。

issued：发表。**sentence**：（法庭之）判决。**banging**：砰的一声关上。

[12]

Tom ran at the door and kicked it, rushed at the engine, picked it up and flung it against the wall. Then he howled at the top of his voice for five minutes. He intended to howl all day. He was suffering from a large and complicated grievance.

[注]

flung（fling 的过去时）：猛掷。**howled**：号哭怪叫。**at the top of his voice**：声音尽量地大。**grievance**：不平之事，委屈。**complicated**：复杂的，不单纯的。

[13]

All at once the door opened and the little girl walked in. She had an air of immense satisfaction as if she had just done something very clever. She said in a tone demanding congratulation. "I've come back."

[注]

tone demanding congratulation：她的音调在要求别人向她道贺。她并没有要求别人来向她道贺，只是她的得意之色，溢于辞表，好像谁听了她这种音调，就该向她道贺似的。她得意些什么事呢？因为她又回来了！两个小孩子一下吵架，一下又和好如初，全篇故事就在这"离""合"之间进展。文章开头时，小女客来访，应该是两人在一起玩了，但事实上两人各人玩各人的，终至哭哭闹闹打架而散。但是分开了没有多久，两人又聚在一起了。故事乃又开一新局面。

[14]

　　Tom gazed at her through his tears and gave a loud sob. Then, he picked up the engine, sat down by the track. But the engine fell off at the first push. He gave another sob, looked at the wheels, and bent one of them straight.

　　The little girl lifted her party frock behind in order not to crush it, sat down under the table, and drew the book onto her knee.

[注]

　　上面没有讲男孩子流泪，现在却已是泪眼婆娑，隔了眼泪向来人凝视（神情如画），心中气愤难平，再高声抽泣了一下。

　　sat down by the track：靠了轨道旁坐下。

　　fell off = fell off the track at the first push：一推就跌出来了。**bent … straight**：用手扳直。

　　他们两人还是各人玩各人的。女孩子怕把衣服坐坏（crush：压皱），先把衣服后面撩了起来，又坐到桌子下面去看书。**onto** = to a position on。

[15]

　　Tom tried the engine at high speed. His face was still set in the form of anger and bitterness, but he forgot to sob. He exclaimed with surprise and pleased excitement, "It's the lines too — where I trod on'em."

[注]

　　his face was still set：满脸怒容，怨愤（bitterness）之色，依然未改。**set**：有"固定不动"之意。

　　exclaimed：喊着说。**pleased excitement**：心中带着喜悦的兴奋。

　　他把火车跌翻的病源找出来了，原来轨道（lines）也出了毛病，就是在他脚踩（trod 是 tread 的过去时）过的地方。'em 即 them，代表 lines。男孩子的问题已经解决,小说已近尾声,再看那女孩子吧。

[16]

The little girl did not reply. Slowly, carefully, she opened the book in the middle and gazed at an elephant. Her eyes became immense, her lips minute. But suddenly, and as it were accidentally, she gave an enormous sigh of relief, a very special happiness.

[注]

女孩子还是只顾自己看书。slowly,carefully 两词前面讲到她看书时已用过两次,此次三度出现,更显出前后照应。女孩子翻书用这两个词来形容,很为恰当,和男孩子的莽撞,正成对比。

女孩子的表情,还是同以前一样,只是眼睛睁得更大了,嘴缩得更小了。作者只抓住眼和嘴两部分来描写,笔墨经济之至,可是效果非常生动。女孩子听见男孩子的"问题"解决了,嘴里不说什么,脸上表情依旧;可是突然地,好像又是(as it were)偶然地("好像是"偶然地,那就并不真是偶然地了),她大大地(enormous)松了一口气,似乎心上的石头也放下了。**relief**:忧虑消失后的轻松。她这声长叹正是表示一种很特殊的快乐。happiness 是同位语;special 和"A Special Occasion"又前后照应。男孩子的问题已经解决,大约不致再辜负今天这个 special occasion 了吧?

Bookshops in Paris
巴黎的书店

Aldous Huxley（1894—1963）

  本文作者奥尔德斯·赫胥黎为英国维多利亚朝思想家赫胥黎（*Evolution and Ethics*〈严复译为《天演论》〉的作者）之孙，家学渊源，才气纵横，为20世纪文坛一大怪杰。论学问之渊博，文思之敏捷，当世恐罕有其匹。识者论其为才华有余，深沉不足。他晚年潜心宗教，作风亦渐从绚烂归于平淡。著作有小说论文诗歌多种，如长篇小说 *Antic Hay* 和 *Brave New World*，散文集 *Music at Night* 等。

  本文选自美国 *Esquire* 杂志1953年12月号，原题 *The French of Paris*，此处所录数段，似可独立成一小品文字。*The French of Paris* 所谈皆有关法国历史文化，读来似亲聆一文坛前辈之闲话家常也。

[1]

  As a child, as a schoolboy, I knew only the physical appearance of Paris and the Parisians. But as my knowledge of French increased, I became aware of other, less obvious aspects of the city. By the time I was eighteen I had developed a passion for French literature. But literature implies books and books imply bookshops, and there are more bookshops to the square mile in Paris than in any other city with which I am acquainted.

[注]

physical appearance：物质方面的外表，指街道房屋等。

aware of：从耳目方面觉察而知。**aspects**：方面。我的法文程度渐渐进步，我觉察出来巴黎城还有比较少受人注意的别的种种方面。

passion：强烈爱好。

implies：关联。文学一定牵连到书本；说到文学，便不得不说到书本。**to the square mile in Paris**：巴黎每平方英里上面书店之多，胜过我所见识过的任何城市。注意介词 to 的用法。

[2]

These bookshops! What an immense profusion! What a blessed cheapness! In those days there were reprints of practically everything at ninety-five centimes. And the latest novel or volume of essays cost only three francs fifty. Except for collectors' items, the price of secondhand books was no less reasonable. In their brown calfskin, if they were of the seventeenth or eighteenth century, in paper or in mottled boards, if they had been published after 1820, they stood there in the deliciously smelly twilight, shelf above shelf, from floor to ceiling. Those dim caverns of forgotten literature, of dead philosophy and superannuated science, were earthly paradises. And when their darkness became a little oppressive, there were the open-air markets on the Quais. Half a mile of books and old engravings, with the river immediately behind and below them, and the Louvre rising majestically in the background.

[注]

第一段文字甚简单，本段则于选词造句，多用功夫。一起头连用三个惊叹句，第一句呼应上段，引起"书店"正文。第二句道书店之多，实文关于"多"这一个概念，可用之词甚多，作者拈出 profusion 一词，则表示"触目皆是，多不胜收"，再加上形容词 immense，则多之极矣。第三句说书店售价之低廉，用一形容词 blessed，则有"为寒士造福"之意。

reprints of practically everything：几乎什么样的书都有翻印本。reprint 常指已丧失版权或得原版权持有人同意后复印之书。

centime 和 franc（法郎）皆法国货币，1 franc = 100 centimes。

collectors' items：藏书家的（珍）品。**secondhand books**：旧书（转让的书）。它们的价钱和新书（包括 reprints 和 latest novel 等）一样地"合理"（reasonable）。

讲起旧书，作者的兴致又提起来了。文章至此，辞藻转趋华丽，作者要把巴黎淘旧书的乐趣，形诸笔墨，非尽力描写，恐不足道出当年情景也。

他举了两种旧书，一种是出版于 17、18 世纪，书皮用棕色犊皮（calfskin），另一种于 1820 年以后出版，书皮用软纸，或用有斑斑点点图画的硬纸（mottled board）。作者所以只描写书皮而不及内容者，因为淘旧书的人第一眼所注意的应该只是书的外表。

书架上一层一层（shelf）地站满了旧书，下起地板，上迄天花板。书店内部情形怎么样呢？作者只用三个词来描写：deliciously smelly twilight。幽暗之中，有异香焉。此处笔墨所以能如此经济，全仗用了 twilight（朦胧）这样一个名词，只说"幽暗"，而不说"幽暗的地方"，这是文章功力所在，善文者当能深体此意。smelly 应该是"臭"（《综合英汉大辞典》即直称之为"臭"），至少是有怪味，然而前面加了个副词 deliciously，只好说是"异香神怡"了。

次句用两个词 dim cavern（幽暗的洞穴），又是说书店里的光线不佳。那样的环境里藏着文学、哲学、科学三科的旧书；作者用了三个形容词 forgotten, dead, superannuated（逾龄的，老朽的），三词除末词稍僻外，首两词均普通，意义均相仿，然在此处用来，似乎个个皆见功夫，被人遗忘了的文学书，丧失了生命的哲学书，老朽无用的科学书。读者细心体会，当可觉得作者选用这三个词的苦心也。

earthly paradise：人间天堂。

their darkness 之 their 指 caverns。**oppressive**：闷人，使人觉得气闷。**open-air**：露天的。**Quai**（法文）：码头，指巴黎塞纳（Seine）河畔的码头。

engravings：版画（石印，木刻等）。**Louvre**：巴黎著名的卢浮宫博物馆。**majestically**：巍然。河畔书摊林立，旧书古书，连绵不绝，长达半英里；塞纳河即紧靠其后，自下流过稍远而雄峙于后方者，则 Louvre 博物馆是也。形容博物馆的"姿态"，不说 standing，而说 rising，文章即更见活泼，本来死的静的东西，被作者说成活的动的了。

[3]

Then came the Deluge. When the tide of blood had withdrawn, when, in 1919, it became possible once more to travel on the Continent, the franc was a thing of paper, worth only a fifth of its gold-based predecessor. But the bookstalls along the river, the secondhand shops around Saint-Sulpice, the huge emporium under the arcades of the Odeon, the Specialists in erudition of the Boulevard Saint-Michel — they were all there, as though nothing had happened.

[注]

Deluge：洪水，本义专指《旧约·创世纪》所记之大洪水，引申义多指划时代的剧变与战祸。例如，相传法王路易十五曾有言曰："朕入灭，洪水崩天。(After me, the deluge!)"后法国大革命果于路易十六王朝发生。文章此处指的是第一次世界大战，第二句即揭示明白。

the tide of blood had withdrawn：血潮退尽。按，第一次世界大战于1918年结束，1919年召开巴黎和会。

a fifth：五分之一。**predecessor**：前身，战前的法郎。**gold-based**：黄金本位的。

Saint-Sulpice：圣叙尔皮斯修道院。**emporium**：市场。**arcades**：环廊。**Odeon**：巴黎著名的奥德翁剧院。**erudition**：学问，尤指博闻强记的学问。那些书店掌柜都很学识渊博。**Boulevard Saint-Michel**：圣米歇尔大道，为巴黎不甚高贵的繁华区域。塞纳河畔，Saint-Sulpice 教堂的四周，Odeon 剧院廊下的市场，Saint-Michel 大道，都是巴黎书店书摊荟萃之区。

as though nothing had happened：好像没有打过仗，法郎也并没有贬值一般。

[4]

Meanwhile, though the economic handicaps are daily increasing, a torrent of new volumes continues to pour from the presses of France. The bookshops are still in business, not merely in Paris, but throughout the provinces. Traveling through the United States, I have found myself in cities of fifty thousand inhabitants, where it was impossible to buy a book. In France you can buy Gide at most railway stations and Valery practically everywhere.

[注]

economic handicaps：经济上的阻碍，书的成本贵了，买书的人经济力量差了。**torrent**：汹涌激流。**presses**：印刷机。此词也可转作印刷厂解，但这里如作印刷机解，似乎更生动，更可传神。经济困难虽与日俱增，但新书还是源源不断地出版。

still in business：照常营业。**provinces**：巴黎以外的各外省。

Gide 即 Andre Gide（1869—1951）：安德烈·纪德，法国小说家、批评家。Valery 即 Paul Valery（1871—1945）：保罗·瓦雷里，法国诗人，哲学家。英文惯例，作家之名即可代表其著作，故不必说 you can buy Gide's works。纪德和瓦雷里都是所谓高级趣味（highbrow）的作家，而其作品在法国几乎（practically）可以随处购得。

A World of Glass
玻璃世界

William Sansom（1912—1976）

本文作者威廉·桑塞姆是英国当代作家，据 *World Writing, 4th Selection* 介绍，桑塞姆 7 岁即开始写作，第一篇作品于 30 岁时始发表。他曾在银行工作，正式写作之外，在音乐（作曲，弹奏钢琴）、电影（编剧）、广播（编排节目）各界均曾干过，可称多才多艺。桑塞姆曾获奖多次，当选为英国皇家文学会会员（Fellow of Royal Society of Literature）。

本文选自 *The Atlantic Monthly*，原为一短篇小说，其开首几节，可作游记文字读，现摘录介绍如下。桑塞姆文字华丽，想象丰富，描写景物，倾全力以赴，能使读者如身历其境。文句尤妙在情境相生，内外交融，此处虽未能将全文录下，但短短数段，似已不同凡响，于写景之外，似另有一番意境，非但能忠实描写，实能境界独创，发人所未发者也。

[1]

We began at Oslo. Throughout the day, we mounted through long Norway, from slush to snow, from snow to deeper snow, proceeding both up the map and onto higher ground.

[注]

Oslo：挪威首都奥斯陆，在挪威南部。本文主角自叙坐火车自南往北旅行。**mounted**：上行，从下往上或从低处行往高处。**long Norway**：挪威地势狭长。

slush：半融之雪。挪威南部气候此时恐尚温和，雪不能积，多成雪水；稍北则见雪，愈北雪愈厚。**proceeding**：行进。地图上的路程是从下往上，事实上地势也是愈走愈高。

[2]

From the warm, almost the hot carriage it was invigorating and fresh to watch the snow. No fierce peaks and sharp summits to disturb a gentle skyline, but instead a good rolling of high distant hills that swam around the wide perspective with a rise and fall of waves: often these were fir-capped, when the snow-back stood fringed against the sky with short rich bristles.

[注]

carriage：火车车厢。**invigorating**：自 vigor 一词衍化而来，意为"增添精神"。车内温暖，几乎令人难受（hot 指高于体温之热度，为人身所难受），望窗外雪景，则使人精神徒增，神清气爽。

地平线上之景物，其线条轮廓（skyline）大致和缓，并无奇峰（fierce peaks）峻岭，矗立突出。纵目四望，天地辽阔（wide perspective），远处高山，升降起伏，犹如波涛滚滚（rolling）四周环绕浮动（swam）焉。

fir-capped：山上植有枞树，如为枞树所覆盖。**snow-back**：山如卧伏地上，其背部皆雪。**fringe**：织物边缘上之流苏。山上皆有树，看来周围似乎有密集短刺。**against the sky**：以天空为陪衬。

[3]

By midday we had passed through the skiing country, where, apart from the beauty of the snow, there was at certain stations a spirit of festivity as red-capped skiers left the train and sought sleighs to take them out to their snowy places of holiday.

[注]

skiing country：滑雪地区。**spirit of festivity**：办喜事那样的高兴。**red-capped**：戴红帽的（红帽子想是滑雪者的"行头"）。**sleigh**：雪橇，雪车。那些来滑雪度假的客人，下火车之后，再坐雪车转往滑雪胜地。

[4]

But some time after that the real country began, the skies changed, a frozen magnificence charged the air with a peculiar magic. Great lakes appeared, ice-bound, their miles to the horizon furred with snow. Icicles as thick as tree trunks hung their green glow from rock ledges, and where waterfalls had been struck solid they hung in rows like monstrous teeth. Over everything the far gleaming sun and its greening sky played strange tricks of transparency.

[注]

  after that：过了滑雪地区后。**the real country**：真正的原野景色，少见人工建设，多是天然之美。**skies**：天空（常用复数形式）。

  frozen magnificence：两词言简意赅，可供有志炼字者参研。magnificence 言宇宙之大与景物之壮丽，添 frozen，则言天凝地冻，一片冰雪。两词联用，颇见巧思，然甚难翻译。

  charged：充电，充塞。冰雪壮丽，不过有形之物，作者文思更进一步，从有形推至无形。无形者，空气（air）也，气氛也。有形之美影响及于无形之气，使空气里都充满了某种神秘之感。

  ice-bound：为冰所封。**their miles to the horizon**：湖面开阔，无际无涯，直接天外（horizon），计程当不止数英里，湖面全部均积雪如绒毛（furred）。

  icicles：冰柱。**trunks**：树干。**ledges**：山崖突出处。此句本来说 Icicles as thick as tree trunks hung from rock ledges 就够，但作者于 hung 之后加上 their green glow（明润绿光）三词。按语法，glow 是 hung 的宾语；按实际，green glow 就是主语 icicles，绿光不能下垂，下垂者仍是冰柱；唯添此三词之后，冰柱形态更见生动。

  where waterfalls had been struck solid：瀑布受寒冻结之处。瀑布此时业已冻结，故动词用过去完成时。struck solid 二词，其声其义，都很显硬性力量，此处用来，较之 frozen 胜过多多。

gleaming：光线微弱的。**greening sky**：greening 是现在分词，从动词 green 变来，但动词 green 可以"及物"，也可以"不及物"，如不及物，则意谓"本身渐渐转绿"，如及物，则意谓"使别的东西成为绿色"，此处当以作不及物动词较妥。

played tricks：耍花样，施法术。日光惨淡，自远处照来，天空似亦渐呈绿色。日色天光，相互为用，凡照射所及，皆起种种奇妙透明作用。**transparency**：透明。日光当不能使不透明者成为透明，但万物皆已多为冰雪所覆，经奇妙光线照射，斯乃彩色奇丽，变化多端矣。

[5]

Such a sun! It hung and traveled all day on the horizon so low that losing heat it grew in complement larger — it gleamed more than shone. It gleamed like a force of great candle-power over the wide land, turning the snow to lavender and pink, greening the icicles and greening the sky; and the sky itself receded infinitely, it became more transparent than itself, it provoked in its pale green a visible sense of infinity.

[注]

挪威地近北极，太阳与我们在温带热带等地所习见者不同，本段以一惊叹短句开始。

low：太阳走不到天当中去，整天只在离地平线不远处巡行，据我们的经验，太阳于甫出或将落之际，离地平线近，不甚热，看来甚大，本文中所叙太阳，则是整天如此。**losing heat it grew larger**：热虽不足，而形体变大。**in complement**：作为补充（似乎以形体之变大，补足其热之丧失）。so...that 是连接词。

日光照耀，本来应该用 shone 一词，但这里的太阳不能说是 shone，只好说是 gleam：与其说是照耀，不如说是微露弱光而已。

a force of great candle-power：烛光（光度之单位）甚强之灯。

lavender and pink：浅紫淡红。此句即照应上段的 strange tricks。日光所照之处，积雪成为浅紫粉红，冰柱成为绿色，天空亦为绿色。

receded：后退。**infinitely**：无限地。天空无限地往后撤退，足见高旷。it became more transparent than itself 颇费解，it 指天空，itself 亦是天空，天空本来是透明的，现在受日光影响，看来较往常更为明澈。**provoked**：引起。**sense of**

infinity：高旷无限的感觉。**visible**：可以肉眼观察得之。

[6]

Yet this was no true arctic sun — although we were traveling near to the polar circle: it shone not on a barren land, but on a snow-laden gentle place rich with cream-colored birch and black fir. On such country its low long beam cast everything into a strange clearness — in the same way, though a thousand times clarified, that a lowering sun on a summer's day clears and stills the air just before evening. Everything seemed set in glass, transplendent, motionlessly clear.

[注]

arctic：北极的。**polar circle**：（北）极圈。**barren land**：荒地。如在北极，则草木不生，一片荒凉。挪威树木甚多，非荒芜不毛之地，气象平和（gentle），亦无凄厉之状。**birch**：桦树。

beam：光线。日光斜照，各物显得特别清晰。在温带国家，夏黄昏日落之前，空气似更觉清澈宁静，挪威情况亦复类此，唯清晰更胜千倍耳。

set（过去分词）：安放。各物如置玻璃之中，纹丝不动，明净耀目。transplendent 为罕见之词，解作 very resplendent（十分光亮）。按，此句上应题意。

[7]

So the day passed as we steamed on through the snows, higher ever north. The sun set early. Then the light was gone, the snows were gray — and soon after we ran into a blizzard. Now from the warm and easy carriage nothing was to be seen: only the drive of snow hailing by, and the white steam and smoke of the forward engine driven down past the windows by the weight of the wind.

[注]

steamed：坐火车进行（火车靠蒸汽推动）。**higher ever north**：愈北则地势愈高。**blizzard**：大风雪。**drive of snows**：雪风猛扑。**hailing by**：势如冰雹，在窗外吹过。

[8]

We steamed out of the blizzard into clear cloud-high height. A hidden moon shone a starshine light over the snow, giving to things mysterious visibility but no exact shape. Then the train passed the last station, and curled round towards Trondheim. A grinding of iron brakes, a jolt of luggage, and the train came expiring its last steam to a halt. Outside, a babel of fresh faces to receive us the stiff and weary.

[注]

cloud-high height：与云高相齐之高地。**mysterious visibility**（神秘的可视性）**but no exact shape**：朦胧可见，疑真疑幻，形体模糊。

curled round：盘旋而行。**Trondheim**：挪威中部海港。

brakes：煞车。**grinding**：摩擦（动作或声音）。**jolt**：晃动。连用两个不定冠词 a——刹车这么"喀啦"一刹，行李这么来回一晃——很能表示停车一刹那间的情形。**expiring**：吐气。**came to a halt**：停止。

babel：嘈杂混乱的现象（原出《旧约·创世纪》第十一章第二节至第九节）。**stiff**：（四肢）僵硬。跋涉一天之后，目的地已到，旅客个个身乏骨直，车外喧哗以迎者，皆"生人面孔"也。

A Hemingway Sample
海明威的写作技巧

Caroline Gordon（1895—1981）

　　海明威是美国最重要的小说家之一，他对小说艺术的贡献，非本文所能详论。本文只是选海氏原文一段，加以评注，也许可以帮助读者对于海氏写作技巧的了解。
　　评注者卡洛琳·戈登为美国当代女小说家，曾有长短篇小说多种问世。本文原题 Notes on Hemingway and Kafka，发表于 Sewanee Review 1949 年春季号。卡洛琳·戈登后与其夫婿 Allen Tate（1899—1979，美国名批评家、诗人，历任北卡罗来纳、普林斯顿、纽约、芝加哥、明尼苏达各大学教授）合辑小说评选集，书名《小说之屋》(The House of Fiction)，书中对于海明威有较详尽之评介，此处所录几段，亦见于该书。

[1]
　　Ernest Hemingway's *A Farewell to Arms* begins:
　　"In the late summer of that year we lived in a house in a village that looked across the river and the plains to the mountains. In the bed of the river there were pebbles and boulders, dry and white in the sun, and the water was clear and swiftly moving and blue in the channels. Troops went by the house and down the road and the dust they raised powdered the leaves of the trees. The trunks of the trees were dusty and the leaves fell early that year and we

saw troops marching along the road and the dust rising and leaves, stirred by the breeze, falling and the soldiers marching and afterward the road bare and white except for the leaves."

[注]

所引海氏原文，请读者先仔细读几遍，看看能不能发现它的优点。读者至少可以发现两点：一、用词皆极简单，全段几乎没有难的词，即使有一、二生词，在普通词典里都可以查到。二、句子结构也很简单，短短一段里面，and 竟用了十几次，好像天下没有别的连接词可以用似的，现在分词用得较多，定语从句出现两次，状语从句一个都没有用。

学英文的人普遍都知道写"simple English"的重要，海明威的英文，如此处所引者，总可以算是 simple 了罢？但是英文要写得像海明威那样简单，实在是多年苦功的结果。海氏生平得益最深的时候，是一战后在巴黎的那几年。那时他勤练写作，更幸运的是他交到了几位良师益友，其中以名诗人埃兹拉·庞德（Ezra Pound）和名散文风格家格特鲁德·斯泰因（Gertrude Stein）（两人皆旅法美侨）给他的启发最深。庞德拿他的文章大刀阔斧地删改，把有堆砌之嫌的形容词统统砍掉。斯泰因则务求精确，力斥虚浮，对写作别具见解，海明威生平对她最为服膺。海氏日后所以能自成一家，文章受万人模仿者，斯泰因教诲之功不小。海氏对于写作的态度极谨严，几乎一笔不苟，他这种认真的习惯是在巴黎那时养成的。

现在再回到海氏原文。《永别了，武器》（*A Farewell to Arms*）（1929）是海氏一部很有名的长篇小说。故事内容讲一个美国义勇救护车队队员在意大利前线服务时，同一个英籍护士发生恋爱，几经波折，终于好梦难谐，后来那个护士因难产在瑞士去世。书有中文译本，译名《战地春梦》，林疑今译。这里且把这一段林氏的译文录下，以供读者参考：

"那一年晚夏，我们住在乡下一间小房子里。从我们那座房子，看得见隔河的平原，那平原同山联在一起。河底有漂石和圆石子，在太阳光下，又白又干，河水则又蓝又清，水流得很快。军队从房子旁边的路上走过，卷起尘沙，洒在树叶上。树干也是积满尘土，树叶早落，军队一开去，尘沙满天，微风一吹，树叶儿就堕。军队走完了后，路上除落叶外，白白漫漫，空无一物。"

林氏译文可以称得上简洁流畅。唯关于河流一句，意义不甚明白。河水既又蓝又清，怎么"河底"的石子会"又白又干"呢？河水应该很浅，"河床"上的大小石头有露于水外者，故能又白又干。in the channels 三词漏译，拟在后面再讨论。

这一段文章字面上的意义，大致已经没有什么问题。我们现在可以看看卡洛琳·戈登如何更进一步地研究它的优点。

[2]

The tone of the whole book is set in the first paragraph. The tone, in this case, is a mood, a dramatization of the wistful rebellion of youth, confronted with the hard facts of life, love and death. This mood is evoked by the very sound of the words in the first sentence:

"In the late summer of that year..." and persists throughout the book.

[注]

tone：调子，情调。所谓调子其实就是态度（对于书中题材所取的态度）。一篇小说的调子可以正经，可以俏皮，可以轻快，也可以忧郁。戈登说《永别了，武器》全书的调子在第一段就表现出来了，本书（in this case）的调子是一种特殊的心情（mood）：是青年人忧郁的反抗心理（wistful rebellion）面对着人生爱和死这两种残酷的现实，主观客观双方冲突，在心头所造成的对峙局面。（**dramatization**：戏剧化。所谓"戏剧"〈drama〉在英文里常常指两种力量的冲突——如忠奸不两立，忠孝不能两全，或天人交战等，这些情形在英文里都可以用 drama 这个词来表示。）我们不妨把海氏原文再读一遍，看看它的调子如何。我们不会觉得它雄壮，也不会觉得滑稽，我们只觉得调子相当沉重，沉重之中似乎还带着一点怅惘，一种无可奈何的神情——《永别了，武器》全书都是照了这个调子进行的。

evoked：唤起。**persists**：坚持不改。戈登说即使开头那几个词的声音，就可以唤起这一种怅惘之感。读者不妨再试读一下，看看有没有她所讲的那种反应。假如一读上去，真会有这种感觉，那么海明威的文字技巧，足以与音乐媲美了，音乐旋律的能不能感动人，据说是没有理由可讲的。但据我个人看来，海明威的第一句的句法的特点是几乎没有顿挫，少变化，多重复，拍子平整徐缓，然而以缓胜速，以拙胜巧。开头 in the late summer of that year，七个词慢慢地拉得很长，隔了两个词，就又出现了 in a house in a village，似乎很笨拙地把 in 重复应用。

looked 一词，遥指句末的 mountains，虽然一气呵成，然而按部就班，不慌不忙，先是 river，再是 plains；而且两词之前，除冠词 the 外，不加任何形容词（这里加形容词的诱惑是很大的，但是加了形容词，拍子就乱了，作者至此，非沉住气克制自己不可）。第一句句法的要义如此，但是这和感情作用有什么关系呢？这就得请读者细心体会了。

[3]

The rendering of the rest of the passage is also admirable. The action of the sun *shows* the pebbles and boulders that lie in the bed of the river to be *dry* and *white*. The river is clear and moves swiftly; the further specification that it was blue where water was deepest (in the channels) makes us see it flow. We are convinced that the troops passed the house by the fact that enough dust was raised to powder the leaves of the trees and even the trunks.

[注]

rendering：处理。

the action of the sun shows：全书第一段，故事可说还没有开始，只是景物描写。景物描写，容易落入呆滞，应该设法于静中见动。又忌笼统模糊，应明确清楚，使读者如亲眼看见一般。原文讲石子之处用的 in the sun 是三词，但实际是太阳照耀的结果，故曰"太阳的动作，使石子显得又干又白"。用了 in the sun 三词，即暗含太阳的动作，而且使读者看得明明白白，清清楚楚。

specification：（特别标明的）品性。**channels**：流水最深之处（the deeper part of a waterway）。该句似作"河水很清，流得很快，水流很深处，则呈蓝色"。这样一解释，水的流动显得更跃然如在目前了。

we are convinced：被动语气，接下面 **by the fact**。由于这件事实，我们才深信……灰尘这么多，使我们不得不深信军队真在那屋子旁边开过。小说（fiction）本是虚构想象之作，唯善写小说者，能使读者把虚构的事情信以为真耳。

[4]

The phrase, "the leaves fell early that year," is an admirable preparation for the climax of the action; that is to say, "My love died young." The whole

Resolution is, in fact, both prepared for and symbolized in this passage: "We saw troops marching along the road and the dust rising and leaves, stirred by the breeze, falling and afterward the road bare and white except for the leaves." A human heart, ravaged by grief, will ultimately become as bare and as quiet as the white road that the soldiers have passed over.

[注]

本段牵涉到象征主义（symbolism）的问题。早落的树叶是象征他的爱人之早夭——作者轻轻淡淡地提了 the leaves fell early 这几个词，想不到其用意有如此之深。乍一看好像是无关紧要的描写风景，而不知作者笔力于一开头即已贯穿全书，其才华其功力实令人钦佩。象征（symbols）的运用，要贴切，要含蓄。如此处改说："我看见了早落的树叶，就想起我那早夭的爱人。"即显浅薄低级。如曰，"我的爱人呀，你的命就像那早落的树叶！"，则会使读者浑身起鸡皮疙瘩。

climax：高潮。**preparation**：准备工作，伏笔。开头提了一下树叶的早落，即为后文"全书故事动作的高潮"（其爱人之死）做一伏笔，而且是很好的伏笔，令人击节称赏（admirable）。

Resolution：解决。此为研究小说技巧之专门术语，故用大写字母开始，一篇小说的结构，通常都可分作两部，前面是 Complication，后面是 Resolution（错综与解决；或系铃与解铃）。《永别了，武器》中，那位救伤队中尉同英国护士认识，是"错综"的开始；他爱人因难产丧生，是小说的"解决"。戈登说，全书第一段的末句已替后文的解决全部做了伏笔，而且这一句话就象征了故事的凄凉的结局。

原来那条"白白漫漫，空无一物"的路，就象征书中主人公痛苦的心（**ravaged**：摧残）。大军过处，烟尘滚滚，军队走完，路上空空荡荡仅余落叶而已；今书中主人公百劫归来，忧患余生，心中除痛苦的回忆以外，万念全消，就像大军走过后的那条公路。这种"隐痛"最应含蓄，说穿不得，说穿了文章品格就低，就有感伤主义（sentimentalism）之嫌了。今海明威此句，粗看之似与感情无关，只是景物描写，然实际上则包含无限隐痛。所以戈登说，《永别了，武器》的"调子"于第一段即贯穿全书，而海明威于写作时所用的苦心，亦可想而知了。

Kant the Man
康德的日常生活

W. Somerset Maugham（1874—1965）

  毛姆的散文，清楚易读，最宜初学模仿。下面所选几段，很少费解之处，实在用不到什么注解。据毛姆在他的《写作生活回忆》(*The Summing Up*) 中说，他自己作文，有三个标准，按其重要性次序说来，第一是达 (lucidity)，第二是简 (simplicity)，第三是顺 (euphony)。达者，就是把话说清楚了，使人一看就懂；简者，要言不烦，少说废话；顺者，音调悦耳，便于上口。这三点——尤其是达——为毛姆一生致力所在。当代作家在这三点上的成就，能够得上毛姆的，实不多见。

  本文选自他的散文集《随心所至》(*The Vagrant Mood*)，原题《某书的读后感》(*Reflections on a Certain Book*)。他所谓某书是康德的美学名著《判断力之批判》(*Critique of the Power of Judgment*) 这样一个书名很可能把一个不学哲学的外行读者吓倒，但是毛姆自己承认对于哲学也是外行，只是对于艺术有兴趣，所以他觉得他对于美学的问题也可以来发表意见。全文分六节，第一节是描写康德的日常生活，就如下面所节录介绍的。后五节是他读康德美学名著后的杂感，都很平易近人，并不比第一节艰难多少。

[1]

  Punctually at five minutes to five Lampe, his servant, waked Professor Kant and by five, in his slippers, dressing-gown and night-cap, over which he wore his three-cornered hat, he seated himself in his study ready for breakfast. This consisted of a cup of weak tea and a pipe of tobacco. The next two hours he spent thinking over the lecture he was to deliver that morning. Then he dressed. The lecture room was on the ground floor of his house. He lectured from seven till nine and so popular were his lectures that if you wanted a good seat you had to be there at six-thirty.

[注]

punctually：准时地。**Lampe**：仆人之名。**dressing-gown**：晨服（闲居时所穿之宽大袍服）。注意：穿（鞋或衣）和戴（帽）都可以用介词 in 来表示。**three-cornered hat**：三角状之帽，康德把它戴在睡帽的外面。**study**：书房。**deliver**：发表（演讲）。

本段句法都很平顺，只有第三句 The next two hours he spent... 中。hours 为宾语，放在动词之前，末句 so popular were his lectures 中主语 lectures 放在动词之后，此种次序之颠倒，大多为加强语气之用；移放在一句前头的词，往往是意义上应该着重的词。

[2]

Kant, seated behind a little desk, spoke in a conversational tone, in a low voice, and very rarely indulged in gesture, but he enlivened his discourse with humour and abundant illustrations. His aim was to teach his students to think for themselves and he did not like it when they busied themselves with their quills to write down his every word.

"Gentlemen, do not scratch so," he said once. "I am no oracle."

[注]

seated 是过去分词。**conversational tone**：普通谈话式的语气（不像在讲学）。

indulged in：任性而为。用了 indulge in 以后，所做的事情大约并不是一件好事，即使并不是坏事，至少也应该加以节制而少去做它的。照毛姆的意思，讲学的时候多做手势一事并不可取，但是康德很少有这个毛病。**enlivened**：使活泼有趣。**discourse**：讲演。**illustrations**：实例，用以说明理论者。

he did not like it 之 it 指学生勤记笔记这种情形。

quills：鸟羽笔。
scratch：原意是"扒，搔"，转作"像扒搔似地写字"，乱写，急写。
oracle：代表天神发言之人。这种人的话才是值得一字不漏地记下来的。

[3]

It was his custom to fix his eyes on a student who sat close to him and judge by the look on his face whether or not he understood what he said. But a very small thing distracted him. On one occasion he lost the thread of his discourse because a button was wanting on the coat of one of the students, and on another, when a sleepy youth persistently yawned, he broke off to say:

"If one cannot avoid yawning, good manners require that the hand should be placed before the mouth."

[注]

judge：判断（前面的 to 省去）。它的宾语是 whether 从句。

distracted him：分他的心。

lost the thread of his discourse：演讲断了线索，讲不下去了。

a button was wanting on the coat：上衣上面少了一个纽扣。注意，中文说法用"上衣"做主语，英文常用"纽扣"做主语。

persistently：（坚持）不断地。**broke off to say**：打断了话锋，改讲另外一件事情。

good manners：礼貌。"假如呵欠非打不可的话，照规矩手也得按在嘴上的。"这是一句幽默的话，幽默之所以为幽默，这里也不妨试一探求其原因：一、康德看见那人不断地打呵欠，心里也许很不高兴，但是他宽恕他的打呵欠，只是批评他不该不把嘴按上。他的宽容也许是勉强的，他的批评只是避重就轻的。但是这种勉强的宽容精神和避重就轻的批评，假如表现得好的话，往往就成了幽默。二、这句话本来是专指某一个人说的，可是康德并不讲明是谁，先用的是 one（任何人），后面连 one 都不用了，只是说 good manners require that the hand... 根本没有提什么人。这样把"专指"化为"泛指"，就显得更为气度雍容。假如改说"...one should place one's hand..."就似乎带一点声色俱厉的样子，也就算不上幽默了。

[4]

At nine o'clock Kant returned to his room, once more put on his dressing-gown, his night-cap, his three-cornered hat and his slippers and studied till exactly a quarter to one. Then he called down to his cook, told her the hour, dressed and went back to his study to await the guests he expected to dinner.

[注]

call down to his cook：他的厨子可能在楼下。he expected to dinner 是定语从句，关系代词 whom 省却。**dinner**：一天中主要的一餐，这里当然是午餐。

[5]

He could not bear to eat alone, and there were always guests, never less than two nor more than five. As soon as they were assembled Kant told his servant to bring the dinner and himself went to fetch the silver spoons which he kept locked up with his money in a bureau in the parlour.

The party seated themselves in the dining-room and with the words "Now, gentlemen," Kant set to. The meal was substantial. It was the only one he ate in the day, and consisted of soup, dried pulse with fish, roast, cheese to end with and fruit when in season. Before each guest was placed a pint bottle of red wine and a pint bottle of white so that he could drink whichever he liked.

[注]

assembled：到齐了。**bureau**：有抽屉之写字台（英国用法，此词在美国作"衣柜"解，毛姆为英人，故此处采用英国解释）。**parlour**：普通住宅的起居室（客厅），兼作会客之用（豪华大宅中正式会客的大厅则称为 drawing-room）。

set to：开始，发动。这里当然是开始用膳，相当于中文的"动筷"。

the only one = the only meal：一天就吃这么一顿。早晨他单喝淡茶抽烟斗，前面已经说过了。

pulse：豆类（黄豆、豌豆、蚕豆等，凡可当饭菜吃的豆都可用这个词）。**roast**：烤肉。**cheese to end with**：末道菜是干酪。**in season**：时鲜的。**pint bottle**：一品脱容量的瓶子（品脱是英制单位，主要是用来便捷地标定液体重量。通常来说，每一英磅重的常见液体如水、酒、牛奶等，其体积基本上就是一品脱）。**wine**：葡萄酒。客人面前置红、白葡萄酒各一瓶，任其自选。

[6]

Kant was fond of talking, but preferred to talk alone, and if interrupted or contradicted was apt to show displeasure; his conversation, however, was so agreeable that none minded if he monopolized it. He would also tell humorous stories, of which he had a rich supply and which he told uncommonly well, so, he said, "that the repast may end with laughter, which is calculated to promote digestion."

[注]

if interrupted or contradicted：他的话假如给人打断了，或是被人驳回去了。was apt to 的主语是句首的 Kant。

agreeable：可喜，有趣。**monopolized**：独占。即使他一个人发言，不容别人插嘴，别人也不会见怪（minded）。

of which he had a rich supply：他能讲的笑话的储备量很足。

so, he said, "that…" 中之 he said 是插入句子，so 跟着后面的 that 一起走。**repast** = meal。**calculated**：预计可以（有某种结果），**to promote digestion**：帮助消化。

[7]

He liked to linger over dinner and the guests did not rise from table till late. He would not sit down after they had left in case he fell asleep, and this he would not permit himself to do since he was of opinion that sleep should be enjoyed sparingly, for thus time was saved and so life lengthened. He set out on his afternoon walk.

[注]

linger：留恋不走。in case 常作 if 解，这里解作 lest（唯恐）。

this he would not permit himself to do：他决不容许自己这样做（午睡）。this 是 to do 的宾语。**was of opinion**：主张。**sparingly**：俭省地。每天节省一个钟头，就好像多活了一个钟头，所以说生命也延长了。午饭后他出门散步。

[8]

He was a little man, barely five feet tall, with a narrow chest and one shoulder higher than the other, and he was thin almost to emaciation. He had a crooked nose, but a fine brow and his colour was fresh. His eyes, though small, were blue, lively and penetrating. He was natty in his dress. He wore a small blond wig, a black tie, and a shirt with ruffles round the throat and wrists; a coat, breeches and waistcoat of fine cloth, gray silk stockings and shoes with silver buckles. He carried his three-cornered hat under his arm and in his hand a gold-headed cane. He walked every day, rain or fine, for exactly one hour, but if the weather was threatening, his servant walked behind him with a big umbrella.

[注]

barely：刚刚够，只有。**chest**：胸膛。**emaciation**：极瘦。介词 to 表示瘦的程度：瘦得几乎只剩皮包骨。

crooked：曲的。**brow**：额。此词亦解作"眉"，但用作"眉"时，常作复数形式（加 s）。**colour**：肤色，气色。

penetrating：锐利的。**natty**：整洁。**blond**：金色（毛发）。**wig**：假发。18 世纪欧洲男人戴假发，为一时风尚。**ruffles**：衣服的褶边。**wrists**：手腕。**cloth**：任何织物，不单指"布"一种。**buckles**：（用以拴带子之）扣子。

本段前五句都是描写康德的仪表。上一段不是刚说到他饭后出去散步吗？怎么会插这几句进去呢？看到第六句："他把三角帽挟在胁下，手持金头手杖，"才知道前面五句出现得并不突兀。康德的散步在他的平淡规律的生活中，是一件大事，所以作者亦极力描写。与其单独地描写他的状貌服饰，不如拿来同他的散步连在一起写。他饭后出去散步——康德在散步的时候是怎么样的一个人呢？于是说到他的身材、仪容、身上脚下的打扮，胁下挟的是什么，手里拿的是什么等。这么一来，文字就更生动。我们读到的不是一个静的康德，而是一个动的康德了。

threatening：有雨意，风云变幻莫测。threaten 原作"威胁"解，但请读者注意英文 threaten 的用法比中文"威胁"来得广。

[9]

The only occasion on which he is known to have omitted his walk is when he received Rousseau's *Emile*, and then, unable to tear himself away from it, tie remained indoors for three days. He walked very slowly because he thought it was bad for him to sweat, and alone because he had formed the habit of breathing through his nostrils, since thus he thought to avoid catching cold and, had he had a companion with whom courtesy would oblige him to speak, he would have been constrained to breathe through his mouth.

[注]

康德的散步，数十年如一日，风雨无间，寒暑不辍。据说只有一次，他收到卢梭（Jean Jacques Rousseau，1712—1778）的《爱弥儿》，读得不忍释手，三天没出门，因此破例没有散步。**tear**：撕，扯。书把他吸引住了，撕都撕不开，其吸引力之强可想。

第二句稍长，但句法仍十分干净。He walked 后接副词 slowly（他怕出汗 sweat，故步子很慢），又接形容词 alone（形容主语，是表语形容词〈predicate adjective〉），该句主干实仅是 he walked slowly and he walked alone 而已。alone 一词放在这里，可称险绝，然而脚头站得很稳，丝毫摇撼不动，作者炼句，实见功夫。alone 离开它所形容的主语 he，已经隔了十几个词，后面又引起四十几个词来说明何以 alone，这样一个词，假如用得不得法，很可能变得无靠无依，交代不清。但是这一句的层次依旧很清楚，我们读到 alone 的时候，自然会大大地换一口气，聚精会神地且看作者在 because 以后要些什么花样出来。

康德散步为什么不带伴儿呢？原来他有鼻孔（nostrils）呼吸的习惯，这样他可以免伤风（catching cold），假如（**had he had** = if he had had）有一个他非敷衍不可的人陪他一起走（替他带伞的仆人，他是可以不必敷衍的），他不得不跟他说话，因此就不得不用嘴呼吸了。

with whom courtesy would oblige him to speak 中的 with 在句法结构上应放在 speak 之后。**courtesy**：礼貌。**oblige**：强使为之。此词与稍后的 constrain 略有不同，oblige 大抵是道义上的约束，constrain 则无论什么样无可奈何的情形，使人不得不受制者，皆可适用之。所以对于朋友，他不得不说话，宜用 oblige；说话时不得不张嘴，则宜用 constrain 了。

[10]

He invariably took the same walk, along the Linden Allee, and this, according to Heine, he strolled up and down eight times. He issued from his house at precisely the same hour so that the people of the town could set their clocks by it. When he came home he returned to his study and read and wrote letters till the light failed. Then, as was his habit, fixing his eyes on the tower of a neighbouring church, he pondered over the problems that just then occupied him. At a quarter to ten he suspended his arduous labour and by ten was safely tucked up in bed.

[注]

walk：散步的地方，供人步行的道路。**invariably**：不变的。**Linden**：菩提树。Allee 原为法文，相当于英文的 alley（巷，胡同），尤指两旁植树之小路。

strolled：逍遥漫步，溜达。**and this ... he strolled up and down**：此句的 this 是宾语前置，语法与前段（见上文）and this he would not permit himself to do 相仿。**up and down**：来回。

Heine 即 Heinrich Heine（1797—1856）：德国诗人、作家海涅，曾著录康德事迹。

issued：出发。**precisely**：精确地，恰巧。**set their clocks**：在他们的钟上拨准时间，对时。

the light failed：日色渐暮，不便工作。

pondered over：思考。**occupied** 本解作"占有"，**the problems that occupied him**：占据了他的头脑的那些问题，他所专心研究的那些（哲学）问题。

suspended：停止。**arduous labour**：费力的工作。**was tucked up in bed**：裹身被中。这样的说法当比 lay in bed 更能使读者觉得床上的安逸舒适。

[11]

Though he lived to be eighty, he never went more than sixty miles away from the town in which he was born. He suffered from frequent indispositions and was seldom free from pain, but he was able by the exertion of his will to turn his attention away from his feelings just as though they did not concern him.

[注]

lived to be eighty：活到 80 岁。**the town in which he was born**：指哥尼斯堡（Königsberg），为东普鲁士首府。

indispositions：身体上的不舒服，小毛病。**seldom free from pain**：身上老是带点病痛。

by the exertion of his will：运用其意志力量。此短语（phrase）插在 able 与 to 之间，其地位亦值得研究。当 able 出现之时，读者自然会等着后面的 to：能够……能够什么呢？可是作者小弄玄虚，偏偏先来 by the exertion of his will 一个短语，再把 to 搬出来。这个用法至少有两点好处：一、意义可以更丰富。多一个短语，当然多一层意义；二、气势可以较舒缓。able 与 to 直接相随，气势迫切，分开了语气就较婉转。然文章之道难有定规，有时文章意义要求单纯，气势要求爽利，这种办法就不合适了。总之，在读者意料不到的地方，插进几个词、一两个短语，或甚一个从句（clause），这就是文章的"装饰"，有助于文辞之美。但是天下一切装饰，运用起来，都要小心，否则随时有可能弄巧成拙。如何运用得好，还得靠多读名家著作，培养正确的品位性情。

to turn his attention away from his feelings：使心另有所属，不去注意身上的痛痒。as though they did not concern him 中的 *they* 指的是 *feelings*：好像身上的不舒服同他没有关系似的。

[12]

He was neither impulsive nor demonstrative, but he was kindly, within his scanty means generous, and obliging. His intelligence was great, his power of reasoning impressive, but his emotional nature was meagre. Twice he thought seriously of marrying, but he took so long to consider the advantages and disadvantages of the step he had in mind that in the interval one of the young women he had his eye on married somebody else and the other left Königsberg before he reached a decision.

[注]

impulsive：凭感情冲动行事。**demonstrative**：喜怒哀乐形诸辞色的，情感外露的。康德为人稳重，情感亦深藏不露。

kindly：待人厚道。**generous**：用钱慷慨。此词之前又插了一个短语 **within his scanty means**：在他菲薄的经济力量容许之下。君子固穷，然苟人有所需，康德亦必尽其微力，乐于周济也。**obliging**：乐于助人。这个词在本文中为第二次出现，前面出现的一个解作"强使人不得不做某一件事"，这里的意思则是"帮助他人，施以援手"。这个词的被动形式常见于书信当中，比如 I shall be much obliged if...（如蒙……不胜感激）。它的主动形式，就是"乐于助人"了。或者说，这个词大概相当于汉语所谓"古道热肠，好行方便"，并无"兜售恩惠，笼络收买"之意。

power of reasoning：推理的能力。**impressive**：（动词 was 省去）给人很深的印象，非常可观。**emotional nature**：情感的天性（天生的情感）。**meagre**：贫乏，薄弱。

advantages and disadvantages：利弊。**the step he had in mind**：他心目中的计划（步骤）。he had in mind 是定语从句。that in the interval 里的 that 与 so long 的 so 相呼应；**in the interval**：在（他考虑的）这段时间内。**he had his eyes on**：又是一个定语从句，"他所看中的"。本句内这两个定语从句运用得很是轻巧自然，随随便便放一个定语从句上去，句子一点儿不觉得累赘笨重，凡是希望把英文写得流利的，在这种地方应该多加注意。

In Dreams Begin Responsibilities
君子好逑

Delmore Schwartz（1913—1966）

　　本文题目应该译作"责任于梦想中开始"（做梦的时候，人生的责任也就开始了），然文中所谓梦想，似指恋爱，所谓责任，似指婚姻，故暂译为"君子好逑"。

　　作者德尔莫尔·施瓦茨为美国当代诗人、小说家，曾任《党派评论》（*Partisan Review*）副编辑。

　　这篇小说原来是在《党派评论》上发表的。该刊搜集历年所发表的短篇小说佳作十余篇，出版选集一本，书名《新体小说选》（*Stories in the Modern Manner*），此处所录即从该书中摘出。

[1]

　　I think it is the year 1909. I feel as if I were in a motion picture theatre, the long arm of light crossing the darkness and spinning, my eyes fixed on the screen. This is a silent picture, in which the actors are dressed in ridiculously old-fashioned clothes, and one flash succeeds another with sudden jumps. The actors too seem to jump about and walk too fast. The shots themselves are full of dots and rays, as if it were raining when the picture was photographed. The light is bad.

[注]

责任于梦想中开始,整个故事亦是"南柯一梦"。

小说中的主人公自称似乎置身于 1909 年,又像是在看电影。**long arm of light**:放映机射至银幕上的一道白光。**spinning**:旋转。**fixed**(过去分词):眼睛全神贯注地看着银幕。

silent picture:无声电影。**ridiculously**:可笑地。**one flash succeeds another**:银幕上的光线,一闪一闪地很不稳定,一亮之后,突然一跳,接着又是一亮。

jump about:东跳西跳。旧时电影的摄制和放映技术均恶劣,演员的一举一动似乎都在跳跃。

shots:一幕一幕的镜头。**dots**:斑点。**rays**:光线,大约指乱七八糟的光线。

[2]

It is Sunday afternoon, June 12, 1909, and my father is walking down the quiet streets of Brooklyn on his way to visit my mother. His clothes are newly pressed and his tie is too tight in his high collar. He jingles the coins in his pockets, thinking of the witty things he will say. He walks from street to street of trees, lawns and houses, once in a while coming to an avenue on which a streetcar skates and gnaws, slowly progressing. It is obviously Sunday, for everyone is wearing Sunday clothes, and the streetcar's noises emphasize the quiet of the holiday.

[注]

银幕上的人物出现了,第一个人是他的父亲。

Brooklyn:纽约市布鲁克林区。

jingles:玩弄而使叮当发响。**witty things**:俏皮话。父亲去看母亲,路上先准备好一套巧妙的言语。

once in a while = occasionally:偶尔。**avenue**:大马路,通衢大道。本来是在小街上走,有时也会碰上一条大马路。**streetcar**:电车。**skates**:滑行(电车在铁轨上像是滑冰似地滑着过去的)。**gnaws**:用劲地慢慢地咬(电车有时候走得不很滑溜,像是在咬什么东西)。skates 和 gnaws,两词用以叙述电车的运动,恐怕是作者创用,并非现成字眼。

那时纽约遵奉安息日的制度似尚未废弛，星期日店铺大多关门，街上静悄悄的，电车的闹声，似乎只是强调了周围的静寂。

[3]

My father has chosen to take this long walk because he likes to walk and think. He thinks about himself in the future. He thinks of my mother, of how nice it will be to introduce her to his family. But he is not yet sure that he wants to marry her, and once in a while he becomes panicky about the bond already established. He reassures himself by thinking of the big men he admires who are married: William Randolph Hearst, and William Howard Taft, who has just become President of the United States.

[注]

panicky：大恐慌。**the bond already established**：两人间已经建立了好的联系。那时其人的父亲还在追求期间，他想不想同他的女朋友结婚呢？他自己也不大清楚。可是偶尔想起他们俩已经相爱得难舍难分了（**bond**：束缚），其势非结婚不可，不由得慌张起来。可是再一想他所崇拜的大人物中也有两个结过婚的（报业大王 Hearst 和 Taft 总统）。这样一想，胆子也就壮了一点。

[4]

My father arrives at my mother's house. He has come too early and so is suddenly embarrassed. My aunt, my mother's sister, answers the loud bell with her napkin in her hand, for the family is still at dinner. As my father enters, my grandfather rises from the table and shakes hands with him. My mother has run upstairs to tidy herself. My grandmother asks my father if he has had dinner, and tells him that Rose will be downstairs soon. My grandfather opens the conversation by remarking on the mild June weather. My father sits uncomfortably near the table, holding his hat in his hand. My grandmother tells my aunt to take my father's hat. My uncle, twelve years old, runs into the house, his hair tousled, He shouts a greeting to my father, who has often given him a nickel, and then runs upstairs.

[注]

embarrassed：窘迫。**answers the bell**：听见铃响，出去开门。**napkin**：餐巾。女方家里还没吃完午餐，小姐的妹妹匆匆忙忙提了餐巾出来开门。情郎到得太早了，突然觉得很窘。

tidy herself：打扮。注意此句时态用的是现在完成时。**has run**：小姐一听见门外的人声，就躲到楼上去化妆了，故此人进屋时，小姐已在楼上了；**Rose**：小姐的名字。

mild June weather：六月天气正是不冷不热。外祖父无话可说，就从天气讲起。

holding his hat in his hand：怪不舒服地靠在餐桌旁坐下，帽子还拿在手里，亏得外祖母体贴，叫姨母把帽子给拿去挂好。

tousled：头发蓬松的。12岁的顽童舅舅从外面闯进来，大声地叫应了一声，奔上楼去了。**nickel**：五分镍币，这位小舅舅常常"受贿"的。

[5]

Finally my mother comes downstairs, all dressed up, and my father being engaged in conversation with my grandfather becomes uneasy, not knowing whether to greet my mother or continue the conversation. He gets up from the chair clumsily and says "hello" gruffly. My grandfather watches, examining their congruence, such as it is, with a critical eye, and meanwhile rubbing his bearded cheek roughly, as he always does when he reflects. He is worried; he is afraid that my father will not make a good husband for his oldest daughter.

[注]

其人之母打扮好下楼来，其人之父正在同外祖父谈天，一时变得很尴尬，不知道该同小姐打招呼呢，还是继续聊下去。

clumsily：笨手笨脚地。**gruffly**：粗暴地。他也这样打了一个招呼，足见外祖父聊天的话锋是打断了。

congruence：合适，相称，和谐。外祖父也不聊天了，索性冷眼（critical eye）旁观。看看这对情侣究竟能够琴瑟谐调到什么程度。未来的事情他看不到，就拿目前他们俩在一起的情形来说吧，究竟是"一对璧人"呢？还是"彩凤随鸦"呢？**such as it is** = such congruence as now exists。**bearded cheek**：蓄有胡子的脸庞。**he**

always does when he reflects：他思索的时候，手就在自己毛茸茸的脸颊上使劲地揉捏。worried：担忧。外祖父择婿甚苛，还怕这位情郎不能做个好丈夫呢。

[6]

At this point something happens to the film, just as my father is saying something funny to my mother. The audience begins to clap impatiently. Then the trouble is cared for but the film has been returned to a portion just shown, and once more I see my grandfather rubbing his bearded cheek and pondering my father's character.

[注]

读者读到这里也许忘了这是在说梦话：上面种种原来都是讲故事的人在梦中看电影看来的。这时候他父亲正在对他母亲说笑话，电影出毛病了，观众开始不耐烦地拍手（示意放映员调整放映机）。

毛病修好了，可是电影又回到刚刚演过的一段（portion）上去了，只见他的外祖父还在抓耳扒腮地权衡（pondering）他父亲的性格。

[7]

My father and mother depart from the house. They walk down the same quiet streets once more. My mother is holding my father's arm and telling him of the novel which she has been reading, and my father utters judgments of the characters as the plot is made clear to him. My mother feels very satisfied by the interest which she has awakened; she is showing my father how intelligent she is and how interesting.

[注]

the same quiet streets：就是他父亲的来路。

the novel which she has been reading：这几天她正在看的那本小说（注意动词的时态）。

characters：小说中的人物。plot：布局。他母亲把故事情节说明（made clear）后，他父亲就开口评论书中的人物。

satisfied：满意。他母亲的谈话，果然引起他父亲的兴趣，心里是很得意。她同他讨论那本小说，正是要让他看看，她是多么的聪明，为人又是多么的有趣。
how interesting = how interesting she is。

[8]

They reach the avenue, and the street-car leisurely arrives. They are going to Coney Island this afternoon, although my mother considers that such pleasures are inferior. My father tells my mother how much money he has made in the past week, exaggerating an amount which need not have been exaggerated. But my father has always felt that actualities somehow fall short.

[注]

leisurely：懒洋洋地。**Coney Island**：纽约布鲁克林之南的一个海滨游乐中心，但品格不高，故他的母亲认为那边的玩意儿都是低级趣味（inferior）的。可是他们还是坐电车上那边去了，这大约是屈从了男方的意思了。

an amount which need not have been exaggerated：这笔数目本来就相当大，用不着再夸大的了。need 在这里是助动词，故虽然主语是第三人称单数，也不加 s。

actualities：现实情形。**fall short** = are insufficient。父亲总觉得实际数目不够大似的，非得要夸张一下不可。

[9]

Suddenly I begin to weep. The old lady who sits next to me in the theatre is annoyed and looks at me with an angry face, and being intimidated, I stop. I drag out my handkerchief and dry my face, licking the drop which has fallen near my lips. Meanwhile I have missed something, for here are my mother and father alighting at the last stop, Coney Island.

[注]

看电影的人忽然哭起来了。父母双双挽臂出游，人生大事快要定局，这应该是好事，并不是噩梦，有什么值得哭哭啼啼的呢？但是好梦方醒，人生之责任也于焉开始。小说中主人公欣赏其父母谈情说爱之余，潸然涕下，也许是喜极而哭，但是更可能的，也许是面对人生现实，心中为之怃然，戒慎恐惧之念一动，不觉悲从中来罢了。

前面几段描写其父去岳丈家求爱情形，轻松有趣，好像是在调侃上一代的求偶风俗，这篇文字似乎该属于 comedy of manners 一类。又如把那对情侣送到花前月下去走走，把爱情多描写一番，那么本文就会成为一篇带牧歌情调（idyllic）的抒情文学作品了。但若就其痴人说梦这一点来说，本文又是一篇幻想曲（fantasy）。可是本文平稳中隐伏紧张，主流底下还有逆流，实应该属于正剧（drama）一类。读者看完全文后自会明白，这里不必多说。其人看电影忽然流泪，似乎来得很突兀，但是就整篇主题看来，这一笔亦不可省。

最煞风景的是电影院里坐在他隔壁的一个老太婆，她看他哭得讨厌，对他怒目相向，其人被她一吓（intimidated），赶快忍气吞声把眼泪擦干，一颗已经掉到他嘴边的泪珠，也用舌头舔去，可是电车上的爱情镜头他大多没有看见，等到他眼泪擦干，电车已经到了最后一站（stop），他的父母二人也在 Coney Island 下车（alighting）了。

[10]

They walk toward the boardwalk, and my father tells my mother to inhale the pungent air from the sea. They both breathe in deeply, both of them laughing as they do so. On the boardwalk's flagpole, the American flag is pulsing in an intermittent wind from the sea.

[注]

boardwalk：海滨沙滩上铺有木板（boards），供人散步的道路。**inhale**：吸入。**pungent**：浓烈的，刺激性的。凡是"钻鼻子，冲脑门"的怪味俱可适用此词，通常指"辛辣"，此处指"咸腥"之味。海风大约有醒脑健身之功，所以男的劝女的多吸些进去。

flagpole：旗杆。**pulsing**（pulse）原指脉搏的跳动，转作一切有规律的动作，此处乃"飘动"。**intermittent**：时发时歇的；吹吹停停的。

[11]

My father and mother go to the rail of the boardwalk and look down on the beach where a good many bathers are casually walking about. A few are in the surf. The boardwalk is full of people dressed in their Sunday clothes and idly strolling. My father and mother lean on the rail of the boardwalk and absently stare at the ocean.

[注]

rail：栏杆。**bathers**：不一定是洗浴的人，凡是在水里游泳，或是浸浸泡泡的人，此词都可适用。**casually**：随随便便地。**surf**：拍岸之浪。

Sunday clothes：平日舍不得穿，专在星期日或重要场合穿着的衣服。

[12]

The ocean is becoming rough. The waves come in slowly, and then crack, dashing fiercely upon the sand, bouncing upward and forward, and at last petering out into a small stream which races up the beach and then is recalled. My parents gaze absent-mindedly at the ocean, scarcely interested in its harshness. The sun overhead does not disturb them. But as I stared at the terrible sun and the fatal, merciless ocean, I forget my parents. I stare fascinated and finally, shocked by the indifference of my father and mother, I burst out weeping once more. The old lady next to me pats me on the shoulder and says, "There, there, all of this is only a movie, young man, only a movie," but I look up once more at the terrifying sun and the terrifying ocean, and being unable to control my tears, I get up and go to the men's room, stumbling over the feet of the other people seated in my row.

[注]

rough：波涛起伏的。**crack**：碎裂，浪花迸发。**bouncing**：跳跃。**petering out**：势力转弱，归于消沉。海水往岸上打来，其势初颇迟缓，继而浪花四溅，声势汹涌，直上沙滩，平地凌空，一跃而前，但终于力竭消沉，化为细流一条，余势未歇。海浪向沙滩上方冲过去（races up the beach），迅即急流勇退，被"召回"（recalled）大海。

harshness：波涛汹涌之状。**disturb them**：扰乱他们的心神。**fatal, merciless ocean**：操生杀之权的无情的海洋。**fascinated**：出神地。**indifference**：漠然，不感兴趣。顶上日光灼目，脚下怒潮澎湃，可是其人之父母只是凭栏眺望，悠然若有所思，对于眼前景物不感兴趣。这样把银幕下的这位看客气坏了。他自己看太阳看海水看出神了,他的父母为什么这样漠不关心呢?想是两人心心相印,神思专一,无暇再顾及外物了。

行文至此,读者可以看出来,这位说梦的痴人是不大赞成他的父母的恋爱的。他的父母如不恋爱,就不会结婚,不结婚就不会有他这样一个人。一个为自己的生命而喜悦的人,应该感谢他父母当初的恋爱。谁要是不赞成自己父母的恋爱,这个人对于人生的态度大概是悲观的。

但是本文并不想提出一种言之成理的人生观,它只是表示一种感情的态度,这种态度可能很不合理,但是感情的态度本无须乎合理。何况整篇故事是一个梦:一个最正常健全的人也常常会做些悖逆荒谬的梦。据现代心理学研究,隐藏于一个人心底下的感情的态度,往往可以左右此人的言行举止乃至思想推理。而了解这种隐藏的感情,梦常常是一种很好的线索。小说假如是反映人生的,那么人生的合理的方面,和不合理的方面,应该统统在反映之列。伟大的作品绝不逃避现实,也决不怕描写人生任何不合理的情形;只是近代小说对于人生不合理的一方面——诸如梦和白日梦,隐藏的爱和憎,遏制的欲望等等情形——特别觉得兴趣,而多加描写而已。

所以读者要欣赏这一篇小说,请且慢责备这个痴人的荒谬。积极的欣赏角度是,考量这种感情的态度是不是人生很普遍的现象?即使有人认为并不普遍,但是照作者写来,这种情形是不是可能的?他写作的处理方式能不能令人信服?他描写轻松的地方,是不是使读者也觉得轻松?他描写紧张的地方,是不是使读者也跟着紧张?他的组织是不是紧凑?他是不是恰到好处地把他的这种感情的态度表达出来了?还有一点很重要:他所提出的人生问题是不是很有意义?读者读过这篇小说之后,会不会对于人生增添一点认识?会不会对于人生多添一点思考?

说到这里,还是回到原文,那人看见父母对于日光海洋漠不关心,心中大为惊奇,又哭起来了(他已哭过一次,见前文)。隔壁的那位老太太拍拍(pats)他的肩说道:"好了,好了(there, there 表示安慰鼓励之意),小伙子,这不过是电影而已,何必因此伤心呢?"可是他看看可怕的太阳和可怕的海洋,眼泪兀是忍不住往下流,因此就起身到厕所(men's room)里去哭个痛快了,出去的时候太挤,还是从同排看客的脚上跌出去的。

[13]

When I return, several hours have apparently passed and my parents are looking for a place to have dinner. My father suggests the best one on the boardwalk and my mother demurs, in accordance with her principles.

However they do go to the best place, asking for a table near the window, so that they can look out on the boardwalk and the mobile ocean. The place is crowded and there is music from a kind of string trio. My father orders dinner with a fine confidence.

[注]

他从厕所里回来，银幕上显然（apparently）又是好几个钟头过去了，他的父母正在找地方吃晚饭。他父亲提议到路边最好的馆子去吃，可是他母亲反对（demurs）。反对也没有什么理由，只是根据她的原则，她大约是不赞成进豪华的餐馆，花费太多的。

mobile：流动的，荡漾的。**string trio**：弦乐三重奏；普通由第一第二小提琴和大提琴各一组织而成，这里是 a kind of string trio（某一种的弦乐三重奏），可能似是而非，并不照此规定。

orders：点菜。**with a fine confidence**：态度很有自信，不慌不忙，指挥若定。

[14]

As the dinner is eaten, my father tells of his plans for the future, and my mother shows with expressive face how interested she is; and how impressed. My father becomes exultant. He is lifted up by the waltz that is being played, and his own future begins to intoxicate him. My father tells my mother that he is going to expand his business, for there is a great deal of money to be made. He wants to settle down. After all, he is twenty-nine, he is making more and more money, and he is envious of his married friends, and then as the waltz reaches the moment when all the dancers swing madly, then, then with awful daring, then he asks my mother to marry him, although awkwardly enough and puzzled even in his excitement, at how he had arrived at the proposal, and she, to make the whole business worse, begins to cry, and my father looks nervously about, not knowing at all what to do now, and my mother says: "It's all I've wanted from the moment I saw you."

[注]

expressive face：善于表情的脸。**impressed**：听后印象很深。how interested she is, and how impressed 这一种句法上文已用过一次：how intelligent she is, and how interesting。

exultant：十分高兴的。**waltz**：华尔兹舞曲。**lifted up**：音乐把人"举"起来了？应该是听得飘飘然而已。**intoxicate him**：使他陶醉。

expand：扩张。**settle down**：成家立业，不再飘荡。

描写求婚的这一句很长，句法略嫌啰唆，但非如此不足尽这位情郎的兴奋与尴尬之妙。请注意连用四个 then（then as the waltz then, then..., then he asks my mother），读者读到这里，当可想象这个情郎吞吞吐吐，欲说又止的神情。**envious of**：羡慕。**swing madly**：疯狂地旋转。**with awful daring**：提起了可怕的勇气。**awkwardly enough**：情形够窘了。**puzzled** 连后面的 **at**：迷惑不解。即使说他那时很兴奋吧，但是他自己也不明白怎么会走到（arrived at）求婚这条路上来的。

to make the whole business worse：他本来已经窘不堪言，她这么一哭，事情更糟了。**looks nervously about**：慌慌张张地东张西望。

[15]

It was then that I stood up in the theatre and shouted, "Don't do it. It's not too late to change your minds, both of you. Nothing good will come of it." The whole audience turned to look at me, annoyed, the usher came hurrying down the aisle flashing his searchlight, and the old lady next to me tugged me down into my seat, saying: "Be quiet. You'll be put out, and you paid thirty-five cents to come in." And so I shut my eyes because I could not bear to see what was happening. I sat there quietly.

[注]

他父母的爱情愈增进，痴人的神情也愈紧张。

nothing good will come of it：不会有好结果的。**annoyed**：觉得很讨厌（过去分

词），形容 the whole audience。**usher**：电影院里领人入座的职员。**aisle**：座位之间的大通道。**searchlight**：电筒（探照灯亦是此词）。**tugged**：用力地拉。**put out**：驱逐出去。**thirty-five cents**：票价（注意 paid 用过去时，因为买票已经是过去的事）。

[16]

But after a while I begin to take brief glimpses, and at length I watch again with thirsty interest. My parents have passed a fortune-teller's booth, and my mother wishes to go in but my father does not. They begin to argue about it. My mother becomes stubborn, and then they begin to quarrel. My mother refuses to budge. She is near to tears, but she feels an uncontrollable desire to hear what the palm-reader will say. My father consents angrily, and they both go into a booth which is draped in black cloth and its light is shadowed. The fortune-teller, a fat, short woman, comes into the room from the back and greets them.

[注]

take brief glimpses：偶然偷瞧几眼。**with thirsty interest**：兴趣极大。**fortune-teller's booth**：算命术士的木棚。

budge：让步（本解作"细微的移动"，大多用在否定句中，相当于中文的"决不移动分毫"，"丝毫不肯移动"等说法）。

near to tears：要哭出来了。**palm-reader**：看手相的，算命的。

draped：（墙上）围（以黑布）。**greets**：打招呼（如说，good evening）。

[17]

But suddenly my father feels that the whole thing is intolerable; he tugs at my mother's arm, but my mother refuses to budge. And then, in terrible anger, my father lets go of my mother's arm and strides out, leaving my mother stunned. She moves to go after my father, but the fortune-teller holds her arm tightly and begs her not to do so, and I in my seat am shocked more than ever, and I get up from my seat and begin to shout and once more the usher comes hurrying down the aisle flashing his searchlight, and the old lady pleads with me, and the shocked audience has turned to stare at me, and I keep shouting:

"What are they doing? Don't they know what they are doing? Why doesn't my mother go after my father? If she does not do that, what will she do? Doesn't my father know what he is doing now?"

[注]

intolerable：令人不能忍受。

lets go of my mother's arm：把她手臂放开（注意中间的 of）。**strides out**：大踏步跨将出去。**stunned**：怔住了。**pleads with me**：恳求我。

父亲求婚成功不久，就同母亲吵架了，此人看得大为着急，大嚷起来。"What are they doing?""他们在干些什么呢？他们不知道他们在干什么吗？母亲为什么不追出去呢？她不追出去，她还想打算干什么呢？父亲做事如此狠心，他自己知道不知道呢？"最后一句叙事很多，但是主要的连接词只用 and 一个，句子虽长，句法并不复杂。

[18]

But the usher has seized my arm and is dragging me away and as he does so, he says: "What are *you* doing? Don't you know that you can't do whatever you want to do? Why should a young man like you, with your whole life before you, get hysterical like this? Why don't you *think* of what you're doing?" and he said that dragging me through the lobby of the theatre into the cold light, and I woke up into the bleak winter morning of my 21st birthday, the windowsill shining with its lip of snow, and the morning already begun.

[注]

领座员已经抓住了他的臂膀，把他拖出去，一面拖，一面说道："你在干什么？你知道不知道一个人做事不能爱闹就闹，爱嚷就嚷的？像你这样一个小伙子，前途正是远大得很，为什么偏这样疯疯癫癫（hysterical）的呢？为什么你不想想你是在干什么呢？"领座员说着，把他拖过电影院大堂（lobby），一直把他送到门外，门外既冷且亮（cold light 寒冷的光亮），与电影放映厅的温暖黑暗大不相同。

到了外面，人就惊醒了。醒来正是此人的 21 岁生辰。冬天的早晨，景物萧索（bleak），窗槛上面堆了一层雪（lip of snow），闪闪发光。黑夜已尽，时间已经是早晨了。begun（过去分词）形容 morning。注意：said 和 woke 改用过去时，表示梦醒以后已进入另一境界。梦醒以前用的都是 historical present。

  一个人 21 岁初度，做这样一个怪梦，大约不算太离奇吧。弱冠之年已过，人生前途正是远大得很，但是人到那时，会起什么样的感慨呢？欢乐和希望，心里当然多少也有一点，但是主要的恐怕还是觉得童年之一去不复返，人生的担子非硬着头皮挑下去不可了。怅惘和恐惧之感恐怕是难免的。在这样情形之下，此人梦见了自己父母当年恋爱的情形。父母恋爱结婚，生儿育女，这事也平常得很，但是转瞬之间，儿子已经 21 岁。要说奇怪，人生的神秘恐莫大于此。这个青年，在生日前夕做了这样一个怪梦，一觉醒来，窗外积雪，晨曦初上，眼前为之一亮，但是被人从戏院里硬架出来，身上又感觉到一阵寒冷，醒来了就不必做梦了，在此寒冷清明的清晨，还是坐起来吧。

A Mountain Adventure

登山遇险记

Gerald Warner Brace（1901—1978）

　　本文选自《贾氏家传》（*The Garretson Chronicle*）第 26 章。《贾氏家传》是一部传记体的长篇小说，作者布雷斯是美国作家。其文字明净洗练，瘦硬遒劲，铸字炼句，俱见功力，堪与 20 世纪任何大家相比。《贾氏家传》全书于描写人物，讨论思想之处，亦皆陈义深远，语句精警。

[1]

　　My friend Tommy Tucker was a senior at Harvard. I used to go to some of the football games with him, and one day we made a plan to go off together with Tommy's roommate John Somes, to climb Mount Washington. John Somes was a veteran mountaineer and had been up Washington several years before. He said that out west they'd hardly call it a mountain.

[注]

senior：大学四年级学生。

Mount Washington：在美国东北部之 New Hampshire，为白山山脉（White Mts.）之最高峰，高达 6,293 英尺。

veteran：老资格的。**out west**：在（美国）西部。**they**：泛指美国西部的人，

照语法的规定，代词一定要明确地代表名词，像这样含混的 they 是悬为禁忌的；但是这种说法常见于日常会话，写小说的要摹写说话的人的口吻，只好不顾标准语法的规定了。

美国西部一万英尺以上的高峰很多，这里六千英尺的山，算不了什么山。they'd 一语中的 'd 是 would 的缩写，隐含虚拟语气，假如他们看见了这座山，也不会叫它是山的。

[2]

We loaded sweaters and windbreakers and knapsacks into the Ford and started north on a bright October afternoon. Motoring twenty years ago was a more rugged adventure than it is now: we had to force a passage through cobbled streets and jammed-up traffic and then jounce everlastingly over the high-crowned washboard roads in the open country, determined to maintain a twenty-five-mile-an-hour average.

[注]

sweaters：运动衫（长袖套头衫）。**windbreakers**：防风运动夹克。**knapsacks**：背包，可背在肩上的帆布包或皮包。**Ford**：福特汽车。

motoring：坐汽车长途旅行。**rugged**：艰苦的。20 年前坐汽车旅行，比今日辛苦得多（这里的 adventure 不作探险解，只是一种不平凡的经历而已）。他们三人坐车从波士顿出发，先经过的是市区，市区的街道是用卵石铺的（cobbled），行人车马（traffic）拥堵（jammed-up），他们挤着往前走（force a passage）。市区过后，进入乡区，乡区开阔（in the open country），然而道路崎岖，路面起伏颠簸（high-crowned），若有棱骨，好像搓衣板（washboard）似的。**jounce**：颠簸，**everlasting**：不停的。

determined 是过去分词，形容主语 we。车子假如比较缓慢地开，也许可以平稳得多。但在路况如此糟糕的情况下，他们仍打算保持每小时 25 英里的速度，就只好先在市区里直冲，后在乡间颠簸着走了。

[3]

To achieve a hundred miles in four hours in a Model T was fine work, but exhausting. Yet on this day the air lay sweetly over the golden countryside, full of balm and peace and the faint taste of leaf smoke. We sang and laughed and drank the rare and mellow distillations of Indian summer, our hearts grew light, our heads giddy with joy: the flames of the northern maples made great chords of splendid music in our spirit. We hailed the northward adventure, the lifting of each higher hill, the spreading miles of forest, the coming of dark spruce, the first glint of rock peaks in the silvery blue, and then the long slow waning of the sun, the golden flow of light from the southwest level across the colored land, the intensity of it, deepening and brightening toward night, the palpable gold on the leaves and grasses, the blue wells of shadows, valleys lost now in dusk and high hills still glowing in smokeless mantles of fire. We turned silent and watched the slow evening climb the slopes of brightness. In the far north a peak gleamed like a luminescent spearhead of pearl, purer than white itself.

[注]

Model T：福特公司的 T 型车，二十世纪初期在美国很流行。**exhausting**：使人筋疲力尽的。车行虽吃力，好在道旁景物很美：时已深秋，田野中满目金色，空气中似含香味（sweetly），笼罩大地，一片温馨（balm 原义是止痛的油膏），宁静之气，充塞宇宙之间，还可以淡淡地闻到乡民焚烧落叶的清香。

Indian summer："印第安的夏天"，指深秋初冬时节出现的短时间回暖。这种亢爽温暖的天气，类似于中文所谓的"十月小阳春"。**distillations**：蒸馏所得的液体，精华（有许多的酒也是蒸馏出来的，这里还使读者联想到酒）。**rare**：稀薄的。**mellow**：圆熟的；和醇的。**drank**：吸收，领略，享受。"我们唱着笑着，欣逢这种亢爽温暖的秋日好天气，更领略到一种清淡醇和的味道，中人欲醉，似乎天气的精华也给我们吸收进去了。"

giddy：眩晕（呼应上句的"酒"）。

maples：枫树。**northern**：长在北方的（车子正往北开）。**flames**：秋日红枫似火。**chords**：和弦（三个或三个以上的乐音同时响）。音乐里几声雄壮的和弦，很有撼人心魄的力量，现在火红的枫叶，在他们心里所起的效果，亦复如此。

hailed：向（人或物）欢呼。这里未必叫出声音来，只是心里非常高兴而已。他们驾车北上，渐入佳境，如入山阴道上，应接不暇，触目所及，无非美景奇观，他们每看见一样新的景致，心里就要喝一声彩。这一句很长，列举眼前的各种景致，精彩的词句一个一个出现，汽车就向山区迈进，而时间也渐近黄昏了。

the lifting of each higher hill：山一个比一个高，一个一个地抬头显露出来。**spruce**：云杉。云杉生在高海拔位置，云杉出现，恐怕是已近山区了。**glint**：闪烁，闪光。先看见的还是些小山，现在初次看见蒙着一层银色的碧空之中，露出一排山峰，峰尖岩石闪闪发光。

the slow waning of the sun：日光渐渐转弱。slow 之前的词是 long，long 的意义与 slow 相仿，不过有了 long 这个词，更能衬托 slow 的程度。

the southwest level：深秋黄昏时候的太阳，应该在西南方，level 大约是地平线。太阳从那边照过来，凡被照耀之处，犹如金光流注；地上原本自有其色彩（colored），经这一照，更显得鲜艳夺目。

the intensity of it：日色渐暮，金光更显浓盛。**deepening**：色彩更深更浓。**brightening**：日落前的回光返照，特别显得明亮。**palpable**：手可以摸得出来的。草上叶上的金光，本是幻相，可是现在看来，宛然真金。**well**：井。回光返照将过，黑夜渐临，低洼之处，黑影渐浓，作深青之色，望之黝然如井。**mantles**：外罩。暮色降临，山谷已消失不见，唯霞光照处，山头仍通体透红，如披火袍，唯不发烟耳。

这句很长，可是只要仔细一看它里面所叙景物之多，这样一句话能包括这许多东西，描写这么长的一段路程，笔墨可说十分经济。

we turned silent：黑夜已临，人亦转趋沉寂，没有刚才那么兴奋了。黑夜来时，先从山脚下黑起，沿坡而上（climb），最后太阳西沉，山头上也是一片黑暗。

可是他们还没有算正式入山。远望极北之处，尚有一峰矗立，状甚尖锐，犹如矛锋（spearhead），隐隐发光，色润如珠，其皎洁胜过一般之所谓白色也。

[4]

Snow, we said.

Snow already? Winter up there in that far point in the sky?

Several peaks — a range of shining pearl like a shimmer of unearthly light. The land below, ourselves, everything, fell away and vanished in the dark.

We plunged into forest and the headlights made a small tunnel in the night ahead.

【注】

长句长段之后，忽来这么短短三个词的一段，自然令人耳目一新。而文章的内容，亦已转换：远处白峰，乃是雪山。山下天气，犹如暖和阳春三月，峰上竟已积雪，未免令人难信。

先看见孤峰一座，后来又看见数峰横列，远处看不真切，仅见珠光耀目，如有天际异光（unearthly light），在空中闪耀（shimmer）而已。

plunged：深入。现在汽车开入森林，林中更是漆黑一团，全凭汽车的前灯（headlights），射出一条狭长的光衖（**tunnel**：隧道），冲破前面的黑暗，往前开去。

[5]

The day and evening remained as warm as summertime. We stopped at Conway for supper in a restaurant, continued on to a place John knew of where we got rooms for the night.

Warm in the morning too; but at first foggy, and sunless, even drizzly. The forests were wet, the sky dark and low. John Somes, the mountaineer, said he thought it would clear. Anyway, unless it really poured we might as well try it.

【注】

John knew of 是定语从句，John 所认识的那个地方。**got rooms for the night**：借宿。**Conway**：地名。

第一晚在山脚下歇过，第二天起来，天还是很温暖，可是起先雾多天暗，甚至于略有濛濛细雨（drizzly 是形容词）。**Warm in the morning** 句主语是 it，动词是 was，二者都被省略。

John Somes 是三人中爬山最内行的一个，见前文。clear 是动词，即 become clear。

poured：倾盆大雨，雨下如注。除非雨真下大了，否则我们怎么也还是要试一试登山。**as well**：试与不试反正一样，还是一试的好。it 指登山之事。

[6]

Then, as we stood waiting and gazing, a vast piece of mountain pageantry occurred. In the overhead darkness a ragged blue hole showed itself, then splashes of pale sun. Mountain shoulders suddenly took shape high among the curtains of light and cloud. The west wind came down over Tuckerman's Ravine and moved the whole cloud-mass before it.

[注]

pageantry：壮观，奇景。我们正在守候眺望之际，忽然一幕山景奇观，浩瀚雄伟，在我们面前展开了。

顶上天空，色本浓重，现在忽然裂出青色一角，在此破碎不整（raged）的裂孔之中，淡淡的阳光，像水花（splashes）似地飞溅下来。

云破天青，在光幕云层之中，群峰（mountain shoulders：山隆起如肩状者）突然显露，耸立高空。**took shape**：成形，现形。本来虚无缥缈，渐渐轮廓显明。

Tuckerman's Ravine：华盛顿山中一峡谷之名。西风从峡谷上方吹来，滚滚白云，俱为吹开。**before it**：云在前面，风在后面，风吹云动。

[7]

We jumped and scurried like starters in a gold rush. Knapsacks were stuffed with food and sweaters and cameras. Matches? Pocket knives? Compass? Yes, all those in spite of a certain disdain on the part of John Somes, who was accustomed to Canadian Rockies. Light of foot, tireless, happy as puppies, we started at mid-morning up the Tuckerman trail.

[注]

天既已转晴，我们可以正式登山了。**scurried**：快跑，急行，仓皇而走。**gold rush**：淘金热。我们上山之前的匆忙与兴奋，好像是一窝蜂地出发去开采金矿的人。

compass：指南针。登山以前，各物都检点一下，看看有什么遗漏的没有。**all those**：要带的东西全带了。**disdain**：鄙夷不屑的神气。Somes 是爬山老手，看见我们出发之前，这样小题大做的紧张，脸上似乎露出一种（a certain）瞧不起的神气。Rockies 即 Rocky mountains，通常译作洛矶山脉，从美国南部新墨西哥州起，纵贯美国、加拿大以迄阿拉斯加。其在加拿大的一部分，高峰甚多，远超这座华盛顿山。

light of foot：脚步轻快。**tireless**：精神抖擞。**puppies**：小狗；**mid-morning**：上午九、

十点钟。**Tuckerman trail**：山上小径之名。

[8]

Of the three who stepped so lightly up the steep trail that brightening October morning, one would not return. But we went in innocence and immense confidence. The sun came out and filled the glades with yellow warmth. Blood ran joyfully in our veins, and we could have climbed to the moon. The cool breeze lifted our damp hair and refreshed the skin under our open shirts. Clouds rolled up over the mountain wall and fanned out into the high blue. The mountain torrents sang through the forests.

[注]

innocence：天真，无知。一行三人，有一个是不能生还的了，但是出发的时候，我们怎么会知道？只是糊里糊涂高兴而已。**glades**：森林中的空旷草地。**yellow warmth**：发着金光的煦暖。

veins：（狭义）静脉，（广义）血管，这里宜译作血管。**could have climbed**（虚拟语气）：照我们那天的兴致，我们会一直爬到月亮上去的。**lifted**：吹起。**mountain wall**：峭壁。**fanned out**：像扇子状地展开。云块冉冉上升，卷过崖壁，散入碧空之中。**torrents**：急湍，激流。**sang**：水声潺潺。

[9]

Up out of the woods we came, to the rocks of the Little Headwall, and stood in a lee in the noon sun to look eastward across the bottomless valley to Carter Dome and Wildcat. All earth and air rang with clear autumn brilliance. White cumulus marched away through the blue to the pale southeastward rim of the world, but the sun kept its warm blaze against us, partly drying our wet skin. In the thin air the white vapor of our breathing took shape.

"Colder than you'd think," John said.

[注]

他们走出林区，登上 Little Headwall（峰名）的乱石山头。**up out of the woods we came** = We came up out of the woods。**lee**：背风之处，风力所不及之处。

他们从九、十点钟开始爬山，到中午已经穿越森林，攀登一小山头，那天吹西风（前面已经说过），他们背西面东而立，身后山石，将风挡住，纵目东望，下临无底深谷，前面 Carter Dome 与 Wildcat 两峰耸立。其时秋高气爽，天色明净，clear autumn brilliance 三词自不难了解，可是动词 rang 一词，则大见功夫。**rang** 者，铿锵有声也；大地太空满目清朗，秋气飒爽，似作金石之声。其有声耶？其无声耶？有待读者之妙悟矣。

cumulus：积云（云之成朵状者，晴朗天气时见之）。白云为西北风所吹，飞过（原文用 marched，声势雄壮，犹如天马行空）碧空，飘向苍茫杳霭（pale）西南方地平线（rim of the world）而去。

blaze：光辉。**the vapor of our breathing**：呼吸时所吐出的白气。人大抵于寒冷之处，始能"嘘气成雾"。该地日光照及之处虽仍觉热，然空气实已稀薄而冷，已是高空景象。

Colder than you'd think：'d 为 would 的缩写，隐含虚拟语气。我不知道你们对这边天气有什么想法，你们也许以为它是热，是不冷不热，是冷，总之，实际上比你们所想象的要冷些。

[10]

I remember how Tommy Tucker danced on the rocky ledge, grinning and making whooping sounds. "I bet that's where God lives," he said, waving up to where the crags of the great headwall dissolved into the silver edge of a rolling cloud. "He sits up on one of those pinnacles and feels like the boss of all creation." Then he cocked his head at John. "Just a dinky little foothill — I realize that. Out west God does things up much bigger — but of course he's a much bigger guy out there than he is here."

"Well, you do get the effect of high mountains, I must admit," said John.

[注]

rocky ledge：山崖之向外凸出部分。**grinning**：露齿而笑。**whooping sounds**：怪声大叫。

waving up to：手挥舞着向上指。**crags**：壁立巨石。**the great headwall**：他们所在之处是 the Little Headwall；the great headwall 应该是另一较大山峰，可是拼法不

用大写，似为普通名词，并非专有名词，但虽为普通名词，在作者心目中亦必专指某一山峰。headwall 此词普通词典不载，想是山峰这一类的东西。**dissolved**：融解。巨石为浮云所掩，终消失于云边银光之中。

pinnacles：尖峰。"我敢说上帝就住在那边。他就坐在那边一座山峰之上，俯瞰万物，自己觉得真像是个万物之主。"

cock his head：侧着头（这样说话，有讽刺之意）。

dinky（俚语）：微不足道，小意思。**foothill**：小山丘。**I realize that**：这个我明白。John 老说这座山不算一座山，而 Tommy 已经叹为观止，怕他又要来讥笑，赶快再向 John 说明一句："我知道这不过是一座小土墩而已。在西部上帝做什么事情，气派都大得多——可是上帝在那边，当然也是大一号的人物，这里只好算是个小人物。"**do up**：原义是"包扎、清理备用"，这里转作"创造"。请注意对白语气逼肖说话人的口吻，相当粗俗，与描写风景文章的典雅大不相同。

effect：效果；味道。"你能说得出这两句话来，我得承认你已经领略到高山的味道了。"

[11]

We ate our lunch there where it was warm. Once a cloud mass obscured the sun, and the shroud of winter settled over us — the harsh and purple cold; I remember how the chill touched my heart and sent a tremor through me of something deeper than cold.

[注]

there where it was warm = at the place where it was warm，他们挑暖和一点的地方，把午饭吃了。足见山上的冷已经相当可怕。

obscured：遮住。**shroud**：尸衣（给人阴森可怕的联想）。太阳一被遮住，立刻冬季降临，我们身上好像罩了一件死人袍子。我们感觉到一种凛厉的冷。太阳忽然隐去，大地景物，泛起紫色；又，紫色使人联想到冻僵的手足。注意前文的 **yellow warmth**，与此处的 **purple cold** 正好遥遥相对，而一秋一冬，一日之内，气候之变化大矣。

chill：寒气。**tremor**：战栗。"我犹记得，寒气侵袭心头，全身一阵战栗，而所以致此之故，似犹不止寒冷也。" **through me** = through my body。**of something**

deeper than cold 形容 tremor。"比冷更凛冽幽森的东西"说的是作者当时隐隐的那种莫名的恐惧感。

[12]

But the sun blazed again, and we pushed up against the funneled wind to the ravine and began the long climb to the top of the vast wall. And wondrous climbing it was, with sun still on our shoulders and small whirls and gusts of mountain wind, and the ocean of space deepening below us. John's boots clashed on the rock; but he went up powerfully, muttering a chant of joy to himself and watching for the turns of the trail.

[注]

pushed up：向上爬。**funnel**：漏斗。**funneled**：四围约束，像在漏斗里漏过似的。山风为峡谷所制，势更猛烈，我们顶风而上，先过峡谷，然后开始向一座大山顶爬去。

whirls：旋风。**gusts**：疾风。**ocean of space**：开阔的空间。

clashed：(鞋钉与山石相接触)叮叮发声。**chant**：歌。**watching for the turns of the trail**：留意山路转折之处。

[13]

Ice appeared in shaded hollows. Some of the north rock faces were enameled with it.

"Maybe you guys shouldn't have sneakers," John said. "They're no good on ice."

"Clouds are lifting!" we shouted. Far ahead through a rift appeared a small dark nub that might have been the top itself.

[注]

rock faces：岩石的表面。**enameled**：像是涂珐琅似地结了一层冰。**sneakers**（美国俗语）：橡皮底运动鞋。他自己穿的是皮靴，上段已说过。

rift：云的隙缝。**nub**：馒头状地隆起一块。他们现在立足之处，已然见冰，可是主峰还是刚刚在云端里隐隐约约露出一小块而已。可是那里是不是就是主峰，现在还没有十分把握。

[14]

But the wind had us. Not the gusty autumnal wind, nor the tree-bending, whirling blasts of earth... not anything known to men or the world of men; rather, it was the released power of all creation, the one irresistible force, a nothing so intensified and materialized and charged that up there on the high cone of the mountain it became the all. In a wind like that no other life existed.

[注]

第一句的 **have**（俗语）= hold at a disadvantage（此解根据 *The American College Dictionary*）。风把我们"控制住"了，"阻挡住了"。

山顶上的风非同小可，它不是劲疾的秋风，也不是地面上常见的把树吹弯盘旋作势的狂风（blasts），这种风是人类从未见识过，人世也从未吹过的。它是宇宙万物所郁结的力量的总发泄（released），它是一种不可抵抗的力量，它本身空洞，并无一物（a nothing），可是在山顶尖峰（cone）高处，它的声势增强（intensified）了，它似乎具有了实体（materialized），它具有了无比强大的力量（**charged**：充斥、装满），以致这种空无一物的风，在这里成了宇宙间一切生命力量的汇总（the all）。在这种风底下，别无他种生物（草木鸟兽），风就是一切。

[15]

We tried to duck back out of it, and prepare. Caps, sweaters, jackets — we fumbled them on, feeling the touch of ice on our skin, in fingers and toes.

Turn back? No one said it. Give it a try, anyway. There's the top, right ahead — a straight and easy slope.

[注]

duck：低头闪避。**fumbled them on**：把它们瞎摸瞎拉地戴上穿上。

give it a try, anyway：不管有风没风，还是往前走着瞧吧。主峰就在前面，山坡很平，不难走。

[16]

We crouched, waiting and beginning to shiver. The wind blast would have to relent, we thought; nothing like that could keep on and on. The sun still shone and the sight of it warmed us. We couldn't feel it.

[注]

crouched：佝偻着身子，等风过去，可是身上已经颤抖不已了。

relent：缓和。**would**：表示"将来"。**have to**：表示"一定"。风一定会缓和下来的，像这样猛烈的东西，不会永久维持下去的。**the sight of it warmed us**：看见了太阳，心里还觉得有点温暖，可是实际上一点暖气都觉不到。

[17]

So the plunge across the rock fields. Tommy shouted, and from the hiss of syllables I decided he was trying to say "excelsior!" Blood and sinews responded, pushed us buoyantly against the wall of wind. We had to bend low and breathe in quick gulps, turning our mouths under the lee of our shoulders. Our lungs felt the raw cold.

[注]

第一句不完整，完整的形式大约是 So we started the plunge…。**plunge**：往前直冲。**rack fields**：乱石岗。

风大得连话都说不清楚了。Tommy 在叫，听不清楚他在说些什么，只是他的音节里丝丝音很多，猜想上去，他一定是想说"再往上爬呀！加油！"（excelsior 即 still higher）。

sinews：肌肉（常用复数形式）。**responded**：响应；努力以赴。**buoyantly**：满怀希望地（此词本有"往上浮"之意）。**wall of wind**：风之阻力极大，犹如墙壁挡路。

breathe in quick gulps：很快地用嘴咽气，鼻子已经无能为力。**under the lee of our shoulders**：拿肩膀挡住风，嘴才可以呼吸。

raw：极冷。寒冷彻骨，连肺里都感觉到了。

[18]

The old notion that it was a cold autumn day still persisted; the gust, we felt, would pass, and our working muscles would spread warmth and life through our bodies. We kept pushing upward with slow and fumbling steps, slipping on ice surfaces like old men. It took a half hour or so for the thought to settle in my mind that we ought not to be there, that the windwall was coming at us more relentlessly, that we were stooping lower and fighting to stay on our feet, and especially that all warmth had withdrawn from feet and legs and hands.

[注]

old notion：旧观念。**persisted**：不退，仍在心头。天虽冷，究竟不过是秋天，冷不到哪里去的。我们觉得疾风就会过去，我们的肌肉活动之后（working muscles），暖气生机，即能布满全身。

the thought to settle in my mind：瞎爬了大约半个钟头之后，我才认清了：第一，我们根本不应该到这里来的；第二，风墙给我们的压力是更汹涌可怕了；第三，我们身子愈俯愈低，拼了命才勉强把脚头站住；第四，我们尤其觉得脚上腿上手上的暖气已经全给吹跑了。

[19]

I tried to speak, then to yell, but made no sound. John Somes went on ahead. Tommy had dropped behind and seemed hardly to be moving. I crouched and waited.

When he came close he put his mouth to my ear and shouted, "I think we're damn fools." The words came faintly and stiffly, but I heard them and nodded. Back to the wind, we looked down the rough slope. My watery eyes were closed slits, and a fine spindrift of snow blew grinning like white smoke over the rocks, but I could still see where the headwall fell away into cold spade.

[注]

dropped behind：落在后面。**faintly and stiffly**：声音模糊而僵硬地。

back to the wind：背对着风。**watery eyes**：眼睛流泪，不能睁开，仅成细缝（slit）。

fine spindrift：很细的浪花。雪为风所吹，如浪花似地凌空飞溅，雪质很细，望之乃如烟雾。**fell away**：人在高处下望，原驻足之山头，渐渐消失。

[20]

"We better get back down there," I yelled.

John had not turned. We saw him dimly in the smoke, a hundred yards above us.

"Can't feel my feet any more," Tommy said — still shouting.

The truth broke suddenly. We are in deadly danger. The illusion of "October" vanished forever and I faced the facts of arctic winter and the ice-created hurricane.

[注]

the smoke：烟状的雪风。

the truth broke suddenly：我这才恍然大悟。

the illusion of "October"：假如还拿平地的眼光，认为天气应该是十月天气，这便成了痴想了，现在这种痴想已经消除净尽。我所面对的事实，乃是北极的酷寒，和冰雪所造成的暴风。

[21]

But there was still John Somes — we ought to stick together. Tommy, I thought, could start back, and I could still keep on and get hold of John, I leaned to yell in his ear, glancing up once more to see if John had turned yet. What happened from that point on is so mingled with my fear and increasing desperation that I can re-create it only as a terrible dream.

[注]

John 一个人走在前头，我们现在要掉头回去，应该把他叫来，三人团结一起（stick together）。我认为 Tommy 可以迳自回去，我再往上爬，把 John 追回来。

I leaned to yell in his ear...：我俯身过去把我的意思高声地对准 Tommy 的耳朵里嚷，一面往高处望，看看 John 是否已经转身回来了。从那时候起，我就记不清楚了。我心中恐惧惶急之情与时俱增（increasing desperation），以后的事情，就和我这种情绪混淆在一起，真幻难分，于今思之（re-create：把当时情形重演或叙述一遍），犹如噩梦一场。

[22]

The mountain slope had glistened remotely above us in the cold sun — not clear to our half-blinded eyes, but palpably there, a visible part of earth's substance. The smoke of snow revealed gray rock and even the cairns set by human hands to mark the trail; and beyond those outposts of earth the blue of sky had given us comfort. But now white and gray masses of cloud came like a cataract, solid, vast, silent in the gale. The sun flashed against it with cold and terrible brightness, but in the hollows and rifts it deepened to dark gray and black. Tatters of it came first like flying arrows, and I saw them flash past the dim, hunched: figure of John Somes; then the mass came down like a solid avalanche of death itself, silver above and black in its caverns, riding the wind. A few seconds of terrifying beauty, and I saw John Somes fade, go under, vanish; and then before I could draw breath or warn Tommy it happened to us too.

[注]

以后发生些什么可怕的事，连当事人自己都说不清楚呢？这事在第三句方才说明，现在先看第一、二句。

他们到了山区高处，见到冰雪之后，只是觉得奇寒难忍，狂风难当，此外景色还和下面差不多，高处山坡在毫无暖气的日光底下，隐隐约约地晶晶发光。他们的眼睛睁不大开，看不清楚，可是前面的确有这么一块地方，似乎伸了手就摸得到的（palpably there），有形有体（substance），宛然可睹，分明是大地的一部分。一阵轻烟似的雪风过处，灰色的岩石便露了出来，还有前人以手堆砌的用以指示路径的石堆（cairns），也看得见了。这些都是大地尽处的前哨（outposts），前哨外面，便是一片碧空，先前看了心中也曾觉得安慰。

注意：这两句的动词时态：had glistened 和 had given（过去完成时）是表示"过去"的事，接着第三句从 but now 起，就是叙述眼前的事了。

cataract：瀑布。gale：大风（gust 是突然发作随时可停的疾风，故常用复数 gusts；gale 则是劲吹不已的大风）。

现在忽然大块雪团袭来，风势既猛，水气又多结成冰雪，因此竟给人以坚硬（solid）的感觉。日光照处，冷光耀目，特别可怕；然云团低洼罅隙（hollows and rifts）之处，则又深暗作浓灰乌黑之色。

云团的碎片（tatters）先到。John 在前，首当其冲，只见前面丝丝碎云，像飞箭似的，射过他拱肩隆背（hunched）模糊的身形，然后大块云团，表面银光闪闪，其凹处黝暗，复如岩洞，挟生杀之威，如雪崖崩落（avalanche），御风而至，当头落下。

这种惊心动魄的奇丽景色，不过是几秒钟的事，John 即为当头罩住，先是身形不清，继则全身掩没（go under），消失不见。我要换口气的功夫都没有，招呼 Tommy 也来不及了，我们两人立刻都被罩住。

[23]

No beauty then. Nothing but wind and our hunched selves. The very rock we stood on lost substance. Air, earth, all reality, was turned into this gray force. I had felt fear like a blade when the cloud charged against us; now in the gray my feelings like my body grew numb.

[注]

no beauty then 呼应上段的 terrifying beauty。

lost substance：化为虚无（脚头站不住了）。

blade：利刃。**charged**：突袭。云团初来袭击时，我觉得恐惧万状，心头刺痛；现在置身云团之中，周身既然僵化，感觉亦复麻木。

[24]

"Time to move!" Tommy yelled.

In ten steps we had lost the trail, so we had to work cautiously over unknown ledges. Visibility, we figured, was ten feet, though it was hard to get our eyes open enough to see at all. We kept the wind square on our backs. It pummeled our bodies and spirits with solid blows, and I felt the life slowly going out of me as a man might who is being beaten by rubber truncheons.

[注]

lost the trail：走出山径之外，找不到路了，因此只好小心翼翼地在不知深浅高低的石壁边缘上爬行。"爬行"原文是 work，走路成了"做工"了，其用心与费力可想而知。

figured：估计。**visibility**：能见度。十英尺以外即不能辨物。

square：恰当（副词）。**pummeled**：（用拳）打。as a man might 后面省去 feel 等词。一个人背上给橡皮棍子（truncheons）不断地打着，会慢慢地给打死的，现在我觉得我的三魂六魄慢慢地都给打得跑掉了。

[25]

But before we quite knew it, the slope dipped steeply downward. Tommy took a little sliding step, then both feet went together. He sprawled out on his side and slid off feet first, flashing his grin at me and saying something I couldn't hear. At once he vanished in the white below.

I crawled from rock to rock after him, and realized that I was holding now to a steep wall. Tommy had gone.

[注]

dipped：倾斜。**steeply**：险峻的。**took a little sliding step**：向前滑了一下。**sprawled out**：四肢没有着落地（跌下）。**on his side**：侧着身子。**feet first**：脚朝下。**flashing his grin at me**：猛地朝我惨笑了一下。

[26]

From then on my memory grows less clear. There are isolated pictures, such as my sudden awareness of the torn whitened flesh of my hands — hardly mine any more, for all feeling had gone from them. And I remember finally the first vague sense of darkness coming on. I had felt forever lost there among the gray rock shapes, as though my small human mechanism had been locked up in everlasting ice; but the fear had grown numb and cold like my body. Now suddenly night meant death itself, as sure as the eastward roll of the mountain.

I started downward at last. I gave up Tommy — abandoned him to wind and night.

[注]

sudden awareness：突然发觉我手上的肉已割裂，色如白纸，而且双手知觉全失，好像不是自己的了。

vague sense of darkness coming on：模模糊糊地觉得黑夜来临。

rock shapes：岩石似乎只余形状，不具实体了。**my small human mechanism**：我的身体这具小小的机构，看来已是封锁在万古不消的冰雪之中了。可是我的身体固然冻僵麻木，我心头的恐惧也已经冻僵麻木——我的恐惧已经不能发生什么作用。可是现在突然醒悟……。请注意动词时态的变换，先是过去完成时 had felt 和 had grown，表示过去；一转而为 meant，表示现在。

as sure as：山岭起伏，滚滚向东而去，本山形势如此，绝无问题；现在如在山间过夜，必定丧生，这也是没有问题的。

[27]

The dusk came fast. Whether wind blew harder and colder I couldn't tell, but I remember groping down into the dark stone crevices. And then after a while a new wave of light seemed to roll up from below and shone against the curtains of mist and roof of dark. And at once I rushed downward into the visible world and saw it stretched out clear and free in the evening light.

[注]

dusk：黄昏暮色。**groping**：摸索而行。**crevices**：隙缝。

a new wave of light：俄而一阵光浪，似自下界涌起，照耀上方，顶上虽云雾结幕，天宇暗黑，下界各物，反清晰可辨，我乃奋身下奔，脱离黑暗世界。夜色清朗，俯视大地山河，历历在目，无遮无拦，向四方伸展焉。

[28]

Below the snow level I tried to move faster, but made only shambling progress. Some parts of me were frozen, and there were more bruises and wrenched points than I had any notion of.

Then a figure appeared in the trail below, and a voice called sharply. John Somes came up in a steady lope, his glistening face all tense and eager.

"Ralph? Is Tommy there?"

[注]

snow level：雪线。这个高度以下就没有雪。**shambling**：蹒跚的，踉跄的。

bruises：青紫肿伤。**wrenched joints**：关节扭伤。我身上青一块紫一块的，关节也扭坏了好几处，我自己本来以为没有受这么多伤。

lope：缓步而跑。**steady**：步履稳定。John 不愧经验丰富，反而先赶到下面去了。
Ralph：即书中主人公 Ralph Garretson。

[29]

They found him on the mountain next morning. He had fallen about fifty feet, had broken both legs and perished from cold.

Meanwhile I had been bundled into a closed car and driven a hundred miles to a hospital, where I was kept for three days.

[注]

bundled：捆起，扎起。**closed car**：门窗关紧的汽车，想是救护车（ambulance）。

Father and Daughter
父与女

James Yaffe（1927— ）

作者亚夫乃美国作家。本文选自《大西洋月刊》1957 年 9 月号。原题《只有傻瓜才生女儿》（*Only a Crazy Man Has Daughters*），文字轻松幽默，对白尤为传神，为家庭喜剧中之佳作。兹录其开头几段如下：

[1]
When a father has a complaint to make about his son, all he has to do is take the boy aside and yell at him:

"What do you mean by getting home at three o'clock in the morning? Your mother was worried to death!"

"Twenty bucks? You want twenty bucks? My God, the way you spend my money, you could be the United States government."

"A car of your own? Listen to him, will you? He's still wet behind the ears, and he wants a car of his own!"

[注]

to make a complaint：责备。complaint 通常译作"诉苦"，但"诉苦"二字易滋误解；complaint 只是使人不满意不愉快的事情，受了委屈固然是 complaint，其他如儿子荒唐，天气冷热不调，火车误点等都可成为 complaint，其表达方式则喃喃低诉与大声斥责均可。

all he has to do：all 之后省去 that 一词，但是照英文口语的习惯，这个 that 以不加为妥。**the boy**：二词极简单，但是用来很好。这里如用 take him aside，则易与主语之 he 相混，如重复 his son 则句法太累赘，如用 the latter，则太像官样文章，风味大减，只有 the boy 二词，才是恰到好处。

下面三小节都是父亲责备儿子的话，第一节是儿子深宵返家时说的。注意：was worried 用的是过去时。"你这么晚回来，你妈着急死了！"母亲的着急，是在儿子回来之前，故用过去时（到了家就不着急了）。这种时间先后关系，中文无需表出，学习时应特别注意。

bucks 即 dollars（美国俚语）。the way 二词有介词的作用：照你这样不断地问我要钱，你简直成了美国政府了。（按，美国政府苛捐杂税之重，时为民众所诟病。）could be 是虚拟式，这里不可以用直陈式 can be，因为一个人是永远不能成为一个政府的。

第三小节，儿子向老子开口要买汽车了，老子说，"你自己要一辆汽车！听听他的话看！乳臭未干的小孩子，自己想要一辆汽车了！"will you 之 you 并不指什么人，只是老子生气时所说的话，旁边未必有第三者在听他说话。**wet behind the ears**：相当于中文的"乳臭未干"，"胎毛未干"，原义是"你还要母亲给你洗脸呢！"

[2]

This is the sort of thing that goes on every day. Sarcasm, grumbling, out-and-out rage — how else should a father in this modern world express his affection and concern for his own son?

[注]

the sort of thing 含混得好。如用 the sort of conversation 反而不确切。thing 的范围比较 conversation 来得广，父亲骂儿子也不好算是 conversation，这里要找一个确切的词很难，用了一个含糊的 thing，读者也知道是怎么一回事了。

sarcasm：讥刺；反唇相讥。**grumbling**：叽哩咕噜地骂人；喃喃怨语。**out-and-out**：完全的，十足的。**rage**：盛怒；大发雷霆。**affection**：亲爱。"这个年头，做老子的还有什么别的法子（how else）可以表示他对于他亲生儿子的慈爱和关切呢?"

[3]

But between a father and his daughter it isn't so easy. Because a father can't yell at his daughter, or wave his fist at her threateningly, or call her a good-for-nothing. More than one father has, of course. But he usually ends up with a terrible feeling of guilt over it. And then, when she smiles up at him and puts her hands on his shoulders and murmurs that pet name which he's always been a sucker for, the most determined father in the world is as helpless as a baby.

[注]

wave his fist at her：举拳头在她面前晃。**threateningly**：威胁状；作势欲打。**good-for-nothing**：无用之人，没出息的。第二句是 because 开头的独立附属从句，照语法书规定，这样写法是有毛病的。因为 because 是个 subordinate conjunction，应该改用 for（它是 coordinate conjunction），但是用 because 开头的独立句，现在很常见到。

more than one father has 后面省去 yelled，waved，called 等词。这一句的 has 也有问题。既然是 more than one，是不是该用 have（动词复数形式）呢？但是这里的 has 没有错，林语堂的《开明英文法》中说：

Each, *many a* and *more than one* with nouns in the singular almost always take the singular verb.

该书又举了两个例子：

More than one person was suspected.

But there are more than one person involved in the matter.

第一例的动词紧跟着 one person，故用单数形式 was；第二例的动词紧接 more，故用多数形式 are。这样的用法合理吗？英文用法，本来只是习惯沿袭而已，并没有人来立过什么"法"。即使是不合理，也只好由它去了。

ends up with：结局。照中文的想法（也是比较合理的想法），应该是"这件事情是如何如何的结局"，可是英文里面偏偏用人（he）来做主语。父亲骂了女儿，结局总是痛自后悔。**feeling of guilt**：歉疚之感。**over** = concerning，about。

smiles up at 之 up 有"抬头"之意。pet name：表示亲爱的称呼，如"好爹爹"之类。**sucker**（美国俗语）：易受欺之人（如上海话里的"瘟生"）。这种特别称呼一叫出来，父亲一向就乖乖地甘愿上当吃亏了。

[4]

Such was the case with Dan Waxman. His daughter, Barbara — Bobby he called her, this was his favorite nickname for a girl — was his only daughter. Ever since she was old enough to cry or flutter her eyelashes, she had very little trouble getting her way with him. But she more than paid him back for this. When she was little she paid him back in laughter and high spirits, in showing him how much she enjoyed her life. "Sarah," he used to say to his wife, "what are we bringing up in this household, a little girl or a wild Indian?" "A wild Indian!" Bobby used to shout out gleefully, and jump around the living room giving war whoops.

[注]

Bobby he called her：转换成常规语序就是 he called her Bobby。**favorite nickname for a girl**：对女孩子的各种昵称之中，他就喜欢这一个。a girl 即 any girl。

old enough：这里的 old 不是老（three months old，five years old 中的 old 也不是老）。**flutter her eyelashes**：（眨眼时）眼睫毛上下颤动。**getting her way with him**：使他听从她。

paid him back：父亲听从女儿（for this），女儿也有报答。**more than**：女儿的报答是使父亲高兴，假使父亲稍稍地依从了女儿，女儿便可使父亲大大地高兴一下，那么女儿便不只是报答亲恩，更是积极地膝下承欢了。注意：more than 后面可以跟动词。

high spirits：兴高采烈。女儿活泼好弄，父亲看了高兴，那便是女儿的报答。

wild Indian：野蛮的印第安人。父亲故意这么问，"我们家里养了一个小姑娘呢，还是小野人呢？"

gleefully：意气扬扬地。**war whoops**：印第安人作战时的呼哨声。小姑娘欣然以小野人自居，并且在起居室里跳跳奔走，嘴发怪声，好像是印第安人出兵打仗一般。

[5]

And now that she was almost grown up, she paid him back in quieter, more ladylike ways. She told him her secrets, the ones she wanted him to hear. She asked his opinion of her clothes and her hairdos. She even laughed at his jokes. Not out of diplomacy either, but heartily and spontaneously, because she thought they were funny and she liked to see him in a good mood.

[注]

now that（连词）：既然。**ladylike**：合乎小姐身份的。

the ones = the secrets。秘密不能全部公开，有一部分她是愿意父亲知道的，她就拿这个跟他来谈。把父亲引为知己，亦是博老人高兴的一个法子。

hairdos：头发式样。这里是复数形式。**even**：父亲所讲的笑话，儿女通常并不觉得可笑，可是她听了竟然也笑。

最后一句并不是完全句子，只是一个副词短语和两个副词，形容上句的 laughed。**not ... either**：此二词连用，有"也不"之意。"她的笑，倒也并不是一种外交手段，而是自发的（spontaneously），真心的大笑。"

they = his jokes。因为她觉得他的笑话真的可笑，再则，她也喜欢看见老人家心里高兴（in a good mood）。

Merry Christmas
圣诞快乐

William Saroyan（1903—1981）

威廉·萨罗扬，美国小说家、剧作家，原为土耳其和俄罗斯交界地区亚美尼亚（Armenia）的移民。他的文字通俗，最善描摹小儿口吻，故事寓于人情温暖，很适宜于初学阅读。本文选自《家政杂志》（*Good Housekeeping*）1953年12月号。

[1]

First I would like to say to you, "Merry Christmas." It is like this — when I say it, I want it to mean what it means. Not just words under a picture on a card, dropped in the mailbox on the corner, or handing you something wrapped up in red paper which I have bought. I want it to say what it says, the way a child says it.

[注]

Merry Christmas：作者这里说"Merry Christmas"隐含有祝愿对方"玩得痛快"的意思。

It is like this：事情是这样的。口语常用。When I say it 之 it 指 Merry Christmas，这两个词人人会说，但是意义或不尽相同，作者所指的是它的真正的意义。

第三句不完全，说完全了大约是 It does not mean just words...

words：祝贺圣诞的文辞。**a picture**：圣诞卡上的图画，文辞通常印在它的下面。**handing**（动名词）：亲手交付。which I have bought 为定语从句，形容 something，圣诞卡上的套语，红纸包扎的礼物，这些都不能代表 Merry X'mas 的真正意义。

the way... 在这里是习惯用法，很难分析它的文法构造，《简明牛津词典》里有这么一个例子：

(I) don't like the way she smiles. 我不喜欢她笑的样子。

she smiles 是定语从句，前面省略一个 relative adverb "that"，同样的用法如 The instant he saw me, he took to his heels（他看见我就逃），he saw me 的前面也省略一个 "that"，但是这种句子的 that 通常都是省略的。

萨罗扬文里的句子同《简明牛津词典》的例子又不一样，在那例句里，the way 是名词，在本文中，the way a child says it 的 the way 也是名词，却有副词的功用，形容 what it says 中的动词 says。

名词可以当副词用吗？可以，而且很普通，随便举两个例子：

I go to school *every morning*.

She lives *next door*.

这两句中的斜体字的用法，都和 the way 相仿。这种名词是属于"宾格"(objective or accusative case) 的，因为兼有副词的功用，语法上称之为 adverbial accusative。

[2]

Christmas is looked forward to by a child with even greater excitement than the excitement with which he looks forward to his own birthday, because Christmas is everybody's birthday, with the party going on all over the world. Christmas is to every child, in his own way, the wonder of the world and the light of life.

[注]

真能领略圣诞节的意义的是儿童。以下就详述儿童心目中的圣诞节。

第一句相当长，但是层次清楚。because 前面是主句，because 后面是从句。

在主句里，把耶稣圣诞拿来同儿童自己的生日相比，儿童过自己的生日，假如有玩，有吃，无不热烈期待（look forward to）这个好日子的；但是他期待圣诞节，其兴奋更甚于期待他自己的生日。这里很多词都是重复的，但是 than 之前用的是被动语态，than 之后用的是主动语态，重复之中还是有变化。

Christmas is everybody's birthday：耶稣圣诞节是每一个人的生日，这句话不一定含有宗教的意义，只是说耶稣圣诞节到处热烈庆祝，好像人人都在过生日。
the party：庆祝会。

the wonder of the world and the light of life：都是些玄虚的字眼，但是读者请不要往玄虚处去想，作者只是要强调小孩子过圣诞节觉得热闹好玩（好像中国过旧历年似的），这些玄虚的字眼无非都表示热闹好玩而已。小孩子对圣诞节，有一种独特看法（in his own way），他们把它看作"宇宙的奇观，生命的光彩"。

[3]

Christmas is odors, brought in from the cold to the fire, a blend of perfume made of the scent of snow mingling with the scent of sanctity; of holly and fir mingling with the gifts of new clothes and new shoes; of Christmas candy and the bright, painted toys mingling with the unmistakable scent of happiness that comes out of people at Christmas, no matter how deeply it is buried.

[注]

以下分从"色、声、香、味"入手，说明圣诞节的所以成为"奇妙光彩"之处。

先说香。作者不说"圣诞节的种种香味是多么的可爱"，他说"圣诞节就是种种香味"。这句话似嫌武断，但是连以下几段的 sounds, tastes, sights 一起看，圣诞节的可爱本来就是种种感觉上的享受，这样的说法也许不算不伦不类吧？

事实上这一段所描写的不尽是嗅觉，如 from the cold 的 cold 为触觉，bright, painted toys 的 bright, painted 为视觉，但是这些东西都有它们的香味，作者就抓住了这一点来描写。假如读者读了这段文章，似乎鼻子里也嗅到这些圣诞节特有的香味，那么作者的写法就成功了。

好的描写文章是要叫读者眼睛能看到，耳朵能听到，鼻子能嗅到，嘴能尝到。这就是所谓"具体描写"。若要文章不空洞不浮泛，平日应多多注意"眼、耳、鼻、舌、身"的感觉经验。

圣诞节的香味一种是从外面来的："从冷空气里飘到火炉边上，雪花的香和天地间圣洁（sanctity）之气所混合而成的一种特别的香味。" **a blend of perfume**：几种香水配合而成的特别香水。这里当然是指特别的香气。

holly：冬青（叶厚角尖，红果小圆如珠，多用于圣诞装饰。按，好莱坞之"好莱"即由此得名）。**fir**：冷杉，想必就是供在屋内的圣诞树。of holly 与前面的 of snow 平行。

unmistakable：不致被人误认的，明明白白的。**scent of happiness**：快乐的气氛。这个跟上面的 scent of sanctity，其实都需要用内心去体会，与感官声色之娱不同。但是作者认为这种圣洁肃穆之气象和融融泄泄的快乐，都是可以用鼻子嗅得出来的。

it is buried 的 it 代表 the scent of happiness。

[4]

Christmas is sounds — the talking and the laughing, the shouting and the singing of childhood's hymns — the tinkling of the music box, which says "Hosanna" in the child's language of gladness, no matter if it is only saying, "This is the way we wash our clothes, wash our clothes, wash our clothes!" in English.

[注]

这一段讲种种声音。

hymns：圣歌。**tinkling**：叮叮咚咚的声音。**music box**：音乐盒，八音盒（拧上发条以后可奏出简单的回旋曲式曲调）。

Hosanna：希伯来文颂赞上帝之声，原意是"求主教苦救难"。

This is the way we wash our clothes...：这是一支简单的儿歌，小孩一面唱一面模仿洗衣服的动作。注意，这里的 the way 同第一段里的 the way 可以相互参证。

儿童不知赞美上帝，但是他们心里的快乐，其实就是对于造物主的一种赞美。八音盒里演奏的虽然只是一支小小儿歌，事实上这就是赞美上帝的颂词。

in English 和 in the child's language of gladness 前后呼应。儿歌是用英文来演唱的，而赞美上帝的颂词——也就是所谓"儿童心里欢乐的语言"——则是由八音盒奏出。

[5]

Christmas is tastes — the round, golden taste of the orange — the taste of the perfect sphere, which has hung among the green leaves in the warm sun.

It is the red-and-white-striped taste of peppermint. It is the sharp, sweet juice of the apple from the toe of the stocking. Many tastes must blend to make the taste of Christmas.

【注】

round, golden taste of the orange：圆是橙子的形状，金黄是橙子的色泽，怎么橙子的味道成了 round, golden taste 呢？这样把感觉印象错综的应用，近人作品（尤其是新诗）中例子很多，望读者善加体会。the perfect sphere：圆满的球形（这里把橙子当作一种几何形体）。

peppermint：薄荷糖。**red-and-white-striped**：红条白条相间隔的（糖的形状）。

sharp：锐利的，这里作"香气浓烈的"解。**juice**：果子里的汁水。**stocking**：盛礼物的袜子。

[6]

Christmas is sights; who can tell of the sights of Christmas reflected in the eyes of a child?

【注】

sights：所看到的东西，形形色色。**tell of**：描述。**reflected**：反映。圣诞节可看的东西太多，作者不一一列举。

[7]

Christmas is being together — gathering together. You do not have to tell a child what this means, and at Christmas, if at no other time, all men are children.

【注】

being together：阖家团圆。**if at no other time**：有些人主张大人和小孩本来没有多少分别，这句话在平时是否恰当，姑且不论，至少到了圣诞节，大人都成了小孩子了。

[8]

Because it is the child's day, the coming of Christmas up the white steps of December transforms mothers and fathers into the children they once were — until at last, on Christmas Eve, their caroling beside the tree I with the earnest voice of childhood. And the tears, in their eyes are once again the tears caused by great expectations of wondrous things come.

[注]

because：既然。

the coming of Christmas up the white steps of December：作者把十二月比作一座白色的台阶，日子一天一天地过去，圣诞节一天一天接近，好像是圣诞节沿着台阶一步一步地走上来似的。这样一个比喻，放在诗里也许是"绝妙好辞"，放在这样一篇散文里，是否妥当，请读者自己评判。不过散文里乱用"诗意的意象"（poetic images），是一种很危险的尝试，至少初学者应该谨慎避免。

transforms：使……变化，它的主语是 coming。**they once were**：（定语从句）大人一度都曾经是小孩子。圣诞节临近，父亲母亲的心情都渐渐返老还童，到了圣诞前夕，变化已经无可再变（**until**：至此为止），他们都成了小孩子；他们在圣诞树边上唱圣诗（caroling）的时候，就是用童年时候纯真的歌喉来唱的。他们唱歌的时候，竟也像童年时候一样（once again），热烈地期待着神奇的事情发生，眼中满是泪水。

[9]

If children could speak — or if anybody could — what would be said on Christmas Day would be the book that all books would be. But who can say, with words, what children feel, what Christmas means to them and to us? There are no words for it.

[注]

if anybody could：谁真能把心里的话讲出来呢？小孩固然不能，大人又何尝能呢？ **could**：违反事实的假定。

what would be said on Christmas day：主语从句，它的动词是紧跟在它后面的

would be。

圣诞节可说的话太多了，可讲的道理太深了，这些话要是说出来，就可以成一部书，这部书可以把天下所有的书的道理统统包括在内。that all books would be 的 that 代替 the book，all books 恐怕是主语补语（subjective complement），放在动词的前面，"这部书将要成为天下所有的书"。

[10]

And yet children say it all — with meaning straight and clear — when they say only, "Merry Christmas."

[注]

圣诞节的意义没有人说得上来，但是小孩子说 Merry Christmas 的时候，就把它的意义直截了当清清楚楚地说出来了。

children say it all 的 it 代替上一段 what children feel，what Christmas means……。**and yet children say it all**：小孩子把这意思完全表达出来了。

[11]

And so, as one of them, and one of you, one of us, helpless with the clumsy words, I say to them and to you: "Merry Christmas." I say it as a child says it.

[注]

as = in the character of（以这样一个人的身份）。

them：小孩。**you**：大人。**us**：大人小孩算在一起——咱们统统都是辞不达意的。**clumsy**：笨拙的。

I say it as a child says it：呼应首段。

D-Day
诺曼底登陆

Winston S. Churchill（1874—1965）

本文选自英国首相丘吉尔所著《第二次世界大战史》第 6 卷 *Triumph and Tragedy*（即最后一卷）的第一章。丘氏文字修养甚深，其历史著作与演说讲稿，不少为可传之作。同书中收其致外交部"手谕"一通，甚饶趣味，现抄录如下：

Prime Minister to Foreign Office 4 Apr. '45
Attention should be drawn to the mis-spelling "inadmissable". I have noticed this several times in Foreign Office telegrams.

丘氏于戎马倥偬，日理万机之余，对于一词之微，也不轻易放过，真可谓心细如发矣。

[1]
Our long months of preparation and planning for the greatest amphibious operation in history ended on D-Day, June 6, 1944. During the preceding night the great armadas of convoys and their escorts sailed, unknown to the enemy, along the swept channels from the Isle of Wight to the Normandy coast. Heavy bombers of the Royal Air Force attacked enemy coast-defence guns in their

concrete emplacements, dropping 5, 200 tons of bombs. When dawn broke, the United States Air Force came on the scene to deal with other shore defences, followed by medium and fighter bombers. In the twenty-four hours of June 6 the Allies flew over 14, 600 sorties. So great was our superiority in the air that all the enemy could put up during daylight over the invasion beaches was a mere hundred sorties.

[注]

long months：很多月以来。long 这个词安得很好。**preparation and planning**：准备和谋划。**amphibious operation**：两栖作战。**D-Day**：预定发动攻击的那一天。本适用于任何战役，现常专门指盟军反攻欧陆，登陆诺曼底的那一天。

preceding night：六月五日夜里。

armada 本为西班牙文，等于英文的 fleet（舰队）。16 世纪时，西班牙曾以"无敌舰队"（The Invincible Armada）侵略英国，英国人谈虎色变，所以现在这个词在英文里的含义，声势似乎比 fleet 更壮。**convoys**：护航队。**escorts**：保护那些商船运输舰的兵舰。

swept（sweep 的过去分词）：障碍物业已肃清的。（"扫雷舰"的英文名称是 mine sweeper。）**channels**：海里可供航行的通道。（此词亦作"海峡"解：The English Channel 即英法之间的英吉利海峡，但此处应作 the deeper part of a waterway 解。）

Isle of Wight：怀特岛，英国南部的一个小岛。**Normandy**：法国西北部的半岛。

heavy bombers：重型轰炸机。皇家空军（Royal Air Force），即英国空军，简写为 RAF。英国的海军是 Royal Navy（RN），英国军舰的前面都加"陛下的舰船"（His or Her Majesty's Ship），如 *H. M. S. Hood*，即为"英舰胡德号"。

coast-defence guns：海岸防御大炮。defence 是英国拼法，美国通常作 defense。

concrete：混凝土（水泥、沙石等）砌成的。**emplacements**：炮兵阵地。

when dawn broke：天亮的时候（天亮是 daybreak，入暮是 nightfall，注意两个动词 break 和 fall 的用法）。第二次世界大战后期，英国空军担任夜间轰炸任务，美国空军白天轰炸。

medium bombers：中型轰炸机。**fighter bomber**：战斗型轰炸机，比中型轰炸机略小。空袭时，重型轰炸机先进行第一轮轰炸，继之（followed by）以中型与战斗型轰炸机。

over 14,600 sorties：超过14,600百"架次"，一架飞机出动一次，称为"架次"（sortie），此词照自法文 sortir，有"出动"之意。一架飞机出动两次或两架飞机出动一次，都是 two sorties。

superiority in the air：空中优势。so great... 连后面的 that。**all the enemy could put up** = all that the enemy could put up：敌方所能发动的飞机飞行架次。**over the invasion beaches**：位于登陆作战区域上空的。invasion 是"进攻"，与 aggression（侵略）不同。侵略是贬义词，进攻攻占只指行动的方向，不涉及行动的是非褒贬。

[2]

From midnight three airborne divisions were alighting, the British 6th Airborne Division northeast of Caen to seize bridgeheads over the river between the town and the sea, and two American airborne divisions north of Carentan to assist the seaborne assault on the beaches, and to check the movement of enemy reserves into the Contentin peninsula. Although in places the airborne divisions were more widely scattered than had been intended, the object was in every case achieved.

[注]

airborne division：空降师。borne 是 bear（载运）的过去分词。**alighting**：着陆。人下车或鸟栖止都可以用这个词。此处用过去进行时，有"不断地降落"之意。

Caen：卡昂，法国地名。**bridgeheads**：桥头堡。**over the river**：这条河大约是指 River Ordon。英国登陆地点是在 Caen 城的北边，初步目标是占领 Caen 城。在 Caen 和海岸之间，有河阻隔，故先用空降部队，到河对岸占领桥头堡，直接压制 Caen 城敌军，并与海岸登陆大军相呼应配合。

two American airborne divisions：两师的番号是第82和第101空降师。**Carentan**：卡朗唐（今或译卡伦坦），也是诺曼底半岛上的一个城市。**seaborne**：请参看前面 airborne 的注。**check**：阻止，抑制。**enemy reserves**：敌方后备部队。**the Contentin peninsula**：科唐坦（今或译康坦丁）半岛，诺曼底半岛上一块凸出的小半岛。敌方后备部队如开入该处，可影响美军的成败。

in places：中国学生喜欢用 in some places 或 in many places，但有时候只说 in places 就够了。**more widely scattered than had been intended**：着陆点范围比原定计划的要大，不能如原定计划那样集中降落。than 此处用如 relative pronoun，做 had been intended 的主语。**in every case**：在每点上，各处统统（完成任务）。

[3]

As dawn came and the ships, great and small, began to file into their prearranged positions for the assault the scene might almost have been a review. Immediate opposition was limited to an attack by torpedo-boats, which sank a Norwegian destroyer. Even when the naval bombardment began, the reply from the coastal batteries was desultory and ineffective. There was no doubt that we had achieved a tactical surprise.

[注]

file：单行纵列行进；鱼贯而驶。**prearranged positions**：预定位置。**for the assault**：准备攻击。**the scene might almost have been a review**：这景象几乎像是在军事检阅。队伍整齐，一切按部就班，几乎不像是在作战，但事实上是在作战，故动词用虚拟语气 might have been。

immediate opposition：当前的抵抗（仅限于……）。这句用了被动语态，句法很紧凑，如用主动语态，就要松懈得多。

torpedo-boats：鱼雷艇。**Norwegian destroyer**：挪威驱逐舰。

naval bombardment：海军排炮轰击。

coastal batteries：海岸炮台。**reply**：还击。**desultory**：断续散漫的。**ineffective**：效率很低，不能命中。这句动词是个很简单的 was，句子重心在 was 后面的两个形容词，这两个词定要用得贴切稳妥才好。作文炼字的功夫，往往见之于 verb to be 后面的两三个形容词。

tactical：战术的。普通英汉词典把 strategy 解释作"战略"，把 tactics 解释作"战术"。详言之，strategy 着眼于全面战争的胜利，tactics 着眼于局部战役胜利。盟军横渡海峡在法国西海岸登陆，假如德国事前毫无所知，便可称 strategic surprise，但事实上，第二战场之说，在那时已甚嚣尘上，德军在西海岸一带早已结阵而待，故此事已经不成为 strategic surprise（此点作者并未言明）。但从 1944 年 6 月 5 日夜间起，联军纷纷出动，机密神速，大举登陆，把德军杀得一个措手不及，这可称为 tactical surprise。盟军登陆诺曼底，在兵法上虽不算是出奇制胜，但是在军事部署调动方面，确是做到"出敌不意，攻敌无备"这一点的。

[4]

Landing and support craft, with infantry, with tanks, with self-propelled artillery, and a great variety of weapons and engineer demolition, teams to deal with the beach obstacles, all formed up into groups and moved towards the beaches. Among them were the D. D. (swimming) tanks, which made their first large-scale appearance in battle. It was still very rough from the bad weather of the day before, and a good many of the swimming tanks foundered on the way.

[注]

landing craft：登陆艇。**support craft**：支援或掩护登陆作战的舰艇。注意，作舰艇或飞机解时，其复数形式通常不加 s。**self-propelled artillery**：自行火炮（无需车辆拖曳）。**infantry**（步兵）和 **artillery**（炮兵或炮）都是集合名词。**engineer**：工兵。**demolition team**：爆破班。**beach obstacles**：海滩上的障碍物。**formed up into groups**：结成队伍。

D. D. tanks：D. D. 二字母为何词之简写不详。唯丘氏恐读者不识此词，已代为注明是 swimming tanks（水陆坦克）。这种坦克正是在诺曼底登陆战中第一次大规模投入战场。

rough：风浪甚大。**foundered**：浸水沉没。

[5]

Destroyers and gun and rocket batteries mounted on landing-craft pounded the beach defences, while farther to seaward battleships and cruisers kept down the fire of the defending batteries. Ground opposition was slight until the first landing-craft were a mile from the shore, but then mortar and machine-gun fire grew. Surf and the partly submerged obstacles and mines made the landings hazardous, and many craft were wrecked after setting down their troops, but the advance went on.

[注]

gun batteries：炮列，排炮。**rocket batteries**：排列成行的火箭炮。这两种炮都架设（mounted）在登陆艇上。**pounded**：轰击。

farther to seaward：离海岸较远处。战列舰（battleships）和巡洋舰（cruisers），吃水较深，船上大炮射程较远，作战时以离海岸较远为宜。**kept down**：压制（对方火力）。

ground opposition：（敌方）地面的抵抗。**first landing-craft**：此处的动词是用复数形式 were，故知 landing-craft 也是复数，是说"第一批登陆艇"，不是"第一艘登陆艇"。**mortar**：迫击炮。

surf：拍岸巨浪。**partly submerged obstacles**：一部分浸在水里的障碍物。**mines**：水雷。这三样东西都使登陆时平添危险（made ... hazardous）。

setting down：放下，送……上岸。军队登岸之后，很多登陆艇也随即被击毁（wrecked）。船舶损坏，有一个专用的词，shipwreck。

[6]

As soon as the foremost infantry got ashore they dashed forward towards their objectives, and in every case except one made good progress. On "Omaha" beach, northwest of Bayeux, the Vth American Corps ran into severe resistance. By an unlucky chance the enemy defences in this sector had recently been taken over by a complete German division in full strength and on the alert. Our Allies had a very stiff fight all day to make any lodgment at all, and it was not until the 7th that, after losing several thousand men, they were able to force their way inland. Although we did not gain all we sought, and in particular Caen remained firmly in enemy hands, the progress made on the first two days of the assault was judged very satisfactory.

[注]

the foremost infantry：步兵的先头部队。

in every case except one：除一处以外，各处进展都很顺利。

"Omaha" beach：诺曼底半岛上 Bayeux 巴约城西北一带的海滩，恐怕本无名称，美军为行军指挥方便起见，给它起了个代号叫 Omaha。（Omaha 原是美国内布拉斯加州的一个城市名。）

the Vth American Corps：美国第五陆军军团。照美国陆军编制，师以上的单位是军团（corps。按，此处 corps 的 ps 不发音），军团以上是军（army），军以上是集团军（Army Group）。担任诺曼底登陆任务的是英美联军的第二十一集团军，由美国第一军和英国第二军组成，美国第一军统辖第五和第七军团，第五军团则统辖第一和第二十九两师。

this sector：这一地段。**taken over**：接防。**in full strength**：实力毫未受减损地。**on the alert**：在警戒状态中。**our Allies**：我们的（美国）盟友。**stiff fight**：艰苦作战。**make any lodgment**：占领任何地点。在敌人土地上占领据点，在军事学上称为 lodgment。

force their way inland：向内陆挺进。这句的结构是 It was not until the 7th that...they were able to force....。after losing several thousand men 只是插进去补充说明之用，和主要结构无关。英文的逗号（comma）常常有括弧（parenthetical）的用处，初学者应该注意。

we did not gain all we sought：我们的目标，没有全部达到。这里的"我们"恐指英军而言。**in particular**：尤其是。英军主要的目标，是袭取 Caen 城，但该城尚在敌军固守中。

made（过去分词）：发动攻击后头两天的进展，被认为很满意。"被认为"恐怕是欧化的说法，谁认为是满意呢？大约是盟军指挥首脑部门，但是英文里不必明言，只要用一个被动语态就够了。

[7]

From the Biscay ports a stream of U-boats, facing all risks and moving on the surface at high speed, sought to break up the invasion. We were well prepared. The western approaches to the Channel were guarded by numerous aircraft, forming our first line of defence. Behind them were the naval forces covering the landings. Meeting the full blast of our defence, the U-boats fared badly. In the first crucial four days six were sunk by air and a similar number damaged. They were notable to make any impression on the invasion convoys, which continued to move with impunity and with trifling loss.

[注]

Biscay：法国比斯开海湾，在诺曼底半岛之南，西班牙之北，湾内著名海港有 Bordeaux，La Rochelle 等。

a stream of U-boats：一连串的德国潜艇。U 是德文 Untersee（水下）的简写。**facing all risks**：不顾一切危险。**sought**（seek 的过去时）：图谋。**break up the invasion**：阻止我们的登陆。**break up** = stop，put an end to。

western approaches：西边入口处。**our first line of defence**：抵御潜艇的第一道防线。

covering the landings：掩护我们登陆。

blast 原意是强风或爆炸，转作"很大的打击"。**the full blast of our defence** 可解作"我方防御武器的全部威力"。

fare = get along（遭逢）。fare well 就是 go well，常用于分别时的祝辞（再会）。welfare（福利）也是从这个词来的。**fared badly**：遭逢不幸，倒霉。

crucial：紧要关头的。在起初四天内，有六艘德国潜艇被空军所击沉；被击损的差不多也有这个数目。

make any impression on the invasion convoys：登陆护航舰队并不受到潜艇的骚扰。**impression**：施压力后所留下的痕迹。潜艇尽管出动，匡奈不发生作用乎？

impunity：此词与 punishment 同源，一人做了坏事不受责罚，可以说 He did something wrong with impunity，但此词又转作"不受损害，并无不良后果"解（freedom from punishment, injury, or other bad consequences），盟军护航舰队，长驱直入，泰然无虞，损失极为轻微（with trifling loss）。

A Student in Economics
勤工俭学生

George Milburn（1906—1966）

本文原题"经济系学生",描写一个半工半读的大学生清苦的生活,文笔朴素,很是动人。作者乔治·米尔本是美国小说家,生于俄克拉荷马州。本文选自《短篇名作二十篇》(*Twenty Grand Short Stories*)。

[1]

All of the boys on the third floor of Mrs. Gooch's approved rooms for men had been posted to get Charlie Wingate up that afternoon. He had to go to see the Dean. Two or three of them forgot all about it and two or three of them had other things to do, but Eddie Barbour liked waking people up.

[注]

approved rooms for men：经学校当局核准的男生公寓。美国有些大学规定,本科学生一定得住学校宿舍,如借住校外公寓者,则该公寓须经学校当局特别核准。Mrs. Gooch 是公寓房东太太的名字。

posted：通知。**had been posted**：事前都经嘱托。**get ... up**：唤醒。

Dean：大学里高层领导,可能是院长或系主任,也可能是教务长。这里是训导长,看下文便知。训导长要找那位学生下午去谈话,那位学生下午要睡觉,恐怕因睡误事，特别拜托同宿舍的朋友叫醒他。到了那时，别人都没有来叫他，只有一位朋友还把这事放在心上。

[2]

"Hey!" Eddie cried. "Come out of that! Wake up there, Charlie! You can't sleep no more if you got to see the Dean at two-thirty. You just about got time to make it."

"Two hours' sleep ain't enough," Charlie said.

"Is two hours all the sleep you got last night?"

"Where you get the 'last night'? I worked all night last night. I had classes till noon today. And darn little more yesterday or the day before. Two hours' sleep is not enough sleep for a man to get."

[注]

come out of that：别睡啦！ that 大约是指 that condition：昏睡不醒的状态。

you can't sleep no more = you can't sleep any more。把双重否定（can't, no）当一重否定用，在英美人口语中是常态。

if you got to see 是 if you have got to see 的省略用法，意即谓 if you have to see。次句的 got 也是 have got 的省略。have got 在口语中常用来代替 have。

这一句 you just about got time to make it 是很常用的口语，但是很难用文法来分析它。**just** = barely：刚够得上，刚来得及。**about**：大约。about 在这里是个副词，用来修饰动词 got，这种用法只见之于口语，在书面语写作时应该避免。**make it**：赶得上。

ain't：这个词是 are not 或 am not 的缩写，但是也可以作 is not 的缩写。**is two hours ...**："two hours" 当一个单位来看，所以动词用单数形式 is。

Where you get the "last night"?："上一夜"这个观念你是从哪里来的？在我跟本无"上一夜"可言：昨晚做了一夜的工，今天上午又是连着上课。Darn 是诅咒的话，表示气愤。**little more** = little more sleep。

[3]

Charlie Wingate loped up the steps of the Administration Building, hurried through the revolving doors, and walked past hissing steam radiators down the long hall to the Dean of Men's office. He was ten minutes late. Before he opened the frosted-glass door he took out a pair of amber-colored spectacles and put them on. Then he went in and handed his summons to the secretary.

"The Dean will see you in a moment," she said. "Please take a chair."

[注]

loped：边走边跳。**Administration Building**：办公大楼。**revolving doors**：旋转门。**hissing**：（热气流通时）咝咝发响。**steam radiators**：水暖器。**hall**：走廊。**Dean of Men**：男生训导长。

frosted-glass：磨砂毛玻璃，可以透光但是不能透过它清晰视物。**amber-colored spectacles**：琥珀色（茶晶）眼镜。**put them on**：戴上眼镜。

summons：（训导处的）通知单。此词语尾为s，然为单数形式，其复数形式作summonses。**secretary**：女秘书。秘书可男可女，但在美国通常为女子的职业，故次句的女性代名词（she said）出现得并不突兀。

[4]

Charlie sat down and gave an amber-hued glance about the outer office. Three dejected freshmen, holding their green caps, were waiting with him. He recognized none of them, so he picked up a week-old copy of the *Christian Science Monitor* and started to read it. But the room was warm and he immediately went to sleep. He had his head propped back against the wall. The newspaper slipped down into his lap. His amber-colored glasses hid his eyes and no one could see that they were closed. He was awakened by the secretary shaking him. She was smiling and the freshmen were all snickering.

[注]

amber-hued glance：向四周一瞥，戴了有色眼镜，所见皆呈琥珀色。**outer office**：训导长在里间，外间供女秘书办公并学生等候传见之用。

dejected：垂头丧气的。训导长召见，可能要受到斥责。**green caps**：美国大学通例，一年级新生要戴特定的帽子。

Christian Science Monitor：《基督教科学箴言报》。那位学生所捡起的是一周前

的旧报纸。

propped back against the wall：头往后仰，以墙作枕。他戴有色眼镜，就是为掩饰瞌睡之用。**snickering**：窃窃低笑。

[5]

"Wake up and pay for your bed, fella!" one of the freshmen called, and everyone laughed heartily.

"I sort of drowsed off. It's so nice and warm in here," Charlie said, apologizing to the pretty secretary.

[注]

pay for your bed：没有交床位费，怎么就在这里打起瞌睡来了？fella 即 fellow（朋友）。

sort of 此处用法类似于副词，意思是"大概，有一点"。例如：I sort of expected it（我多少料到了这事）。sort of 和 kind of 可以通用。**drowsed off**：迷迷糊糊打瞌睡。但是他不承认真的在打瞌睡，加上 sort of 两词，意思就较有伸缩，可以译作："不知怎么的"。

[6]

The Dean of Men got up as he entered and with his eyes on the slip bearing Charlie's name, said, "Ah, this is Charles Wingate, isn't it?" He grasped Charlie's hand as if it were an honor and pressed a button under the edge of his desk with his other hand. The secretary appeared at the door. "Miss Dunn, will you bring in Wingate's folder—Charles W-i-n-g-a-t-e. How do you like college by now, Wingate? Eyes troubling you?"

"Pretty well, sir. Yes, sir, a little. I wear these glasses."

[注]

slip：纸条，即训导长传见的通知条。**bearing Charlie's name**：上面有他的名字。Charles 是他的学名，Charlie 是朋友熟人间的昵称。**as if it were an honor**：握手的方式很亲热，好像 Charlie 是什么大人物，仿佛训导长会觉得跟查理握手很光荣似的。

Miss Dunn：女秘书的芳名。**folder**：文件夹，里头是这个学生的一应文件。

W-i-n-g-a-t-e：训导长把字母一个一个地拼出来，方便秘书去找寻档案夹。

by now：上了这几个星期的课（到了现在这个时候）。**college** 可译作"大学生活"。Charlie 也是一名新生。Eyes troubling you？训导长看见学生戴茶晶眼镜故发此问。

pretty well：恐怕是答复第一个问题，很喜欢大学生活。**a little**：眼睛有一点儿毛病。**I wear these glasses**：我经常戴这一副眼镜。wear 是现在时（present indicative），照语法书上说，这种时态可以表示"习惯，经常"之意。**sir**：学生叫老师，士兵叫长官，都用这个称呼。

[7]

The secretary came back with the folder and the Dean looked through it briefly. "Well, Wingate, I suppose you're anxious to know why I sent for you. The unpleasant truth is, Wingate, you don't seem to be doing so well in your college work. Your freshman adviser conferred with you twice about this, and this week he turned your case over to me. My purpose, of course, is to help you. Now, to be quite frank, Wingate, you're on the verge of flunking out. Less than a third of the semester remains, and you have a failing grade in English 101, conditional grades in Psychology 51 and Military Training, three hours of F and four hours of D, almost half your total number of hours. On the other hand, you have an A average in Spanish 1 and B in Economics 150. Wingate, how do you account for your failing English when you are an A student in Spanish?"

[注]

sent for you：找你来谈话。注意时态用过去时，学生已在面前，"召唤"已为过去之事。

unpleasant truth：谈起来使人很不愉快，但事实真相是如此。**to be doing**：注意它的进行时态。

freshman adviser：大学一年级导师。**conferred**：同你谈过。

on the verge of：在边缘上，即将。flunking 是美国词汇，学业成绩不及格。**flunking out**：因学期成绩不佳而被勒令退学。

less than a third：点明时候，这一学期所剩不到三分之一的时间了。**English 101**：大学课程通常都用号码代表课程名称，通常来说，数字越低的课越简单。比如文中 English 101 应该就是大学一年级语文（英文）课，大学二年级散文可能叫做 English 201。当然，课程号码的编制，各学校并不相同。

conditional grades：即丁等，或 D。F 是不及格（failing grade），某课程如得 F 即不给学分。得 D 者，在某种条件之下（如补考得 C 以上，或与其他得 B 以上之课程相平均）仍可得学分。故 D 可称为"成问题的分数"。**three hours of F**：3 个学分（学时）得 F，即 English 101 的成绩是 F。hours 是每星期上课的时间，通常每周学时数就是该课程的学分值。**four hours of D**：大学一年级心理学课和军训一共是 4 个学分。

A average：平均分数得甲等。**Spanish 1**：大学一年级西班牙语课。

account for：说明。怎么英语考了一个不及格，外国语（西班牙语）反而得甲等呢？

[8]

"To tell you the truth, sir, I got behind on my written work in English, and I've never been able to catch up. And I don't really have to study Spanish. My father is a railway section foreman in my home town, and he's always had a gang of Mexicans working for him. I've been speaking Mexican ever since I was a kid. I probably know as much Spanish as my professor."

[注]

got behind on my written work：欠缴作文，欠缴练习。**catch up**：赶上；作文练习太多，补缴也不及。

railway section foreman：铁路某一段的工头。父亲手下工人大多数为墨西哥人，墨西哥人说西班牙语，学生耳染目濡，从小就会说墨西哥话（西班牙语）。

[9]

"How about this B in Economics? That's a fairly high grade."

"Yes, sir. Doctor Kenshaw — he's my Ec professor — doesn't give exams. Instead he gives every one a B until he calls for our term papers. We don't recite in his class. We just listen to him lecture. And the grade you get on your term paper is your semester grade."

[注]

fairly high grade：相当高的分数。学生承认这个分数不算坏，故答曰："Yes, sir"。

Ec 是 economics 的简称，exam 是 examination 的简称。这位教授不考试，平时给每个人的分数都是 B，视"期末论文"而给出最后成绩。现在还没到交期末论文的时候，所以这个学生的平时成绩得到了 B。按，中国大学的教师在学期终了才把分数送交教务处。本文所述的那家美国大学，平时成绩随时送教务处或学生的导师，可以说是很认真的了。

recite：背诵。上课不背书，只要听教授讲述即可（lecture 是 infinitive）。

[10]

"Ah! What you students term a pipe course, eh, Wingate?"

"Not exactly, sir. We have to do a lot of outside reading for the term paper. But I'm counting on keeping that B in Ec."

"That's fine, Wingate. But it appears to me that it's high time you were getting busy on some of these other grades, too. Why can't you dig in and pull these D's up to B's, and this F up to at least a C? You've got it in you. You made an unusually high grade on your entrance exams, your record shows. Graduated from high school with honors. What's the trouble, Wingate? Tell me!"

[注]

训导长和学生这段对话，入情入理，两人口吻，均恰如其身份，是很好的戏剧对白，也可用作会话练习。

pipe course（美俚）：容易对付的课程。

it's high time：这该是时候了。**high** 解作 **far advanced**：已到最后关头，不可再因循坐误。学生希望他的主系功课（经济学）能够维持乙等，但是别的功课他也该用功。were getting busy 是虚拟语气（subjunctive mood），学生是否真的回去用功，尚不可知；英美人说话把"直述"和"虚拟"两种语气分别得很清楚。

dig in（美国俗语）= study hard。**pull...up**：把这两个丁等"拉"高，成为乙等。**D's**：照语法书规定，一个单独字母的复数形式，于 s 之前，还要加一省字号（'）。

got it 的 it 代表"能考到好分数的学养、天分等"。

your record shows：据我这里的记录看来。这一句照语法分析起来，这三个词可算是"主句",前面 you made... 是从句,做 shows 的宾语。事实上,训导长说这句话的时候,恐怕没有考虑到前后的主从关系,他先说了"你入学考试的成绩非常之好"——何以见得呢?有记录为凭。这三词用以附加说明,应该是一种插入成分(parenthetic construction)。

graduated ... with honors:中学毕业成绩优异。主语 you 省却。honors 作"成绩优异"解时,一定用复数形式。

[11]

"I don't know, sir, except I work at night and..."

"Oh, I see it here on your enrollment card. Where do you work?"

"I work nights for Nick Pappas down at The Wigwam."

"How many hours do you work?"

"Ten hours, sir. From nine till seven. The Wigwam stays open all night. I eat and go to eight o'clock class when I get off."

"Very interesting, Wingate. But don't you suppose that it would be advisable to cut down a bit on this outside work and attend a little more closely to your college work? After all, that's what you're here for, primarily — to go to college, not work in a cafe."

[注]

enrollment card:注册登记卡,学生如课外有兼职,注册时要注明。

nights 即 every night。Nick Pappas 大概是以店老板的名字。**The Wigwam**:咖啡馆(cafe)的名字。wigwam 原意为印第安人的茅屋,该店可译作"茅屋咖啡馆"。**down at** 的 down 似指本城或本街的某一方向,在 downtown 附近的地方。**get off**:下班。

advisable:值得一做。it would be advisable 是虚拟语气,有"不妨如此"之意。**cut down ... on**:减少。**attend ... to**:用心对付。**more closely**:多用一点心。

primarily:主要地。你到这里来,主要为的是要上学念书。

[12]

"I couldn't work fewer hours and stay in school, sir. I just barely get by as it is, I get my board at The Wigwam, and I pay my room rent, and I've been paying put on a suit of clothes. That leaves only about a dollar a week for all the other things I have to have."

"Can't you arrange for a little financial support from home?"

"No, sir, I'm afraid I couldn't. I have two brothers and two sisters at home younger than I am. It wouldn't be right for me to ask my father to send money out of what he makes."

[注]

I couldn't work 是虚拟语气，意谓"即使我想这么做，也办不到"。既想减少课外工作时间，又想不辍学，两者不可兼得。

just barely get by：只是勉强对付过去。by 有"过去"之意。**as it is**：就现状来说。

board：膳食之"膳"，此词原意为木板，转为桌子，又转为专指饭桌，再转为饭桌上陈列的膳食。

paying out on：分期付款（注意时态，钱还没付清）。**a suit of clothes**：一套西装。

all the other things I have to have：其他必须用的。I have to have（定语从句），我所"不得不用"的东西。

I am afraid I couldn't 的 couldn't 也是虚拟语气。

younger than I am：英文里没有姐姐和妹妹，哥哥和弟弟的分别，所以要加这四个词来说明，中文翻译起来，只要说"我有两个弟弟，两个妹妹"即可，不必说"我有两个年龄比我轻的兄弟和姐妹"。

It wouldn't be right 又是虚拟语气。我不向父亲去要钱，假如去要钱，那是不对的。虚拟语气日常会话中用处很大，读这一段对白便知。out of what he makes，从父亲的收入里俭省出钱来给我。make 有"赚钱"之意。

[13]

"Well, there's this about it, Wingate. The university is here, supported by the taxpayers of this State, for the purpose of giving the young men and women of this State educational opportunities. The university is not here for the purpose of training young men to be waiters in all-night restaurants. And, as far as I can see, that's about all you are deriving from your university career. So it occurs to me that you should make a choice: either find some way to devote more attention to your college work or drop out of school altogether.

The fact is, you are on probation right now. As you must know, any student who is passing in less than half his work is automatically suspended from the university and must return to his home. Now one F more and out you'll go, Wingate. That's just being frank with you."

[注]

there's this about it 中的 it 指"因兼职分心而耽误学业"一事，this 指下文所说明的那一段道理。

taxpayers：纳税人。州立大学系赖本州人民纳税而维持的。**educational opportunities**：受教育的机会。

all-night restaurants：通宵营业的餐馆。

as far as I can see：据我所知道的。语气中有保留，事实也许并不如此。**that's about all** 的 that 指"当餐厅服务员"一事。**university career**：在大学读书这段过程。**deriving**：获得。你在大学读书所得益者，不过是在餐厅当服务员而已。**about all**：几乎尽在于此，此外别无收获。

it occurs to me：我有这个想法。**devote more attention to**：更用心。**drop out of school**：退学。**altogether** 词典上解作"完全的"，其实即相当于普通话的"干脆"退学算了。

on probation：试读，试用（人员）。录用与否，视成绩而定。**right** 用以加强 **now**。**automatically**：自动地，根据学校规定，不必另外有什么手续。**suspended from the university**：停学。**half his work**：及格学分不到全部所修学分的一半。

out you'll go = you'll go out。out 放在前面是不是念起来更为有劲？ out 在这里，是全句重心所在。**one F more**：只要再多一个不及格。这种句法结构（后面跟 and：只要如何如何，就如何如何的结果），很常用。

being frank：跟你说老实话。being 是动名词（gerund）。

[14]

"I'd hate to have to go back home like that, sir."

"Well, you'd have to. If you flunk out, the university authorities are obliged to see that you return to your home immediately."

"I'd hate that, sir. I'd hate to go back home and have to live off my family, and that's probably what I'd have to do. You know there are not many jobs to be had nowadays, sir, and I'd hate to go back home and loaf."

[注]

like that：这样子（被学校除名）回家。

you'd have to：假如不用功，就非被除名不可。You'd 的 'd 是 would 的缩写，虚拟语气。

are obliged：有此责任。**to see** = to make sure：做到这一点。you return 的 return 也是虚拟语气；假如主语是 he 或 she，return 也不用加 s。

I'd hate that：我不愿意那样（假如真有那一天的话）。**to live off my family**：依赖家庭为生。

to be had（被动式 infinitive）：可能找到的事情并不多。**loaf**：闲荡。

[15]

"It is a problem, I'll confess, Wingate. But what's the point in your coming to your university and working all-night in a cafe and then flunking your class work? Moreover, your freshman adviser reports that you make a practice of sleeping in class. Is that true?"

"Well, yes, sir. I suppose I do drop off sometimes."

[注]

第一句的 is 重读："我承认这的确是一个问题。"

point：目的。**make a practice of**：有此习惯。

I suppose：我想。suppose 在此处即等于 think，并无"假设"之意。**do drop off**：的确瞌睡。**drop off** = fall asleep；这两个词的意义比上文 drowse off 更重，drowse off 不过是瞌睡而已。

[16]

"Pretty impossible situation, isn't it, Wingate? Well, I've given you the best advice I can. Unless you can alter your circumstances I suggest that you withdraw from the university at once. We have six thousand other students here who need our attention, and the university has to be impartial and impersonal in dealing with these problems. Unless you can find some means to avoid flunking out I suggest withdrawing beforehand."

[注]

第一句：这种情形，岂不是令人相当难堪？ **impossible** = intolerable。

you withdraw 请你自动退学。这是训导长的建议，所以 withdraw 还是虚拟语气的动词。

impartial：不偏不颇。**impersonal**：公事公办，客观地。**means**：法子。

[17]

"I believe I'll try to stick it through, sir. I'll try to remove the conditional grades, and maybe I can luck through on my finals."

"I hope you can, Wingate. As you feel that way about it, good luck to you."The Dean of Men stood up. Charlie stood up too.

The Dean put out his hand and showed his teeth in a jovial smile and bore down on his knuckles. "I'm counting on you strong, old man." he said, encircling Charlie's shoulders with his left arm. "I know you have the stuff and that you'll come through with flying colors one of these days."

"Thank you, sir," Charlie said, grinning tearfully while the Dean gave his shoulder little pats.

[注]

stick it through：坚持下去。

luck through：凭运气闯过去。luck 当动词用。**finals**：大考。**feel that way about it**：对这件事情有那种想法。

jovial smile：友善的一笑。**bore down on**：用力地握。bore 是 bear 的过去时。**knuckles**：手指骨节，尤其指连接手掌的根部骨节。按，这一句的句法似乎欠妥，前面 his hand 和 his teeth 都是指的训导长，最后 his knuckles 又指那学生了，代名词 his 所指不清，谨慎的作家应该避免这种毛病。

counting on you strong：满心希望要看你表现你的实力。strong 是宾语补语 (objective complement)，old man 相当于"朋友"。

encircling：左臂围着学生的肩膀（右手在握手）。

stuff：天分，实力；相当于普通话：你是个念书的"料"。**flying colors** 原意是"飘扬的旗帜"，转作"胜利，辉煌的成绩"。**one of these days**：将来有一天。

grinning tearfully：满眶眼泪，强颜欢笑。**little pats**：轻轻地拍他的肩膀。

[18]

At one o'clock Charlie finished cleaning off the last of the tables. The Wigwam was empty, so he opened the book he must read for Ec 150. He had read a few lines when a bunch of girls from the Theta house down the street came charging in, giggling and talking in gasps and screams, their fur coats clutched over their sleeping pajamas. It was long after the closing hour, and they told Charlie to keep an eye out for the university night watchman.

[注]

时已子夜一时，咖啡馆顾客渐少，Charlie 乃可展诵他的经济学指定参考书。

a bunch of girls：一群女生。**Theta house**："姊妹会"自营宿舍之名。美国大学本科男生通常有"兄弟会"（fraternity），女生有"姊妹会"（sorority）之组织。会名大多用希腊字母标识，这里的 Theta 就是一个希腊字母。姊妹会有自备宿舍者，会员即寄宿在内。**down the street**：该会宿舍在街的某一头，想必离那咖啡馆不远。charge 原意是"冲锋"，这里借作"冲进来"。**giggling**：傻笑。**talking in gasps and screams**：有的讲了半句就要换气，有的尖了嗓子怪叫。

fur coats：皮大衣。**sleeping pajamas**：睡衣。**clutched**：裹紧。**the closing hour**：本可指咖啡馆的打烊时间，但咖啡馆既通宵营业，这里当指学校宿舍关门时间，过了这个时间，照规矩学生不可再上街进食，查出要受罚的，所以这辈女生叫 Charlie 留意街上大学所雇的巡夜人（night watchman）。

[19]

They took up the two back booths and they consulted The Wigwam's printed menu card without failing to read aloud the lines "We Employ Student Help Exclusively," and "Please Do Not Tip. A Smile Is Our Reward" with the customary shrieks. Nearly all ordered filets mignon and French fries, which were not on the menu, but two or three ordered pecan waffles and coffee, which were. When he had served their orders Charlie went back to his book again, but the low buzz of their talk and their sudden spurts of laughter disturbed him and he could not read. At a quarter of two they began peering round comers, of their booths. They asked Charlie in whispers if the coast was clear.

[注]

booths：小间，雅座。**printed menu card**：印好的菜单。**consulted** 普通解作"请教"，这里是"看菜单"。**without failing to**：点菜之前，少不了要把这几句话朗诵出来。这几句话是："本店专雇学生兼理店务。" **help**：集合名词，指的是 the whole force of hired helpers。**exclusively**：只雇这一种。"请不要给小费。诸君惠赐一笑，本店服务生即觉心满意足。"

with the customary shrieks：念了这几句话，那几个女生照例要哈哈狂笑（这几句话本没有什么可笑，但女学生聚在一起，喜欢大笑，此殆中外一理），shrieks 和 screams 都是尖声叫喊，都可解作尖声大笑，但 shrieks 的叫声笑声更为可怕。

ordered：点菜。**filets mignon**：菲力牛排（无骨的嫩牛肉片）。**French fries** 即 **French fried potatoes**：油炸薯条。

waffles：华夫饼。**pecan**：是一种胡桃，壳薄形长，味甘芳。**which were** = which were on the menu。菜单上没有的菜，大约店里平常也准备，所以也可以点。

buzz：嗡嗡之声。**sudden spurts of laughter**：突发的笑声。**spurts**：（水等之）激射。

a quarter of two：一点四十五分。一点五十分也可说 ten minutes of two。

peering：张望。**whispers**：低声说话。**if the coast was clear**：街上是否有巡夜的走过。所以用 coast（海岸）者，据说这是当年海边私枭把风者语。

[20]

Charlie went to the door and looked out on the street and beckoned widely with his arm. They trooped, out with their fur coats pulled tight, their fur-trimmed silken mules slapping their bare heels. They had left about thirty cents as a tip, all in cents and nickels. The coins were carefully imbedded in the cold steak grease and gluey syrup and putty-colored cigarette leavings on their plates. Charlie began stacking the plates without touching the money. He carried the dirty dishes back and set them through the opening in the kitchen wall. Fat Kruger came to the opening and Charlie went back to his book. Fat called, "Hey, Charlie, you leavin' this tip again?"

[注]

beckoned：做手势（widely 有"挥动"之意）。

trooped：一堆人从咖啡店迅速走出去。

fur-trimmed：毛皮滚边的。**mules**：穆勒鞋（高跟拖鞋）。**slapping**：拖鞋松垮，走路时鞋底一下一下拍打脚后跟。

imbedded：镶嵌。**steak grease**：牛排的油脂。**gluey**：粘而且腻的。**syrup**：糖浆。waffles 上常常浇了糖浆才吃，故盘子里剩有糖浆。

putty：油灰（用以补漏等）。**cigarette leavings**：香烟头（浸在油里，故呈油灰色）。

stacking the plates：把盘子叠起。

dirty dishes：dish 是餐具的总名，盘、碗、盅等均可。plate 是浅底的盘子。小姐们把钱丢在"盘子"的油汤里面，Charlie 所叠起的也是"盘子"，但这里他要把所有的碗盏等都送进厨房里去洗，故用 dishes。洗碗碟的人，叫作 dishwasher。

the opening in the kitchen wall：厨房墙上的窗洞。

Fat Kruger：在厨房里做工的学生之名。

you leavin' = you are leaving。此人发音把 ng 读作 n，小说家为求写生逼真起见，亦把 g 给吃掉了。**again**：足见他不收小账已不是一次了。

[21]

"You're right. I'm leaving it!" Charlie said. "I can get along without their tips. They leave it that way every time. I guess they think I'll grabble on their filthy plates to get a lousy thirty cents. It takes a woman to think up something like that."

[注]

get along：维持下去。

that way：总是把赏钱放在油污里面。

grabble：用手乱摸。**filthy**：脏（比 dirty 更多一层"可憎"的意思）。**lousy**：这个词在美式英语中常用，形容可恨可厌的东西，相当于中文"这几个臭钱"中的"臭"字。**a lousy thirty cents**：三角钱当作一个单位，故前面可用冠词 a。

it takes a woman：赏钱还赏得不干不净，这种脏主意，只有女人才想得出。那几个女生的嘻嘻哈哈，他看在眼里，心里当然非常不舒服，一肚子气，到现在才发泄一下。

[22]

He sat down on a counter stool with the economics book before him, trying to fix his mind on it. He read a page, The print became thin, blurred parallels of black on the page. He propped the muscles with his palms at his temples, trying to keep his eyes open. His head jerked forward and he caught it and began reading again. Soon his face lowered slowly through his hands and came to rest on the open book.

[注]

子夜以后咖啡馆中已无顾客，他开始专心用功。

counter tool：靠着柜台的高脚凳子，和前面所说的雅座不同。

print：书上的字。**thin blurred parallels of black**：一行一行的文字成了稀稀的模糊的平行黑线——他犯困，眼睛看不清了（这是描写简单朴素之处，希读者注意）。

propped：撑住（太阳穴 temples 上的肌肉）。

jerked forward：往前一冲。**he caught it**：收住前冲之势，止住不动。

lowered slowly：慢慢地俯首下去。**through his hand**：他的手掌不是撑住了太阳穴吗？但是头慢慢地滑下去了。**rest**：头伏在书上。

[23]

Fat Kruger came through the kitchen swinging door and tiptoed up front. Fat gave his head a gentle shove, and Charlie started up to catch his balance.

"What time is it?" Charlie said, yawning and arching his back.

"Half past two. Charlie, I wouldn't put my eyes out over that book if I was you, when you're dyin' for sleep," Fat said.

[注]

swinging door：可以朝内开也可以朝外开的弹簧门。**tiptoed up front**：蹑着脚

走向前来。

a gentle shove：轻轻一推。**started up**：猛然一惊。**to catch his balance**：怕跌下凳子去，赶快坐稳了。

yawning：打呵欠。**arching his back**：把背拱起。

put my eyes out over that book：读书。if I was you 普通语法教科书作 if I were you，但 if I was you 现在也不算错。

dyin' for：渴欲。此人说话没有 ng 的音，前面已经说过了。

[24]

"I've got to get it read, Fat. It's my outside reading in Economics and the whole semester grade depends on it. It's the hardest book to keep your mind on you ever saw. I've been reading on it for over a month and I'm only half through, and he's going to call for these reports any day now. If I flunk Ec I flunk out of school."

[注]

第一句的 read 是过去分词："非把它读完不可"。

semester grade：学期成绩。

第三句的 you 是泛指，实在还是说他自己，并不一定指听话的对方，you ever saw（定语从句）你所看见过的书中，这本书读起来最费劲。saw 是过去时，照语法书规定，用现在完成时 have seen 较妥，但口语习惯用过去时亦可。**I've been reading on it**：（注意时态）一直在读，尚未读完。**reading on it** 大约相当于 **working on it**：用心研读。

half through：读完一半。

he's going 中的 he 指教授。**call for**：要求学生上交报告。**any day now**：学期所剩只有三分之一，这几天教授随时都可能要求学生上交报告。

I flunk out of school：照语法书规定，应说 I'll flunk out of school。但这里前一从句与后一从句都用 flunk，亦有简练动人的效果。

[25]

"Charlie, I just can't figure you out. You never do get any real sleep. You sure must want a college education bad. It don't look to me like you would figure it's worth it."

[注]

figure out：了解，弄明白。

第三句的 sure 和 bad 都当副词用，前者即 surely，后者即 badly（非常之需要）。

第四句的语法很成问题，但是这正好印证了小说故事中 Fat Kruger 的文化水平不高，所以不妨分析一下。Don't 是用错了，应作 doesn't；前面的 It 代替后面 like 以后的从句。like 在口语中常用以代替 as 或 as if，这里似乎是代替 as if（后面的动词 would 是虚拟式）。It's worth it 中的第一个 it 代替 college education，第二个 it 代替牺牲睡眠的艰苦生活。全句可译作：据我看来，你这样吃苦来读大学，总有一天你会觉得（figure）是划不来的。

[26]

"Oh, it's worth it! It's a big satisfaction, to my folks to have me in college. And where can a man without a college degree get nowadays? But I'll tell you the truths I didn't know it was going to be like this when I came down here last fall. I used to read *College Humor*, in high school, and when fellows came home from university for the holidays, all dressed up in snappy clothes, talking about dates and footballs and dances, and using college slang — well, I had a notion I'd be like that when I got down here. The university publicity department sent me a little booklet showing how it was easy to work your way through college. So here I am. I haven't had a date or been to a dance or seen a football game since I enrolled. And there are plenty of others just like me. I guess I'm getting a college education, all right — but the only collegiate thing I've been able to do is go to sleep in class."

[注]

my folks：家里的人（我进了大学，他们心里很觉得安慰）。

where can a man get？他能爬到哪里去？混不出头的！ **college degree**：大学学位。 **nowadays**：这年头。

last fall：时已冬令，秋天已成过去，故称 last fall，并不是"去年的秋天"。秋季入学时，我并不知道大学生活会这么（like this）清苦的。

College Humor：杂志名，内容都是介绍大学生活的轻松的一面。

all dressed up ...：是 absolute phrase。**snappy** = smart。**dates**：(谈恋爱的) 约会。

well：转换语气之用。这句的从句（when ...）很长，这里起转入主句。

I had a notion：我当时以为（注意动词的过去时）。**like that**：生活可以跟他们所讲的和杂志上所看到的一样。

university publicity department：大学的对外宣传部。**booklet**：小册子。

work your way through college：半工半读地读完大学课程。**plenty of others**：像我这样不交女友，不跳舞，不看足球的学生多得很。

I guess = I think。**I'm getting a collegiate education**：有"我（算是）在大学里读书"的自嘲之意。**all right**：就算这样吧。

the only collegiate thing：唯一称得上大学教育的事情。I've been able to do 是定语从句。

[27]

"How you get by with sleeping in class, Charlie?"

"I wear these colored spectacles and prop myself, and the profs can't see I've got my eyes closed."

Fat waggled his heavy face mournfully. "Boy, it sure is tough when a man don't get his sleep."

"Yeah, it is," Charlie said, looking down at his book again. "I'll get a break pretty soon, though. I'd rather chop off a hand than to flunk out of university before. I'd even finished one semester."

[注]

第一句应作 How do you get by ... ？：怎么对付过去的呢？**prop myself**：身体往后靠。**profs** = professors。

waggled：摇。**mournfully**：愁容满面地（摇他的头）。这一句的 sure 仍是 surely；don't 仍应作 doesn't。**tough**：艰苦，不好过。Boy 这里并不是"堂倌"之意，而是个发语叹词，类似于"老天"。

Yeah, it is = Yes, it is tough。

break：休息。这里恐是指圣诞假期而言。**though** = however。
rather...than：宁可砍断一只手，也不情愿在第一学期终了之前，就被学校勒令退学。**I'd finished** = I had finished，这个动词也是虚拟语气，并不是直述语气的过去完成时。

[28]

The tardiest of the hundred students enrolled in Dr. Sylvester Kenshaw's Economics 150 straggled into the lecture room and made their ways to alphabetically assigned chairs with much scuffling and trampling of toes and mumbled apologies. Ec 150, renowned as a pipe course, was always crowded.

[注]

enrolled in Economics 150：选这门课的。**tardy**：行动迟缓的。**tardiest**：上课到得最迟的（那些学生）。这个词是本句的主语，动词是 **straggled**：三三两两悠悠荡荡地进入（教室）。**alphabetically assigned chairs**：依字母次序排列的指定的课椅。**scuffling**：碰撞。**trampling of toes**：踩着别人的脚趾，教室拥挤，许多学生业已入座，迟到的学生在他们身边挤过去，难免有碰撞和踩人脚趾之事发生。**mumbled apologies**：含糊的道歉。
renowned as a pipe course：以分数宽出名（pipe course 前面已有说明）。**crowded**：教室挤，就是选课学生多。分数打得宽，学生都来选。作者对此，恐不无感慨焉。

[29]

Dr. Kenshaw was late that morning. Charlie Wingate sat in his chair on the back row in an agony of waiting. He had on his amber glasses and he could fall asleep as soon as Dr. Kenshaw opened his lecture. But he had to stay awake until then.

[注]

on the back row：他的姓是 W 字母开始，故座位排在后排。**in an agony of waiting**：等候得焦灼不安。agony 是大痛苦，或"痛苦万状"。

he had on his glasses = he had his glasses on：戴上了眼镜。**to stay awake** = to remain awake：教授没有来，他还不能睡。

[30]

When the clock on the front wall showed nine after eleven the seated class began stirring as if it were mounted on some eccentric amusement-park device. Excited whispers eddied out on the warm air of the steamheated lecture room. "He's giving as another out!" "He's not meeting this class today!" "He's got one more minute to make it!" "Naw; six more! You have to wait fifteen minutes on department heads."

[注]

the seated class：业已就座的全班学生。**stirring**：骚动。底下跟一个从句，形容骚动之状，好像全班学生（**it** = the class）都跨上了游乐场中的翻天椅或逍遥椅。**some**：某种。**eccentric**：特别的。**amusement-park device**：游乐场里的设施，如旋转飞椅、过山车、摩天轮等。

excited whispers：声音虽低，可是情绪兴奋。**eddied out**：声音像水花似的，一圈一圈向四周散布出去，把声音比作水之漩涡，而把空气比作水。说到了空气，又用 warm 来描写空气是"暖"的。

引号里几句话的 he，指的都是教授。**cut**：缺席。**meeting the class**：来上课。**to make it**：赶得及，再过一分钟，就是十一点十分，教授迟到了十分钟，学生就要一哄而散了，前文有过 You just about got time to make it 这样的句子。

naw 即 no。平常的教授等他十分钟就够，系主任应该等他十五分钟。这位先生是经济系主任，这里点明。

[31]

There was a seething argument on this point, but when the clock showed fourteen minutes after eleven a bold leader sprang up and said, "Come on, everybody!" All but five or six especially conscientious students rose and milled after him toward the door. Charlie Wingate followed, thoroughly awakened by the chance of getting to bed so soon. The leader yanked the door open and Dr. Kenshaw stumbled in, all out of breath, his eyeglasses steamed, his pointed gray beard quivering, a vain little man in a greenish-black overcoat.

[注]

seething：沸腾状的。**argument**：争论。七嘴八舌，各执一词，有的主张等满十分钟就不再等了，有的主张应该等足十五分钟。**a bold leader**：勇敢的领袖，首先发难者。**sprang up**：从座上一跃而起。

especially conscientious students：特别奉公守法的学生。这种人只有五六个，他们还安坐不动，余人都唯那位领导人物马首是瞻，纷纷站起，向门口走去。**milled**：（像牛羊似地）四处乱走（move around in confusion）。

awakened 是过去分词。既然可以早些回去畅睡，这么一兴奋，反而神清气爽了。**thoroughly**：足见他来上课的时候还是想瞌睡，现在方才完全醒过来。

yanked（美国俗语）：使劲一转旋钮，然后把门拉开。**stumbled in**：跟跄地进来。**steamed**（过去分词）：教授从冷空气里进来，室内的热汽在眼镜上结一层薄雾。**quivering**：抖动。因匆忙之故欤？抑见学生不耐久候而发怒耶？ **vain**：虚荣心重的，自以为了不起的，这里可解作"盛气凌人的"。a vain little man 是同位语，说明主语 Dr. Kenshaw。

[32]

"Go back to your seats!" Dr. Kenshaw commanded sternly as soon as he could get his breath. He marched over to his lecture table and planked down his leather brief case. He took off his overcoat and began wiping the steam from his eyeglasses while the students hurried back to their chairs. "It does seem to me," he said, his voice quavering with anger, "that it would be no more than courteous for the class to await my arrival on those rare occasions when I am delayed."

[注]

sternly：严厉地。**get his breath**：上文不是说过他 all out of breath 吗？

planked down：用力放下。**briefcase**：公文包。

quavering：（声音之）颤动。教授的谈吐很典雅。本文诸人物的谈吐，此公的和前文训导长的属于同一类型，都是受过高深教育者的口吻；只是训导长的显得诚恳，此公的显得尖刻。说话尖刻的人，于用字练句方面，一定也特别讲究。

no more than courteous = only courteous。"我难得有事情，因此迟到，诸位多等一会儿，据我看来，未必就委屈了诸位，这不过是礼貌问题而已。"

[33]

A few students exchanged meaning glances. They meant, "Now we're in for it. The old boy has on one of his famous mads."

[注]

exchanged glances：互相看看。**meaning glances**：眼光的意思，心照不宣。**they meant** = the glances meant。**in for it**（用于口语）= unable to escape from a danger, penalty, etc：挨骂是挨定的了。in 是副词。

the old boy 即教授。mad 在口语用法中，有 angry 的意思；但这里当作名词用，颇见特别。**one of his famous mads**：老先生的脾气是出了名的，今天可又要发作了。on 是副词，用法同前文的 He had on his amber glasses 相仿。

[34]

"Today, I believe I shall forego delivering my prepared lecture," Dr. Kenshaw went on in a more even voice, "and let you do the talking. Perhaps it would be moot to hear a few outside reading reports this morning. All of you doubtless are aware that these reports were due last week, although I had not expected to call for them at once. Let us begin forthwith. When your name is called, you will rise and read your report to the class."

[注]

教授用了几个典雅的词,如第一句的 **forego**（= abstain from, 这里似以译作"暂停"为妥）和第二句的 **moot**（= debatable, 该不该这样做是值得讨论的）。

a few outside reading reports：几篇课外阅读的报告。**due last week**：上星期就该催你们交了。**I had not expected …**：我本来不打算马上就催你们交。**forthwith** = immediately。

[35]

"Mr. Abbot!" he called, Mr. Abbot stammered an excuse. Dr. Kenshaw passed coldly on to Miss Adams, making no comment. All through the A's it was the same. But with the B's an ashen, spectacled Miss Ballentyne stood up and began reading in a droning voice her report on "The Economic Consequence of the Peace." Obviously Dr. Kenshaw was not listening to her. His hard little eyes under craggy brows were moving up one row and down the other, eager for a victim. On the back row, Charlie Wingate's propped legs had given way and he had slipped far down into his seat, fast asleep. When Dr. Kenshaw's preying eyes reached Charlie they stopped moving. Someone tittered nervously and then was silent as Dr. Kenshaw jerked his head round in the direction of the noise. Miss Ballentyne droned on.

[注]

stammered an excuse：结结巴巴地说了一个理由（例如"做好了忘了带来了"或"上星期有病了"等）。

making no comment：教授"不加评论"；并不责备他。

all through the A's：凡 A 字母开头的学生，统统无法应命。

ashen, spectacled：脸色灰白，鼻架眼镜的。**droning**：很单调的声音。她的读书报告的题目是："和平对于经济上的影响"。

hard little eyes：小小的冷酷的眼睛。**craggy brows**：像岩石似的凸出的眉毛。**up one row and down the other**：一排一排地看。**eager for a victim**：一心要找个学生来出气。

given way：软了下来（本来是挺直的）。

preying eyes：虎视眈眈择人而噬的眼睛。**they stopped moving**：学生已经捉到，教授的眼睛也无劳左右搜索了。

tittered nervously：神经紧张地偷偷笑了一下。**jerked his head round**：脑袋突然转了过去，追查谁在偷笑。

[36]

When she had finished, Dr. Kenshaw said dryly, "Very good, Miss

Ballentyne, very good indeed. Er...ah...would someone be kind enough to arouse the recumbent young gentleman in the last row?"

There was a murmur of laughter while everyone turned to look at Milton Weismann nudging Charlie Wingate. Charlie sprang up quickly. Dr. Kenshaw was running down the list of names in his small record book.

[注]

dryly：冷淡地。**recumbent**：身体躺着的。这也是一个典雅的词。这一句话的礼貌很周到，但是也很刻薄。全句用虚拟式，不用命令式。这是非常客气的请求，不知哪一位……？称学生为 young gentleman，很典雅，但是语带讽刺。

Milton Weismann：Wingate 的邻座同学。**nudging**：用肘轻推。

running down the list of names：名字一个一个地看下去。**record book**：记学生成绩的小册子。

[37]

"Mr. ...ah...Wingate, isn't it? Mr. Wingate, your report."

"Pardon me, sir?"

"Mr. Wingate, what was the title of the book assigned to you for report in the class?"

"*Theory of the Leisure Class* by Veblen, sir."

[注]

教授拿教室座位次序和点名册子名单次序一对照，知道这位学生名叫 Wingate，但没有十分把握，所以前面吞吞吐吐了一下。

Pardon me, sir?：学生恐怕没有听清楚教授的话。

Thorstein Veblen (1857—1929)：美国经济学家凡勃伦，他的那本《有闲阶级论》(1899) 是经济学名著，据说非常艰深难懂，无怪那个学生读得叫苦连天。

[38]

"Ah, then that's the explanation. So you were assiduously engaged in evolving your own theory of the leisure class. Is that right, Mr. Wingate? You have evidently concluded that Economics 150 is the leisure class."

The class rocked with laughter. Dr. Kenshaw pleased with his pun and flattered by the response to it, found it hard to keep his face straight.

[注]

教授在这里大大地挖苦了那学生一番。**that's the explanation**：这就是说明；这一下我可明白了。

assiduously：勤勉地。**engaged in**：从事于。**evolving your own theory**：发明你自己的理论。

evidently：明显地。**concluded**：得到这样一个结论：来上我们这班课的都是有闲阶级。

rocked with laughter：笑得前仰后合。

pun：双关语。上文的 class 既解作"阶级"，又解作"班级"。教授妙语解颐，自己也很欣赏自己的机智。**the response to it**：对他妙语的反应全班大笑，笑话没有白说，因此更为得意了。**hard to keep his face straight**：脸板不下来，自己也想笑。

[39]

"Mr. Wingate's theory is quite apparently one to which the majority of this class subscribes. Now these reading reports were assigned to you last September, and you have had ample time to prepare them. I'll not call for any more of them today, but at the next session of this class I expect every one of these papers in. As for you, Mr. Wingate, if you'll see me directly after class. I'll be glad to hear any explanation or apology that you may wish to make."

[注]

is quite apparently one = is quite apparently a theory。to which 之 to 连后面的 subscribes。**subscribe to** = agree to：这位同学的有闲阶级理论，全班同学大多数显然都赞成的。

ample time：充分的时间。

the next session of this class：下次上课的时候。**I expect every one of these papers in**：我希望统统交齐，一份不漏。

[40]

"Thank you, sir," Charlie mumbled. He entered a slow torture, trying to keep awake until the class bell rang. But fifteen minutes had to pass before the bell would ring.

When the bell rang the class rose quickly and began clumping out. When the last had gone out, Dr. Kenshaw unscrewed his fountain pen and opened his roll book. He ran his finger down the list until he came to "Wingate, C."and in the space opposite under "Smstr Grd" he marked a precise little F.

[注]

slow torture：慢性地受罪。还有十五分钟才得下课，他又不敢再在课堂上睡觉。

clump = walk heavily。

unscrewed：取下笔套。**roll book**：点名册子，就是 record book。**Wingate, C.**：点名册以姓氏排列，故首书是 Wingate, C. 是 Charles 的缩写。

Smstr Grd 是 Semester Grade 的省写。前文已经说明，他再得一个 F，就要被除名了。**precise**：清清楚楚的。

[41]

A whiffling snore escaped Charlie Wingate in the back of the room. Dr. Kenshaw took his overcoat from its hanger, slipped into it, and strapped up his brief case. He put on his hat and strode out of the lecture room, slamming the door. The noise made a hollow echo in the empty room, but it did not disturb Charlie Wingate. He slept on behind his amber glasses.

[注]

whiffling：轻轻的如微风之声。**snore**：鼾声。**escaped**：从他（鼻子里）发出来。

hanger：衣架。its 代替 overcoat's。**slipped into it**：穿上大衣（全身滑进大衣里面去）。**strapped up**：把皮带扣上。

strode（stride 的过去时）：大踏步地走出去。**slamming the door**：把门砰地一关。

hollow echo：空洞的回声。但是可怜的 Charlie 又睡熟了。

Prescott
史学家普雷斯科特

Van Wyck Brooks（1886—1963）

  本文作者布鲁克斯是美国当代文学批评家，著作很多，最重要的是皇皇五巨册的《美国文学史》(*Makers and Finders: A History of the Writer in America, 1800—1915*)。布氏以生动华丽的文字，传记家的笔法，描写美国过去的文坛实况和文人言行，使得读者有身历其境、面对古人之感。所以有人说他这部文学史读来和历史小说一样有趣。

  本文选自《新英格兰的盛世》(*The Flowering of New England, 1815—1865*)(1936)。这一本书在他全部文学史里按出版年份来说是最早的一本也是最成功的一本。在《新英格兰的盛世》这一时期里，美国文坛名家辈出，如朗费罗、爱默生、霍桑、梭罗等皆是，史学家普雷斯科特的成就也许比不上他们这些人，但普氏以半盲之人，全凭苦心毅力，完成他的那部巨著 *The Reign of Ferdinand and Isabella*，实在也值得介绍于中国读者之前。

[1]

  Suddenly, in 1837, out of the throng of historical studies, honest and laborious, some of them fervent, none of them august, a great work appeared, like – a wonder of nature, as it seemed to American readers, — *The Reign of Ferdinand and Isabella.* It was a brilliant performance, as any child could see and no scholar was ever to deny. Its limitations were obvious enough. It was not a philosophical history. The author had no great leading views, nor any profound feeling for human motives. There were depths upon depths behind and beneath the story that he had never plumbed. But, as a work of art, a great historical narrative, grounded at every point in historical fact, and with all the glow and colour of Livy and Froissart, it was a magnificent success. Its outlines wore as firm as those of a cartoon of Raphael, and its pageantry of picturesque detail was calculated to feed as never before the starved imagination of the country. The book had been planned like a battle and built as stoutly as a Salem clipper, destined to sail through many enchanted minds for generations to come.

[注]

throng：大量，很多种。1837 年前几年间，美国出了好多种历史研究著作，都是老老实实苦心经营（laborious）之作，有几种热情充沛（fervent），但是没有一本是令人叹服（august）的杰作，忽然在那一年，从（out of）那一堆书里，出现了一本巨著，据美国读者看来，就像是一件奇迹（wonder of nature）。

伊比利亚半岛上阿拉贡国（Aragon）国王 Ferdinand 于 1469 年娶 Isabella 为后，Isabella 于 1474 年复继位为卡斯蒂利亚国（Castile）女王，这两国的联合奠定了今日西班牙的基础。15 世纪的西班牙在他们统治（reign）之下，国势极盛，哥伦布发现新大陆，就是在他们俩赞助下完成的。普氏的巨著，就是以这个时代为题材。

brilliant performance：精彩之作。这一点小孩子都看得出来，专家学者也从没有人否认过。

limitations：限制，缺点。虽然是本巨著，但并非十全十美，缺点很明显。

philosophical history：哲学历史，从哲学观点来写的历史，历史中包含哲学思想者。

leading views：主要的观点。great 这里应作"高明"解。**human motives**：人类行为的动机。普通历史家只研究事情本身，有心理学修养的历史家，还要研究事情后面的动机。但是普氏在这方面并没有深刻的认识。

depths upon depths：故事的后面，故事的底下，一层复一层的，深藏着人心的奥秘，但是普氏从来没有往深处去探测。普氏只对于故事本身发生兴趣。

这部历史虽然缺乏深刻的哲理和心理动机的分析，但是我们拿它当作一件艺术品来看或是一部伟大的历史叙事作品来读，我们不得不承认这是部了不起的著作（magnificent success）。

grounded 是过去分词，形容 narrative，意为"建立"。这部历史所讲的许多事迹，没有一处是向壁虚构，每一句话都有根据："每一点都建立于历史事实之上"。

Livy(59B. C.—17A. D.)：李维，罗马历史家。Froissart(1337？—1410)：傅华萨，法国历史家。他们的文章都是有光彩的（glow and colour），普氏的文章也可以和他们的媲美。

最后几句话都是赞扬普氏巨著的优点。他这本书的轮廓明确，就像拉斐尔的画稿一样。cartoon 现在通常译作"卡通"或"漫画"，这里解作"画稿"，即油画、壁画、织锦等动工以前，先在厚纸上用笔所画的草稿。拉斐尔是文艺复兴时期意大利画家。这部书的"轮廓明确"，说的是它的计划周密，叙事次序井然，无轻重偏颇之病。

picturesque detail：如画的细节。本书的组织完整，各处小节描写，又生动美丽如画，使人目不暇接，犹如盛大赛会，化装游行（pageantry）一般。

calculated = fit，suitable（足以产生某种结果）。**to feed the imagination of the country**：给美国人民以精神食粮，激发他们的想象力。**starved**：饥饿的。19世纪初叶，美国人的精神生活很是贫乏，所能想象的东西很有限。普氏此书，活龙活现地描写西班牙国势最盛的一段时期，大多为美国人见所未见，闻所未闻的事情，美国人欢迎这本书，无异是饥民之得美食。**as never before**：以前所出的书，从来没有像这本书那样能满足美国人者。

like a battle：本书写作以前，设计周密审慎，犹如参谋部计划一场战斗一样。

Salem：塞勒姆，美国马萨诸塞州的海港，当时是美国造船业中心。**clipper**：快帆船。本书的结构完美，颠扑不破，如塞勒姆快船一般地结实（stoutly built）。按，普氏为塞勒姆地方的人，这个譬喻用得很适当。

destined 原意是"命中注定的"，但通常并不含有"命运"的意义，只是指"将来有某种结果"而已。他这只船造成以后，将要在未来世世代代（for generations to come）读者的心灵中航行。**enchanted**：着迷的。这本书可以使人入迷，使读者犹如置身于15世纪的西班牙一般。船在很多人的心灵中航行，就是说很多人要读它（读了还要着迷）。

[2]

It was the work of William Hickling Prescott, Ticknor's young friend, the charming, amusing son of Judge Prescott, who lived in his ample house in Bedford Street, overlooking a beautiful garden. Prescott? — who could believe it? He was partly blind, and he had an extravagant love of jolly parties. He talked with a joyous abandon, running over with animal spirits, laughing at his own inconsequences, with always some new joke or witty sally. He could be happy in more ways, in spite of his defective eyes, and happier in every one of them, than anyone else his friends had ever seen. One met him in the street, with his gay blue satin waistcoat, tall, graceful, with light brown hair and a clear and ruddy complexion. He seemed to look younger everyday. It was known that, for twenty years, he and a group of his friends had carried on a literary club, reading their papers over a merry supper. He had printed a few essays in the review. But this was in a dilettantish spirit, everyone supposed. One of his relatives, meeting him on the street, not long before his book appeared, urged him to undertake some serious task. It would be so good for him. It would be more respectable than leading this unprofitable life.

[注]

George Ticknor (1791—1871)：乔治·蒂克纳，当时有名学者，曾任哈佛大学法语、西班牙语教授。学识渊博，喜奖掖后进。普氏年龄比他轻5岁。

第一句说明普氏家世，其父任法官，家里房子很大。社会人士对他的认识如此。作者并不直叙普氏的家世与为人，这里只是描写当时的人看见普氏的巨著后的惊奇心理，凭这样一个人也能写出这样一部书来吗？

partly blind：半盲。**jolly parties**：热闹的社交宴会。

abandon：随便（名词）。说起话来总很高兴，想说什么就说什么。

animal spirits：活泼好动的劲儿（此二词为习语）。**running over**：全身洋溢着。

inconsequences：前言不对后语，自己也觉得好笑，running 和 laughing 都是形容主语 he，描写他说话的情形。**sally**：隽语，俏皮话。

in more ways：他的眼睛虽有病，但他作乐的方法很多，他的朋友们再也没有看见像他那样会多方面寻快乐的人了。his friends had ever seen 是定语从句，关系代名词 that（或 whom）省掉。**in every one of them**：in every one of these ways，别

人也许也有这么多作乐的方法，但是他寻起快乐来，不论任何方式，总比别人还要高兴。本句 than 一字，既照应前面的 more，复照应稍后的 happier。

接着一句描写他的服饰容貌。作者还不是直接描写，还是借用当时人的看法。

one met him 的 one 没有确指什么人。**gay**：色彩鲜艳的。**satin**：缎子。**graceful**：态度文雅的。**clear and ruddy complexion**：面色清朗红润，看他样子，似乎愈活愈年轻了。

literary club：文学联谊会。**merry supper**：大家一起吃晚饭，谈笑欢乐，同时再宣读各人的论文。

the review：指当时有名的杂志 *The North American Review*。

dilettante：以文学作为消遣之人。**in the dilettantish spirit**：他的举办文学联谊会，发表文章，大家认为他只是搞着玩的，并不是真正用心研究或埋首写作。

undertake some serious task：着手干一样正经的工作。**respectable**：为人所重视。他那时所过的生活，对他自己太没有好处了。

[3]

Every evening the light from his study window glimmered through the pear-trees in the garden. But only George Ticknor, outside the household, knew that, for at least ten years, Prescott had been hard at work, harder, Perhaps, than any Boston merchant. And, if everyone bought this book for a Christmas present, it was only because the author was so attractive. One of his cronies, who was not a reader, rose before dawn, on the day it was published, to buy the first copy; but, while everyone saw at once that it was good, no one was aware how good it was. There were scarcely twelve men living who were able to know. Within a year or two, the electoral returns came rolling in, from England, France and Spain. The book had been born a classic.

[注]

study window：书斋的窗户。**pear-trees**：梨树。写这部文学史的布鲁克斯，把人家花园里种的什么树都考证出来了，但只是像小说家那样的随手拈来，并不在卖弄考据之学。

outside the household：除了他家里人以外，只有好友蒂克纳知道他在那里用功写作，而且已经花了"十年寒窗"的功夫了（前文那位亲戚不知道，所以还要劝他干正经事）。

harder 用以加强 hard。他的用功之苦，比之波士顿孳孳为利的商人，也许有过之而无不及。

everyone 是夸大的说法，即"很多人"。大家都去买他的书，作为圣诞礼品送人。买的人所以如此之多，因为作者为人很可爱，平日人缘很好，至于书写得好不好，大家并不关心。

crony：好朋友。此人平日并不读书（not a reader）。

while 有"虽然"之意。大家都看出来这是一部好书，但是到底好得怎么样，那些买书的人没有人知道。当时资格评定这部书的优劣者，全世界仅有（scarcely）十二人而已。

electoral returns：各地选举的开票结果。这虽并没有谁在举行选举，作者只是借用一个习语，表示各地的好评源源不断而来。

a classic：名著，不朽之作。这是个主语补语：一出版就成了名著。

[4]

It was a conquest of personality. Prescott was a first-rate-human being, exuberant, gallant, wilful, firm, devoted, far removed from the clerkly sort of scholar, painstaking but wanting in vigour and sinew, who, in a world in which the most virile types adopted careers of enterprising action, ruled over the sphere of books.

[注]

it：本书的成功。**conquest of personality**：人格的胜利。conquest 原意是"征服"。这本书所以能够如此成功，全凭作者个人特殊的人格。这句话照应上文的 ...if everyone bought his book...it was only because the author was so attractive，可是作者的性格，不只是 attractive 而已。

a first-rate human being：第一流的人物。**exuberant**：精力充沛的。**gallant**：此词有"勇敢"，"高贵"之意，相当于中文的"潇洒不群"。**wilful**：任性行事的。

the clerkly sort of scholar：注重钞录稗贩的那一种学者。**clerkly**：像个小书记似的，没有见解，没有气魄。普氏绝不是这一类人。**painstaking**：非常用功的。**sinew**：筋络，转作"体力"。可是体力（vigour and sinew）稍差。

who 还是代表主语 Prescott，它的动词是 ruled。在那时的美国，凡是以体魄胜人（virile）的那一种人，都去从事（adopted：采用）于带点冒险性（enterprising）的事业了，如经商、航海、从军等，普氏体力既不如人，只好在书 it 里称王（统治了书本的领域）。

[5]

He did not like to get up in the morning and had to instruct his servant, the faithful Nathan, to pull away his bed-clothes. He did not like to work. He had to make bets with his secretary that he would write a certain number of pages or carry out some other resolution. He was always making resolutions, never too old to make them; and he was never old enough to keep them.

[注]

原来普氏的用功，也很勉强。早晨懒得起床，非得吩咐忠仆 Nathan 不可，叫他把被子掀掉。

make bets：赌东道。他的决心（resolution）常常不能付诸实行（carry out），他不得不同他的秘书打赌，规定自己要写多少页书，或者干些别的什么事情，为了怕输东道，只好硬着头皮苦干了。

was always making resolutions：常常在下决心，定计划。**never too old to make them**：自己从来不觉得老，所以计划（them 代替 resolutions）层出不穷，假如自己承认老朽，那么也许就得过且过，不再下什么决心了，never old enough to keep them：老人自觉岁月所余无多，心上如有未了之事，总希望在生前把它做掉。这种人可说是 old enough to keep their resolutions 了，可是普氏并不觉老之将至，也不想偿宿债，还宿愿。

[6]

The refractory horse makes the most mettlesome charger. Prescott had a formidable will, and he had bridled and harnessed his indolent nature. Every morning, in the dead of winter, to wind himself up for the day. he mounted his horse and rode to Jamaica Plain, to see the sun rise from a certain hill. As for his blindness, which was never total, he made an advantage of it. One might have thought that blindness was a blessing. He could not read for more than ten minutes, — an hour or two a day at the best of times. And how could a blind man write a history, based on unpublished documents, in two or three foreign languages?

[注]

第一句用现在时,表示一般情形。凡顽劣不驯(refractory)之马,如经名手训练,常成为最刚健之良驹(**charger**:战马,用以冲锋陷阵者)。

formidable will:坚强的意志。他用毅力驾御了自己懒惰的个性。**bridled**:替马装上羁勒。**harnessed**:替马装上马具,备驾车之用。**indolent**:习惯性的懒惰,怕吃力,喜悠闲。这里把他的个性比作一匹马,所以可以 bridled,又可以 harnessed。

in the dead of winter:三九严冬。dead 作名词用,解作"死气沉沉的时候"。万籁俱寂的深夜,可以译成 a dead of night。**to wind himself up**:替自己"上发条";振作精神,准备一天的工作。**Jamaica Plain**:波士顿附近的地名。这样一个懒得起床的人,冬晨居然能骑马到郊外山头看日出,精神自是不凡。

which was never total:盲虽盲,但从未完全失明。which 代替 blindness。**as for blindness**:至于他的瞎眼吧……。**make an advantage of it**:他把短处转化为长处;本来不利于自己的缺陷,反而转变成为对自己有利的优点。

one might have thought:我们几乎可以这么说;虚拟语气,隐含这么一个条件从句:假如我们能够看见他这么用功的话。**a blessing**:天赐恩典。

based on unpublished documents:他这部历史所根据的是些未经发表的文献(如书札、日记、手稿之类),这些东西是用两三种外国文字写成的。他双目不灵,一天最多只能读上一两钟头的书,每读十分钟就要休息,他怎么能披阅这许多未经整理的原始史料,写出这么一部伟大的历史呢?

[7]

He made his ears do the work of his eyes, with the aid of a friend and a sister and later of a competent secretary. Blindness had always favoured contemplative habits. Had not Malebranche closed his shutters in order to drive the sunlight out? Had not Democritus, as the legend said, blinded himself deliberately to stimulate his thinking? Blindness was good for invention, as many poets proved, from Homer to Milton. The blind were famous for their patience, especially for their feats of memory.

[注]

他用耳代目，使耳朵做眼睛的工作。他是请人把书读给他听的；先是请一位朋友和自己的姊妹，以后又找到了一位很能干（competent）的秘书。of a competent secretary 的 of 连前面的 with the aid。**blindness had always favoured…**：从历史上看来，目盲非但不足为害，而且大有助于深思冥想的习惯。动词时态 had favoured 表示在普氏以前已经如此。

接着用两句问话，这种句子形式虽为问句，事实上答案不言自明，在修辞学上称为 rhetorical question，相当于中文的"反问"。

Nicolas de Malebranche（1638—1715）：尼古拉·马勒伯朗士，法国哲学家。他总把百叶窗拉下，不让阳光进屋，免得周围景物，分了他用功的心（中国也有"十年目不窥园"的佳话）。

Democritus：德谟克利特，公元前4、5世纪间的希腊哲学家。据古人传说（as the legend said），他故意（deliberately）把眼睛弄瞎，为了要激发自己的思想。invention：这里不是指科学上的发明，而是文学家的想象。创造人物，制作故事。希腊大诗人荷马据说是个瞎子，弥尔顿的《失乐园》等巨著都是在失明以后写成。许多诗人可以证明，目盲有益于文学创作。

the blind：瞎子，形容词作名词用，相当于 the rich 表示所有的富人。瞎子都以耐心出名，不会心浮气粗；他们的惊人的记忆力，尤为世人所乐道。**feats**：特殊技能，如力能扛鼎，百步穿杨，一目十行等。**feats of memory**：能记普通人所不能记的东西。

[8]

Prescott taught himself to use a noctograph, by means of which, with the aid of an ivory stylus, pressing on a sheet of carbon-paper, he took his notes and wrote his manuscripts. The secretary copied the notes in a large, round hand, which Prescott was sometimes able to read. Meanwhile, he had learned to memorize, composing in his memory to such an extent that he could often carry in his mind as many as three chapters of one of his books, seventy-two pages of printed text. He could hold it there for several days, turning it over and over, remodelling every sentence. One chapter he thus remodelled sixteen times, before committing a word to paper.

[注]

noctograph：盲人用的写字机器，构造不详，想必是利用触觉代替视觉的。**ivory stylus**：象牙制的尖头笔。**carbon-paper**：复写纸。**pressing on**：加压力于其上，即"写"。**took notes**：记笔记。**manuscripts**：文稿。

round hand：圆形字体，笔画清楚，不倾不斜，各字母间都分开的，相当于中文的"正楷"，易于辨认，与"行书"（running hand）不同。**sometimes**：秘书把他的笔记这样清清楚楚地抄了下来，普氏还只是"有时"能读得出来而已，其目力之不济可想而知。

composing in his memory：用他的记忆来作文。写下的稿子自己不能读，如何能修改补正呢？只好把文章都记在脑子里。**to such an extent that**：普通人也有会打"腹稿"的，可是比起普氏来，真是小巫之见大巫。普氏打腹稿，能够做到把好几十页书都记在头脑中的"程度"。关于"记住"，这两句里用了两个动词，都值得称道。一个是 carry：头脑中把一本书整整三章文章（排印起来要占 72 页之多）都"背"下来。还有一个词是 hold：放在那里，牢记不忘。**hold it** 的 it，指那几章文章的"整体"。

turning it over and over：心里翻来覆去地想它。**remodelling every sentence**：腹稿未必妥当，句句都在头脑中仔细地修改。remodelling 所指，不单是更动几个词而已，硬是把句法都要彻底地改过的。

committing a word to paper：写一个词在纸上。先是一字不落，想之又想，改之又改，然后再落笔。有一章他的腹稿改了 16 次之多。committing 有"付托"之意。

[9]

His blindness had another effect. It increased the sensitivity that lay behind the judgments he conveyed — as an artist ought to convey them — by subtle modulations of tone and style. He spoke of the careless indifference with which men who would never abuse a dog crushed, without a thought, insects whose bodily agonies were imperceptible to the naked eye.

[注]

the judgments he conveyed：他所下的判断。**convey**：表达。西班牙那时盛行"异教裁判"，对于思想罪犯百般凌虐，普氏写这一段的历史，对于此种暴行，甚表不满。"不满"就是他的判断，他如何表达他自己的见解呢？他既是一个讲究行文措辞的"艺术家"，他并不直言责斥，他用的是艺术家的办法。在他文章的语调（tone）和风格（style）之中，自有其不可捉摸（subtle）的抑扬顿挫（modulations），他就在这种地方，暗加褒贬。

他的见解基于他对人类的同情，所以说在他的判断的后面（that lay behind the judgments）有他对于人生是非苦乐的敏感之心（sensitivity），而盲人又是特别的敏感。

men who would never abuse a dog：从不肯虐待猫狗的人。这种人应该是很仁慈的了，可是他们会不假思索地（without a thought）踏死小虫！（crushed 后面虽有逗号，但是在语法结构上，它应该连它的宾语 insects），因为猫狗的痛显而易见，虫豸的痛苦，非大慈大悲极具同情心者，不能体会。它们身体上的苦楚（bodily agonies）为肉眼所不能见。**naked eyes**：肉眼，普通人的眼睛。所以有眼睛的人，未必能体贴入微，而盲人可能特别敏感，乃知蝼蚁之亦贪生也。

the careless indifference with which men ... crushed ... insects：人踏死小虫的时候，带一种马虎、满不在乎的态度。普氏在某一篇文章里，就讨论到（spoke of）这一点，足见盲目反而增加了他的敏感。

[10]

He had first acquired these mental habits when, as a young man with failing sight, he had been sent abroad, to London and Paris, to consult the doctors there, and had spent a quiet winter in the Azores. People were surprised, in later years, that Prescott, who had never visited Spain, or Mexico or Peru, knew so much about these tropical scenes and was able to fill his books with such glowing pictures, — Spanish gardens, myrtles, laurels, lemons, the box-tree and the rose, mountain vistas, wildly picturesque, the Cordilleras and the Sierra Nevada, with convent bells ringing in the valleys. A young man who had grown up in Boston, under cloudy skies, lashed by the east wind, have had little imagination if he had not received vivid impressions during these June-like months in the Azores.

[注]

these mental habits：这些心理上的习惯，即上文所说的记忆，拟腹稿等。**acquired**：获得。"养成一种习惯"可说 to acquire a habit。**with failing sight**：目力渐渐丧失。**to consult the doctors there**：请教伦敦、巴黎两地的名医（普氏游欧，在他 19 岁到 21 岁之间）。**Azores**：大西洋中岛屿，属葡萄牙。群岛前面，该加冠词 the。普氏的外祖父那时是岛上的美国领事。

本文文章的特点，是长句子相当多，可是句子虽长，停顿也多，很少有一气呵成的，读了几个词读者就可以换一口气，调子缓慢，不慌不忙，有闲散轻松之妙。调子既慢，装饰用的词可以随时插入，句法内容因以丰富，而句法变化亦变幻莫测矣。以第一句为例，when 以前的句法是直截了当的，到了 when 以后，从句的主语 he 还不见出来，反而添了一个逗号，逗号之后又来 as a young man with failing sight 这样一个短语，这六个词紧凑得好，假如初学写来，写成 when he was young and his sight was failing 就显得笨拙而啰唆矣。六个词过后，再说他到海外去。去哪里呢？（语气一顿）伦敦、巴黎。去干什么呢？（语气又一顿）是去瞧大夫的。

这样写法在第二句中更为明显。如 surprised 后，语气一顿，接 in later years （普氏成名以后），that Prescott 之后，隔了好多词，动词 knew 才出现；而 knew 之前，语气又要停好几次；Spain 之后一顿，or Mexico 后一小顿，or Peru 后又一顿。如中间取消一个 or，改说 Spain, Mexico or Peru 句法较直截干脆，唯韵味不同矣。总之，文章无定法，调子快有调子快的好处，调子慢有调子慢的好处。本文调子很慢，作者苦心所在，尚望读者仔细体会。

普氏从来没有去过西班牙，也没有去过墨西哥和秘鲁（普氏继 Ferdinand and Isabella 之后，复完成两大巨著：Conquest of Mexico 与 Conquest of Peru），可是他对于那些热带国家的风光景色知道得非常清楚，犹如曾经身历其境一般，所以以后读者很觉奇怪。他的书里面到处是南欧和中南美洲风景的描写，色彩鲜明，生动如画（**glowing**：发光的）。

myrtles：桃金娘，其叶、花与浆果均可作为香料。**laurels**：月桂。**lemons**：柠檬，又是一种香味浓郁的树。**box-tree**：黄杨树。**mountain vistas**：山岭间的远景。**wildly picturesque**：粗犷而入画（形容 vistas）。**the Cordilleras**：山脉名，在秘鲁。the Sierra Nevada 是西班牙的山名（美国加利福尼亚州有大山，亦名 Sierra Nevada）。

convent：修道院。深山古寺，幽谷钟声，普氏历史书中，偏多这种描写，无怪本文第一段中说本书的 pageantry of picturesque detail 可以满足美国人饥饿的想象力了。

a young man：即普氏。他生长在景色单调的波士顿，天空是阴沉沉的时候多，整年受着东风的鞭打（lashed）。这样一个人假如不在热带住过一阵子，得到很生动的印象，是不会有多大的想象力的，更不必说是描写风光旖旎的西班牙了，**June-like months**：他在 Azores 的时候是冬天，可是那里大约是四季如夏；虽在冬天，气候仍温暖如六月。

[11]

After his taste of the Azores, he returned to Boston. His friends rallied about him in his blindness and read to him aloud, six or eight hours at a time, especially the inseparable Ticknor, absorbed in the study of Spanish literature, on which he was lecturing at Harvard. Ticknor, to amuse him, read his lectures to him, three or four afternoons every week, along with his favorite classics and historical works and the old English romances.

[注]

rallied about him：集合在他的四周。普氏欧游之行，未能将双目医好，回国后朋友们帮助他（rally 除"集合"外，更有"支持"之意），读书给他听。**inseparable**：不可分离的，形影不离的（好朋友）。**absorbed**：（过去分词，形容蒂克纳）专心致志于。蒂克纳是哈佛大学西班牙语教授，前文已经说过。

his lectures：蒂克纳在哈佛的讲稿。非但念自己的讲稿，而且把普氏所爱读的（his favorite 的 his 恐是代表普氏）古典文学、历史名著、英国古代英雄传奇等都连带念给他听。

[12]

Prescott was reading for pleasure, with Ticknor's Spanish library as his hunting-ground. He had in mind no scheme for a composition, but he was planning a literary career, for which he proposed to lay a firm foundation. English grammar first, as if he had never gone to school or college. For style, Sidney, Bacon, Browne and Milton. One hour a day for the Latin classics, Tacitus and Livy for elevation: he knew them by heart already, but this was a different matter. A year devoted to French, from Froissart to Chateaubriand. A year for Italian, another year for Spanish. There he paused, there he felt at home, too much at home to carry on with German. His eyes were not equal to the Gothic script.

[注]

reading for pleasure：为消遣而读书，念着玩的。**Spanish library**：西班牙文的藏书。**hunting-ground**：打猎的场地。他不断地借阅蒂克纳的藏书。

he had in mind no scheme = he had no scheme in mind，作者所以先说 in mind，后说 no scheme 者，为的是使 for a composition 这个形容词短语可以紧跟着它所形容的名词 scheme。composition 所指不仅是一篇作文，一本书亦可。动词 compose 是"写作"，composition 就是"作品"。**a literary career**：文学生涯，以文学为终身事业。既有志写作，不可不有准备，所以他想先扎好根基：筑好（lay）结实的基础。

English grammar first：此句为不完全句，前面所省掉的大约是 he studied 两词。普氏是哈佛大学毕业生，文学修养本来已经很深（他的眼睛是在大学里弄坏的），可是现在先从英文语法学起，好像自己从来没有进过学校似的，把英文语法从头研究一遍。这种功夫，无非为他日后写作作准备。

style：文章风格。语法只教人文章的规范，真要写得好，还得精研名家的作品。普氏所精读的是四家的作品：**Sir Philip Sidney**（1554—1586）：菲利普·锡德尼爵士，伊丽莎白时代作家。其 Arcadia 以辞藻华丽，想象丰富著称。**Lord Bacon**（1561—1626）：培根，他的散文简洁老辣。**Sir Thomas Browne**（1663—1704）：托马斯·布朗爵士，17 世纪英国散文家，他在中国不大出名，但英国 19 世纪散文家如 Lamb 等，受他的影响很深。他的文章风格可说是辞富理赡，音调节奏之美，英国散文作家很少有比得上他的。**Milton**（1608—1674）：弥尔顿，大诗人，但散文也有名，热情充沛，气势雄浑。

Tacitus（55？—117？）：塔西佗，罗马历史家。普氏精读这两家的作品，为的是求风格高超（elevation），不作庸俗语。其实这两家的作品，他早已熟读，可是以前读的时候，也许只注意事实的记录，现在是专从文章方面用功，两种用功方法完全不同，不可混为一谈也（this was a different matter）。

Chateaubriand（1768—1848）：夏多布里昂，法国作家，是浪漫运动的中坚人物之一。他的历史著作很能激发怀古的幽情。

paused：稍歇，不再往前继续研究别种文字。**at home**：有如鱼得水之乐。

Gothic script：哥特式字体。英文法文所用的都是罗马字体，近代德文书亦有用罗马字体印者，但普氏那时的德文书都用哥特式字体。所谓 Goth 原是日耳曼一种人种之名，其字体锋芒毕露而多曲折，没有罗马字体那样易于辨认。**equal**：力能对付，读来不吃力。

[13]

For a while, he thought of writing a history of Italian literature. But, no, an Italian subject would not be new: Sismondi had covered the ground too well. He wished for a theme that was new as well as great, Spanish history, if it was not unknown, had not been explored at its most vital point, the reign of Ferdinand and Isabella. Theirs was the momentous reign during which the scattered kingdoms were brought together, the age of the conquest of Naples, the founding of the Spanish Inquisition, the opening of the Western hemisphere. Thanks to the present government of Spain, the archives had been thrown open to Spanish scholars. They were busily publishing documents, chronicles, memoirs. But the decrepit kingdom humbled by the loss of its foreign empire, rising from its ancient lethargy, was yet in too chaotic a state to foster any vigour of expression. Spain with all its historiographers, had not produced a master-mind who could assimilate for a greater purpose all these documents that had come to light.

[注]

Sismondi（1773—1842）：西斯蒙迪，瑞士历史家。他的关于意大利文学的著作内容很是详尽（covered the ground too well），没有留下多少东西可供后人发挥的了。

theme：题材。他需要的是一个新颖的题材，可以发人所人所未发，而且是个大题目，可以大加发挥的。

the most vital point：最重要的一点。**explored**：研究，西班牙历史不算是个冷门（not unknown），可是这一段的历史却没有人写过。

theirs = the reign of Ferdinand and Isabella。**momentous**：非常重要的（时期）。**scattered kingdoms**：西班牙本来分几个小国，现在是统一（brought together）了。

Naples：那不勒斯；意大利那时小国林立，所谓"城邦政治"也。那不勒斯是现代意大利的一个城市，在那时是一个小国，法国和西班牙为了争取该地的统治权，于1494年发生战争，西班牙先败后胜。**Inquisition**：异教裁判所。那时的西班牙虐待异教徒（包括犹太人和非正统的基督教徒）很是厉害。**the Western hemisphere**：西半球。哥伦布的探险是由 Ferdinand 和 Isabella 赞助成行的。新大陆于1492年发现。

the present government：普氏当时的西班牙政府。

archives：档案。**thrown open**：打开。学者可以自由阅览抄录。

they 指的是 Spanish scholar。学者们整理结果，印行了很多有关15世纪末叶和16世纪初叶西班牙历史的文件，编年史和回忆录。

decrepit：衰弱的。到了19世纪，西班牙国势削弱，殖民地纷纷独立，海外帝国因以丧失（loss of its foreign empire），备受屈辱（humbled），声威大落；虽然力图扫除积弊，奋发自新（**lethargy**：暮气），然而国事仍旧混乱（chaotic），不能培养（foster）创造伟大著作的生气活力。（**expression**：表达，即文学写作）。

historiographers：历史编著家，着重整理编订，和史学家（historians）有区别。**master-mind**：第一流的头脑。**assimilate**：吸收。它的宾语是 documents。**for a greater purpose**：为了更大的目的。利用这些文献，写出一部巨著。**come to light**：（经学者整理后）重见天日。西班牙既然没有人动手写一部融会贯通、可读可诵的历史书，只好由别国人来越俎代庖了。

[14]

The great theme was at Prescott's disposal. In order to feel sure-footed in the language, he went over his Spanish grammar again. Then he began to read all round the subject. Beginning with the general, laws of nations, the constitutional history of England, the histories of the continental countries, France, Italy, Germany, Portugal, the general history of Spain, before he settled on his special field.

[注]

at his disposal：听他调遣，任他应用。**sure-footed**：脚跟站稳，有充分把握。**went over**：从头研究一遍。

all round the subject：一切有关本题的书籍。

constitutional history：宪法史。

the continental countries：欧陆各国，以别于英国。

his special field：特定的范围，即 Ferdinand 和 Isabella 统治西班牙的那一段时期。

[15]

The book was a ten-year task: three and a half years of study before he wrote the opening sentence, three months for chapter one, seven months for the final chapter, two years for condensing and abridging. He had the text set up in type and caused four copies to be printed, for his friends to correct and criticize. Prescott, as he painfully scrawled his chapters, never guessed how hungry his countrymen were for the brilliant glow and colour that he gave them, the pageantry of kings and queens and battles. This was the romance that America longed for. When it was published, the book was a universal triumph.

[注]

ten-year task：费时十年的工作。

condensing：缩短。**abridging**：节略。材料太多，书虽写成，可删之处尚多，最后费了两年功夫，大加修削。

text：书的正文（不连附注或图片等）。**set up in type**：排印成书。type 是印刷用之活字（铅字）。

caused four copies to be printed：先印四本，并不发卖，专供朋友评阅正误之用，为的是要精益求精。

scrawled：潦草地写。并不是普氏写得潦草，其耐目力不济，写不清楚乎？

hungry...for：嗷嗷待哺。

the brilliant glow and colour：光华夺目，色彩绮丽的文字。that he gave them 是定语从句，他所写给他们看的。the pageantry 和 glow and colour 是同位语。帝王后妃和各处战事的描写，无不有声有色，热闹有趣，一幕接着一幕，无异是化装游行或盛大赛会。普氏辛辛苦苦写这部书时，决想不到他这一类的描写会受到美国人这样的欢迎。

Man and Woman
男与女

Erskine Caldwell（1903—1987）

厄斯金·考德威尔生于美国佐治亚州。他是美国当代最伟大的小说家之一，与海明威、福克纳、斯坦贝克等齐名，描写美国南部（尤其是佐治亚州）贫穷没落的农村生活，最擅胜场。

这里所选的一篇短篇小说，篇幅无多，文字十分简单，几乎无需注解。然而其深刻动人之处，却耐人寻味。其描写、结构都值得我国短篇小说作家的参考。本文选自 The Pocket Book of Erskine Cadwell Stories。

[1]

They came slowly up the road through the colorless dawn like shadows left behind by the night. There was no motion in their bodies, and yet their feet scuffed up dust that settled behind them as quickly as it was raised. They lifted their eyes with each step they took, peering toward the horizon for the first red rays of the sun.

[注]

第一段点出小说的时间和地点，时间是黑夜已过，旭日未升，地点是公路上。人物只是模模糊糊的 they。有多少人呢？是些什么人呢？这里尚未说明，但标题是"男与女",我们可以暂且假定是一男一女。他们的身形我们还看不清楚,他们只是像"黑夜所遗留下来的影子"。他们的动作我们也看不见,只是他们的脚步拖起(scuffed up)了灰尘,脚步步步向前,灰尘也在他们身后旋起旋落(settled)。

scuffed 本是不及物动词,解作"拖着脚步走路",这里是及物动词。**peering**:眯着眼睛看。

描写文最难运用的是形容词,以及由形容词转化出来的副词。本文形容词用得很少,都很简单。这一段里可以说只有两个形容词是用作描写的,一个是 colorless (dawn),一个是 red (rays),都很传神而有力量。描写黎明景色,中英文都有很多滥调,如"天空露出鱼肚白色"、"美丽的朝霞"等,这种美丽的字眼,比之本文的两个简单的形容词,到底哪一种更为妥贴,哪一种更能显出作者炼字的功夫,请读者自己下判断吧。同样的,slowly 是个很简单的副词,但这里用这么一个词也够了,作者可说是惜字如金。

slowly 前面的 came,是从读者的立场而言,假定读者看他们往前走"来"。用了 went,就变成愈走愈远,came 则表示愈走愈近。

[2]

The woman held her lower lip clamped tightly between her teeth. It hurt her to do that, but it was the only way she could urge herself forward step after step. There was no other way to drag her feet one behind the other, mile after mile. She whimpered occasionally, but she did not cry out.

"It's time to stop and rest again," Ring said.

She did not answer him.

They kept on.

[注]

the woman:我们猜想一男一女在赶路,果然有一个女人,我们大约是猜对了。(下文 Ring said,Ring 是那男人的名字。) **clamp**:作名词用,解作"螺钉夹",作动词用,解作"像螺丝钉那样地夹着"。这里是过去分词,作形容词用。

it hurt her:她并不觉得好受。可是她已精疲力尽,非咬紧牙关,无法再继续前进,咬痛嘴唇,在所不惜了。

one behind the other = one foot behind the other foot。

mile after mile：天没亮就在赶路，可能是他们刚刚出门，但是由这一段文章看来，他们已经赶了不少路了。

whimpered：低声呜咽。

[3]

At the top of the hill, they came face to face with the sun. It was a quarter of the way up, cut like a knife by the treeless horizon. Down below them was a valley lying under a cover of mist that was rising slowly from the earth. They could see several houses and farms, but most of them were so far away they were almost indistinguishable in the mist. There was smoke rising from the chimney of the first house.

[注]

第一段第一句里说 slowly up the road，看到这里，我们知道他们原来是在登山。

quarter of the way up：太阳尚未全部露面，只有四分之一升在地平线上。地平线上没有树，太阳好像被刀切似的。脚下有谷，谷中雾气冉冉上升，把山谷盖了起来。

so far away：后面照语法规矩应接 that 一词，但近代作家有把这个 that 省掉的。

indistinguishable：房屋农田在雾中看不清楚。

smoke：景物朦胧，单提出"炊烟"一事，引起下面文章。**the first house**：最近他们的那座房屋。

[4]

Ruth looked at the man beside her. The red rays of the sun began to color his pale face like blood. But still his eyes were tired and lifeless. He looked as if he were balancing himself on his two feet with great effort, and as if the next moment he might lose his balance and fall to the ground.

[注]

女人的名字叫作 Ruth，在这里点出。

color（动词不定式）：着色。初升的阳光，把男人苍白的脸照得血红。

balancing himself：费了好大的劲，两条腿才站得稳。**lose his balance**：失掉平稳，

脚站不住。**the next moment**：现在虽然勉强站稳，但是似乎一不小心，随时都可以倒下去。

[5]

"We'll be able to get a little something to eat at that first house," she said, waiting minute after minute for him to reply.

"We'll get something there," she said, answering for him, "We will."

[注]

上一段已经描写那男人面色苍白，双目无神，步履不稳，这一段里他连口都不开了。女人提议到前面那家人家去讨些东西吃，她等了好久（minute after minute），男人默不作声。最后还是女人自己替他回答（answering for him）。

we will：我们"一定"讨得到东西的。这个 will 应该重读，有些语法家主张这里应该用 shall。

[6]

The sun came up above the horizon, fast and red. Streaks of gray clouds, like layers of wood smoke, swam across the face of it. Almost as quickly as it had risen, the sun shrank into a small fiery button that seared the eyes until it was impossible to look at it any longer.

[注]

streaks：丝，条。**wood smoke**：柴木的烟。

shrank：缩小。太阳升离地平线以后，很快地就显得缩小了，现在看上去只像是一颗"火一般的小纽子"。**seared**：炙伤。**until**：这一个词表示他们两人一直在看着太阳，刚才那个男的不理会女人的说话，大约是看太阳看得出神了，但是现在阳光炽烈，他们不能再看了。

[7]

"Let's try, anyway," Ruth said.

Ring looked at her in the clear daylight, seeing her for the first time since the sun had set the night before. Her face was paler, her cheeks more sunken.

[注]

anyway：不管怎样。

Ring 不看太阳，望望他身边的女人。**since the sun had set**：昨晚日落以后，他还没有仔细看过那女人的脸。可能他们两人已经赶了一夜的路——可是为什么呢？他们要往哪儿去？这是个闷葫芦，作者故弄玄虚，要到最后方始把谜底揭穿。读者的兴趣已被引起，非往下读不可，这也是小说家的手法。

[8]

Without words, he started forward down the hill. He did not turn his head to see if she was following him, but went down the road drawing one foot from behind and hurling it in front of him with all his might. There was no other way he could move himself over the ground.

[注]

男人还是不说话，恐怕是疲惫已极。他一直往前走，也不回头看看女的是不是在后面跟着。他走起路来用全力（with all his might）把后脚拖过来，再用力踏到前面去。**hurling** 原意是"投"或"掷"，他的脚步跨出去要用这么大的劲，其步履之不稳可想而知。**way**：方法。不用这么大的劲，他是没法往前走了。

[9]

He had stopped at the front of the house, looking at the smoke that floated overhead, when she caught up with him at last.

"I'll go in and try," she said. "You sit down and rest, Ring."

[注]

作者对于这一男一女的描写，很是经济，他们的服饰、籍贯、身材、年龄等，一概置之不理，他只是强调他们的疲乏和衰弱，还有一点就是他们的视线。他们看太阳，互相看对方的苍白的脸，看山谷下的田庄民房，现在男的又在看飘在头顶上的炊烟——想必是十分饥饿了吧？**caught up with**：追上。男的走路已如此费

Man and Woman | 285

力，可是女的走路还要慢，好容易才把他追上。

[10]

He opened his mouth to say something, but his throat became choked and no words came. He looked at the house, with its worn doorstep and curtain-filled windows and its smoke-filled chimney, and he did not feel like a stranger in a strange country as long as he kept his eyes upon those things.

[注]

这一段又是描写那男人的视觉，他的情感也轻轻地提了一笔。

choked（过去分词）：塞住。

doorstep：台阶。**worn**：磨旧了的。**curtain-filled**：窗帘拉满的。

这些东西使他联想起自己的家，他的眼睛老看着这些东西，他就不觉得是"身在异乡为异客"了。

[11]

Ruth went through the gate, and around the side of the house, and stopped at the kitchen door. She looked behind her and saw Ring coming across the yard from the road.

Someone was watching them from behind a curtain at the window.

[注]

gate：园门，和屋子不相联属的。**kitchen door**：厨房门，后门。

someone：本文的第三个人物，可是此人的态度是猜疑的、不友善的、慢客的，此人只是在窗帘后面窥望。那一男一女看见这种举动，怎么会不觉得自己是 strangers in a strange country 呢？

[12]

"Knock," Ring said.

She placed the knuckles of her right hand against the side of the house and rapped on the clapboards until her hand began to hurt.

She turned around and glanced quickly at Ring, and he nodded his head.

Presently the kitchen door opened a few inches and a woman's head could be seen through the crack. She was middle-aged and brown-faced and had a scar on her forehead.

"Go away," she told them.

[注]

rapped：拍击。**clapboards**：木屋墙上的横条木板。

she turned around：他们两人一起赶路，互相关切，女的打门的时候还要转过头来看男的，男的颔首赞可。作者对于这种小地方不肯错过。

presently：不久。**crack**：缝。

go away：疲乏的旅人受到逐客令。作者尽量避免情感的描写，可是读者自然而然地对于小说中一男一女的命运发生关切之感。屋中人的态度想必很不客气，这里短短两个词，不借任何描写，已使读者如闻其声，如见其人了。

[13]

"We won't bother you," Ruth said as quickly as she could. "All we wanted was to ask you if you could give us a little something to eat. Just a potato, if you have any, or bread, or something."

"I don't know what you are doing, here," the woman said. "I don't like to have strange people around my house."

She almost closed the door, but in a moment the crack widened, and her face could be seen once more.

"I'll feed the girl," she said finally, "but I can't let the man have anything. I don't have enough for both of you, anyway."

[注]

bother you：麻烦你。

all we wanted：我们所需要的（不过是）。这句话的动词都用过去时，表示她拍墙叫门时候所需要的是什么东西。

I can't let the man have anything：孤身男女清晨在山野间赶路，是惹人疑心的，屋中人不肯施舍给那男的，不是没有道理。又从 I'll feed the girl 一句看来，那个女人年龄想必很轻。

[14]

Ruth turned quickly around, her heels digging into the sandy earth. She looked at Ring. He nodded his head eagerly.

He could see the word forming on her lips even though lie could not hear it. She shook her head.

Ring went several steps toward her.

"We'll try somewhere else," she said.

"No," he said. "You go in and eat what she'll give you. I'll try the next house we come to."

She still did not wish to go into the house without him. The woman opened the door a foot or more, and waked for her to come up the steps.

Ring sat down on a bench under a tree.

"I'm going to sit here and wait until you go in and get something to eat for yourself," he said.

[注]

digging：转身时脚后跟（heels）在沙土上钻了一下。

the word：大约是"no"。**forming on her lips**：嘴唇已经圆起来，预备说这个词了。**she shook her head**：又是简单的叙述，可是包含很深的情感：何忍自己得食，而见那男人被摈诸门外呢？她预备到别家人家去试试。**opened the door a foot or more**：呼应前面的 opened a few inches。

[15]

Ruth went up the steps slowly to the porch and entered the door. When she was inside, the woman pointed out a chair by a table, and Ruth sat down.

There were potatoes, warmed over from the night before, and cold biscuits. These were put on the table, on front of her, and then the woman poured a cup of hot coffee and set it beside the plate.

Ruth began to eat as quickly as she could, sipping the hot black coffee and chewing the potatoes and bread while the brown-faced woman stood behind her at the door, where she could watch Ring and her by turns.

Twice Ruth managed to slip pieces of bread into her blouse, and finally she got half a potato into the pocket of her skirt. The woman eyed her suspiciously when she was not watching Ring in the yard outside.

[注]

steps：台阶。**porch**：门的入口处，上面通常有屋檐盖住。

warmed over：昨夜煮的马铃薯，早晨再热一次。

sipping：啜饮。**bread**：恐怕不是前面的 biscuits。**watch**：监视。**by turns**：轮流地。一下子看着屋内的女人，一下子看着屋外的男人。

managed：设法。**slip**：滑下去。轻轻地放进去，由面包自动落下。**blouse**：女装的上衣，腰间有带拴住，东西放在里面，不会掉出来的。blouse 和 skirt 是西洋女子普通的服装。这个女人的服装本文开始时并未描写，这里假如她不演出一幕"陆郎怀橘"的故事，作者恐怕仍旧要略而不提的。

eyed 这个词当动词用，有"监视"或"冷眼旁观"的意思。**suspiciously**：猜疑地，用猜疑的眼光。

[16]

"Going far?" the woman asked.

"Yes," Ruth answered.

"Come far?" the woman asked.

"Yes," Ruth said.

"Who is that man with you?"

"He's my husband," Ruth told her.

The woman looked out into the yard again, then back at Ruth. She did not say anything more for a while.

[注]

很简洁的一段对白。可是屋主人的猜疑，乞食女人的无意对答，已跃然纸上。如多用文字描写，恐怕反而要减少这场面的紧张和尴尬了。

本文一开始就描写那一男一女的视线，现在这几段所着力描写的也是那屋主人的眼光，她来回地看那一男一女。

[17]

　　Ruth tried to put another piece of potato into her skirt pocket, but by then the woman was watching her more closely than ever.

　　"I don't believe he is your husband," the woman said.

　　"Well," Ruth answered, "he is."

　　"I wouldn't call him much of a husband to let you walk through the country begging food like you did just a little while ago."

　　"He's been sick," Ruth said quickly, turning in the chair to face the woman. "He was sick in bed for five weeks before we started out."

　　"Why didn't you stay where you were, instead of making tramps out of yourselves? Can't he hold a job, or don't he want to work?"

[注]

　　by then 的 by = at or before(a specified limit)。by now 与 by then 的用法很常见，now 或 then 在这里是名词，作宾语用。单用 then，只表示"那时"，by then 有双重意思："在那个时候"，或者"甚至在那个时候以前"，Ruth 又要伸手偷马铃薯，可是"到了那个时候"，屋主人监视得更严了。

　　I wouldn't call 比 I will not call 客气，用了 would（虚拟式），态度比较多保留、少武断。**much of a husband**：够得上做丈夫。to let 作形容词用，大约是形容 him。做丈夫的让妻子在山野间走路，登门乞食，还算得上是丈夫吗？

　　like 应作 as。英美人教育程度不够的，说起话来，常用 like 代替 as。did 即 walked through the country begging food。

　　turning in the chair to face the woman：那个女人本来又饥又倦，又要想法偷藏食物，无意多说话。可是现在那男的受到诬蔑，她不得不严辞辩驳，因此她的话说得快了，身子也转过来了，脸也冲着那个多疑的主人。虽然没有用 indignantly 这类的词，其神情已可想而见。

　　stay where you were：相当于"留住在家乡"，但是"以前所住的地方"不一定就是"家乡"：你们为什么不留住在你们的老地方呢？

　　tramps：流浪人。**making tramps out of yourselves**：使自己成为流浪人。instead of 普通英汉词典解作"代替"，但是这一个介词短语的意义很多，在这里的意思约相当于"反而要"，你们为什么"反而要"出来流浪呢？

hold a job：守住一项职业，保持饭碗。**don't**：按照语法规矩，应该说 doesn't。

[18]

Ruth got up, dropping the bread in her hand.

"Thank you for the breakfast," she said. "I am going now."

"If you take my advice," the woman said, "you'll leave that man the first chance you get. If he won't take a job, you'll be a fool…"

"He had a job, but he got sick with a kind of fever."

"I don't believe you. I'd put you down for lying about him."

[注]

dropping the bread in her hand：Ruth 想必是不愿再听那人唠唠叨叨的话，站了起来，拿在手里的面包也掉了下来（本来也许还想多吃一点呢）。

you'll leave that man the first chance you get：一有机会，就同那个男人分手。the first chance 是副词短语，you get 是定语从句，形容 chance。

If he won't take a job：屋主人一口咬定那男人是游手好闲之徒。**fever**：发烧。那个男人的脸容苍白，步履维艰，前文已一再言之，其故为何，现在要逐步地揭穿了。

I'd = I would。**put down** = reckon（认为）。我可要认为你是在替他撒谎。

[19]

Ruth went to the door, opened it herself, and went outside. She turned around on the porch and looked at the woman who had given her something to eat.

"If he was sick in bed, like you said," the woman asked, following her past the door, "why did he get up and start tramping like this with nothing for you and him to eat?"

[注]

opened it herself：来不及等人家来替她开门了。

turned around…and looked at her：既然她想赶快夺门而出，不愿再多停留，为什么又要转过身来，岂是言有未尽吗?

like you said 应作 as you said。屋主人还要追出来，问这么一句话。这个闷葫芦非打破不可。套一句金圣叹批《水浒》的笔法:"我亦欲问。"

[20]

Ruth saw Ring sitting on the bench under the tree, and she was not going to answer the woman, but she could not keep from saying something.

"The reason we started out walking like this was because my sister wrote and told me that our baby had died. When my husband first got sick, I sent the baby to my sister's. Now we're going to see the grave where she's buried."

[注]

not going to answer the woman:那个男的想必是不堪饥饿了,何况他们赶路要紧,那种唠唠叨叨的话何必置答,但是话到嘴边,不说又不能(could not keep from…)。

we started out walking like this 为名词性从句,前面省掉一个连接词 why。

to my sister's = to my sister's house。这种用法很常见,如"在王先生家里",英文单说"at Mr. Wang's"即可。

这一男一女有这么一段悲惨的经历,可是作者描写时仍旧不带半点情感,文字简单之至,"赤裸裸"的事实就有感动人的力量,何必多说伤感的话呢?

where she's buried:照一般习惯,baby 的代词可用 it,但是那是不知婴孩是男是女时才用。身为父母者,一定知道自己的孩子是男是女的,所以这里仍用 she。

[21]

She ran down the steps and walked across the yard as rapidly as she could. When she reached the corner of the house, Ring got up and followed her to the road. Neither of them said anything, but she could not keep from looking back at the house, where the woman was watching them through the crack in the door.

After they had gone a hundred feet or more, Ruth unfastened her blouse and pulled out the pieces of bread she had carried there. Ring took them from her without a word. When he had eaten all there was, she gave him the potato. He ate it hungrily, talking to her with his eyes while he chewed and swallowed.

[注]

through the crack in the door：从门板的裂缝里（张望）。

unfastened：解开，打开。走了一百多英尺之后，屋中人应该看不见他们的行动了，她才把"私货"拿出来。

all there was 的 there was 是定语从句，关系代词 that 省掉：所有的东西，私藏面包的全部。

talking to her with his eyes：用眼睛说话，嘴是忙不过来了。**hungrily**：很传神的副词，可解作"狼吞虎咽状地"。

[22]

They had walked for nearly half an hour before either of them spoke again.

"She was a mean old woman," Ruth said. "If it hadn't been for that food, I'd have got up and left before I ate what she gave me."

Ring did not say anything for a long time.

Ruth choked back a sob.

"How much farther is it, Ring?"

"About thirty or forty miles."

"Will we get there tomorrow?"

He shook his head.

"The day after?"

"I don't know."

[注]

mean 原意为"卑鄙，小气"，这里可解作"可恶"。**I'd** = I would。

choked back a sob：想哭出来，可是用力忍住了。

[23]

"Maybe if we get a ride, we might get there tonight?" she asked, unable to hold back any longer the sobs that choked her throat and breast.

"Yes," he said, "If we could get a ride, we would get there a lot sooner."

He turned his head and glanced down the road behind them, but there was nothing in sight. Then he looked down at the ground he was walking on, counting the steps he took with his right foot, and then his left.

[注]

get a ride：有便车坐。

choked：此词与上段的 choked 意义略有不同。这里解作"塞住"。

glanced down the road behind them：看看后面有没有车子来，可以顺便搭乘的。

he was walking on：定语从句。

counting the steps：两人重上征程。长途漫漫，这样一步一步地数着走，哪一天才走得到呢？

A Pretty Girl
美丽的姑娘

Max Beerbohm（1872—1956）

  马克斯·比尔博姆出生于维多利亚女王统治下的英国，逝于意大利。比氏寿登耄耋，久无作品问世，很多读者以为他早已不在人世了。事实上，按他的文章风格和生活趣味来说，他和19世纪末叶所谓唯美主义作家如王尔德等比较接近，同我们这一代确是疏远了。他的文章，大抵近乎"游戏人间"一路，俏皮、幽默、机智，但不一定深刻。他有过人的聪明，在文字修饰上所用的功夫却极大，作品数量不多，大多是经过精心雕琢之作。

  比氏的小品文最有名，但他也写小说。这里所选的几段采自他的长篇小说 *Zuleika Dobson* 的第二章。*Zuleika Dobson* 是一部胡闹的讽刺小说，Zuleika 是个十分美丽的姑娘，她在牛津住了一个时候，牛津的大学生都被她弄得神魂颠倒，但是谁也得不到她的青睐，结果大家跳河自杀，集体殉情以死！学生都死完了，牛津大学也开不下去了。

[1]

  She was a nymph to whom men's admiration was the greater part of life. By day, whenever she went into the streets, she was conscious that no man passed her without a stare; and this consciousness gave a sharp zest to her outings. Sometimes she was followed to her door — crude flattery which she was too innocent to fear. Even when she went into the haberdasher's to make some little purchase of tape or riband, or into the grocer's — for she was an epicure in her humble way — to buy a tin of meat for her supper, the homage of the young men behind the counter did flatter and exhilarate her.

[注]

nymph：希腊神话中的仙女，常借用作"年轻貌美的女子"。

men's admiration：男人的爱慕。这种女子，生活中主要的事情（greater part），就是给男人爱慕。

no man passed her without a stare：路人看见她，都要张大眼，对她注视。

no ... without：两重否定，等于一重肯定。

this consciousness 照应前面的 was conscious。她知道人家都要看她。出门游散（outings）时，分外有劲。**zest**：（很浓的）兴味。

she was followed：从这一句里，可以看出被动语态胜过主动语态的地方。"她被跟随"——（by whom）谁在跟？这可不必说了，总是街上那些男子。**crude flattery**：这一个短语用得很见功夫。男人觉得女人长得美，这是一种恭维（flattery），但是用眼睛看看，或嘴上赞美足矣。那种人尾随不舍，一直盯到她的家门，未免显得粗野（crude）。**innocent**：盯梢的人可能不怀好意，但是小姐一派天真，只引以为得意，并不觉得恐惧。

haberdasher：贩卖针线等小装饰品的杂货商。他的"店"，英文里不用说，只要加 apostrophe s ('s) 即可。同样的，贩卖食品的杂货商是grocer，这一种店就是the grocer's。**tape**：布带。**riband**：是ribbon（丝带）较古的拼法。**to make some purchase of**：这一个短语相当古雅，我们普通说话作文，只要用to buy some (tape or ribbon) 就够了。

epicure：讲究饮食的人。**in her humble way**：那个时候，她并没有钱，可是在她的经济情况许可的范围之内，她还是很讲究的。

young men behind the counter：柜台后面的青年人；伙计。**homage**：大恭敬。**exhilarate**：使（她）高兴。

[2]

As the homage of men became for her, more and more, a matter of course, the more subtly necessary was it to her happiness. The more she won of it, the more she treasured it. She was alone in the world, and it saved her from any moment of regret that she had neither home nor friends. For her the streets that lay around her had no squalor, since she paced them always in the gold nimbus of her fascinations. Her bedroom seemed not mean nor lonely to her, since the little square of glass, nailed above the wash-stand, was ever there to reflect her face. Thereinto, indeed, she was ever peering. She would smile, frown, pout, languish — let all the emotions hover upon her face; and always she seemed to herself lovelier than she had ever been.

[注]

a matter of course：当然之事，没有什么稀罕的了。第一句中的主句的主语置于动词之后，正当的次序是it (= the homage) was necessary to her happiness。the more 的the是副词，有"因此"(on that account) 之意。这种用法很常见，如nevertheless即为never the less (并不因此减少) 三词合成的。**subtly**：subtle的副词形式，解作"微妙的，神秘的，不可捉摸的"。她的快乐，更不可思议地有赖于男人对她的恭敬了。

第二句的 **the more ... the more** 也是常见的句法结构，第一个 the = in whatever degree；第二个 the = in that degree。那边增加，这边也同样地增加。of it 连前面的 The more, it 代替 the homage，她所得到的恭敬愈多，她对于这种恭敬也愈为珍视。

it saved 的 it 仍是代替 the homage。有了男人献殷勤，她也用不着为身世兴悲了。

squalor：污秽（此词的形容词是 squalid, squalid 比 dirty 更多"未经扫除，无人清理"之意）。**paced**(及物动词)：走过。**paced them** = paced the streets。**nimbus**：(神佛头上的) 光轮。她走在街上，遍体似有彩云环绕，令人目移神夺（fascinations），她自己因此也看不出街上的污秽了。

mean：寒酸相。她的卧室本来是寒酸而又寂寞的，但是现在看来却并不如此，因为洗脸架子上面，钉了一面方镜子，常得美人照看，镜中玉容，就足使陋室生春了。

thereinto = into that (glass)。**indeed**：说真的。indeed 这个词很常见，但是不易应用。这里大约是怕读者不相信上面一句所说的 the glass was ever there to reflect her face, 特再补充说明一句："这是真的，"这位小姐老是在照（peer into）镜子的。ever 本来和 always 一样，解作"无论何时，永远如此"，但是这种副词（另外的例子如 perpetually, constantly 等）倘若和进行式动词一起用，那就表示"常常，老是这么做"了。**she ever peered into the glass**：是说不通的，因为一个人不可能什么事情不做,"永远"看着镜子的。**she was ever peering**:表示她"常常"这么做,现在看一下,过一会又看一下,再过一会又看一下。

peer解作"凝视",意义大致同gaze相仿,但gaze常常指看的人因爱慕而看得出神,peer则指仔细地看,或吃力地看,或带着好奇心地看,或看的人和所看的东西中间隔了一层什么东西。人和镜中的影像之间隔了一层玻璃,用peer是很合适的。

frown:皱眉。**pout**:撅嘴。**languish**:做出娇憨之态。这些动词前面的助动词would表示"习惯"。

let = she would let。hover本指鸟类不振翼远飞,而在某一地点拍翅盘旋;或云雾等浮挂在一个地方。现在她故意对镜子做出各种"表情",那些情感也好像在她脸上低回飞翔。

lovelier:每对镜子看一次,总觉得自己比以前更可爱了,注意时态seemed和had been之间的先后关系。

[3]

Yet was there nothing Narcissine in her spirit. Her love for her own image was not cold aestheticism. She valued that image not for its own sake, but for the sake of the glory it always won for her.

[注]

yet was there nothing = yet there was nothing。Narcissine是Narcissus的形容词。Narcissus:水仙花。据希腊神话,此花原是一美少年,见水中自身倒影而悦之,顾影自怜,憔悴不堪,天神将他化身为花,俾得永远临泉自照也。变态心理学中有一种病,叫作Narcissism,这位小姐可没有这种"自恋"的病。

aestheticism:唯美主义。前面所以加形容词cold者,表示唯美主义不注重情感;看见美的东西心里用不着激动,美是应该冷静地欣赏的。

for its own sake:只因为这个影子的美,才觉得它宝贵,此外别无其他情感掺杂在内。这位小姐并不如此。她长得美,博得无数男人的追求,她为了这种"光荣",才对于镜子里自己的影子看个不厌的。it always own for her是定语从句。

[4]

Though Zuleika bad never given her heart, strong in her were the desire and the need that it should be given. Whithersoever she had fared, she had seen nothing but youths fatuously prostrate to her — not one upright figure which she could respect. There were the middle-aged men, the old men, who did not bow down to her; but from middle-age, as from eld, she had a sanguine aversion. She could love none but a youth. Nor could she love one who fell prone before her. And before her all youths always did fall prone. She was an empress, and all youths were her slaves. Their bondage delighted her, as I have said. But no empress who has any pride can adore one of her slaves. Whom, then, could proud Zuleika adore?

[注]

given her heart：把心送人，陷入情网。第一句中主句又是倒装的，动词 were 在前，主语 the desire and the need 在后。这许多男人爱慕她，她没有爱慕过任何男人，可是她很想恋爱，也很需要恋爱。**it (the heart) should be given**：她的心该"奉献给"一个男人。

whithersoever she had fared：她不论走到哪里。**fare** = go，这是比较古雅的字眼。**fatuously**：痴呆地。**prostrate**：匍匐在地。事实上当然不一定有人向她三跪九叩首，这不过引申前面的 homage（青年男子都对她臣服）而已。

one upright figure：一个站直的身躯。有自尊心不向她表示爱慕的男人，这种人才是使她尊敬的。

bow down：还是引申 homage 的意思。

eld = old age，这是个古词。我们现在只有 elder 和 eldest 这两个形容词，名词 eld 很少有人用了。sanguine 在这里应该解作"热忱的"（warm or ardent），也即是 strong。

aversion 连前面的两个 from (from middle-age, from eld)，中年人、老年人对她不一定"服贴"，但她也很讨厌中年人、老年人。中年人、老年人她不要，青年人毫无骨气，对她恭而敬之，俯首贴耳，这种人她也是不能 (nor could) 爱的。prone 是形容词，解作"俯伏的"，是主语补语，形容 who。fall prone 二词常连用，是习语。

did fall prone 的 did 用以加强语气。

bondage：奴役。

but no empress 一句，用现在时态，表示一般情形。**adore**：敬爱，崇拜。love 的含义广泛，adore 一定是一种很崇高的情感。

[5]

It was a question which sometimes troubled her.

To be able to love once — would not that be better than all the homage in the world? But would she ever meet whom, looking up to him, she could love — she, the omnisubjugant? Would she ever, ever meet him?

[注]

她老是受人家的爱，她到底还能不能爱别人呢？不一定见了男人就爱，只要她能爱一个男人，只要她能主动地爱一次——这不是比全世界的恭敬都集中在她一人身上还要强吗？**to be able to love once**：是不定式短语，作名词用。这句的主语 that，就是代替这个不定式短语（infinitive phrase）的。

后面一句的语法结构，也是比较古的用法。照现在通用说法，应该说 But would she ever meet the man whom 但是按古时的用法，the man 这个先行词（antecedent）是可以省掉的。**looking up to him** 是 participial phrase，形容从句中的主语 she。**looking up**：她要"仰首"才看见他，足见这个男人是不向她俯首称臣的。

she, the omnisubjugant：she 是重复 she could love 中的 she。omnisubjugant 是个罕见的词，词典里都不一定查得到，但意义不难了解。omni 是个前缀，表示"全体"（如 omnipotent, omniscient 等，这些词的解释请查词典）。subjugant 是 subjugate（征服）的形容词形式，ant 是个后缀，表示 present participle 的意思（如 defiant, pliant 等）连在一起，这个词的解释应作"征服一切的"。

最后一句 ever 重复地用，非但是为了音调好听，而且也加强情感上绝望的意义。这样一个男人，"这一辈子"还找得到吗？

[6]

It was when she wondered thus, that the wistfulness came into her eyes. Even now, as she sat by the window, that shadow returned to them.

[注]

wistfulness：一种"若有所思"的神态。她心里思量，能不能找到一位如意郎君的时候，眼睛里就露出这种表情了。这种表情不是一种快乐的表情，它像一种"阴影"。现在她凭窗闲坐，这阴影又回到她眼睛里来了。

Her Graduation Day
毕业的那一天

Nancy G. Chaikin

本文作者南希·蔡金系美国女作家，1945 年毕业于密歇根大学。她的作品不多，但是她的短篇小说曾两度选入《美国短篇小说佳作选》。本文原题"*Bachelor of Arts*"，刊载于 The Best American Short Stories 1955，长达六七千字，这里所选的只是短短的几段。蔡金的作风，大抵属于"婉约"一派，本文描写一个大学女生毕业那一天的种种心理变化，细腻熨贴，丝丝入扣。这一派作家可以说都是私淑 Henry James 的。

[1]

In the morning, with the sun slanting across the floor of her room, she put on her cap and gown and stood before the mirror looking at herself, pleased with how right they looked on her. She could never remember which way the tassel went, but she'd see when she got down to the procession. Now she would only have to come back to this room to collect her bags — they were all packed — and they stood alone in the middle of the floor of the half empty room.

[注]

slanting：斜（照），斜（射）。此词为动词的分词形式。

cap and gown：学士帽与学士服。美国大学生通常只在举行毕业典礼那天，才戴方帽子，穿学士袍。

how right they looked on her：她穿戴上(on her)这种衣帽，看起来是多么的合适。名词性从句，作 with 的宾语（她看了心里很高兴）。

the tassel：流苏。学士帽顶上的那束丝穗，该披（went）在左边，还是右边呢？别人也许指教过她，但是她是永远记不得的。

she'd see = she would see. **the procession**：行列，由校长、教授所率领的毕业生行列。他们排队进入大礼堂，是毕业仪式的一部分。流苏管它偏左还是偏右，她走到队伍里，看见别人的样式，自己也就知道了。

to collect her bags：检取行李。collect 有"一件一件捡起来,归聚在一处"之意。**bags**：凡是皮包衣箱等，都可称为 bags。**packed**：装好，理好。

[2]

She thought of calling the Union, where her parents had presumably spent the night after arriving very late, but decided, instead, to go directly over there and meet them for breakfast.

[注]

calling：打电话。**the Union**：即下文的 the Union Building。美国大学校园里有很多这样一座座大楼，大楼里有餐厅，有各种社交娱乐设备，也有旅馆房间。来参观毕业典礼的学生家长和校友大多借住在里面。Union 是 Students Union 的简称。

presumably：可以这么假定。**arriving very late**：晚上到得太晚，来不及和女儿见面，直接到"招待所"去投宿了。**instead**：不打电话了。

[3]

She knew they would expect her to be excited and pleased and loving, that they would not understand She was their only child — the next best thing to a son; if she could not be a professional she could at least be a Bachelor of Arts. They were unbearably proud of her, and she was embarrassed by their open, unashamed pride, their overstated affection, their naive conviction that in giving her a college education they had attained the peak of parental obligation.

Instead, she thought sadly, they had driven her further and further from them — with their strange emotional way of life, their pathetic ignorance of everything she had come to love.

[注]

这一段描写父母与女儿间心理上的距离。父母看见女儿大学毕业，一定非常高兴；可是女儿自己前途茫茫，心事重重（一方面舍不得离开学校，一方面回到家里又怎么样？）实在提不起兴致，可是又不得不陪着父母高兴。父母和女儿之间竟然还有这种隔膜吗？这种隔膜的确是存在的，这就是"现实"，小说家假如要描写现实，一定不会忽略这种现象的。

loving：（看见父母）表示亲热。她知道在她父母意料之中，她一定是这样高兴的；她知道父母是不会了解的（understand 这里作不及物动词用）。按用法习惯，假如有一个以上的名词性从句作为宾语之用，第一个从句的连接词 that 可以省掉，但是第二个第三个名词性从句一定要用连接词 that。在这里，She knew 后面有两个名词性从句，第一个名词性从句 they would expect ... 前面没有 that，但是第二个名词性从句 they would not understand 前面就有 that。第一个从句没有 that，读者不难判知它的语法地位；假如第二个从句没有 that，读者怎么知道它是 knew 的宾语呢？

the next best thing to a son：她是独生女儿，在她父母心目之中，女儿虽然比不上儿子，但是比儿子也仅差一级，儿子算是 the best thing，女儿就算是 the next best thing 了，to a son 的 to 是连 next 的。

a professional：专门职业人才。美国的父母大多希望儿子成为一专门职业人才（enter a profession），如医生、律师、教授、牧师等。女儿虽然成不了专门职业人才，她至少也可以成为一个文学士（B.A.），父母也可以聊以自慰了。

unbearably：父母引女儿以自豪，但是女儿忍受不了。

open, unashamed pride：父母讲起女儿来，其骄傲自得之状，溢于辞表（open），不知害羞为何物。

overstated affection：父母爱子女，本出天性，但是爱(affection)不必放在嘴上讲，这两位父母把爱说得有点肉麻了。

naive conviction：天真的想法（信念）。他们以为把女儿栽培到大学毕业，已经尽了最大的责任——达到尽父母之责（parental obligation）的最高峰。他们这种态度是使她很窘迫难受（embarrassed）的。

she thought sadly：是插入的说明（parenthetic），在本句语法结构中没有地位。

instead：此词在本段中第二次出现。这里的意思大约是，她的父母"非但没有"尽父母的责任，反而使她疏远起来了。他们把她"赶得愈来愈远"。

父母的骄傲得意，他们的过分亲爱，这就是他们的以情感为主的"奇怪的生活方式"。**pathetic**：可怜的。**everything she had come to love**：文学、思想、美术等，她本来也不一定能欣赏，进了大学后，她就喜欢这些东西了。had come to 表示今昔之间的变迁。可是这些东西，她父母可怜地仍是一无所知。with their strange... 是形容词短语，形容前面的 them。

[4]

She walked slowly over to the Union Building, feeling the unfamiliar folds of the black robe about her legs, the pressure of the four-cornered hat upon her brow. And they were there in the lobby of the tall white building, huddled close to one another on a leather sofa, watching anxiously for her through the crowds of noisy alumni and polished, expectant looking fathers and mothers, and eager black-gowned graduates.

[注]

unfamiliar：不习惯的。学士服下半截有好多道"褶子"，包在腿部周围（about her legs），走起路来，觉得很不习惯。**four-cornered hat**：方帽子。

lobby：前厅。huddled 是过去分词，形容主语 they：父母二人正紧紧（close）地依偎着，坐在皮沙发上，在人群之中，焦急地张望着他们的女儿。alumni 是 alumnus（校友）的复数形式。返校参观毕业典礼的校友，声音很吵闹。**polished, expectant looking fathers and mothers**：家长们服装很整洁，神态上若有所待。**eager black-gowned graduates**：毕业生穿着黑袍，亟盼参加典礼。

[5]

When they saw her, they smiled broadly, looking slowly down her, from the stiff top of her cap with its ridiculous displaced tassel, to her shoes, just showing from beneath the gown. Then they were kissing her and saying the things she had known they would say.

[注]

smiled broadly：虽然是微笑，可是笑得很明显，"笑容可掬"。英文也有 a broad smile 这样的习语。

looking slowly down her：慢慢地把她从头到脚地看（这里是从头上的帽子看到脚下的鞋子）。注意：looking down her 和 looking down upon her（瞧不起）不同。 **stiff**：僵硬的。**ridiculous**：可笑的。**displaced tassel**：放错了地方的丝穗。**showing**：学士服长可掩足，鞋子只露出一点来。**beneath the gown** 是个介词短语，但是这个短语又是介词 from 的宾语（从学士服下面显露出来）。这种用法很普通，如 The cat came out from under the table。

they were kissing her（动词进行式，使动作显得特别生动）：他们现在吻起她来了。

the things she had known they would say：她早知道他们会说出来的那些话。

本文的句子大多拖得很长，该断的地方不断，再加上许多词去补充说明前面的话。如本段第一句：they smiled broadly，照语法结构，句子断于 broadly 亦无不可，但作者在后面加上 looking... 这么一个分词短语，到 to her shoes，句子也可停住了，但作者另加 just showing... 这么另外一个分词短语。这种句法，修辞学上称为"松散句"（loose sentence）善用 loose sentence 者，修饰描写，不厌其详，必定使句子内容更为丰富，而且句子尾巴拖得很长，欲尽不尽，回味无穷。"松散句"读来有种懒洋洋的感觉，好处是宽舒平易，和"戛然而止"斩钉截铁式的"尾重句"（periodic sentence）不同。本文这位小姐百无聊赖，面临喜事而兴趣索然，多用"松散句"，和全篇小说的情调也是很调和。

[6]

They had their breakfast in the big oak-paneled dining room of the Union, but no one was very hungry. Her parents simply kept shaking their heads and looking curiously, proudly, about the big room. And for Anne, she did not know what there was for her to say to her parents — but they did a good deal of talking themselves.

[注]

oak-paneled：不是普通泥灰墙，墙上精镶橡木板。很讲究的房间，才有这种装饰。

no one was very hungry：真不饿乎？抑因精神兴奋而无暇进食乎？或因心事重重而食不下咽乎？

kept shaking their heads：不断地摇头（叹为观止的神情）。

the big room：大学招待所竟有如此富丽堂皇的餐厅，而女儿就在这所大学毕业，父母看来，既觉得新奇，又觉得得意。**what there was**："有"什么话可说的。

did a good deal of talking：女儿虽不开口，他们自己却说了很多话。themselves 用以加强主语 they。

[7]

"You know, Anne, what a great day this is for us — our own daughter graduating. We want you to know how proud it is for us." Her father laid his cool, old hand over her perspiring one, then passed it swiftly, lightly over her cheek.

"Yes, Pa, I know, *I* know."

[注]

how proud it is for us：proud 在这里解作"值得骄傲的"。

her perspiring one：她的出汗的手。passed it 中的 it 代替 his hand。pass the hand over 有"抚摸"之意。

第二个 I know 的 I 印作斜体，表示需重读，显出不耐烦的语气。

[8]

She left them there, indicating the building to which they were to go and arranging to meet them again at the Union for lunch. So she stood in line with the others, under the blazing sun, her head throbbing beneath the cap — and watched their figures moving toward the doorway of Blane Auditorium. Then the procession started and she felt nothing except the burning of the sun through her gown, the hot pavement through the soles of her thin summer shoes.

[注]

indicating：用手指点。**the building**：即大礼堂。**arranging**：约定。

stood in line：排队。**blazing sun**：火热的太阳。**throbbing**：(胸口，太阳穴等处)反常的、剧烈的跳动。

their figures：父母的身影。**Blane Auditorium**：这座大礼堂大约是纪念一个叫做 Blane 的人的。

pavement：不一定是马路边上的人行道，这里只是指铺过(水泥、柏油或石板等)的路。**soles**：鞋底。队伍行进时，除了身上脚下热以外，别的什么都感觉不到。

[9]

She was grateful that, in the huge auditorium, with the visitors all sitting behind the graduates, she could not see the faces of her parents or hear their murmured wonder and pride when the honors were announced.

[注]

grateful：来宾都坐在毕业生的后面，她因此看不见父母的脸，听不到他们低声赞叹（wonder）和得意的话，心里好受得多。她对于这样的安排，心里是感激的。

when the honors were announced：发表优秀学生名单时。她自己也在优秀之列，可是她自己并不觉得得意，她也不愿意看见父母得意的样子。**honors**：优异的学业成绩。此词此义永远是用复数形式的。

[10]

Then, at last, they were singing the Alma Mater — and she sobbed as if she were a slobbering old alumnus at a reunion dinner who had too much to drink.

[注]

they：泛指全体师生来宾。**the Alma Mater**：拉丁文原义是"鞠我育我的母亲"，转作"母校"。这里是"校歌"。

sobbed：啜泣。**slobbering**：唾液直流或语无伦次的。**reunion**：校友返校重聚。**drink**：专指"喝酒"而言。老校友重聚时，饮酒过多，感怀今昔，鲜有不怆然涕下者，现在这位小姐忽然也像这种人一样，呜咽地哭起来了。

Emergency Landing
紧急着陆

John Cheever（1912—1982）

本文原题"The Country Husband"是一篇很长的短篇小说，和前面的"Bachelor of Arts"一样，原载《一九五五年美国短篇小说佳作选》。作者约翰·奇弗是美国颇享盛名的短篇小说作家，美国马萨诸塞州人。

本文主要描写一个乡村大夫的各种人生问题以及夫妇之间的关系。这里所选的几段，是全文的开头，读者拿它当作普通叙事文读可也。

[1]

The airplane from Minneapolis in which Francis Weed was travelling East ran into heavy weather. The sky had been a hazy blue, with the clouds below the plane lying so close together that nothing could be seen of the earth. Then mist began to form outside the windows, and they flew into a white cloud of such density that it reflected the exhaust fires. The color of the cloud darkened to gray, and the plane began to rock.

[注]

Minneapolis：美国中西部明尼苏达州的一个大城市。**East**：美国的东部，这里用作副词，等于 eastward。**heavy weather**：阴沉沉的天气，恶劣气候。

the sky had been：注意动词时态。过去完成时表示此事已成"过去"。**hazy**："雾霾"的形容词形式。

mist：雾气比 haze 更进一层。hazy 不过表示天气不够清明，视野不够远。

they flew 中的 they 泛无所指（语法家是不赞成这种用法的），大约是代表这群旅客。

density：密度。**exhaust fires**：飞机后面排气管 exhaust pipe 里所喷出来的火。这种火旅客平常是看不见的，但是现在白云厚密，排气不甚舒畅，把火光反射回来，旅客也可以看见云中的隐隐红光了。exhaust 在这里是名词，解作"排泄"，转作形容词用。**rock**：摇摆。

[2]

Francis had been in heavy weather before, but had never been shaken up so much. The man in the seat beside him pulled a flask out of his pocket and took a drink. Francis smiled at his neighbor, but the man looked away; he wasn't sharing his painkiller with anyone.

[注]

flask：酒瓶。**sharing**：与人共享。**painkiller**：本解作"止痛剂"。这里是酒或解忧剂。

[3]

The plane had begun to drop and flounder wildly. A child was crying. The air in the cabin was overheated and stale, and Francis' left foot went to sleep. He read a little from a paper book that he had bought at the airport, but the violence of the storm divided his attention.

[注]

drop：往下落。**flounder**：颠簸。**cabin**：舱房。**stale**：混浊。**went to sleep**：恐怕是"麻木"的意思。

a child was crying：短句子，但有此一句增加了紧张的气氛，文章就特别有神。

a paper book：纸面小书。**divided his attention**：分散他的注意力。

[4]

It was black outside the ports. The exhaust fires blazed and shed sparks in the dark, and, inside, the shaded lights, the stuffiness, and the window curtains gave the cabin an atmosphere of intense and misplaced domesticity. Then the lights flickered and went out. "You know what I've always wanted to do?" the man beside Francis said suddenly. "I've always wanted to buy a farm in New Hampshire and raise beef cattle."

[注]

ports：窗洞。port 或 porthole 本来是船上的窗洞，这里借作飞机上的窗洞。

blazed：发强烈的火光。**shed sparks**：发火花。shed 是过去时。**shaded lights**：暗淡的灯光。shaded 可能解作"有灯罩的"，但飞机上的灯，据我所知，并无灯罩。**stuffiness**：闷气。**domesticity**：家庭风光。飞机上本来是地方宽畅，空气散漫，现在在昏暗的灯光之下，窗幔都拉上（文中未明言，但如未拉严实，这里不必特别提出 window curtains 二词），空气混浊，不像在空中旅行，反而有一种强烈（intense）的家庭气氛（atmosphere），可惜这种气氛是放错地方了（misplaced）。

flickered：闪动一下。**went out**：熄灭。

the man beside Francis：就是喝酒的那个人。**New Hampshire**：美国东北部州名，新罕布什尔。**raise**：饲养。**beef cattle**：供食用之牛。与"供取乳之牛"（dairy cattle）不同。

灯光忽灭，危机将临，机上人士自必紧张万分，可是作者于百忙中偏来此闲笔。一个取瓶独饮之人，忽然讲起他生平志愿，乃是退隐农场，畜牧为生。如今飞机安危莫卜，万一因失事丧生，则平生志愿，无从实现，岂非抱恨终身？借这两句淡淡的话，作者明白表示：机上乘客已经意识到他们面临生死关头了。

[5]

The stewardess announced that they were going to make an emergency landing. All but the child saw in their minds the spreading wings of the Angel of Death. The pilot could be heard singing faintly, "I've got sixpence, jolly, jolly sixpence. I've got sixpence to last me all my life..." There was no other sound.

[注]

stewardess：女乘务员，空中小姐。

the child：想必就是刚才哭的那个孩子。小孩不知道死之将临。**the Angel of Death**：中国人好称"死神"，西洋人信基督教者，只相信一神，"死"并不是神。又，angel 可善可恶，魔鬼即 fallen angel 也。中国人一讲到安琪儿，即有美丽温柔的联想，但基督教神学中，angel 的含意甚广。善学英文者，非但把每一个词的意义要弄清楚，而且把每一个词可能引起的联想，都要把握得住。**spreading wings**：安琪儿据说是有翅膀的。

pilot：驾驶员。**jolly**：（俗语）非常之好的。**to last me all my life**：够我用一辈子。

there was no other sound：飞机即将紧急着陆，机上寂无声息，唯有驾驶员唱歌之声。这也是用"闲笔"来反衬紧张之法。作者当然可以插写机上各人紧张之状，但这样费墨多，而效果恐未必能及这里淡淡的几笔也。

[6]

The loud groaning of the hydraulic valves swallowed up the pilot's song, and there was a shrieking high in the air, like automobile brakes, and the plane hit flat on its belly in a cornfield and shook them so violently that an old man up forward howled, "Me kidneys! Me kidneys!"

[注]

hydraulic valves：液压阀。**groaning**：本来解作"呻吟之声"，这里应该是"沉重的轰隆之声"。**swallowed up**：吞没。**shrieking**：尖声怪叫。**high in the air**：高空中。**cornfield**：玉米田。**up forward**：坐在很远的前排。**me kidneys!**：me 想是 my 之误，说话的老人可能犯了语法错误。他大叫，"我的腰子（快要震碎了）！"

[7]

The stewardess flung open the door, and someone opened an emergency door at the back, letting in the sweet noise of their continuing mortality — the idle splash and smell of a heavy rain. Anxious for their lives, they filed out of the doors and scattered over the cornfield in all directions, praying that the thread would hold. It did. Nothing happened. When it was clear that the plane would not burn or explode, the crew and the stewardess gathered the passengers together and led them to the shelter of a barn. They were not far from Philadelphia, and in a little while a string of taxis took them into the city.

[注]

flung open the door：把门用劲拉开。**emergency door**：紧急时应用之门,太平门。

mortality：这个词在这里应译作"生命",原意是"早晚必死的"。西洋哲学里最有名的三段论法是"凡人必死,苏格拉底是人,苏格拉底必死。""必死"成了人的一种特性了。**continuing mortality**："必然要死"的性质还是继续存在着,那就是说人还没有死,人还活着。**letting in**：让（声音）传进来。noise 就是横线后面的雨声。**sweet**：听见外面雨声,知道自己没有死,这是使得人觉得安慰。

splash：水花四溅之声。**idle**：雨"懒洋洋地"下着？**smell**：splash 和前面的 noise 是同位语。但是乘客在飞机上已经气闷了好久,一旦机门打开,他们一定也会嗅得到雨的气息,这个词放在这里虽然在语法上说不大通（因为 smell 并不和 noise 同位）,但是仍旧是好的描写。

filed out：鱼贯而出。**the thread**：英文有 their life hangs by a thread 这样的习语(生命系于一线)。hold 在这里是不及物动词,解作"维系不断"。旅客从飞机里出来,在玉米田里四散逃命,一面祷告上苍,不要再出乱子。

it did = the thread did hold。

it was clear 中的 it 代替后面的"that"从句。**explode**：爆炸。**the crew**：飞机（或船舶）上工作人员的总称（集合名词）。

shelter：隐蔽。**barn**：在美国是"草料房和马棚"合用的一座大房屋。

Philadelphia：美国东部大城,有名的"费城"。**a string of taxis**：一队出租汽车（想必是航空公司去叫来的）。

Romeo
情圣

Charles Jackson (1903—1968)

 本文作者查尔斯·杰克逊是一个谨慎用心的作家,他在40岁的时候方才出版他的第一部作品,《失去了的周末》(*The Lost Weekend*)。这部描写酒徒心理的小说,至今仍被公认是一部杰出的作品。杰克逊生于美国新泽西州,早年曾因患肺病,在疗养院休养六年之久。杰氏著有长篇小说四种,短篇小说若干篇,他不是一个多产的作家。
 这篇"情圣"选自他的短篇小说集《众生相》(*Earthly Creatures*),原文有很多处描写精彩的地方,因为篇幅所限,不能备录,这是要向读者道歉的。我们在这里所读到的,只是故事的轮廓。故事的主题是一个梦想的幻灭(disillusionment),题目"情圣"是一个"反语"(irony)。

[1]
 As Alice Harvey hung up the receiver, her first thought, luckily, was a practical one: Now I've got to really do something about dinner.

[注]
 receiver:电话听筒。**hung up**:挂好。**luckily**:侥幸地。电话里所听到的是什么消息,读者暂时并不知晓。可以猜得到的是,消息很不平常,引起了那个女

人很多思想；很侥幸的，第一个思想只是一个实际问题的考虑（**a practical one** = a practical thought），并没有牵涉到别的问题，否则的话，她恐怕要顿失常态，连说话的气力都没有的。

I've got to = I have to：不得不。**to really do**：副词放在不定式 to 和 do 的中间，语法家称为分离不定式（split infinitive），引为大忌。事实上，英美人说话作文时，常这么用，这里只是那个女人心里的思想，更不可以谈严格的语法规则了。
dinner：我们可以猜想，电话里所说的大约是有人要来吃晚饭。

[2]

She stepped into the tiny kitchen.

"Gladys," she said, "I hate telling you so late, but Ralph just phoned from uptown that he's bringing somebody home. He's a kind of, well, celebrity. Could you run over to Gristede's and get some steak or something?"

[注]

Gladys：女佣之名。**I hate**：没有早通知你，害得你临时张罗，有道歉之意。**Ralph**：是那个女人的亲人，关系在稍后即有说明。**uptown**：城里地势较高的区域。中文里无相当的字眼，中国人思想里也没有这个概念。普通常以为 downtown 指热闹市区的，但不一定。uptown 也可以很热闹的。up 和 down 犹如火车之上行下行，并无一定标准。

well：说到这里，想不到一个适当的字眼，语气在这里停顿一下。**celebrity**：有名人物。**a kind of celebrity**：可以说相当有名的人物。

could：这样说比用 can 客气，主人对佣人用这种说法，足以表示说话者的修养，无损说话者的尊严，胜过颐指气使的命令句也。

Gristede's：商店名。**steak**：牛排。临时来了客人，菜肴还需添购。

[3]

Back in the living room, she sat on the sofa and lit a cigarette. Perhaps now I can let myself think about it, she thought.

What does a woman do when faced with the prospect of seeing the man she fell in love with more than twenty years ago, fell in love with but never met?

[注]

她的第一个念头只是厨房添菜的问题,现在一个人静静地坐下,想起主要的问题来了。

what does a woman do:动词用现在时,表示一般情形。**prospect**:期待或期待中的事情。这个男人,她二十多年前曾经爱过(爱过,但是没有见过面),现在面临着同他见面的机会,在这种情形之下,做女人的该怎么办呢?

[4]

Ralph had phoned that he'd run into Gavin Douglas and could he bring him home to dinner. She had cried, "*Who* did you say? You can't mean the *actor*!" and he had replied in that infuriating unimaginative way he had, so like his father: "Why can't I mean the actor?" If the prospect of meeting and knowing Gavin Douglas had arisen when she was eighteen, she would have died. Now, after some twenty years, here he was, about to walk into her living room, the dream made flesh ...

[注]

这一段是补叙电话里的话。但是这并不是小说家在这里补充说明,这里仍旧是那个女人的心理活动——她坐在沙发上的回忆。

run into:碰到,不期而遇。**could he bring him home to dinner**:这句话语法有问题,但是为了要模仿打电话的口吻,这样说也未尚不可(按规矩来说,大约应该如此:and had asked whether he could bring him home to dinner)。

the actor:天下同名同姓的很多,Gavin Douglas 是位名伶,但是现在这位 Douglas 可能另有其人。

in that ... way:这几个词说明了 Ralph 的个性,也说明了他父亲(**so like his father**:多么地像他的父亲!)的个性。他们父子二人都是缺乏想象力的(unimaginative),令人气恼(infuriating)。这几个词又暗示:她对于她丈夫,并不完全满意。母亲听到 Gavin Douglas 这个名字,情不自禁,大叫出声,可是儿子不觉察到母亲的音调有异,还侃侃地在电话里答辩:"为什么不可以就是舞台名伶

Douglas 呢?"不能替别人设想,这就是做人缺乏想象力的地方。

if the prospect ... had arisen:这样一个机会假如在她 18 岁时候发生的话,她会死掉的。这是一句很标准的假定句子,请注意动词的形式。prospect 并不解释作"机会",这里为凑中文的方便,勉强译作"机会"。

some twenty years:约摸 20 年。**about to**:将要。**the dream made flesh**:这是一个 nominative absolute phrase。made 是过去分词,flesh 是主语补语:梦想实现,梦中人将以血肉之躯和她相见了。

[5]

She had no idea that anyone she knew would actually know Gavin Douglas, least of all her son. But she didn't need to think twice to know where and how her son had met him.

During the past summer Ralph had had his first job. He had been assistant stage manager at a summer theater on the Cape, as a kind of apprenticeship for the work that he thought he wanted to take up later. He was eighteen but he was interested in the theater as a business. And that is how he must have met Gavin Douglas; the Cape playhouse was famous for its guest-stars, though these were usually tired or retired actors; stars of the past rather than the present. Odd that Ralph had never mentioned him before; but how could he have known what it would mean to his mother? He was too young to appreciate the name and fame of the great matinée idol of twenty and thirty years ago, the star who had been an idol of hers when she was Ralph's age.

[注]

她不知道,任何她所认识的人,会真的认识这位名伶;她尤其不能(least of all)相信,她儿子会认识他。

didn't need to think twice:用不着想两遍,一猜就中。

the past summer:过去的夏季,可能仍旧是今年。**his first job**:美国学生暑假期间多有做短工赚钱的。

assistant stage manager:助理舞台经理。注意:前面不用冠词 the。冠词最为难用,不容易用规则来概括说明。大抵主语补足词(predicate nominative)的名词,前面可以不加 the，如 Wordsworth 的名句：

The Child is father of the Man.

此句中的 father 前面就没有冠词。又，职位前面，常有无需冠词 the 者，如 Queen of England，headmaster of a school 等，这里的 manager 这个词，既然用在动词 had been 之后，是个主语补足词，又是一个职位的名称（经理），不加 the 并不是一种奇怪的用法。但这种用法并不是一定的规则，读者还得于读书时随时留意为要。**summer theater**：美国的夏季是戏剧季节，平常不大演戏的小城小镇，到了夏天就会有剧团租场演出，这种戏院就叫作 summer theater（恐怕是为吸引避暑游客而设的）。

the Cape：cape 原意是海岬。这篇小说的背景大约是美国东北部一带，所指海岬恐怕是马萨诸塞州的避暑胜地 Cape Cod。

a kind of apprenticeship：一种实习。这位青年希望干戏剧活动（the theater），暑假里先实习起来。

guest-stars：客串明星。**tired or retired actors**：厌倦舞台生涯或业已退隐的伶人，广东话有个较能传神的说法，过气老倌（tired 和 retired 两个词连用，很巧妙）。那些小剧院所能请到的大明星，无非是些过时人物。

odd：当系 It was odd 的简略，"这是很奇怪的"。

what it would mean：这个人的名字有什么意义呢？

appreciate：欣赏，了解。**matinée idol**：舞台名伶。**matinée**：原义是"日戏"（下午上演），但 matinée idol 二词连用为一习语，与"日戏"无关，只是"名伶"而已。

文章写到这里，一个是母亲，一个是儿子，已经说得明明白白了。

[6]

Idol was not the word. She had fallen in love with him. And it was not too much to say that she had never really fallen out of love. Her love had never been requited or fulfilled, had never even been communicated. Gavin Douglas had been unaware of her very existence — except as a pair of clapping hands among all those other clapping hands that had become routine to him.

[注]

说他是她的偶像，还不完全对。她不仅是像普通女学生那样崇拜这位大明星而已，她是真"爱"他的。

it was not too much to say：说这样的话也不算过分，事实的确如此。她于20年前陷入情网，迄今犹未自拔。

requited：得到报答。"单恋"是 unrequited love。**fulfilled**：圆满实现。**communicated**：表达出来。这一句里三个动词用得都很有劲。

unaware of her very existence：根本不知这天下有她这么一个女人。very 是形容词。

她虽然盲目痴恋，台上人只知道台下纷纷鼓掌，在掌声雷动之中，有她这么一双手掌，他怎么能分别得出来呢？假如他知道有她这么一个人，也无非是知道台下有一双手掌而已。

other：这个词在逻辑上是说不大通的，可是英文里确有这么个习惯用法。在"别的"许多手掌之中，有她这么一双。既然是"别人的"，她就应该不包括在内，怎么还能用 among 呢？英文另有一个类似的习语 among the rest（这些人或物之中），rest 并不作"其余的"讲。**routine**：习以为常的事实，"家常便饭"。

[7]

She never told her love except to Smith Harvey, the boy she married. She had had to tell someone and it was Smith she told inevitably. Smith was a junior at the university of Rochester when she was a freshman. They had met during her first year and, with no thought of the marriage that was to take place later, had started going together. One Saturday he took her to the matinée at the Lyceum to see the famous Constance Hope and her leading man Gavin Douglas in *Romeo and Juliet*. She had fallen in love at sight with the handsome actor, and through him (though no two men in the world could have been more unlike) with Smith Harvey.

[注]

她私下恋慕之情，不得不对人说，她那时有一个男朋友，很自然地（inevitably）她就对他说了。

junior：三年级学生。**University of Rochester**：纽约州的罗切斯特大学。

started going together：开始一同出去玩。他们以后结为夫妇，但是在开始的时候，他们并没有想到婚姻之事。**take place**：发生或举行。

the Lyceum：戏院名。此词原指雅典一处花园，亚里士多德讲学之所。戏院的 Theater 可以不写出来，但冠词 the 非加不可。

同样的，长江的英文名称，可以不说 River，但是冠词 the 非加不可。Constance Hope 想是比 Douglas 更有名的女伶。**leading man**：男主角。

through him：因为爱舞台上的罗密欧，也连带地爱上了台下的男同学。虽然这两个人绝不相像，天下人之间个性的不同，无有过于他们两个人者。一个是热情奔放的罗密欧，至于另外一个，我们前面已经有了一点认识，他同他的儿子一样，是缺乏想象力的。

[8]

She loved her husband and had always loved him, but somehow married love had never quite come up to what she had seen and felt that afternoon across the footlights. What puzzled her was the question that baffled her to this day: What was the nature of that youthful ardor, what did love of that kind really consist of, what was it? Illusion, perhaps; poetry and Shakespeare and the actor's art. But could make-believe — make-believe and nothing more — cause her to experience love, really experience it, so powerfully that it still held after twenty years of a marriage which, at its worst, had never been unhappy? No, she could not believe it had been illusion merely. It was something in the nature of Gavin Douglas, a special ardor he possessed that other men did not, a mysterious and ineffable quality in the artist. What she and Smith had together had lasted and would always last; it was durable and sound. Yet the other was durable, too; how else could she respond to, and even feel again, at this very moment, that powerful emotion that Romeo had given her from the stage? — pure, heart-piercing, like the poetry he spoke ...

[注]

这一段分析夫妻之爱和浪漫的爱之间的不同。但这不是说理文章（小说中最好不要插入说理文章），这里仍旧是在描写女主角的心理，她觉得爱情有两种，夫妻间的恩爱似乎还不能满足她心里的要求。

somehow：不知怎么的。**married love**：夫妻之爱。**come up to**：达到（她所见

所感的那种热烈的情形）。**footlights**：舞台前面的一排照明灯。**across the footlights**：隔了这么一排的灯，（台下人）所看到的台上。

that baffled her to this day：这个问题她至今不能索解。这个问题作者用三种方式来表达，那种青春热情（youthful ardor）的性质是什么？那一种的爱到底是什么东西所组成的？它到底是什么东西？

illusion：幻觉。

make-believe：假戏，以假作真的东西。台上所看到的只是演员的艺术，所听到的只是莎士比亚的诗句，这些并不是真人真事——但是这种以假作真的东西竟能使她经验到"爱"吗？**really experience it, so powerfully（experience it）**：这种话重复地说，更可以表示女主角强烈的感情。**held**（不及物动词）：保持不失。

at its worst：20 年的婚姻，当然不能说一无阴翳，但是在最坏的时候，她的婚姻并不是不快乐的。**a marriage**：冠词 a 用得很好。先用不定冠词，范围不加限制，然后接着用一个限制性的定语从句（restrictive 从句），把性质确定。这一种用法是很常见的。

no：这一段是心理描写，难免有自问自答的话，戏台上的爱情只是幻觉吗？不是的。**had been illusion**：动词时态表示，这是专指"那天下午"所看到的戏。

it was something 中的 it，仍是代替 love。这种爱是那演员性格（nature）里的某种性质（something）。a special ardor 和 something 是同位语。**other men did not** = other men did not possess。

something 这个词用处很大。凡是抽象的性质，作者怕一下子说不清楚，都可暂时用这个词来代替。多用抽象的名词和形容词，文章可能成为古板。something 是一个容易为读者所接受的词，用了它，文章就较流畅。但是 something 意义宽泛，作者仍旧应该设法用比较确定的字眼把意义说明白，这里作者用了两个同位格的词，加以说明补充，一个是 a special ardor，第二个是 a mysterious and ineffable（言语所难表达的）quality。

代替抽象名词的除 something 外，更可以用"what"从句，本段第一句 what she had seen and felt 就是一个例子。这里 what she and Smith had together 也是一样。"她和她丈夫所共有"，是什么东西呢？当然是夫妻之间的恩爱。但是作者为了避免多用 love 之类的抽象名词，用了这样一个名词性从句。读者诸君于习作英文论说文时，如觉得抽象名词运用不易，这里所介绍的补救办法，不妨一试。

他们夫妻间的爱情,历久不衰(had lasted);以后始终如一,也是在意料之中。这无疑是一种持久(durable)健全(sound)的爱。

respond to:感应。请注意,英文逗号的用法和中文不同。我们写中文时,很少把动词和它的宾语用逗号分开来的。这里 respond to 的宾语是 that powerful emotion,但是二者隔得很远,中间用了三个逗号,舞台上那种浪漫的爱,也是能持久不变的;要不然的话(else),她怎么此刻(at this very moment)对于那种强烈的感情,仍旧能发生感应呢?非但发生感应而已,她心里还能够体会到那种感情。

最后几个词形容 emotion:纯洁而摧人肝肠的感情,如同他所念的(剧中的)诗句一般(按,莎士比亚的戏剧中的对白均系诗句)。

[9]

To this day she had only to pick up the play at any time and read again that passionate but plaintive plea

O, wilt thou leave me so unsatisfied?

to remember how, shivering in the half-dark of the theater, she had turned compulsively toward Smith at her side, holding her hand absently, as he thought was expected of him — unaware, and sweet, but not Romeo! — and how she felt at the time such a strange, such a confused and confusing fear that love of that kind was not to be given to her; that, so to speak, art was one thing and life was another...

[注]

plaintive:悲伤的,悲诉的。**plea**:恳求。这里连用三个 p 开首的词,后两个又都是 pi 开首的,这在韵律学里称为"头韵"(alliteration),这里要描写一种强烈的感情,句法和普通口语式的散文不同,音调起伏,已经接近莎翁的无韵诗了。

O, wilt thou 原句出自《罗密欧与朱丽叶》第二幕第二场,这就是最有名的"后花园私订终身"那一场。罗密欧在恳求朱丽叶:"啊!你就这样离我而去,不给我一点满足吗?"

she had only to pick up the play ... to remember:她只要捡起莎翁原剧,重读到这个地方,心里就会记起两件事情。这两件事情是用 how 连接的两个宾语从句。

第一，在光线黯淡的戏院里面，她身体颤抖，不由自主地（compulsively）靠向（恐怕是心理上的靠向）她身旁的男同学。男同学心不在焉地握住她的手（他知道她所求于他者为此），他情意缠绵（sweet），但是他不是罗密欧！

第二，她在那时候有一种奇怪的恐惧之感，它本身是混乱不清的（confused）同时却使她心思更为昏乱（confusing），她觉得像戏台上的那种爱情是没有人会给她的。

最后一个"that"从句仍是说明 fear。她觉得可以这么说（so to speak）：艺术是一回事，人生是另一回事。

[10]

The door opened and Smith came in. He crossed to the sofa, bent down and kissed her. Then he stood up and gazed at her in a curious way. "What's eating you?" he said.

"Me? Why nothing. Why?"

"You look all ..." He shrugged.

"All what?"

"... Peculiar."

"Smith, Listen to me. Sit down. Who do you suppose is coming to dinner tonight?"

"Alice, what the hell's the matter with you?"

"Gavin Douglas, Ralph called up. He's bringing him home for dinner."

"*Who* did you say?"

"Gavin Douglas. The actor Romeo."

"My God ..."

"Why do you say that?"

He laughed. "I'm saying it for you."

"Well, you can stop it right now. This isn't a bit funny!"

"The dream made flesh..."

In spite of herself, she smiled. It was exactly she had thought, to the very words. "But what am I going to do?" she all but cried. "What under heaven am I going to do? ..."

[注]

刚才是回忆,是情感的起伏,现在又回复到现实生活里来了,文字也几乎换了一种。

eating:用文言来说,当是"啮蚀",译成白话,该是"伤你的脑筋"。**what the hell's the matter** = what is the matter。the hell 为咒骂之词,但咒骂之意可强可弱,视语气而定,这里咒骂之意当然很弱。

Ralph called up. He's bringing ...:注意时态的用法。虽然是家常谈话,也一点不可马虎。

to the very words:词都用得一样的。她听说那伶人要来吃饭时,曾经想到过 the dream made flesh(见前面本文)。现在她丈夫也有同感,把她的思想一字不易地说了出来。

all but cried:几乎要哭。**under heaven**:用以加强 what,别无他意。

[11]

Her attention was drawn to a car just driving up below. The apartment was on the third floor, and she stood close to the window behind the curtains, and looked down.

It was a Ford convertible. Her son Ralph got out, from the other side stepped a hatless youngish man in a reversible overcoat. It couldn't be Gavin Douglas; it was certainly not Romeo. He rounded the rear of the car and disappeared with Ralph into the small foyer.

[注]

attention was drawn:注意力被吸引。**driving up**:开到门口。**convertible**:篷车。这一切都是从她的眼睛里看到的。**youngish**:年纪不算大。**reversible overcoat**:正反两用大衣(反穿就是雨衣)。

it couldn't be:这样一个人怎么可能是她记忆中的情圣呢?**rounded the rear**:从车子后面绕过来。**foyer**:公寓房子楼下的小客厅。他们两人走进来了(disappeared)。

Romeo | 323

[12]

　　She heard them in the living room, heard Smith being hearty and cordial. A minute later her bedroom door opened and Ralph came in.

　　"Thank God you didn't dress up," he said.

　　"And why would I dress up?" she replied airily. "It isn't a dinner party, after all."

　　"Come on out. Dad's making drinks ..."

　　When she came into the living room, Gavin Douglas sprang up from the chair.

　　"I'm Ralph's mother," she said. "How do you do ..."

[注]

living room：上了楼进了房了。**being hearty and cordial**：正在热忱招待。verb to be 通常并没有动作的意思，但是 being 这个现在分词也表示一点动作。例如：

　　I am being a fool，我正在说傻话（或做傻事）。

　　cordial 其实和 hearty 同一意义，都解作"恳切"，不过 cordial 的词源是拉丁文的"心"，hearty, 的词源是盎格鲁—撒克逊文的"心"，cordial 比较近于文言，意义亦较弱。

dress up：穿上礼服。西俗妇人参加正式宴会(dinner party)，当穿晚礼服(evening dress)。

airily：轻快地。

making drinks：调鸡尾酒。美国人于晚餐之前，喜饮鸡尾酒。鸡尾酒是两种酒调和的饮料，种类繁多，两种酒之间配合的分量又可因人而异，都是临时调和的。通常还都是由主人亲自动手。

[13]

　　Was it truly Gavin Douglas? Why, he looked no more like an actor than — why, than her husband did; and scarcely older. With inexpressible relief she noted that he was still handsome, very masculine-looking, and he might have been, anybody; anybody, that is, with a certain background and breeding. He was of medium height; his complexion was ruddy and healthy; his eyes were blue as a robin's egg. His voice was resonant and deep but not thrilling — not as it had been in the theater; his diction was no better than it should be. But what amazed her most of all was his dress. He looked just like Smith on a weekend in Connecticut.

[注]

　　这是她第一次正式见到在台下的情圣。他的模样可真不像个演员。本段首二句是模仿口语的，这位主妇虽不开口，但心里自问自答却如同说话一般。第二句的两个 why 就是说话时才用得到的感叹词。why 作感叹词用，据《简明牛津词典》解释，至少有五种意义（详情请查该词典）。此处第一个 why 用以表示一种"使人惊讶的发现或认识"（surprised discovery or recognition），相当于中文的"啊"（原来如此！），第二个 why 用以表示"停顿而加以思索"（pause for reflection），相当于中文的"嗯"（让我想想看）。她丈夫既不类伶人，客人看来也不像，两人年龄似乎也相仿。

　　relief：心头觉得说不出的安慰。她只怕她心目中的情圣已经白发苍苍，老态龙钟，破坏了她的美丽的梦想。

　　might have been：后面跟一破折号，表示她想到这里，又停顿了一下。**anybody**：照那人的样子看来，她决看不出他的身份，他可能是任何人，但先说任何人，又嫌太泛，她又替自己做注解：那就是说（that is）任何有某种生活背景（background）和高尚教养的人。

　　robin's egg：知更鸟蛋。知更鸟在美国东北部是很常见的一种鸟，它的蛋有一种美丽的蓝色，作者拿来和那人的眼睛颜色相比，是很好的譬喻。

　　resonant：响亮的，余音袅袅的。**deep**：深沉的。**thrilling**：动人的。

　　diction：所用的词，措辞（dictionary 就是从这个词衍化来的）。**no better than it should be**：恰到分寸，并不见得特别出色。

　　on a weekend：美国男子大约有几套服装。上写字间是一套，正式宴会是一套，度周末假期又是一套。她丈夫周末去康涅狄格州（离纽约非常近的一个州）时所穿的衣服并没有什么出奇之处，现在来客所穿的也不过这么一套，并无大明星派头。

[14]

"It's delightful meeting Rafe's parents," he said. "I can scarcely believe it. Neither of you seem old enough to have produced such a strapping young man."

Rafe? Had she heard correctly? But of course! It was the British pronunciation.

"Are you English, Mr. Douglas?"

"Heavens no. I was born and brought up in the tiny town of Two Buttes, Colorado. My father had a small mine. I used to say that after I left, they changed the name to One Butte, but I've long since gotten over such lousy jokes — I hope."

[注]

第一句主语 It 代替动名词短语 meeting Rafe's parents。

neither of you 后面的动词用复数形式 seem，不用单数形式 seems，这是合乎语法的。**strapping**：高大的。这一句话是在恭维他们夫妻二人长得年轻，看不出老。

Rafe：儿子的名字是 Ralph，这个词在美国的读音，读者不难从拼写上猜测出来。但是英国人把它读成 Rafe（读 a 长音），听来很特别。

heavens no：heavens 恐怕是 Good heavens! 之略。good heavens 没有中文"天呀！"那么严重，语气相当于普通话的"是英国人才怪呐"。

mine：矿。

Butte：美国西部用语，解作"山岗"。他的家乡就是科罗拉多的双岗镇了。接着他还讲一个笑话，他说他离开家乡之后，家乡人士就把镇名改为单岗镇。他的幽默所在，是把 butte（u 长音）当作 butt（u 短音）来读。butt 的意思是屁股。"两个屁股"的小镇，打自己拍屁股走人后，就只剩"一个屁股（one butt）"了。这两句主要表示的是：此人有他的幽默感，而且不惜拿自己来挖苦的。

gotten over：有超越或克服之意。"我已经有很久（long since）不说这种低级笑话了。" **lousy**：这是一个应用很广的 American slang 词。

这个人的说话，既然按英国音读 Rafe，又用美国人的 gotten 和 Lousy。我们可以说他所表现的有两方面，一是他的艺术家与众不同的一方面，一是他平易近人、善于"做人"的一方面。

[15]

"Really a mining town?" she said. "How did you happen to go on the stage, Mr. Douglas?"

"After all, one has to do something. And one night in Pueblo, when I was sixteen, I saw a road company of *Way Down East*. After that there was no holding me. My father kicked like a steer but it was no use. Green as I was, the stage was for me, from then on."

"When you were sixteen? It doesn't seen possible ..."

"Why not?"

[注]

to go on the stage：从事舞台生活。

after all：说来说去，人总得要做事（我就挑选了戏剧）。

Pueblo：科罗拉多州的城市名。**road company**：走江湖跑码头的戏班。***Way Down East***：美国20世纪初很有名的戏，为 Lottie Blair Parker（1858—1937）所作，中文译名似为《赖婚》。

there was no holding me：there is 的后面跟一个动名词，解作"没有办法"，这里是"从此以后，没有办法管得住我了"。我就想投身戏剧界了。

steer：小公牛。**green**：嫩，没有经验。

[16]

"You seemed hardly sixteen when my husband and I saw you in *Romeo and Juliet*."

"Oh, did you see that? Imagine!"

"I've never forgotten it, Mr. Douglas."

"Well, I was *twice* sixteen during my Romeo period," he said, and smiled charmingly. "Do you know how old I am now? Fifty-three, no less."

... Twice sixteen, she was thinking. That youth — that slim young lover? A Romeo of thirty-two? Incredible it seemed; it was possible, perhaps, but not probable.

She got up. "I — think it's time for dinner," she said. "Mr. Douglas, won't you bring your drink in to the table?"

[注]

imagine!：请想想看！怪不怪？

during my Romeo period：我演罗密欧那个时期。

that youth — that slim young lover：这是指舞台上所看见的罗密欧，演员本人则是已经 32 岁了。

incredible：令人难信。**not probable**：不近情理。

bring your drink in：把鸡尾酒一块儿带来。

[17]

"So you saw our *Romeo and Juliet*," he said, "Fancy that. You must have been kids."

"We weren't. We were both in college at the time."

"About Rafe's age. I should imagine," he said. "Wouldn't you call him a kid?"

[注]

fancy that：同上文的 imagine 一样，是一种自言自语。

must have been：从现在的立场，猜度过去的事情所用的动词形式。**kids**：小孩子。

I should imagine 和 Wouldn't you 两个虚拟式动词，都是比较客气而不武断的说法。

call him a kid：大学生还算是小孩子，其人显然有点倚老卖老。

[18]

"... We played *Romeo and Juliet* thirty consecutive weeks at the Morosco," he was saying, "and then took it on the road for another whole season. You can imagine the bang it gave me when we played Pueblo, Colorado. After the American tour, there was a three months' run at the Haymarket in London. I'm telling you, I was never so sick of anything in my life as I was of Romeo when we finally quit. Bored stiff."

"Bored? But you couldn't have been! I can't believe it, Mr. Douglas?"

[注]

he was saying：只听他在那里滔滔不绝地说。

thirty consecutive weeks：连续演 30 个星期（卖座如此持久不衰，在纽约百老汇不是一件稀罕的事，一出戏可能演一年多的）。

Morosco：百老汇的戏院名。上文说 Alice 和 Smith 是在"兰心"戏院看的戏。"兰心"戏院想是在纽约州罗切斯特，那时候戏班已经出发巡回表演了。

took it on the road：各处巡回公演。road 有一个特别意义，专指戏班跑码头而言。请参照上文 road company。

bang：感触（原义是"猛烈的打击"）。他自己是 16 岁的时候，看见了戏班子在那里演出，而决心献身戏剧的，现在的戏班也在那里演出了。**played**：play 作及物动词用，这种用法比较特别。根据 *The American College Dictionary*，此词的解释是：（戏班）在（某地）公演 (to give performance in, as a theatrical company does)。词典中还举了一个例子：

> to play the larger cities（在大城市公演）

这里 We played Pueblo, Colorado, 用地名做 played 的宾语，意义亦不难了解了。

run：连续演出。**the Haymarket**：伦敦剧院名。该戏院有悠久的历史，1705 年落成，首任经理为 William Congreve，在英国文学史上是有它的地位的。

sick of：厌倦。**as I was of** = as I was sick of。so sick 连后面的 as。

quit：这个词是 quit 的过去形式（用 quitted 亦可）。各处巡回演出之后，他对于罗密欧这个角色厌烦到了极点了。

bored stiff：恐怕是 I was bored stiff 的省略。stiff 当是主语补语，形容主语。**bored**：厌烦（到使人要命的程度）。

[19]

"Sorry to disillusion you, Mrs. Harvey, but I was *thoroughly* bored by that time. Forcing myself, putting it on, faking. But then, art is nothing if it's not make-believe. You build a performance out of artifice and tricks, and then you bring into play whatever skills you have, to make it true, convincing, or if you will, realistic." He laughed, that pleasant, hearty laugh. "The world of art is different from the actual, the facts. As for the artist himself — or the actor or writer or whatever — well, the less said about him, perhaps, the better."

[注]

disillusion you：使你的迷梦幻灭。

forcing 等三个词是现在分词呢？还是动名词？句子没有做完，很难下判断。假如是现在分词，那么这三个词可以说是形容上一句的主语 I 的。假如是动名词，那么这三个词前面大约省了 What I had been doing was 这几个词。**forcing myself**：强迫自己做戏背台词。**putting it on**：装得煞有介事（putting on 是假装，it 大约是指演戏那一套，所指较泛）。**faking**：冒名欺骗。所作所为，无非如此，怎不叫人厌倦呢？

make-believe：上文已有解释。"可是艺术就是以假乱真，假如艺术不是如此，艺术根本就一无所有了。"

artifice：人工，技巧。**tricks**：手法。演戏就是利用种种技巧手法（从种种技巧手法里面，建立你的演技）。

bring into play 是个习语，解作"发挥作用"。play 在这里并不作"戏"解。artifice 和 tricks 是演戏的基本条件，此外演员各人有不同的演技才能，你就把你所有的技能全拿出来，使你的表情（**it** = your performance）宛然像真的，一般使人见了信服，或者你喜欢用这种字眼（or if you will），我们可以说你的表情可以更"现实化"（realistic）。这里的"你"，当然是泛指，并不是指听话的人。

这许多话无非要表示，演戏虽然是作假，但是"假"里面还有道理。

he laughed 后面跟一个逗号，这表示 that pleasant, hearty laugh 并不是 laughed 的宾语（没有那个逗号，laugh 就成了 laughed 的宾语）。现在这样标点法，that pleasant, hearty laugh 该是一个补充说明（parenthetical）的短语，说明 laughed 的。

the less said：关于艺术家本人，愈少讲起他愈好。艺术家的贡献是他的艺术，我们只需注意他的艺术，不必注意他的本人。

[20]

All but breathless, thrilled to her fingertips, Alice Harvey was only able to ask: "Why do you say that?"

"Well, I don't mean to hold the floor too much, but the artist is both scoundrel and angel. He's gifted and cursed, happy and in despair, parasitic and productive, neurotic and brilliant, antisocial and socially aware to the very heart of him — and always intensely interesting, because there's a little of the artist in us all." Biddy used to say "Give me the man of talent to act with, but the mediocrity to live with — every time."

[注]

all but：差不多，几乎（作副词用）。**breathless**：透不过气来。她并没有真的透不过气来的，但是除此以外，一切透不过气来的现象都有了。又例，all but drowned：几乎淹死。thrilled：激动。前面那个伶人的一段话，在她是闻所未闻，她听见了全身颤动，一直到手指尖都有一种异样的感觉。她难以张口，最后只能问这么一句话。

floor：国会里发表议论的地方。**take the floor**：发言，参加讨论。**hold the floor**：老是一个人在讲，不让别人发言。

scoundrel：坏人。注意：scoundrel 和 angel 连用，因此前面没有冠词 a。在两个或两个以上的名词（成分）连用的场合，通常不用 a 或 an，例如：

  We are brother and sister.

艺术家（the artist 中的冠词 the 并不表示某一个艺术家，而是表示这一类的人）是有矛盾的性格的，说他可恨（scoundrel）固然可以，说他可爱（angel）也可以。

gifted 和 cursed 二词都是从过去分词转化而成的形容词。假如问：By whom is he gifted and cursed？据说是 by God。**gifted**：天赋独厚的。**cursed**：受诅咒的，上帝规定艺术家不得过好日子。

艺术家是幸福的人，也是没有希望的人；他是社会的寄生虫，同时也是有创造天赋的人；他精神失常，可是又是才华出众，他离群索居，不喜社交，可是心底里决丢不掉社会。**socially aware**：有"社会意识"；明白个人对于社会的责任等等。

interesting：艺术家总是可以引起人家很大的兴趣，因为我们谁都有一点儿"艺术家的气质"（a little of the artist）。

Biddy 那句话可以这么译："同我一起演戏的，我希望是一个天才；和我共同生活的，我希望是个庸人。"艺术家或天才固然有趣，但是平时是很难处的。**mediocrity** = a person of but moderate ability（才艺平庸之人）。

[21]

"Biddy? Was she your wife?"

"Good heavens no! Biddy was the glamorous, the beauteous Constance

Hope. Juliet herself."

"But — why Biddy? Was that really her nickname?"

"It's what I called her. You see, Biddy was fifteen years older than I. Forty-seven when we played Shakespeare."

[注]

这位伶人脱口而出地说起了 Biddy 这个名字。这是个昵称，又像是个女人的名字，无怪听的人以为是他太太的名字了。

glamorous：美得迷人的。glamorous 原义是"有魔力的"，有些出版较早的词典，恐怕还只列这样一个解释。近年来这个词似乎专指"惑阳城，迷下蔡"的那种"妖艳"，和"魔法，妖法"已经脱离关系了。beauteous 用作"美"解，则古人诗中常见，是一个比较有书卷气的字眼。总之，glamorous（作这个解释）是个通俗的新词，beauteous 是个古雅的老词，这位伶人是这两种词都喜欢用的。

[22]

Alice Harvey shook her head in bewilderment, and then, in spite of herself she laughed; but only because it was also fantastic, beyond belief. "About that business of make-believe," she managed to say, "do you really, Mr. Douglas, do you actually expect me to take you seriously when — " She flushed, trying to find an illustration for what she meant. "Well, for instance, the thrilling scene where Juliet comes on alone and launches that long speech that ends with something like

> Give me my Romeo; and, when he shall die,
> Take him and cut him out in little stars, ...

I mean, do you actually mean to sit there and tell us, Mr. Douglas, that — that Constance Hope wasn't moved when she spoke those lines? Wasn't carried away?"

[注]

舞台上的朱丽叶，事实上已经是 47 岁的中年妇人了，难怪我们这位女主人摇摇她的头，不知所措了。

in spite of herself：不能控制自己。

47岁的妇人能演14岁的朱丽叶，而且演得非常之好，看戏的人大受感动，现在想想，未免好笑。但是另外还有一点可笑之处（because ... also），虽然这位伶人不会骗人，但事情毕竟荒唐（fantastic），令人难以置信。

she managed to say：好容易才想出这句话来说。她虽然想了这句话来说，但是话说得还是断断续续。这句话很长，句法转了好几次。

do you actually 是重复 do you really。**to take you seriously**：相信你不在开玩笑。when 以后，句子做不下去了，她就换一种说法。

flushed：脸红。**an illustration**：用以说明的例子。

thrilling scene：动人的一场戏。原剧第三幕第二场，朱丽叶一个人出场。开始（launches）大段独白。这段话是朱丽叶的祷告，她求太阳快些下去，夜快些来。"把我的罗密欧给我！等他死了以后，你再把他带去，分散成无数的星星……。"

well, for instance …：这句话没有说完，她又换了一句。**I mean**：这两个词是很有用的习语，自己觉得话说不清楚，不得不反复说明时，这两个词就用得着。

sit there：坐在那里（餐厅的那张椅子上）。

朱丽叶那一段话是很动人的，岂有演员自己反不受感动之理？**carried away**：出神，着迷。

[23]

"I'll tell you how carried away she was," he said. "Naturally I remember that scene well — God, I hear it in my sleep, to this day, Capulet's orchard, just before intermission. Biddy hadn't been in the previous scene, but I was. When I came off-stage, I always found her standing there in the wings waiting, smoking a cigarette — against all the rules, of course, but that was Biddy, a law unto herself. When she heard the cue, she handed me the cigarette and went on. It was a long scene, with the Nurse. Biddy kept on hoping, but in vain. She always had to light a new one, and cursed the Nurse for being so slow with her lines that she wasted a whole cigarette."

[注]

hear it：这一段戏词，他念念不忘，现在时隔多年，他在睡梦中似乎还听得见。**Capulet's orchard**：Capulet 是朱丽叶的姓氏，他们家的果园，是那场戏的背景。

intermission：休息时间。

the previous scene：第三幕第一场，即罗密欧击毙 Tybalt 的那一场。那场戏中没有朱丽叶的戏。

off-stage：这是个形容词（这里应该是形容主语 I），解作"在后台"。

wings：舞台的侧面（此词用复数形式）。**against all the rules**：翻遍后台管理规则，没有一条是容许演员在那种地方抽烟的。可是这位演员与众不同。她是 Biddy，她可以率性行事。**unto** 就是 to，这是个古词。a law unto oneself 是习语，解作"不可以常理来规定"。例如：A child is often a law unto itself. 小孩常有小孩自己的办法。

cue：上一场的最后几句话（朱丽叶听见了，就预备出场。此词也可解作同一场另一演员一段对白的最后几个词，演员听见了，就预备接口说话）。

Nurse：朱丽叶的乳娘是戏里一个重要角色。

kept on hoping：这句话意义不大清楚，但看后面两句，便知她是希望这场戏早点结束，回去抽那枝香烟！

to light a new one：重新点一支香烟。原来那一枝已经烧完了。**so slow with her lines**：乳娘背台词（lines）背得太慢，害得朱丽叶糟蹋一支香烟。

[24]

Poor Alice Harvey — her head was swimming. She didn't believe, almost didn't dare listen; and certainly didn't dare to glance at her husband by now, who was probably grinning at her with his own particular brand of fiendish delight. "But if Constance Hope," she faltered, "wasn't affected by the scene, wasn't deeply moved inside, then why ... now ... why was I moved?"

[注]

her head was swimming：眩晕。

dare listen 二词之间，原文没有 to，这种用法很奇怪。照普通用法，用 dared not listen 时不用 to，用 didn't dare 后面就得用 to。本段接着就是 didn't dare to glance，用 to 是不错的。

她一向所崇拜的演员，原来把演戏看得如此随便，她怕她丈夫在窃笑。**grinning**：露齿而笑。**brand**：种类。她丈夫有一种特别的"恶毒的取笑"。所谓"恶毒"者（**fiendish**：魔鬼的），就是看见别人窘迫了，他就引以为乐。
faltered：吞吞吐吐地说。

[25]

"My dear Mrs. Harvey," he said, with his gentlest, his most intimate smile. "If Biddy had been moved herself — carried away by the emotion of the scene, swept off her feet, whatever you want to call it — *you* wouldn't have been moved at all. You'd have sat there cold and impassive, resisting it with your whole being, irritated, in fact, by the spectacle of a woman making a holy show of herself."

[注]

gentlest：最温柔的。**most intimate**：最亲切的。If Biddy ... herself 中的 herself 用以加强主语 Biddy。moved 是"感动"，说话的人怕这个词意义不够清楚，换了两种说法："假定她被戏里的情感支配了，假定她演得忘乎所以了……" **swept off one's feet**：（习语）感动得忘乎所以，兴奋过度。**whatever you want to call it**：不论你用 moved 也好，用别种说法也好。假如演员自己大受感动，观众就不受感动了。

impassive：不感痛痒，无动于衷（形容词，形容主语 You）。**resisting it** 中的 it 大约指的是戏。**with your whole being**：用你的全力来反抗，你就要看不下去了。**being**：要素，本性，存在。**your whole being**：精神身体统统算进去。**irritated** 仍是形容主语 you，"你看见了要生气的。"此词连后面的 by。in fact 是插进去补充说明的。**spectacle**：奇观，惨相，好戏。

making a show of herself：炫耀，表现自己。holy 原义是"神圣"，这里是反语。a holy show 该是"出丑，出洋相"。一个女人当着大庭广众，真正地大哭大笑起来，别人是忍受不了的。

[26]

Shortly after ten, Gavin Douglas rose to leave.

He was at the open door leading to the hall and the stairs, his reversible coat over his arm. He turned back momentarily, then, and Alice Harvey was delighted to see that he was about to make an exit, so to speak. He took her outstretched hand in both of his and gave her a long, searching, and very complimentary look. She waited, pleased.

"Mrs. Harvey," he said, his voice dropping a full octave lower and thrilling her through and through, "all summer long I've wondered where Rafe got those eyes. Now I know ..."

[注]

open door：公寓的大门，不是房间的门，所以这里说是"通到门堂（hall）和楼梯的那扇门"。**over his arm**：挽在臂上。

then：那时候他本来已经预备跨步外出，现在忽然回转身来。**to make an exit**：（演员）下场。下场的时候演员常常要念两句"下场诗"。现在当然不在舞台上，但是在女主人心目中，他现在的姿势，可以说（so to speak）是在准备下场，正要说什么精彩的话，或者做什么精彩的表情。

outstretched：伸出来的。**both of his** = both of his hands。

look 前面有三个形容词：long（时间长），searching（仔细——似乎在寻些什么东西），complimentary（带着恭维的意义）。

pleased：过去分词作形容词用。

dropping a full octave lower：声音忽然低了八度，即本来唱 do re mi 的，现在唱低音的 do re mi。**thrilling**：这个词又出现了，这里可以解作"使她心神荡漾，全身的汗毛孔都觉得异样的舒服"。

where Rafe got those eyes：我一直猜不透令郎怎么会有一双这样美的眼睛，现在我明白了……。

Dialogues of A. N. Whitehead
怀特海对话录

Lucien Price（1883—1964）

怀特海（Alfred North Whitehead）是当代大哲学家，1861 年生于英国，出身剑桥大学，早享盛名，1924 年受美国哈佛大学之聘，任教十余年之久，1937 年退休，1947 年逝世。怀氏生前喜与青年朋友交谈，青年人聆其教诲者，自然增长智慧，然而怀氏虚怀若谷，认为和青年人谈论，亦大有助于他自己的思想。他曾经说过，"It is all nonsense to suppose that the old cannot learn from the young."

Lucien Price 是《波士顿环球报》(The Boston Globe)的记者，亦是好学深思之士，他从 1932 年起经常访问怀特海，讨论学术思想、人生各种问题。后来他把讨论的话，随时笔录，二十余年来，居然成一本厚书，Price 自云对于记录谈话，有特殊训练，非但谈话要旨，可以保持不失，连谈话时所用语句，都可以照式录下。他的记录，大部分曾经怀氏寓目，认为无误。怀氏态度诚恳，吐属隽雅，思想深刻，学识渊博，他的"语录"可以和 Boswell 的《萨缪尔·约翰逊传》以及 Eckermann 的《歌德对话录》相比。Dialogues of Alfred North Whitehead 1954 年由 Little Brown 图书公司出版。

[1]

"Suppose our American culture were wiped out: whom have we produced so far who would stand as a lasting contribution to the world?"

"Walt Whitman."

"Not Emerson?"

"I read Emerson a good deal when I was younger, but if my good neighbours, the Forbeses, will pardon me for saying so (they are grandsons of Emerson), he was not so original. But Whitman brought something into poetry which was never there before. Much of what he says is so new that he even had to invent a new form for saying it. Whitman seems to me to have been one of the very few great poets that have ever lived. He can stand easily beside the really great European poets."

[注]

our American culture：问话的人（Price）是美国人。**were**：虚拟式动词。**wiped out**：扫除，消灭，

whom 是疑问代词，who 是关系代词，代替 whom，到今天为止（so, 美国到底出了什么人才，可以算是对全世界是一个永久的贡献呢？**stand**：别的东西都消灭了，他可以屹立不移。

Whitman(1819—1892)：惠特曼，美国诗人，《草叶集》的作者。**Emerson**(1803—1882)：爱默生，美国诗人，思想家。

the Forbeses：怀特海的邻居 Forbes 一家人。Forbes 指的是 Cameron Forbes，美国外交官，曾任美国驻日大使，驻菲律宾总督。他是 Emerson 的外孙。

pardon：批评人家的祖先，当然应该请人家原谅，即便他们人不在左右，听不见我的话。**not so original**：没有什么独创的贡献。

brought something：这两个简单的词，用处很大。something 在本书前文中已经讨论过，这里可能代表一种"美""力量""风格"或"思想"。brought 可能表示"灌输""创造""倡导"种种意思，这两个词都可以用比较艰深专门的词代替，但是在普通谈话中，这样也就够用了。**which was never there before**：以前所没有的。定语从句，形容 something。

what he says：他所说的（内容）。what 的用法，在本书前文中曾讨论过。is so new 的主语是 much。saying it 的 it 代替 much。

form：（诗歌的）形式。这句话用两种不同的时式，be says 用现在时，话虽说

过了，但是话还留传人间；古人说话，大多可用现在时以表示之，例如 Confucius says。又 is so new 也用现在时，对于今日的读者，还是新鲜的。had to invent 用过去时，惠特曼创造新形式以表现新思想，是在过去。

seems to me to have been：分词用完成时，表示惠特曼现在已不在人世。**can stand easily beside**：足与（欧洲大诗人）相比。

[2]

"You must remember that at Winchester the boys are a selected group, with a very special kind of training to which they are well adapted. In that groove they acquire astonishing proficiency, but they would be quite ignorant out of it. They would know a great deal about Roman customs in the period of the Punic Wars, but very little, perhaps nothing, about urgent problems of their own land and time. They do well at the universities and make names in the professions and as colonial administrators and civil servants. The creative arts? I do not think you will find many of them excelling there. They write very well, but not very imaginatively, American students are less well-informed but more eager to learn; English boys are less eager but more informed. The American boy knows less about what interests him more, the English boy knows more about what seems to interest him less." He said this with a laughing twinkling in his bright blue eyes.

[注]

本段怀特海讨论英美两国青年的知识程度。Price 曾去参观英国有名的 Winchester College（中学），发现高年级中学生都能阅读希腊名著的原文，可是美国哈佛大学的学生都不一定有这样高的程度，怀特海即就此点发表意见。

selected group：经过挑选的一群人，优秀分子。adapted 连前面的 to which，这辈青年很能适应于这种训练。**groove**：原意为"沟"或"槽"，转作"故辙"、"规定的路子"、"刻板文章"。这里指英国中学的训练方法。

proficiency：精通，熟练。是动词 acquire（获得）的宾语。

would be：虚拟语态，说话的人不敢说定。**out of it** = out of the groovy 在规定课程范围之内，他们知道得非常之多；在这范围之外，他们的知识可能很浅陋。

Roman customs：罗马人的风俗习惯。

Punic Wars：罗马与迦太基之战（Punic 就是腓尼基，迦太基是腓尼基人立的）。
urgent problems：迫切的问题。他们对于本国目前的大问题，可能知道得很少，甚至一无所知。

do well：成绩很好。

make names：扬名，露头角。

excelling：出人头地。他们干律师、医生、牧师等（所谓 professions）行业，到殖民地去做官，或者在本国做公务员（civil servants），成绩都很好，但是他们在创造性的艺术方面，却很少有人能有杰出的成绩。

they write very well：训练严格，故写作技巧很好；但思想可能窒塞，想象力不够活泼。

eager to learn：求知欲旺盛。**informed**：学识丰富。

less ... more：美国学生对于学问（what）所知不多，但是兴趣较浓。**twinkling**：闪光。

[3]

"It strikes me that our writers don't *know* enough."

"It is true that most great writers did know quite a lot. But it is possible to know too much. What is wanted is an immense *feeling* for things. And the danger in old civilizations is that the teaching may be *too* good. It damps students down. They know too much about what has been done, they write well, but without freshness. It is so fatally easy for a good period in art to die in scholasticism and pedantry, for the life to go out of it. Oxford has taught the classics for centuries, and for centuries Cambridge virtually refused to teach literature and taught mathematics, and yet twice as many poets came out of Cambridge as out of Oxford."

[注]

our writers：美国作家。这一段又是 Price 发问。

did know：过去时，did 用以加重语气。过去大作家学识的确是丰富的。

to know too much：若从充实学识着手，可能中了书毒，对于艺术创作反有妨害。

an immense feeling for things：学识并不重要，重要的是对于万事万物，有一种极大的"体会的能力"。

old civilizations：civilizations 可以解作"国家"。在文明古国，教书先生过分道地，这是有危险的。

damps：使潮湿；挫折学生的锐气，打消学生的热忱。**what has been done**：前人的作品。

scholasticism：（中世纪的）繁琐哲学。对于枝节问题，不惮辞费地讨论不休。

pedantry：卖弄学问，掉书袋子。这两种现象，都是"遗神取貌，买椟还珠"，有害于艺术创作。一个艺术上有成就的时代，假如发生了这种现象，它的生命就算完结了。**fatally easy**：非常容易，因此也是非常之不幸。本句结构仿照下列形式，It is easy for（someone）to do（something）。本句前后两节，前节是 for a period to die，后节是 for the life to go out of it，末一个 it 代表 period。

virtually：事实上（虽不一定如此，也相差不远）。

Cambridge：剑桥大学教育不以文学为主，反而诗人辈出。剑桥出身的大诗人有斯宾塞（Spenser）、弥尔顿（Milton）、华兹华斯（Wordsworth）、柯尔律治（Coleridge）、丁尼生（Tennyson）等，人数比牛津出身的多一倍（twice as many）。

[4]

"How about the possibility of one or two great artists exhausting an epoch or an art-form? The Renaissance takes a drop after Michelangelo, and grand opera since Wagner has been a 'Tristan, Junior.'"

"That does happen. Such figures come at the end of an epoch. The danger is when the great themes have been superlatively well done, and the later workers come to secondary themes or refinements or niceties, and art or thought gets down off into shallows. That is fatally easy. I mean such themes as a mother's love for her child, something so universal that to express it sounds trite, and yet the medieval sculptors and Renaissance painters could express it with unbelievable beauty: but it is no good trying to imitate them."

[注]

exhausting：用尽，汲干。一二大艺术家可以把一个时代（**epoch**）的才气吸干，或者使用某一种艺术形式（**art-form**），达到尽善尽美的境地，使后人难以企及。这种艺术形式就算给"用绝"了。

Michelangelo（1475—1564）：米开朗琪罗，意大利画家、雕刻家、文学家、科学家。他是文艺复兴时代的大师，他死以后，文艺复兴就此没落（**takes a drop**）。

grand opera：纯正歌剧。Wagner 以后，纯正歌剧就少有伟大作品，只有轻松歌剧（light opera）点缀门面。

Tristan, Junior 照字面上讲应该是"Tristan 之子"，出典不详。瓦格纳（Wagner）的名著为 *Tristan and Isolde*，"Tristan 之子"应该比不上 Tristan 的。

figures：人物。great themes：艺术上重要的题目（如母爱，下文有举例）。**superlatively well**：好得无以复加。done：（艺术）制作。

later workers：以后的艺术工作者，自忖比不上过去的大师，只好挑次要的题目来发挥。**refinements or niceties**：这两个词都解作"精致"，纤巧而不雄壮，注重小节而忽略精神。（中国诗词的没落，所走的似乎也是这个路子。）

gets down off into shallows：驶入浅水，不复有海阔天空的雄风矣。

something：同位语，就是"母爱"。**universal**：人人皆知，四海皆有的。如母爱之类的题目，再要用来作为艺术题材，未免使人觉得（sounds）是陈腐（trite）了。

medieval sculptors：中世纪的雕刻家。他们以及文艺复兴时代画家大抵喜欢用"圣母和圣婴"作为题材。

it is no good 中的 it 代表动名词短语 trying ...。模仿那些大师们是没有用的。他们把母爱表现得如此之好，叫以后的艺术家如何下手呢？

[5]

There had been another wartime commencement, and the College Yard, where I crossed it, was being cleared of scaffold timber, which had been put up for the out-of-door ceremonies. The grass plot looked trodden into hard ground. Academic Cambridge, like any other academic town out of term-time, seemed suddenly deserted.

[注]

commencement：大学的毕业典礼（这里是指哈佛大学的）。**wartime**：其时第二次世界大战尚未结束。**another**：珍珠港事变以来，在战争中举行毕业典礼已经不是一次了。**there had been**：毕业典礼已经举行过。

College Yard：哈佛大学部门众多，其大学本科部分称为 Harvard College。

Yard 是校园。别的美国大学大多用 Campus 一词,哈佛则称 Yard。College Yard 就是哈佛的"校本部"。

where I crossed it: 我所走过的地方。

was being cleared: 正在清理卸除。用中文来写,"工人"、"木匠"这种主语大约是省不掉的,英文的被动句法就比较简单了。

timber: 木材。**scaffold**: 木架,台。**put up**: 架设。**ceremonies**: 毕业典礼是在户外举行的,临时要搭一座台,事过后拆除。

plot: 一片地。**trodden**: 过去分词作形容词用。毕业典礼参加的人很多,草坪看来都好像践踏成一块硬地了。

Academic Cambridge: 剑桥(哈佛所在地)的学术地区。**Academic town**: 大学城,拥有一所大学的小城。**out of term-time**: 学期终了之后,假期。**deserted**: 人都走完了。

[6]

It was a loury evening with rain in brew and a rising wind. The Whiteheads were alone and seemed more than usual at their ease. In no time at all we were out beyond the harbour jetties and into the conversational open water. It was about the gap between written and spoken language, between literature and vernacular.

[注]

loury: 阴沉沉的。**in brew**: 这个习语和中文"酝酿中"是巧合,brew 原意是"酿"。**a rising wind**: 风正起。

the Whiteheads: 他们这一家人。**alone**: 没有客人。"我走到他们家里……"这种话是不必说的;这是文章经济之法。

at their ease: 优游自得。平常本来如此,今天晚上益见闲散。

in no time: 很快的。at all 用以加强 no。**harbour jetties**: 港口边上的码头。**conversational open water**: 码头种种,都是"暗喻"。谈话来开始时,好像船未启碇,开始之后,立刻畅谈无阻,好像驶入汪洋大海。

gap: 歧异。**vernacular**: 白话,口语。这个词通常作形容词用。

[7]

"It is quite unlikely," said Whitehead, "that Cicero spoke to his friends in the language of his letters, to say nothing of his orations."

"A slave population complicates it, too," Mrs. Whitehead added. "No matter how vivid or picturesque the vernacular may be, if it is used by a servile class it is avoided by the educated."

[注]

Cicero（106B. C.—43B. C.）：西塞罗，拉丁文文章大家。他的文章流传于世，他的谈话失传。据怀特海看来，西塞罗的谈话，不大可能（quite unlikely）像他的书札一样地文绉绉的，因为谈话用的是白话，书札可能用的是文言。至于西塞罗的演说稿，那更是句法整齐，音调铿锵，和平常谈话差别之大，那更不必说了（to say nothing of ...）。

a slave population：罗马社会中的奴隶阶级。这使得问题（it）更为复杂。不论白话是多么的生动（vivid）如画（picturesque），不过它既为贩夫走卒（servile class：贱役阶级）所用，就为士大夫所不取了。

[8]

I said that the gap seemed particularly wide in English.

"Not so wide as you might think," said he. "The London poorer classes, for example, have an extraordinary appreciation for Shakespeare. His language doesn't put them off at all: their sense of humour is about the same as his; they think the things are funny. All this is not surprising for they were the sort of people for whom the plays were originally written. There is a school of technology in the East End for which I used to be on the visiting committee, and I saw a good deal of it. One evening a teacher was going over a page of literature in a textbook with his class; and asked the meaning of an unusual seventeenth-century word. One of the young men answered correctly. He was asked how he happened to know. 'I saw a play of Shakespeare's (he named the one) at the Old Vic last Thursday night, and that word was used in it in the same sense as here.'"

[注]

particularly wide：拉丁文文言、白话之间既有如此差别，英文的文言、白话之间的差别似乎尤其大。gap 原意是"空隙，裂痕"，形容它的"大"，应该用 wide。

怀特海的意思，差别没有此君所想象那样的大。莎士比亚在今日读来，总算是"文"的了，但是伦敦比较贫苦的人（受教育不多），对于莎士比亚，特别能欣赏。

put off 有"阻止"之意。莎翁的文字并不能把他们"推开"。

sense of humour：幽默感。莎翁剧本里不乏下流的俏皮话和低级趣味的滑稽场面（但这无损莎翁的价值，此处不讨论），他的幽默感与伦敦贫苦阶层的口味大体一致（about the same）。

the things：莎翁剧本里的滑稽的东西。他们认为这些东西的确是滑稽的，这一切并不奇怪，因为莎翁剧本本来是为这辈人而写的。

school of technology：工业职业学校。**East End**：伦敦的东区，居民大多为社会中下阶级，与上流社会所居之西区（West End）不同。

visiting committee：监督委员会。委员经常到校视察（visit），监督校务。任委员之职，可说 on the committee。**saw a good deal of it**：关于学校情形，我所见甚多。

an unusual seventeenth-century word：文学教本里一个冷僻的，17 世纪的古词。

happened：照这班学生的程度，这种古词他们不该认得的，怎么这个学生"碰巧"会认得呢？

he named the one：莎翁那部剧本的名字，那个学生是说出来的，但是怀氏在这里并没有复述。**the Old Vic**：伦敦老维克剧院，以演出莎翁戏剧闻名于世。英国电影明星，出身 Old Vic 剧院者，颇不乏人。

that word：莎翁死于 1616 年，他所用的词，17 世纪诗文中常常可以见到。那个学生虽然读书无多，但是看了莎翁的戏，居然把戏里的生词记得，到课堂上来应用，足见莎翁剧本之深入人心。

[9]

"If I may say a good word for American slang," said I, "it is that, besides being fresh and vigorous, it is almost always sweet and clean, pure animal high spirits."

"That is true," he assented, "and very much to your people's credit."

[**注**]

他们又讨论到美国俚语（slang）的问题，作者是美国人，他要替美国俚语说一句好话，但是怀氏夫妇是英国人，对于美国的东西未必赞成，所以作者先请他们原谅："假如容许我……的话"。这种谦逊的态度，是一个受过高尚教育的人应有的风度。一般学习英语会话的人，即使能够说得口若悬河，舌生莲花，假如风度不够，仍旧没有学到家也。

it is that 的 that 是连接词，引起下面的名词性从句。照作者看来，美国俚语除了新鲜有劲之外，差不多都是清洁而可爱（前面他们刚讨论过，法国的俚语常隐含一种恶俗的意义：French slang generally has a nasty innuendo behind it），只是纯粹表示一种生命的活力。**animal spirits**：天生的兴高采烈。**high spirits** 兴致高，起劲。

to your people's credit：是贵国人民的光荣。credit 解作"好名誉"，to one's credit（此人博得别人的称赞）是习语。讲起美国俚语，1957 年 2 月 18 日的 *Time* 杂志有一段讨论文字，颇有趣。英国一位 Lord Conesford 对于"美国英文"大肆攻击，他认为美国人把 face, meet, check 这三个简单的动词，累赘地说成 face up to, meet up with, check upon 是不足为训的。还有几个"美国词"，也是要不得的：如 underprivileged（贫穷），hospitalized（住医院），alibi（借口），bi-partisan（共和、民主两党联合一致的）等。但是这些都算是美国的正式英文。对于美国 slang，这位爵爷倒颇表首肯。他认为俚语常常都是"雄健可喜"（virile and admirable）的。他举的例子：

bulldozer：声威逼人、欺凌弱小之人，开路机。

blurb：大事吹擂的广告或声明。

debunk：揭破流行的谬说。

这些词并非正式英文，然而这些词如用正式英文的字眼来代替，读起来就没有俚语那样"有劲"了。

[10]

"Dialogue, as actually spoken, seldom goes into print effectively unless something has been done to it — often quite a little. It must sound the way people talk, but if you try setting down their talk verbatim, you may find that it doesn't seem as lifelike as it ought."

"Art," said Whitehead, "is the imposing of a pattern on experience, and our aesthetic enjoyment in recognition of the pattern. The mistake is to think of words as entities. They depend for their force, and also for their meaning, on emotional associations and historic overtones, and derive much of their effect from the impact of the whole passage in which they occur."

[注]

现在讨论的题目是小说中的对白。前一段恐怕是作者说的，他认为对白真照口头所说那样地印在书里（goes into print），谈起来效果是不大会好的（seldom ... effectively）。如要效果好，作者必须要加工改造（原文是被动句法），通常要花点功夫改写。

对白一定要读起来像（sound）真人说话那样（这一句按语法分析起来，people talk 前面也许该有 in which 二词，但照实际用法这两个词是用不着的。

setting down：记下来。**verbatim**（副词）：一字不易地。照人家的说话，照式录下，读起来总该（ought）像真人说话了吧？事实可并不如此。

第二段怀氏发表他的艺术思想。他说：艺术者，是在经验上面加上（imposing）一种形式，以作诗为例，我们喜怒哀乐的情感，可以说是一种经验，诗的长短、字句的排列、平仄的安排就是形式（pattern）。单有经验，不成艺术，一定要把形式套上去，才是艺术。**aesthetic enjoyment**：审美的快感。我们读到一首好诗，觉得很快乐，这种快感是美丽的文字给我们的，我们就在对于形式之美的认识里面（in recognition of the pattern）得到快乐。enjoyment 之后，省了个动词 is。

the mistake：通常人都犯的错误，是把文字当作"实在的东西"（**entities**：这是个哲学名词）。事实上，文字所以有力量（force），所以有意义（meaning），是有赖于情感的联想（如"家"这个字可以唤起我们很多的联想）和自古相传的暗示的意义（如"雪"这个字便有很多附属意义；**overtones** = additional meanings）。

再则单词本身效果也不强，词必须见于（occur）整段诗文（the whole passage）之中，才有动人的力量；整段诗文给我们一种刺激（**impact**：打击）。单词的效果，大部分是从这种整个的刺激中得来（derive）的。

Michael and Mary

金船

Seumas O'Kelly（1881—1918）

  本文选自《爱尔兰短篇小说故事集》（*Irish Stories & Tales*）。爱尔兰人与英格兰人种族不同，其地虽久为英国所统治，然其人对英国素乏好感。19世纪末，随爱尔兰民族主义之抬头，爱尔兰文学也力求表现其民族之特色。所谓"爱尔兰文艺复兴"（The Irish Literary Revival）之目的，即为摆脱英国文学之传统，以新形式表现爱尔兰人之思想与信仰。现在南爱尔兰为一独立国（不属英联邦）。爱尔兰文学在戏剧、诗歌、小说方面亦颇多表现，为英语文学放一异彩。20世纪最伟大小说家之一乔伊斯（James Joyce），即为爱尔兰人。《爱尔兰短篇小说故事集》所收诸人，如王尔德（Oscar Wilde）、萧伯纳（Bernard Shaw）、乔治·摩尔（George Moore）、肖恩·奥法莱恩（Sean O'Faolain）、弗兰克·奥康纳（Frank O'Connor）等，皆文坛俊彦。谢默斯·奥凯利（Seumas O'Kelly）之名声，虽不如上述诸人，然此篇细腻动人，允称佳作。

[1]

  Mary had spent many days gathering wool from the whins on the headland. They were the bits of wool shed by the sheep before the shearing. When she had got a fleece that fitted the basket she took it down to the canal and washed it. When she had done washing it was a soft, white, silky fleece.

She put it back in the brown sally basket, pressing it down with her long, delicate fingers. She had risen to go away, holding the basket against her waist, when her eyes followed the narrow neck of water that wound through the bog.

[注]

本文题名 Michael and Mary，现在 Michael 尚未出现。**gathering wool**：拾羊毛。**whins**：金雀花。**headland**：山岩，想是牧羊之所。

shed：褪脱，羊在修剪（shearing）之前，自己会褪毛。毛落山野间，贫家女子捡来，亦有微利可博。

a fleece：原意是"一次剪下之羊毛"，这里当然是"一次拾来的羊毛"。**that fitted the basket**：篮子里盛得下的。**sally**：柳枝，这个词是 sallow 的变体。**pressing down**：用力塞进去。**long, delicate fingers**：关于这个女子的美，只有这几个词形容。

neck of water：水道，即上述之运河（canal）。**followed**：眼睛跟着河道望去。**bog**：潮湿之泥炭地。运河在这种沼泽地上蜿蜒（wound）流过。

[2]

She could not follow the neck of yellow water very far. The light of day was failing. A haze hung over the great Bog of Allen that spread out level on all sides of her. The boat loomed out of the haze on the narrow neck of the canal water. It looked, at first, a long way off, and it seemed to come in a cloud. The soft rose light that mounted the sky caught the boat and burnished it like dull gold. It came leisurely, drawn by the one horse looking like a Golden Barque in the twilight. Mary put her brown head a little to one side as she watched the easy motion of the boat. The horse drew himself along deliberately, the patient head going up and down with every heavy step. A crane rose from the bog, flapping two lazy wings across the wake of the boat, and, reaching its long neck before it, got lost in the haze.

[注]

本段是风景描写，有几个有关色彩的形容词，尤其要请读者注意。色彩并不艳丽，然而很醒目。本文的浪漫情调是很明显的，但是这里到底只是乡村风光，并非仙境，这河也只是一条"黄流"，并非碧绿的。

天色将暮，日光渐暗（failing），她看不远。

Bog of Allen：这块沼泽地大约不小，居然有它的专用名字。爱尔兰北部有湖名 Lough（= Lake）Allen：这块沼泽地想必离此不远。level 是形容词，形容主语 that。沼泽地平平地向四周伸展开来。

the boat：这里不用 She suddenly saw … 等字样，这种写法在英文里并不显得突兀。**loomed**：朦胧中突然出现，通常用于形体庞大的东西。boat 虽是小船，但是四周雾气（haze）低垂，船穿雾而出，疑是驾云（in a cloud）而来，也会使人觉得很大的。

soft rose light：雾气中看出来的霞光，用这几个词恐怕是最为妥贴。**mounted**：升（空），空中霞光，应该普照万物，但是周围都是平平的地和水，没有突出的东西，单单照在船上，好像霞光只有一道，专照（**caught**：捉住）这艘小船的。**burnished**：摩擦（金属），使光亮，小船在雾气之中，为霞光所照，色彩一定很美，但是假如真说它灿烂若黄金，未免显得过火，这里 dull 一词用得最为恰当。

leisurely：船并不急驶。**horse**：中国有用民夫拉纤行船的，爱尔兰恐怕是用马拉纤的。马在岸上走，船在水中行。**Golden Barque**：典不详，想必爱尔兰民间传说中有"仙舟"这种东西，乡村女子在暮色苍茫之中（in the twilight），逢此奇景，很可能往这方面联想上去的。barque 即 bark，小船。乡间小船，认作仙人金槎，这就是我所谓"浪漫情调"。

brown head：头发的颜色。**put … to one side**：侧着头。

drew himself：马往前走，马本身也有重量，所以可以说"马拉自己"。**deliberately**：不慌不忙地。**patient**：任重道远，马的头表现着"耐心"。**going up and down**：忽俯忽仰。

crane：鹤。四周本来一片静寂，小船出现，打破了这种沉寂，作者特别叫一只野鹤受惊飞起，描写就更有生气。中国旧诗中这种"画龙点睛"之法很常见，读者不妨参照。**lazy wings**：和前面船的 leisurely 以及马的 deliberately 相呼应。**wake**：船身后边的水流。**reached its neck**：伸长它的头颈。**before it** = before the crane。

[3]

The figure that swayed by the big arm of the tiller on *The Golden Barque* was vague. and shapeless at first, but Mary felt her eyes following the slow movements of the body. Mary thought it was very beautiful to sway now and then by the arm of the tiller, steering a Golden Barque through the twilight.

[注]

figure：人的身形。朦胧中还看不仔细。swayed 是不及物动词解作"摇摆"。
tiller：舵柄；想必粗而且长，故说 the big arm。
The Golden Barque：小船的名字，我们不知道。但是在 Mary 想象之中，她觉得它很美，就干脆叫它金船了。**slow movements**：一摇一摆，姿态很美。
every now and then：一下又一下地，常常。**steering**：掌舵，驾驶。

[4]

Then she realised suddenly that the boat was much nearer than she had thought. She could see the figures of the men plainly, especially the slim figure by the tiller. She could trace the rope that slackened and stretched taut as it reached from the boat to the horse. Once it splashed the water, and there was a little spout of silver. She noted the whip looped under the arm of the driver. Presently she could count every heavy step of the horse, and was struck by the great size of the shaggy fetlocks. But always her eyes went back to the figure by the tiller.

[注]

她忽然发觉（realised）船已行近，各人的身形都可以看清楚（plainly），她起初还以为很远呢，这几段描写，都以船的行动为线索，由远而近，驶过她的身边，然后消失。
slim：细长的。那个在舵柄旁的人非但摇摆的姿态优美，身材也是细长的，值得一看再看。
the rope：拉纤的绳，从船上伸（reached）到马身上。马走得快，绳子就绷紧（stretched taut）；船滑得快，绳子就松（slackened）。
splashed：纤绳一张一弛，有时候局部落在水里，水花四溅。spout of silver（银色水花）和 golden barque 有相得益彰之妙。
driver：赶马的。他的鞭子弯成环状（looped），夹在肋下。

presently：不久之后（船渐驶渐近）。

was struck by：见所未见，印象很深。**shaggy**：蓬松松的。**fetlocks**：马脚后跟上的毛。马距毛如此之盛，是她以前所没有注意到的。

最后一句很有力量：她的注意力是集中到那个掌舵的身上去了。

[5]

She moved back a little way to see *The Golden Barque* pass. It came from a strange, far-off world, and having traversed the bog went away into another unknown world. A red-faced man was sitting drowsily on the prow. Mary smiled and nodded to him, but he made no sign. He did not see her; perhaps he was asleep. The driver who walked beside the horse had his head stooped and his eyes on the ground. He did not look up as he passed. Mary saw his lips moving, and heard him mutter to himself; perhaps he was praying. He was a shrunken, misshaped little figure and kept step with the brute in the journey over the bog. But Mary felt the gaze of the man by the tiller upon her. She raised her eyes.

[注]

船行近了，她反而要退后几步，才可看得仔细。船虽到了眼前，但是它的神秘性仍未丧失。它来自奇异的远方,穿过沼泽地（这是现实），再驶向不可知的世界。

drowsily：睡眼惺忪地。**prow**：船头。

船上有两个人，岸上有个赶马的。这三个男人之中，只有那个掌舵的是在注意她。而且一个是虽然经她招呼对她也不理会，一个则是状貌猥琐，相形之下，那个掌舵的更显得杰出。

赶马的身材瘦小（shrunken）而佝偻（misshaped），一步一步地赶着马（brute），在沼泽地上走。

Mary 正在看着这两个人，可是她发觉掌舵的那人眼光正落在她身上，她抬起眼睛来了。

[6]

The light was uncertain and his peaked cap threw a shadow over his face. But the figure was lithe and youthful. He smiled as she looked up, for she caught a gleam of his teeth. Then the boat had passed. Mary did not smile in return. She had taken a step back and remained there quietly. Once he looked back and awkwardly touched his cap, but she made no sign.

[注]

光线模糊，那人戴了一顶鸭舌（peaked）帽，脸为黑影笼罩，看不清楚（throw a shadow 是习语）。可是这个人的身体看来是年轻的，而且刚柔适中，富于弹性（lithe）。

as she looked up：呼应上段的 she raised her eyes。

此人是否在笑，她并不确切知道，可是他的牙齿露了一下白光，像是笑了（原文只用 gleam，不用 white，white 这个词在这里是可以省略的）。

Mary did not smile in return：船头上的那个红脸汉，没有理她，她却向他微笑领首。现在掌舵的向她一笑，她反而不作表示，这是女人心理微妙处。是少女的矜持乎？抑是感触太深，不知所措乎？

船已行远，可是她还是以目送之。她看见那人回过一次头，很笨拙地以手触帽，向她致敬（**awkwardly**："不知怎么是好"的尴尬表情）。

[7]

When the boat had gone by some way she sat down on the bank, her basket of wool beside her, looking at *The Golden Barque* until it went into the gloom. She stayed there for some time, thinking long in the great silence of the bog. When at last she rose, the canal was clear and cold beneath her. She looked into it. A pale new moon was shining down in the water.

[注]

by 有 past 之意。some way 也是作副词之用：走得相当远了。**bank**：河岸。她坐下来，看金船消失于暮色之中。

thinking：她在想些什么呢？她所想的内容如果写了出来，小说的格调恐怕反而要庸俗了。

the canal was clear and cold：clear 者，河上已经没有船。cold 一词尤见分量，意味深长。此刻唯有天际淡淡新月，空照流水而已。

[8]

Mary often stood at the door of the cabin on the headland watching the boats that crawled like black snails over the narrow streak of water through the bog. But they were not all like black snails now. There was a Golden Barque among them. Whenever she saw it she smiled, her eyes on the figure that stood by the shaft of the tiller。

[注]

cabin：木屋之类的敝庐，这大约就是她的家。**snails**：蜗牛。船本来都像蜗牛爬行，可是现在在她心目中，有一条船是与众不同的了。**the narrow streak of water**：就是那条运河。

shaft：柄。她看船，其实只是要看那条金船。船上也只有那个掌舵的人可看而已。她笑，她的眼光落在那个人的身上——心事全在不言中。

bog：前文我把 bog 译作"沼泽地"，这是有词典为凭的。1957 年 2 月 26 日的 *The New Yorker*，内有"Bog for Sale"一文，读后才知道爱尔兰的 bog 和一般英美人所了解的 bog 并不相同，爱尔兰的 bog 大约并不潮湿，只是"泥炭地"而已。bog 的泥土是可以用来当煤炭烧的，现在把该杂志的原文抄录几句如下：

> An Irish bog is not what people imagine. It is not a swamp. It is simply land — usually low-lying and heather-covered — from which turf has been, or can be, cut. Turf, which is called peat outside Ireland, is a layer — perhaps, fifteen or twenty feet deep — of decomposed primeval forest; when cut into rectangular slabs and dried, it is in demand as domestic fuel.

现在再让我们看看"家居泥炭地，眼望金槎船"的 Mary 在做些什么。

[9]

One evening she was walking by the canal when *The Golden Barque* passed. The light was very clear and searching. It showed every plank, battered and tar-stained, on the rough hulk, but for all that it loft none of its magic for Mary. The little shrunken driver, head down, the lips moving, walking beside the horse. She hear: his low mutters as he passed. The red-faced man was stooping over the side of the boat, swinging out a vessel tied to a rope, to haul up some water. He was singing a ballad in a monotonous voice. A tall, dark, spare man was standing by the funnel, looking vacantly ahead. Then Mary's eyes travelled to the tiller.

[注]

searching：搜索性的；发隐抉微的；无孔不入的。初次看见金船，是在暮色苍茫雾气低迷之中。这次虽然仍旧是黄昏，光线却特别明亮，她对于金船有更进一步的认识。

plank：船身（hulk）上的板条。木船上一条条的板都可看得清清楚楚，那些板条已经破烂（battered），沾有柏油污迹（tar-stained）。木船敝旧如此，其非"金船"殆无疑义。但是即使如此（for all that），木船仍旧有它的魔力（magic）。

前面所介绍过的几个人，这里重又出现，只是状貌声音都比较清楚了，第一个是那小个儿赶马的，她现在看得见他嘴唇的动作，听得见他在喃喃自语。另一个是那红脸汉子，他俯身船舷之外，用一只吊桶样的东西（**vessel**：器皿）在河里打水。一面取水，一面唱着山歌。还有一个高挑身材黑瘦（spare）子，那是以前没有出现过的，此人站在烟囱边上，茫然地往前方注视。

眼睛向三个人身上一转，然后又落到掌舵那地方。注意：travelled 这个词是从"旅行"衍生出来的意义。这个词《简明牛津词典》解释作"用心的或是有次序的一件一件东西看过去"，该词典并举了这样一个例：his eye travelled over the scene。

[10]

Mary stepped back with some embarrassment when she saw the face. She backed into a hawthorn that grew all alone on die canal bank. It was covered with bloom. A shower of the white petals fell about her when she stirred the branches. They clung about her hair like a wreath. He raised his cap and smiled. Mary did not know the face was so eager, so boyish. She smiled a little nervously at last. His face lit up, and he touched his cap again.

[注]

她看见那个男人，总觉得有点不自在，现在仍旧如此。

backed：这个词可以作动词用的，她往后一退，以山楂（hawthorn）的枝叶掩身，河岸上孤零零的（all alone）就是这么一棵树，人入花丛，树枝受震，群英纷落（a shower），附着（clung）在她的头发上，她好像戴了一顶花冠（wreath）。这是她同那个男子第二次见面，作者对于 Mary 的美，并没有描写，但是她的娇羞，加上头发上的白花瓣（petal），她那时的美，我们也不难想象了。

raised his cap：脱帽高举行礼。

帽子一脱，那人的脸就看得清楚了，Mary 想不到他的脸竟是如此的热情流露（eager），如此的稚气可掬。

at last：人家对她行礼，她没法再矜持，最后只好窘迫地微微一笑。她笑了，他的脸上也容光焕发（lit 是 light 的过去时）了，那时他的帽子已经戴上，他就举手触帽行礼。

[11]

The red-faced man stood by the open hatchway going into the hold, the vessel of water in his hand. He looked at Mary and then at the figure beside the tiller.

"Eh, Michael," the red-faced man said quizzically. The youth turned back to the boat, and Mary felt the blush spreading over her face.

"Michael!"

Mary repeated the name a little softly to herself. The gods had delivered up one of their great secrets.

[注]

hatchway：甲板上的出入口。going 形容 hatchway：这个出入口是通到船的底部（hold）的。

quizzically：开玩笑的样子，那红脸汉已经猜到那男人的心事了。

Michael：这个名字第一次出现。女的对于那个男的，已有好感，可是不知道他的名字。她恐怕非常想知道他的名字，可是作者对于这种心理状态，绝不用一字描写（一写恐怕就"俗"）。但是她听见了这个名字，脸就红到耳朵根（spreading over her face），还轻轻地自言自语念这个名字——这种暗示，不就够了吗？（这种暗示的写法，中国旧诗里很常见。）最后还说了这么一句话：天神总算把一件大秘密让凡人知道了。为什么是"大秘密"呢？她的亟于想知道那人的名字，不言而喻。从此以后，那人不再是 the figure beside the tiller，而是 Michael 了。

gods：想是爱尔兰古时的神，不是基督教的神。基督教的神应该用大写 G，而且也没有复数形式的。**delivered up**：交出，献出（不再吝啬）。

[12]

She watched *The Golden Barque* until two square slits in the stern that served as port holes looked like two little Japanese eyes. Then she heard a horn blowing. It was the horn they blew to apprise lock-keepers of the approach of a boat. But the nearest lock was a mile off. Besides, it was a long, low sound the horn made, not the sharp, commanding blast they blew for lock-keepers. Mary listened to the low sound of the horn, smiling to herself. Afterwards the horn always blew like that whenever *The Golden Barque* was passing the solitary hawthorn.

[注]

船又驶远，她还是以目遥送。**slits**：孔；通常指"长条的裂口"，但是这里是"正方形的"。**stern**：船尾。**port holes**：船上的窗洞。船走远了，船尾的两个窗洞也渐缩小，最后看来只像日本人的两只小眼睛。西洋人通常以为东方人的眼睛小，好像东方人以为"高鼻子"是西洋人的特征一样。

horn：号角，喇叭。they blew 的 they 泛指"那地方船上的人"。这种用法为语法家所不取，但是很常见。**apprise**：通知。

lock：运河中由水闸控制的一段水道。运河是人造的河，水面可能有几段高，有几段低。高低水道间，有水闸控制。船行至高低水道差异之处，先得用信号（如吹喇叭）通知管闸的人（lock-keeper）把水闸放开。

船上忽然吹起喇叭来了，那是为什么呢？水闸还远得很呢。再则，要通知开闸，喇叭的声音是尖锐短促，带着命令（commanding）的意味，这是 Mary 所知道的，但是现在喇叭的声音是悠长迟缓，这种低声的喇叭是吹给谁听的呢？Mary 笑起来了。

以后船还在那棵树下过，行到那地方，船上就轻轻地吹起喇叭。男方的情感，作者也不直接描写，只是用暗示。笔墨如此经济，而情感已跃然纸上，作者真写情好手也。

[13]

Mary thought it was very wonderful that *The Golden Barque* should be in the lock the one day that she was travelling with her basket to the market in the distant village. She stood a little hesitantly by the lock. Michael looked at her, a welcome in his eyes.

"Going to Bohermeen?" the red-faced man asked.

"Ay, to Bohermeen," Mary answered.

Mary hesitated, as he held out a big hand to help her to the boat. He saw the hesitation and turned to Michael.

"Now, Michael," he said.

[注]

后来又有一天，Mary 提了篮子到远处村庄的市场上去，路过水闸，那船恰好停在那边，Mary 觉得真巧（wonderful）。看见了船，她踌躇了一下，脚步停住了。Michael 对她看，眼睛里表示欢迎。可是他还不好意思开口，由那红脸汉代表发言的。

Bohermeen 想必就是那 distant village 的名字。

红脸汉要扶她上船，送她一程，可是 Mary 不要他扶。这里 hesitate，hesitantly，hesitation 三种形式都用上了。

[14]

Michael came to the side of the boat, and held out his hand Mary took it and stepped on board. The red-faced man laughed a little. She noticed that the dark man who stood by the crooked funnel never took his eyes from the stretch of water before him. The driver was already urging the horse to the start on the bank. The brute was gathering his strength for the pull, the muscles standing out on his haunches. They glided out of the lock.

[注]

红脸汉来扶，她不要；Michael 伸手过来，她就接住了上船（on board），其中必有文章，无怪红脸汉要笑了。

到了船上，她又看看四周的人。烟囱是弯曲的（crooked），她这才注意到。站在烟囱边上的黑汉子，想必是负航行之责，所以眼睛老是看着前面那条水道。

现在又要开船了，所以赶马的在岸上赶马动身。

马（the brute）起步之前，先鼓足了劲，后股（haunches）上的肌肉都凸了起来。前面描写过马的距毛（见前面本文）。据我臆测，这种大动物的"雄姿"，对于春情业已发动的 Mary 多少有点挑逗作用，当然这都是"暗示"，无丝毫恶俗之气。

[15]

It was half a mile from one lock to another. Michael had bidden her stand beside him at the tiller. Once she looked up at him and she thought the face shy but very eager, the most eager face that ever came across the bog from the great world.

[注]

别人都看过了，最后向 Michael 抬头一望。Michael 的脸是羞涩的，可是很 eager，Michael 是从外乡来的（是从"广大的世界"来的），行船经过她家乡的泥炭地，这种人 Mary 以前也见过，可是论到脸上神情的热烈殷切，那是要数 Michael 第一了。

[16]

Afterwards, whenever Mary had the time, she would make a cross-cut through the bog to the lock. She would step in and make the mile journey with Michael on *The Golden Barque*. Once, when they were journeying together, Michael slipped something into her hand. It was a quaint trinket, and shone like gold.

"From a strange sailor I got it," Michael said.

[注]

make a cross-cut：走对角线穿过。按正路走，也许路径要长了。**step in**：上船。**make the mile journey**：航行那一英里路程；mile 是名词，但英文中名词作形容词用（即作定语）的情形很多。

slipped：偷偷地放。slip 本有"滑"的意思，这个词当然比 put 更传神，比 gave her something 也好多了。slipped 表示一种确切的动作，这是炼字的功夫，用心写作的人，决不以能用 put，give 这类的词就满足的。

quaint：别致的。**trinket**：首饰。

Michael 送她东西，可以说是表示爱情。但是他说 from a strange-sailor I got it，又为全文结束，作一伏笔。他同那些大船上的水手是有来往的，关于 Michael 的生活，我们所知道的就是这么一点。但是这一点渐渐加强，就决定了这篇小说的结局。

[17]

Another day that they were on the barque, the blinding sheets of rain that often swept over the beg came upon them. The red-faced man and the dark man went into the hold. Mary looked about her, laughing. But Michael held out his great waterproof for her. She slipped into it and he folded it about her. The rain pelted them, but they stood together, Michael holding the big coat folded about her. She laughed a little nervously.

[注]

another day that 中的 that 有 when 之意。**sheets of rain**：猛雨。**blinding**：使人睁不开眼睛。

the dark man：就是那"高挑身材黑瘦子"。

Mary 不畏风雨，反而大笑。这和她的个性以及当时她喜悦的心情有关。作者的描写，就是这么一触即走，不多叙述。

waterproof 此处作名词用，就是稍后的 **big coat**：雨衣。

slipped 此词第二次出现，大致可以使人想到娇小玲珑的身材，"钻"进一件大雨衣里的神情。**about**：在（她）周围，替她裹好。**pelted**：密集打击（石子、冰雹、雨点等）。holding the big coat folded 中的 folded 是过去分词。

[18]

"You will be wet," she said.

Michael did not answer. She saw the eager face coming down close to hers. She leaned against him a little and felt the great strength of his arms about her. They went sailing away together in *The Golden Barque* through all the shining seas of the gods.

[注]

Michael 那件雨衣，让给 Mary 穿了，自己淋雨。这一方面是描写男人强毅的个性，一方面表示他们的爱情又进一步。现在他们俩相偎相依，这种热情场面不易描写，稍一不慎，就可能流为恶俗。但是作者笔墨经济，只重复前面所用过的 eager 一词。最初她只注意男人的身材，后来她看清楚他的脸，他的脸可能是很英俊的，但作者故意不用 handsome 等字样，只说是 eager。现在 the eager face 向她贴近。他们的爱情就分这么三个阶段。

在运河里他们只可以共航一英里左右，但是外面风吹雨淋，男人拥抱着她，她已有"陶醉"之感。所以她觉得他们是在"神圣光亮的海上"航行，驶向远处（sailing away）。

[19]

"Michael," Mary said once, "is it not lovely?"

"The wide ocean is lovely," Michael said. "I always think of the wide ocean going over the bog."

"The wide ocean!" Mary said with awe. She had never seen the wide ocean. Then the rain passed. When the two men came up out of the hold Mary and Michael were standing together by the tiller.

[注]

这几段又从梦想回到现实，而小说不快乐的结局也渐渐接近了。Mary 在陶醉之中，觉得这样行船很可爱。Michael 是否和 Mary 同样的陶醉之感，我们不知道；因为这篇小说以 Mary 为主体，思想情感等，皆以 Mary 的观点为出发。但是从对白之中，我们可以看见：Mary 所想的是缥缈仙乡之海，而 Michael 所想的是现实的五大洋。两种境界也许都是浪漫的，但是两人的想法不易接近。Mary 发现两人虽相偎相依，然而是"同床异梦"，Michael 有他自己的理想，并不能把全部精神贡献给她；所以她凛然惊觉地（with awe）说："The wide ocean!"

going over the bog 是形容主语 I 的。going 有"行船"之意。

[20]

Mary did not go down to the lock after that for some time. She was working in the reclaimed ground on the headland. Once the horn blew late in the night. It blew for a long time, very softly and lowly. Mary sat up in bed listening to it, her lips parted, the memory of Michael on *The Golden Barque* before her. She heard the sound dying away in the distance. Then she lay back on her pillow, saying she would go down to him when *The Golden Barque* was on the return journey.

[注]

go down：她所住的地方较高，运河那边地势较低。

reclaimed ground：本系荒芜，后经垦殖适于耕种的土地。

sat up：夜已深，Mary 想已入睡，听见喇叭轻柔缓慢的声音，她坐了起来。

her lips parted：这是 nominative absolute phrase。嘴唇张了开来，或者用句文言老调"樱唇微启"，这样一个简单的动作，表示她谛听的神情，她的期待，她的欲望。以这几个简单的词，代替大段心理描写，非高手莫办也。

on the return journey：船回来时，在水闸那个地方，还要停留一个时候。她决心（注意作者不用 resolved 等比较难以捉摸的词，只是用很简单的 saying 一词）时再到船上去一次。

[21]

The figure that stood by the tiller on the return was not Michael's. When Mary came to the lock the red-faced man was telling out the rope, and where Michael always stood by the tiller there was the short strange figure of a man with a pinched, pock-marked face.

[注]

"若干时候以后，船回来了，Mary 又赶去了……"这种话在叙事明快的文章里，是可以省去的。

掌舵的已经换了一个人，远远一看身材就知道不对。

telling out the rope：船上的绳本来是圈好的，现在用到它，一圈一圈地（telling 有"计数"之意）把它拉出来。

现在舵工换了一个矮小个儿，一脸苦相（pinched），且有麻子（pock-marked）。

[22]

When the red-faced man wound the rope round the stump at the lock, bringing the boat to a stand-still, he turned to Mary. "Michael is gone voyaging," he said. "Gone voyaging?" Mary repeated.

"Ay," the man answered. "He would be always talking to the foreign sailors in the dock where the canal ends. His eyes would be upon the big masts of the ships, I always said he would go."

[注]

绳拉出来是预备碇泊之用，现在绳是绕在木桩之上，**bringing to a stand-still** 是习语：使停止。

voyaging：通常指"长程航海"。

foreign sailors：呼应前面的 a strange sailor。

dock：船坞。**where the canal ends**：运河的终点。

masts：桅杆。ships 和 barque 有大小之别。

红脸汉几句简单的话，很清楚地把 Michael 的理想说明了。

[23]

Mary stood there while *The Golden Barque* was in the lock. It looked like a toy ship packed in a wooden box.

"A three-master he went in," the red-faced man said, as they made ready for the start, "I saw her standing out for the sea last night. Michael is under the spread of big canvas. He had the blood in him for the wide ocean, the wild blood of the rover." And the red-faced man, who was the boss of the boat, let his eyes wander up the narrow neck of water before him.

[注]

据 Mary 看来，斯船已不复是金船。小船在水闸里停着，只像是一只装 (packed) 在木盒里的玩具船。

three-master：三桅大船。

they：泛指船上的人。**made ready**：管水闸的人把水位调整好了，船又可以启航了。

her：船习惯用阴性代名词代替。**under the spread of big canvas**：巨帆张起，Michael 站在下面。

in him：在他身体里面。the wild blood 加强前面的 the blood ... for the wild ocean：他有爱好海洋的血，流浪人的血。

boss：主人。红脸汉虽不能出海远航，他的心未尝不追随 Michael 于海上焉，所以他的眼睛往前看。

[24]

Mary watched *The Golden Barque* moving away, the grotesque figure standing by the tiller. She stayed there until a pale moon was shining below her, turning over a little trinket in her fingers. At last she dropped it into the water.

It made a little splash, and the vision of the crescent was broken.

[注]

船又开走了，可是掌舵的是那个怪模样（grotesque）的人了。

a pale moon：这个景致前面已出现过。景犹是也，船犹是也，唯人事之变迁大矣。

a little trinket：不用 the，而用 a，好像这是任何一件首饰而已。事实上，读者当然知道这是那一件了。

the crescent：新月。河里起了一些水花，新月的影子也破碎了。这是具体生动的描写，然而也有象征的意义。象征些什么，这里也不用说了。

University Days
大学生活

James G. Thurber（1894—1961）

瑟伯生于美国俄亥俄州之哥伦布市。他是美国现代幽默大师，文画双绝。他创作的漫画，以臃肿而懦弱的男人，臃肿而凶横的女人，以及神经质的狗为题材，颇能反映西方文明社会的病态。他的著作很多，如 *Further Fables for Our Time*，所收为供成人阅读的伊索寓言式的故事。这篇"大学生活回忆"原为他的自传 *My Life and Hard Times*（1933）里的一章，现在选择"植物学课"和"经济学课"的几段，选自《美国最佳幽默小说集》（*Best American Humorous Short Stories*），美国式的幽默，通常以胡闹与胡说（nonsense）为主，不一定有什么尖刻的讽刺，或是高尚的含义。中国近代知识分子，大多推崇高级的幽默，而鄙视低级的滑稽。其实喜剧与悲剧，历史同样久远，喜剧主要的目的是叫人笑，并不一定有什么明确的教训。莎士比亚的幽默、胡闹与胡说的成分很多，但是莎士比亚的喜剧天才，是同他的悲剧天才一样受到举世的称颂的。这几段文章的描写可能夸张，记事不一定忠实，问题是看读者觉得好笑不好笑了。

[1]

I passed all the other courses that I took at my university, but I could never pass botany. This was because all botany students had to spend several hours a week in a laboratory looking through a microscope at plant cells, and

I could never see through a microscope. I never once saw a cell through a microscope. This used to enrage my instructor. He would wander around the laboratory pleased with the progress all the students were making in drawing the involved and, so I am told, interesting structure of flower cells, until he came to me. I would just be standing there. "I can't see anything," I would say. He would begin patiently enough, explaining how anybody can see through a microscope, but he would always end up in a fury, claiming that I could *too* see through a microscope but just pretend that I couldn't. "It takes away from the beauty of flowers anyway," I used to tell him. "We are not concerned with beauty in this course," he would say. "We are concerned solely with what I may call the *mechanics* of flars." "Well," I'd say. "I can't see anything." "Try it just once again," he'd say, and I would put my eye to the microscope and see nothing at all, except now and again a nebulous milky substance — a phenomenon of maladjustment. You were supposed to see a vivid, restless clockwork of sharply defined plant cells, "I see what looks like a lot of milk," I would tell him. This, he claimed, was the result of my not having adjusted the microscope properly, so he would readjust it for me, or rather, for himself. And I would look again and see milk.

[注]

that I took 的 took 有"修读"之意。my University 指 Ohio State University。

botany students：修植物学的学生（同样的，English students 指修读英语的学生）。**microscope**：显微镜。**plant cells**：植物细胞。

I could never see：事实上，Thurber 确有眼疾。他写稿时，字写得很大，一张纸上只写寥寥数十字。但他仍写文作画不辍，精神可佩。

instructor：狭义是"讲师"（大学教员的一个等级），广义是"授课的先生"。这儿用的是广义，因为这位先生是一个教授。

he would：这一段里 would 用得很多，表示过去的习惯。pleased 是过去分词，形容主语 He，教授看见全班学生在画细胞图，心里很高兴。**the progress all the students were making**：这里 progress 的意思，不是"进步"，而是"进行"，先画了一个轮廓，然后愈画愈详细。**structure**：（花卉细胞之）结构，这种结构是复杂的（involved），据说（so I am told）也是有趣的。

standing there：大家都在埋头作画，我只是站着。

end up：他开头很耐心地对我解释，显微镜里的细胞是人人看得见的，可是到后来总会大发雷霆（fury），说我一定也看得见的，只是假装（pretending）看不见而已。**claim** = to assert or maintain as a fact。

it takes away from 中的 it 指在显微镜中看花这件事。takes 在这里是不及物动词。**take away from**：减损。**anyway**：不管显微镜里看得见看不见细胞。

concerned with：所关心者，所注意者。

mechanics：机械结构之学。花是有生命的东西，当然和没有生命的机械不同，但是细胞的结构，其配合整齐，亦可与机械结构相比。故教授说"我可以称之为花的机械结构的学问"。**flars**：教授读 flowers 时，嘴张得太大，读成了这个音。

now and again：有时。**nebulous**：云雾状的。**milky**：牛奶状的。**a phenomenon of maladjustment**：因调整不良（显微镜的焦距没有对好）而产生的现象。

you：泛指看显微镜的人。**restless**：活动不息的。**clockwork**：发条机械，呼应前面的 mechanics。**sharply defined**：轮廓鲜明的。

for me, or rather, for himself：与其说为我调整，不如说为他自己调整。教授调整好了，他自己先看。

[2]

I finally took a deferred pass, as they called it, and waited a year and tried again. (You had to pass one of the biological sciences or you couldn't graduate.) The professor had come back from vacation brown as a berry, brightened, and eager to explain cell-structure again to his classes. "Well," he said to me, cheerily when we met in the first laboratory hour of the semester, "we're going to see cells this time, aren't we?" "Yes, sir," I said. Students to right of me and to left of me and in front of me were seeing cells; what's more, they were quietly drawing pictures of them in their notebooks. Of course, I didn't see anything.

[注]

deferred pass：重修后给学分（延迟的及格）。

as they called it：学生手则有这样一个名称（they 系泛指）。

you 同上段的 you 一样，也是泛指。在那所大学里读书，必须选修一门生物科学（动物学、植物学、生理学、遗传学等），否则不得毕业。

vacation：美国人喜欢到山上、海边去度暑假，回来的时候，皮肤晒得红红的（应该说是"棕色的"，但是中国人不大说"棕色的"）。

the first laboratory hour：本学期第一堂实验课。

were seeing：see 用进行时，是不常见的。但这里应该用进行时：教授和我谈话的时候，同学们都在看显微镜，非但是看（looking through），而且都从显微镜里看见细胞。

[3]

"We'll try it," the professor said to me grimly, "with every adjustment of the microscope known to man. As God is my witness, I'll arrange this glass so that you see cells through it or I'll give up teaching. In twenty-two years of botany, I — " He cut off abruptly for he was beginning to quiver all over, like Lionel Barrymore.

[注]

grimly：教授的脸沉下去了。

known to man：全人类所知道的调整显微镜的方法本来只有这么几种，教授都要给用上了。

as God is my witness：赌咒的话：你这次再看不见细胞，我就不吃这碗教书饭了（give up）。

cut off abruptly：话突然停住，教授愈说愈气，全身发抖。

Lionel Barrymore：当年有名的性格演员，擅演暴躁易怒的老人。

[4]

So we tried it with every adjustment of the microscope known to man. With only one of them did I see anything but blackness or the familiar lacteal opacity, and that time I saw, to my pleasure and amazement, a variegated constellation of flecks, specks and dots. These I hastily drew. The instructor, noting my activity, came back from an adjoining desk, a smile on his lips and his eyebrows high in hope. He looked at my cell drawing. "What's that?" he demanded, with a hint of squeal in his voice. "That's what I saw," I said. "You didn't, you didn't, you *didn't*!" he screamed, losing control of his temper instantly, and he bent over and squinted into the microscope. His head snapped up. "That's your eye!" he shouted. "You've fixed the lens so that it reflects! You've drawn your eye!"

[注]

with every adjustment：套用前面教授的话。

with only one of them：用各种调整方法，我所看见的只是一片黑暗，或是平常那种牛奶状（lacteal）的模糊一圈（opacity）。opacity 的形容词形式是 opaque。lacteal 意同前面的 milky；只是 lacteal 的词源是拉丁文；milky 的词源是盎格鲁—撒克逊文。可是有一次调整对了，我所见不同。那一次，我看见了很多斑斑点点（flecks, specks and dots），聚成一堆（**constellation**：星座），形状斑驳复杂（variegated），我大为惊喜。

noting my activity：见到我在画图了。**adjoining desk**：隔壁那张桌子。**his eyebrow's high in hope**：教授满怀希望，眉毛抬得老高。

a hint of squeal：声音里有点尖声惨叫的味道。**you didn't**：似为 you didn't see that 之略。

squinted：眯着眼睛往里看。

snapped up：头猛地一抬。

lens：透镜。**reflects**：反射，这里用作不及物动词。笨学生所看见的，原来是自己眼睛的镜像！

[5]

Another course that I didn't like, but somehow managed to pass, was economics. I went to that class straight from the botany class, which didn't help me any in understanding either subject. I used to get them mixed up. But not as mixed up as another student in my economics class who came there direct from a physics laboratory. He was a tackle on the football team, named Bolenciewicz. At that time Ohio State university had one of the best football teams in the country, and Bolenciewicz was one of its outstanding stars. In order to be eligible to play it was necessary for him to keep up in his studies, a very difficult matter, for while he was not dumber than an ox he was not any smarter. Most of his professors were lenient and helped him along. None gave him more hints, in answering questions, or asked him simpler ones than the economics professor, a thin, timid man named Bassum.

[注]

another course：生物学之外，经济学他也不喜欢，但是他总是不知怎么想法子"弄"（managed）及格的。

straight：直接的；一上完生物学，就去上经济学。

either：两样东西之任何一样。

get them mixed up：把两门功课混淆起来。

but not …：此句不完全，仅是补充前句的 mixed up。

direct：这个词同前面的 straight 一样，用作副词。

tackle：截球员（美国式足球球员中之一）。

Bolenciewicz：此人恐怕是波兰裔，名字的读音很难。

eligible：有入选资格。**to keep up in his studies**：各门都及格，有一门不及格，就不可以参加比赛。

dumber：较笨。**smarter**：较聪明。

lenient：宽；特别客气。**helped him along**：帮他及格。注意：along 有"前进"之意。

thin, timid man：这样一个"瘦怯怯"的教授，同这个其笨如牛的学生，正好成一滑稽的对照。教授要帮学生及格，发问的时候，大多给他暗示（give him hints），免得他多费脑筋思索，或者问些很容易的题目（**simpler ones** = simpler questions）；但是讲到暗示之多，题目之容易，没有一位教授比得上这位经济学教授的。

[6]

One day when we were on the subject of transportation and distribution, it came Bolenciewicz's turn to answer a question. "Name one means of transportation," the professor said to him. No light came into the big tackle's eyes. "Just any means of transportation," said the professor, "any medium, agency, or method of going from one place to another." Bolenciewicz had the look of a man who is being led into a trap. "You may choose among steam, horse-drawn, or electrically propelled vehicles," said the instructor, "I might suggest the one which we commonly take in making long journeys across land."

[注]

transportation and distribution：运输与分配（经济学的一个题目）。

it came Bolenciewicz's turn：这里的 it 用语法家奥托·叶斯柏森（Otto Jespersen）的术语，应该是 preparatory "it" 的一种。it 就是 turn，不过这个词先出来，为名词 turn 作一准备。句法结构大致同下句相仿：

It's no use crying over spilt milk.

means of transportation：交通工具（教授的用词太深，为笨学生所不能了解）。教授看见学生瞠目不知所对（眼睛里没有光），就换一种说法：any medium, agency, or method of going from one place to another，那时学生更觉糊涂，脸上的表情就像一个被人家设圈套愚弄的人一样。

教授叫学生任意举一种交通工具，后来缩小范围，叫他任意举一种"车辆"（vehicles）：在蒸汽推动，马力拖曳，电力推动各种车辆中任举一种。

the one：这种车辆。在陆地上长距离旅行乘坐的车辆应该是火车。

[7]

There was a profound silence in which everybody stirred uneasily, including Bolenciewicz and Mr. Bassum. Mr. Bassum abruptly broke this silence in an amazing manner. "Choo-choo-choo," he said, in a low voice, and turned instantly scarlet. He glanced appealingly around the room. All of us, of course, shared Mr. Bassum's desire that Bolenciewicz should stay abreast of the class in economics, for the Illinois game, one of the hardest and most important of the season, was only a week off, "Toot, toot, too-toooooooot!" some student with a deep voice moaned, and We all looked encouragingly at Bolenciewicz. Somebody else gave a fine imitation of a locomotive letting off steam. Mr. Bassum himself rounded off the little show. "Ding, dong, ding, dong," he said, hopefully. Bolenciewicz was staring at the floor now, trying to think, his great brow furrowed, his huge hands rubbing together, his face red.

[注]

题目问得如此之浅，而学生仍旧答不出来。班上虽然大家不开口，但是人人都有点不安的骚动。

Choo-choo-choo：火车的声音。教授模仿了这种声音，自己觉得不好意思，脸上立刻绯红。

appealingly：请求（帮助）地。教授没有办法了，且看同学中有没有人能够打开这个僵局。

shared Mr. Bassum's desire：同具此感。教授的尊称用 Mr. 在美国大学里是很普通的。通常美国各大学的概况里课程名称与内容一章，对于授课教员一律称之为 Mr.，不管他的身份是教授或副教授。**stayed abreast of**：跟得上；不留级。

the Illinois game：大概是和 University of Illinois 比赛的一场足球赛。**the season**：足球季节；美国通常是在秋季。**only a week off**：还有一个星期就要比球了，假如此君这个题目答不出来，校队就要少一员大将。

toot, toot ...：这个声音更像火车了。

encouragingly：以鼓励的眼光看他。

letting off steam：火车头排汽的声音。

the little show：上课成了口技表演了。**rounded off**：使圆满结束。**Ding, dong**：火车站的钟声。**hopefully**：期待地（这下子他总该答得出来了）。

great 和 huge 二词表示其人的魁梧。**brow furrowed**：蹙额。

[8]

"How did you come to College this year, Mr. Bolenciewicz?" asked the professor. "*Chuffa* chuffa, *chuffa* chuffa."

"M'father sent me," said the football player.

"What on?" asked Bassum.

"I git an 'lowance," said the tackle, in a low, husky voice, obviously embarrassed.

"No, no," said Mr. Bassum. "Name a means of transportation. What did you *ride* here on?"

"Train," said Bolenciewicz.

"Quite right," said the professor. "Now, Mr. Nugent, will you tell us — "

[注]

M'father = my father。**What on?** 教授问他是坐什么车，但是 on 词意义很多，学生误会是问他靠什么来维持生活的（例如 live on），所以回答说是"有一笔津贴"。git 当是 got，这位学生发音是不准的。**an 'lowance** = an allowance。

最后总算答对了，教授又问另一个学生 Mr. Nugent 别的问题了。全班那时当然松了一口气，这些话都不必说。作者的文字很简练，要言不烦，幽默而不流入油滑，作者自己似乎是板起了脸来叙述这一段有趣的故事的。莎士比亚说：Brevity is the soul of wit. 旨哉斯言。

British Bicycles in Spain
英国自行车在西班牙

Robert Graves（1895—1985）

格雷夫斯是英国当代著名诗人。他又是历史小说家，小说中有 I, Claudius（《朕，克劳迪乌斯》），Wife to Milton 等。1975 年他还出版了一本 They Hanged My Saintly Billy，故事是重述一百年前英国的一桩凶杀案。

在 20 世纪 50 年代，格氏对于考古学大有兴趣。写了 The White Godness 和 The Nazarene Gospel Restored 等。1955 年他为"企鹅丛书"写了两厚册的《希腊神话》（The Greek Myths），用人类学考古学的视角来看希腊神话，发掘传说故事中的社会意义。

格雷夫斯著作等身，这里所选的只是他的杂文中一段。本文原题是 A Bicycle in Majorca，发表于 1957 年 6 月 22 日的 The New Yorker 杂志。Majorca 是西班牙所属地中海一个岛，格氏卜居于此，已历有年数。这篇文章叙述他孩子的自行车失窃的故事，文字轻松，挖苦西班牙人，可是不失作者的绅士风度。

[1]

The Spaniards certainly know how to ride bicycles; they are heroic racing cyclists, and the mortality among leaders of the profession is a good deal higher than among bullfighters. A recess at the back of the Palma Cycling Club provides a shrine for one of its members killed on a mountain road during the Tour of Spain — his pedals and shoes hung up beneath a plaque of St. Christopher, with candles perpetually burning. Other members, who have died in lesser contests, are not so commemorated. But we British at least know how to make bicycles. I hasten to say that I am not criticizing Spanish workmanship. The British just happen to be experts in this particular trade; they even export vast quantities of bicycles to the choosy United States.

[注]

西班牙人是 Spaniard，西班牙的是 Spanish，英文"某国的人民"（名词）和"某国的"（形容词）大致都形式相同（如 Chinese，Japanese 等），西班牙是少数例外之一（波兰人，Pole；波兰的，Polish；芬兰人，Finn；芬兰的，Finnish）。

骑自行车的人（不论是赛车专家，或是普通乘骑的人）是 cyclist，bicyclist 这个词不常用。**racing**：赛跑的，长距离比赛的。

mortality：死亡率。**bullfighters**：斗牛士。斗牛士西班牙文为 torero（徒步的）或 toreador（骑马的）。斗牛士易为牛所伤，死亡率颇高；但是赛车这一行（profession）里面的重要人物，其死亡率之高，远胜（a good deal higher）于斗牛士，注意本句中 among 这个词的用法。

recess：壁凹。**Palma**：马略卡岛（Majorca）上之城镇。**Cycling Club**：自行车协会。联谊性质之社团，英文大多是 club，如"留美同学会"为 American University Club，"哈佛同学会"为 Harvard Club 等。**shrine**：神龛。**Tour of Spain**：环游西班牙自行车比赛。会里有一个会员，在一条山路上失事身死。死后会员把他的跑鞋和他的车上的踏脚板挂在会所后面的一座神龛里，作为纪念。龛里本来供的是 St. Christopher 之像，像刻在一块板（plaque）上，终年蜡烛供养。鞋和踏板挂在神像的底下。

lesser contests：小规模的比赛，然而亦有失事丧生的，这种人会里就不这么隆重地纪念（commemorate）了。

make：此词重读。英国人骑车拼命的劲儿，也许赶不上西班牙人，但是英国人至少会造自行车。

workmanship：制造技术。作者是英国人，现在要赞美英国的自行车，但是自吹自擂，有失风度，赶快（hasten）声明，他不是在批评西班牙的自行车坏。英国自行车制作精良，举世闻名，作者说话很谦虚，可是读者不得不承认，他的态度的大方。

happen：恰巧是。英国人别的东西也许全不行，这一行（制造自行车）偏偏是内行。

choosy：口语词汇，意思是"好挑剔的"。美国人买外国货。当然挑好的买，英国自行车是美国人所喜欢的。

[2]

The Spanish government will not, of course, agree that anyone else in the world can make anything better than Spaniards do, and surely a government's business is to foster faith in the nation's industrial proficiency. This attitude, however, makes it difficult for a Spaniard or a foreign resident in Spain to import a British bicycle, especially when Spanish sterling reserves are low.

[注]

本段讲西班牙政府不允许英国自行车进口。作者对于此事，很可能并不赞同，但是他多用反语（irony），事事就西班牙政府立场说话，结果把西班牙政府挖苦得很惨。

西班牙政府当然认为西班牙的国货，绝不会比外国货差。他们绝不会同意，说是别国人造出来的东西会比西班牙人造的好。注意本句中 anyone else 二词，如改用 any other nation，就笨得多了。

a government's business：business 是"责任"或"天职"。这词同前面的 anyone else 相仿，都是口语习用之词，读之令人起亲切之感。如此处改用 responsibility 等词，句子又要显得笨了。我们学 idiomatic English，主要的是要学这些简单的词的用法。**foster faith**：培养信心。**industrial proficiency**：工业技术之(熟练)程度。

however：此种态度虽好，但是对人民亦有不便之处。**makes it** 中的 it 指下面 to import（进口）... 。**foreign resident**：外侨。

sterling reserves：英镑外汇储存量。**low**：不足。向英国买东西，就得动用英镑外汇。国际贸易大约有两大集团，即英镑集团（sterling bloc）和美元集团（dollar bloc）是也。美元外汇储存量是 dollar reserves。

[3]

Such a person must fill out fifteen forms in quintuplicate, supplying all his own vital statistics, with those of his relations in at least the nearer degrees, and showing a just cause why he should be allowed a British bicycle (despite the hundred-percent Spanish import duty) instead of a much better, locally manufactured machine, which can be bought at half the cost.

[注]

such a person：申请购买英制自行车的人。**fill out fifteen forms**：填十五种表。**in quintuplicate**：每种表填同式五份。同式双份是 duplicate，三份是 triplicate，四份是 quadruplicate。**vital statistics**：《四用字典》解作"人口统计"。但此词亦有"履历"之意，包括出生年月日，出生地点，婚姻状况等。**those of his relations**：those 仍是 statistics。亲有远近，以 degree 表示之。**relations in the nearer degrees**：近亲或家属。**at least**：虽然不致把"三代""九族"都填进去，至少父母妻子的"履历"都要填写清楚的。**just cause**：正当理由。**allowed**：请求政府批准。注意，allowed 后面不必跟 to buy 等字样。allow 本身就含有 to have 的意思。**import duty**：进口税。进口税高达百分之一百，你还要去申请外汇购买英国自行车，一定有理由，试于表格上详述之。**much better**：反语。自行车是一种 machine。**at half the cost**：西班牙制自行车价钱只需英国的一半，何况它的质量又比英国的好得多（在西班牙政府看来）。

[4]

When he has waited fifteen months for an answer, while sterling reserves continue to fall, the chances are that the answer will be "We lament to inform you that last year's bicycle import quota has already been satisfied; we therefore advise you to fill out the necessary forms in quintuplicate for the present year's quota" ... this year which, as a matter of fact, ended three months before.

[注]

申请表送上去后，如石沉大海。一年零三个月后（同时，西班牙政府外汇更形缺乏，他们更舍不得批准了），批复来了。

the chances are that：很可能的。引号中文字模仿"官样文章"。lament 原意是"悲悼"，这里只是"深表遗憾"。此词改用 regret 亦可，regret 亦有"悲悼"、"惋惜"之意。

import quota：进口定额。**satisfied**：满足（额度已满）。

the present year's quota：本年的进口定额。可是回信离开填发日期已有十五个月，换言之，公文里的所谓"本年"，已经过了三个月。西班牙政府的"公文旅行"，把事情一搁置，就是一年三个月。

[5]

The most painless way, therefore, to import a British bicycle, as I learned from a friendly clerk at the Town Hall, is to arrive with it at the frontier, prepared to pay the import duty in rash, and insist on entry.

[注]

painless：作者没有说申请人的痛苦，这里用了个 painless，前面那种填表、等候，最后还碰了一鼻子灰的痛苦，都包含在内了。

Town Hall：市政府议事厅，或市政府。

arrive with it at the frontier：入境的时候，就把车子带来。prepared 是过去分词。**in cash**：用现款付。**insist on entry**：同海关人员交涉，坚持要把车子带进来。

The Reigning Royalty of Europe
欧洲之王室

David Cecil（1902—1986）

　　戴维·塞西尔为现代有名批评家，在牛津大学任教多年。著有 *The Stricken Deer*（诗人 Cowper 传），*Early Victorian Novelists, Hardy the Novelist* 等。本文原发表于《生活画报》（*Life*）1957 年 8 月号。原文甚长，此处摘录数段。题目中 reigning 一词，意为"在位的"。法国、意大利、西班牙等国王室后人，今仍在世，他们仍旧保持王室的尊号，只是他们并不"在位"。又如，英女王为 reigning queen，其母（王太后）亦有 queen 的尊号，可是就不是 reigning 了。

[1]

　　European monarchies of today are a very different thing from those of the past. For one thing they are constitutional. They also thrive in liberal democracies, where the government is conducted by the heads of the majority party in the elected chamber of government. Theoretically the king is head of the state. But he always acts on the advice of his ministers, so this does not amount to much. The one important occasion in which Britain's constitutional monarch can influence events is when a party takes power without an accepted leader. The monarch can then choose, as Queen Elizabeth II did recently when she named Harold Macmillan to be prime minister, rather than Richard Austen

Butler. But even here a monarch is unlikely to act against the wishes of the substantial body of the party in power. And though the monarch can advise the government, which may pay attention to the king's wisdom and experience, he does not direct policy.

[注]

monarchy：君主政体；君主国。those 仍是指 monarchies。第一句里的 thing 的用法应加以注意。有了这个词，文章显得更为亲切，因为这个词是太普通了。

for one thing：今古君主政体不同之处可能很多，今举一点来说。

constitutional：合宪法的。君主立宪（constitutional monarchy）与君主专制（absolute monarchy）不同。

liberal democracies：自由民主的国家。

theoretically：理论上说来。**head of the state**：国家元首。

acts on the advice of his ministers：按照大臣的劝告而行事。注意句中 his 一词。minister 在中国译作"部长"，英文原意是"仆人"；大臣者，帝王之仆人也。**this**：纵为国家元首（事实上不发生什么作用）。**amount to**：（加起来）得到（什么样的数目）。**does not amount to much**：没有多少价值。

occasion：场合。此词前面的介词常用 on（如 on one occasion：某一次），但是这里用的是 in which。**events**：大事；国家大事。**takes power**：执政。when ... 是名词性从句，与前面的 occasion 相等。英国某一政党虽已掌握政权，但是群龙无首（没有公认的领袖），那时英国受宪法限制的君主，就可出来干涉，左右大局。

choose：常用作及物动词，这里是不及物动词，君主可以为政党选拔领袖，组织内阁。**did recently**：did 为 did choose 之略。**Macmillan**：麦克米伦，英国前首相。方艾登辞职之际，Butler 是副首相，继任希望本来甚大，但是保守党内部拥护麦克米伦者和拥护 Butler 者，分成两派。女王经咨询元老丘吉尔和 Marquess of Salisbury（此人可能与本文作者是一家人）后，决定任命麦克米伦组阁。

even here：即使在这种场合之中。**the substantial body**：大多数人。国王不大可能（unlikely）违反执政党多数意见，独断独行。**pay attention to**：国王有其智慧与经验，他的指示，政府人士可以注意倾听；但是国王不能指导政府的政策，他的话可能毫不起作用。

[2]

Monarchy today has also lost its religious halo. The religious conception does not fit with the secular views that lie behind modern democracy — all the more so because a large number of the citizens of these democracies no longer believe in any religion.

[注]

halo：神光（神、佛、天使、saints 头上的光）。在君主专制的时候，帝王自命君权神授（中国的皇帝自称"奉天承运"），英国国王在加冕时大主教还要背这么一段话："Receive this kingly sword brought now from the altar of God and delivered to you by the hands of us the bishops and servants of God." 君主政体本来有一种神圣的光华，现在可是没有了。

secular：非宗教的。**all the more so**：尤其使这两种观念格格不入者。so 是"不合"，more 是"更不合"，the（副词）= on that account，因此而更为不合。

[3]

Only in England is the institution still sacramental, the monarch being crowned in church and still recognized as head of the national church. Other countries manage to forego the religious ceremony of coronation: the monarchs of Europe mark their accession by swearing an oath in the legislative assembly, according to a constitutional concept that does not accept any idea of divinely appointed monarch.

[注]

institution：（王室的）制度。**sacramental**：含有神圣意味的（**sacrament**：圣礼，或是任何有神圣意味的东西）。第一句是倒装法。句子重心在前三个词，主语放在动词的后面。又本句用了一个 absolute phrase (the monarch being...)，这种短语用作轻描淡写的说明，最为合适。**crowned**：加冕。这个词的名词形式是 coronation。 **head of the national church**：国教的教主。in church 的 church 是"教堂"，national church 的 church 是"教会"。

manage：想办法。**forego** 或拼作 **forgo**：取消。**Europe**：广义的欧洲，包括英

国在内。狭义的欧洲，仅指欧洲大陆。这里所用的是狭义。**accession**：登基，就位。这个词的动词形式是 accede。**mark**：举行仪式以表示。**swearing an oath**：宣誓。**legislative assembly**：立法议会。他们所以在议会里宣誓，而不在教堂加冕者，是根据一种宪法观念，这种宪法观念不承认君主是上帝任命的（不接受这种想法）。

[4]

Has the king's social and personal position changed with the decline in his religious status and political power? The answer to this question is different in different countries. In Scandinavia it has. The general sentiment is democratic. The Norwegians, the Swedes and Danes do not like the idea that the royal family is something apart, leading an existence of courtly formality and stately splendor. The royal families, so far as we can gather, agree with them. Certainly they fall in with their wishes. The kings and queens of these countries perform their public functions with traditional state and dignity; but when these are over, they return to a home life which differs in no essentials from that of their subjects.

[注]

social and personal position：社会地位与个人地位。**religious status**：宗教上的地位。status 和 position 没有多少分别，不过 status 是法律名词，更能引起庄严的联想。国王的宗教地位和政治权力都衰落了（decline），他的社会地位与个人地位是否也因此改变呢？

Scandinavia：指挪威、瑞典、丹麦三国（还有冰岛）。按地理位置说来，丹麦是不在斯堪的纳维亚半岛上的。**it has** = his position has changed。

do not like the idea：idea 这个词很常用，中文不易表达（上一段有 does not accept any idea of）。这一句直译应该是"他们不喜欢这个想法"，照中国习惯说法，其实就是"他们不喜欢这个办法"。**something apart**：高高在上，和老百姓判然不同。leading an existence 中的 existence 就是 life：过这样的生活。**courtly formality**：宫廷的繁文缛节。**stately splendor**：庄严华丽。"庄严"和"华丽"这两个观念在中文里是平行的，但在英文里，可以用一个为主（名词），一个为从（形容词）。这是中英文用法不同之处，亦是英文较多伸缩性的一个例子，请读者注意。

so far as we can gather：就我们所知者。**gather**：从事实上推断。那些君主，是否真正赞成"君民平等"的想法，我们不敢断言。就事实上表现看来，他们是赞成的。有一点我们是敢断定的（certainly），他们的确是依从（fall in with）老百姓的意志而行事的。

perform their public functions：执行公务（如接见外国使节，主持国庆大典等）。**state and dignity**：这两个词连用时，意义上没有多大分别。state 有"庄严"之意。

when these are over = when these functions are over：公务执行完毕。

differ in no essentials：其主要之点并无分别。**that of their subjects**：他们"子民"的家庭生活。

[5]

In Belgium and England the story is different because there the traditions of aristocratic society and court life are still alive. The British royal children are privately educated; the queen of England does not go out unattended and the Belgian king rarely does; there are courtiers and splendor. Yet even in England royal life has modified a great deal. An English princess will now dine out with friends without a lady in waiting in attendance. The little Duke of Cornwall is beginning his education not at home under the care of a tutor but at a school. It seems possible, too, that when he is older he may become the first heir to the British throne to attend a public school. Altogether the English royal family today leads a life which, while retaining many of its old forms, is growingly democratic in spirit.

[注]

story 原意是"故事"。the story is different 是习语，与"故事"无关，意为"情形是不一样的"。**aristocratic society**：贵族社会。alive 这个词是可以形容 tradition 的。**are still alive** 当然比 still exist 来得好。

privately educated：请"太傅"教授。

does not go out unattended：没有侍从跟随，是不出门的。unattended 形容主语 queen。

... rarely does：比利时国王出门，难得没有侍从跟随。**there are ...**：宫廷供奉

之臣和宫廷生活的华丽，迄今犹存。

modified：改变，程度减轻。

will dine out 的 will 是表示"习惯"。**a lady in waiting**：侍从宫女。**in attendance**：从旁侍候。

Duke of Cornwall：就是现在英国的王子 Charles。英国太子的封号是 Prince of Wales，当时这个王子尚未正式封为 Prince of Wales。

under the care of a tutor：受私人教师指导。

heir to the throne：储君。**public school**：英国的 public school，不是"公立学校"，只是"公众可以就读的学校"。以前英国的储君，从来没有上学校念书的。

a life which：这句话的重心是在 which... 这个定语从句上。a life 可以说没有什么意义，它的意义借"which"从句而完成。这种生活虽然（while）旧日规模仍旧保持不少，可是在精神上，已是日益民主了。同样的句法，见于上一段之末句，a home life 的意义亦是借"which"从句而完成的。

A Professor in Retirement
退休教授

Jean Stafford（1915—1979）

  珍·斯塔福是美国当代名女作家。她的第一部长篇小说 *Boston Adventure*（1944），一举成名。后来，她又写了 *The Mountain Lion*, *The Catherine Wheel* 等长篇，以及短篇小说多种。珍·斯塔福是个很精细的作家，描写不厌其详，可是笔触轻灵，同情的态度中还略带讽刺。美国当代作家，文字风格的差别很大，有极端的粗犷，也有极端的细腻。珍·斯塔福是用精细的手法，来表现她对世界的看法的。

  本文原题 *A Reasonable Facsimile*，刊于 1957 年 8 月 3 日 *The New Yorker* 杂志。讲一个老教授和一个青年人的故事。这里选录几段，读者虽不能观全豹，但是她的英文还是可以叫人喜欢的。

[1]

  Far from withering on the vine from apathy and loneliness after his retirement as chairman of the Philosophy Department at Nevilles College, Dr. Bohrmann had a second blooming, and it was observed amongst his colleagues and his idolatrous students that he would age with gusto and live to be a hundred. He looked on the end of his academic career — an impressive one that had earned him an international reputation in scholarly quarters — as simply the end of one phase of his life, and when he began the new one, he did so with fresh accoutrements, for, as he had been fond of saying to his students, "Change is the only stimulus."

[注]

第一句相当长，但是内容也丰富。读者试把第一句里所讲的事情，一一列出，然后再把这些事情，集在一个句子里面，这个句子读起来，又要流利漂亮，你就会发现：不要说写篇好文章是件难事，写一句好句子也是不容易的。

这位 Bohrmann 博士，是 Nevilles College 的哲学系主任，现在因年老退休了，但是他的精神老而弥健。这一句分前后两节，两节以 and 联系。

普通人到了退休的年龄，因为对于世事冷淡（apathy），而且亲人凋零，生活孤寂（loneliness；老教授甫丧妻，这点以后就要说到），不免像一颗干瘪的葡萄，在藤上（on the vine）萎谢了，但是这位教授不然。本句用 far from 开头，很见力量。普通人是这样的，他可不是这样。

Dr. Bohrmann 是主语。**had a second blooming**：第二次开花。第一次开花大约是在青春时期，那时人做事有劲，肯用心学习，老教授退休以后，重新表现青春的活力。blooming 当然是和 withering 对比的。

observed：观察；也解作"发表意见"。it 代表下面的"that"从句，amongst 就是 among：在这些人中间，有这样一个意见。**idolatrous**：崇拜的（此词之根是 **idol**：偶像）。学生们平日把这位教授，敬崇之若神明，在庸手写来，这件事大约又需要一句句子，但是这里只用一个词就够了。**age**：动词，年龄老下去（aging〈形容词〉：垂老，渐老）。**gusto**：（做事、做人）津津有味的精神。

the end of his academic career：学术（教授）生涯的结束。looked on 连后面的 as：他把退休这件事只看作是生活一个方面（one phase）的结束。career 后面，有一个说明。两条横线的作用，等于括弧。**an impressive one** = an impressive career。**impressive**：给人深刻印象的，不平凡的。他教了几十年书，替他在学术圈子里挣来了国际上的声誉。him 是 indirect object；但是这种 indirect object 和普通 indirect object 不同。普通的间接宾语，可以说是省掉了介词 to，这一种（语法书上称为 dative of interest）间接宾语可以说是省掉了介词 for，例如：

He has built me a house. 他替我造了一所房子。

It will last the owner a lifetime. 用这件东西的人，用它一辈子也用不坏。

the new one = the new phase。**he did so** = he began the new one，先用了一个"when"从句，然后再把从句里的话，在主句里面重复一遍，这个办法可以使文字流利。

accoutrements（此词通常用复数形式）：配备。新的"配备"是些什么东西，下文有说明。

change is the only stimulus：变化是唯一的刺激。这句话他是常常喜欢对学生们说的。他退休以后为怕精神颓唐，力求改变生活方式与生活环境（新的配备），以"改变"作为刺激自己的方法。

[2]

He took up the study of Japanese; he took up engraving and lettering (designed a new bookplate, designed a gravestone for his dead wife); he began to grow Persian melons under glass; he took up mycology, and mycophagy as well, sending his fidgety housekeeper off into shrill protests as he flirted with death by eating mushrooms gathered in cow pastures and on golf links. He abandoned chess for bridge, and two evenings a week played a cutthroat game with Miss Biossom Duveen, the bursar's blond secretary, as his partner and as his opponents Mr. Street, the logician, and Mr. Street's hopelessly scatterbrained wife.

[注]

took up the study of Japanese：开始研究日文。**engraving**：镌刻（一种艺术）。**lettering**：刻美术字。**bookplate**：藏书票。西洋藏书家，喜欢印一种凭单，粘贴在书的内封里。单上有图案画，并有"EXLIBRIS so-and-so"（某某之藏书）等字样。这位教授既然学了镌刻之术，便替自己设计（designed）了一种新的藏书票。
gravestone：墓碑。他的太太已故，此处顺便提一笔。

grow（此处为及物动词）：培育。**under glass**：在花房（greenhouse）里种波斯瓜。

mycology：研究蕈菇这类东西的学问。这种学问，研究研究倒也无所谓，可是他吃起野草来了。**mycophagy**：普通词典中可能不载此词。此词源自希腊，myco原义是"蕈"，phagy原义是"吃"，两者连起来，就成"食蕈"。

sending ... off into protests：使（某人）提抗议。(send one crazy 是英文习语：使某人发疯。) 他那管家婆，原来就容易激动 (fidgety)，看见他从放牛场 (pastures)

和高尔夫球场（golf links）上找野草来吃，觉得这是在跟生命开玩笑（**flirted with death**：和死神调情），不由得尖声大叫：使不得。

bridge：桥牌。原来下象棋的，现在改为打桥牌。

cutthroat：形容词，竞争激烈的，谁也不肯饶谁的（*American College Dictionary* 引有 cutthroat competition 这样一个习语）。**bursar**：（大学的）出纳主任。**blond**：金发的。这位秘书小姐是教授打桥牌的 partner。Mr. Street 和 Miss Blossom Duveen 一样，都是 with 的宾语。可是 as his partner 放在 Duveen 的后面，as his opponents（对手方）放在 Mr. Street 的前面，这样句法就不呆板。**logician**：逻辑学家（逻辑教授）。**hopelessly scatterbrained**：心神不集中到不可救药的程度，这两个词一用，他们每星期两次牌局的情形，也稍为提到一点了。

[3]

But the radical thing about his new life was the house he had built for himself in the spring semester of his last year at the College. It was a house of tomorrow — cantilevered, half glass — six miles out on the prairies that confronted the mountain range in whose foothills lay Adams, the town where the College was. The house, though small and narrow, was long, and it looked like a ship, for there was a deck that went all the way around it; from certain points Dr. Bohrmann could see Pikes Peak, a hundred and fifty miles away, and from every point he could watch the multiform weather: there dark rain, here blinding sunshine, yonder a sulphurous dust storm, haze on the summit of one peak, a pillow of cloud concealing a second, hyaline light on the glacier of a third. The house amazed that nondescript, stick-in-the-mud Western town, which from the day it was founded, had been putting up the worst eyesores it could think of. Whoever on earth would have dreamed that the professor, absent-minded and old, riding a bicycle, wearing oldfangled gaiters and an Old World cape, would make such an angular nest for himself and drastically paint it bright pink? The incongruity between the man and his habitat could not possibly have been greater.

[注]

上面这许多改变，还不算特别。根本性的（radical）改变是他造了一所新房子。

a house of tomorrow：设计非常新颖的房子。

　　cantilevered：这是建筑学上的名词。cantilever 是"悬臂梁",墙上横伸出来的梁,一头悬空。和两头有靠的正梁（beam）不同。他这座房子,可能是只用悬臂梁,不用正梁的。half glass：半是玻璃。这两点都是新式建筑的特点。**prairies**：大草原。他的房子造在大草原上,离镇六英里。**mountain range**：山脉。**foothills**：山脉下面的丘陵。他们的大学所在地,名 Adams 镇,镇倚山而建。

　　that went all the way around it：房子的样子像船,周围有甲板,人可以在上面散步。went 有"伸张"之意。around it = around the house。

　　Pikes Peak：Rocky mountains（后面要讲到）的高峰之一。在"甲板"上散步,从某几处远望,可见高峰矗立。可是无论从哪一点望出去,四时昼夜天气之变幻,尽收眼底(**multiform**：形状有多种的)。那边黑沉沉的在下雨,这边太阳亮得叫人睁不开眼睛,再远一点(yonder)是尘土飞扬,黄而且热,同硫磺相仿(**sulphurous**)；某一座山峰顶上是暖暖雾气；巨云一朵(**pillow** 是枕头,好比喻)把另一个山头遮掩住了,再有一个山峰上冰河一片,发出玻璃样的光(hyaline light)。

　　镇上的人(town)看了这座奇怪的房子大为惊奇。原来他们那个处在美国西部的镇,落后而不随时代前进,好像是插在泥里一样(stick-in-the-mud),外表也是非驴非马的难看(nondescript)。**eyesore**：看了使人眼睛不舒服的东西。镇上的人能够想到有多难看的房子,就造(putting up)多难看的。

　　这样一个教授,怎么会造这样一座奇形怪状的房子(angular nest),而且更过激地把它漆成明亮的粉红色呢(**drastically**：激烈地)? 这一句里面还把教授的服饰,顺便描写了一下。他是骑自行车的,腿上扎了老式的裹腿(oldfangled gaiters),身上披了一种旧式披风(cape)。**Old World** 原指旧世界(东半球),这种披风该是欧洲人的服饰,美国人很少穿的。披风裹腿都是骑自行车时候的装束。

　　habitat：住地。这样一个老派的老人,住这样一座新派的房子,其不调和(incongruity)已达极点(不可能有更不调和的东西)。

[4]

Imagine this character, with his silver beard, wearing a mussed green tweed suit, those gaiters, a stiff-collared shirt, a Tyrolian hat, sitting in a black sling chair on the front deck of this gleaming, youthful house, drinking ginger beer out of an earthenware mug and looking through binoculars at eagles and the weather. Or look at him pottering in his pretty Oriental garden, shading himself with the kind of giant black bumbershoot one associates with hotel doormen in a pouring rain. No matter where you placed him in that house, he simply would not match. It was the joke of Adams, but a good-natured one, for Dr. Bohrmann was the pet of the town.

[注]

this character：这个人，这个"角色"。**character**：行为乖僻的人（例如：he is a character，他是个怪人）。**mussed**（美国俗话）：皱而脏的；邋遢的。**tweed**：毛糙的花呢。**those gaiters**：上面所说的裹腿。**stiff-collared**：硬领。**Tyrolian**：大约是指奥地利 Tyrol 地方的。这种帽子以及种种打扮都是旧式的。**sling chair**：可折叠的椅子。**gleaming, youthful**：这两个词形容这座粉红色的新派房子，很贴切。**ginger beer**："姜汁啤酒"，一种碳酸饮料，虽叫作 beer，其实并不含酒精成分。**earthenware mug**：陶器大杯。**binoculars**：双筒望远镜。**eagles**：此词点明了远处的高山和辽阔的空间。**pottering**：吊儿郎当地工作。**Oriental garden**：中国式或日本式的花园布置，在美国是时髦玩意。**bumbershoot**：一种大帽子，可张开收拢如伞。教授在花园里作杂工，就戴这样一顶帽子，以避阳光（shading himself）。此词后面省了一个关系代词。这种帽子通常是旅馆的看门人在大雨倾盆（pouring rain）时候戴的，我们（one）看见这种帽子，就会把它同那种看门人联在一起。**associates**：联想。

placed：不论你把他"放"在这座房子的什么地方，他总是不相称的。"你"是指读者，前面两句用命令式，也是请读者"想象"，请你来看。

joke：镇上的人把这座房子引为笑谈。可是笑话里面并不含有挖苦的成分（good-natured），因为镇上的人都喜欢这位教授。**pet**：被人爱抚的动物或人。

[5]

Dr. Bohrmann and his wife, who died two years before his retirement, had arrived in Colorado from Freiburg by way of Montreal, where, just as he was beginning to make his presence felt at the university, he was halted in his stride by a sudden, astounding hemorrhage of the lungs. When, after seventeen wan, lengthy months, he was discharged from the sanitarium, not as cured but as arrested, his careful doctors counseled him to go West, to the Rocky mountains, under whose blue, bright skies he could, in time, rout the last bacterium. On their further recommendation he applied for an appointment at Nevilles College, since Adams was famous for the particular salubrity of its air. And providence was pleased to accommodate him, having a few months earlier created a vacancy on the staff through the death — from tuberculosis — of a young instructor.

[注]

第一句所包含的内容又很丰富。教授太太是在他退休之前两年故世的；他们两本来是从德国的弗赖堡（Freiburg）地方来到美洲，卜居在美国的科罗拉多州。在来美国之前，曾在加拿大的蒙特利尔教过一阵书，**by way of**：经过（蒙特利尔来到科罗拉多）。在蒙特利尔的大学教书刚刚露点头角（**to make his presence felt**：使自己的"存在"被人家觉得，使人家知道有他这样一个青年教师），他忽然咯血。**hemorrhage of the lungs**：肺出血。**his stride**：他的大踏步往前迈进（教育界的地位蒸蒸日上），忽然被咯血所阻止。**sudden, astounding**：突如其来的，吓人的。

这许多事情，要写在一句之内，不是一件容易的事情。读者如要揣摩何谓"用英文思想"（to think in English），对于这种句子应该细心模仿。作者风格的特点还是她的松散自然，从容不迫。她并不因为句子内容丰富而显得手忙脚乱，无法应付。所以如此者，恐怕是因为她多用 loose construction 的缘故。讲起教授的太太，作者就随随便便地插一个定语从句（non-restrictive 从句），说明她已经死了。句子到 Montreal 本来可以完了，作者又加了个定语从句（where...），说明他的如日方升的事业，忽受扼于肺疾。中国学生作文时，如能把定语从句任意活用，于文字通畅之道，已思过半矣。

教授咯血后，在疗养院（sanitarium）里住了17个月（过了惨淡〈wan〉漫长的17个月），此后他出院了（**discharged**：释放），病是没有医好，只是算已经停止恶化（**arrested**：已被遏止）；他的医生（**careful**：怕他旧病复发）劝他到西部去，到洛矶山去。说到这里，作者为维持一贯的 loose construction 的作用，又用了一个定语从句。洛矶山区，天空明亮作纯蓝色。他住在那里，隔了相当时候，可以把体内最后一个结核杆菌（bacterium）消灭（**rout**：击溃）。本句下半句连用好几个逗号：计 West 后有一个，mountains 后有一个，blue 后有一个，could 后有二个，

time 后有一个,这许多逗号使句子的进行缓慢,吞吞吐吐,有言尽而意不尽之妙。若求句子爽利,当然不是用这个写法的了。

迁居不难,但是生活也得维持。医生们有更进一步的建议,他根据(on)这个建议,向 Nevilles College 申请谋职(**appointment** = office assigned:指派职位),因为该校所在地 Adams 镇空气清新,有益健康(salubrity 的形容词形式是 salubrious),是向来有名的。

providence:上帝。代替 God 的词有好几个,如说上帝可以为人安排一切,这种场合我们可以用 providence,上帝很高兴把他好好安插(accommodate him),原来该校在几个月以前,有个年轻教员害结核病故世:上帝在该校的教职员群(staff)中制造了一个空缺(having created a vacancy)。

[6]

Adams was high above sea level and its prospect of soaring palisades and pinnacles of rock was magnificent, if, at first, dismaying to European eyes that had been accustomed to grandeur on a smaller scale. Moreover, the faculty of its college was remarkable — was, in part, illustrious — because so many of its members had come here for Dr. Bohrmann's reason; if their distemper had been of a different nature, they would have lectured in much grander but moister groves — in New Haven or Princeton; in Oxford or Bonn, For the most part, they accepted their predicament with grace — it is no myth that the tubercular is by and large a sanguine fellow — and lived urbanely in rented houses, year by year meaning it less and less when they stated their resolve that as soon as their health was completely restored they would go back to the East or to their foreign fatherlands.

[注]

Adams 海拔甚高,悬崖壁立,奇峰插云,气势壮阔。**prospect**:广阔的风景。**soaring**:高入云表的。**palisades**(此词在此场合常用复数):悬崖绝壁,排成一排的。**pinnacle**:尖峰。

这种奇景,即使(if)欧洲人初来,看来要目眩神移(dismay),但是总可以说是壮观(magnificent),欧洲人的眼睛也认识伟大,但是他们所见惯的伟大,格局要比美国的小（grandeur on a smaller scale）。这句话其实就是说，欧洲人惯见的"山"，气势格局却不如美国的，但是这里不说 accustomed to mountains，而说 accustomed to grandeur。中文用具体名词的地方英文常常可用抽象名词。这里的 grandeur 范围当然不限于"山"，欧洲的伟大的东西，格局上大多不如美国的。if 后面省了 it（= the prospect）was 二词。

faculty：大学教员（集体名词）。上一段有一个 staff，此词通常意义是"某一个机关的职员的总称"，范围较广；faculty 一个意思是"学科"，另一个意思是"某学科或某大学的教员的总称"，教员则是 member of the faculty。Nevilles College 地虽偏僻，它的"教授阵容"却相当可观（remarkable），有一部分还是赫赫有名的（illustrious）人物。**for Dr. Bohrmann's reason**：Dr. Bohrmann 到这里来，是一半教书，一半养病，教授中有很多位也是抱了养病的目的来的，所以该校容易招得到好教员。

distemper：病。假如那辈教授害的不是肺结核（假如他们的病换了一种性质），按他们在学术界的声望，应该在有名的大学任教，不会到这个小地方来的。**New Haven**：纽黑文，在美国的康涅狄格州，耶鲁（Yale）大学所在地。**Princeton**：在美国的新泽西州，为普林斯顿大学所在地。**Bonn**：通常译作"波恩"，曾经是冷战时期的德意志联邦共和国首都，该地也有著名的波恩大学。

groves：古希腊雅典城附近有丛林（grove）一所，名 Academy，为柏拉图讲学之所。现在英文里的 Academy 解作"学校"或"研究院"，稍"雅"的说法有 the groves of Academe，解作"学校"（或"学园"、"学府"），连带地，groves 这个词都代表"学校"了。耶鲁等大学，规模是较大，可是那些地方空气较潮湿（moister），不宜肺痨病人疗养。

predicament：倒霉的命运（生肺病）。这辈教授,大部分不怨天不尤人地（with grace）承受了自己的命运。**grace**：洒脱乐观的态度。

by and large = in every way，in all respects。有人说，结核病人（the tubercular）是十足的乐天知命的人（a sanguine fellow），这句话并不是瞎说（no myth）。他们承受了自己的命运，租了房子住（住在租来的房子里），过一种高雅的生活（**urbanely**：意思是说，虽然那地方是偏僻的，他们还可以讲究派头）。

他们常常向人表示决心（stated their resolve）：一俟病躯全部康复，他们就要回到东部去（美国东部开发较早，文化程度较高），或者回到他们在外国的老家去。可是一年一年过去（year by year），他们的病可能养好了，但是他们也爱上了这块地方，不想迁移。因此嘴上虽说要走，心里要走的意思越来越少了。**mean it**：真心地说这句话（例：I meant it，我不是开玩笑）。**meaning it less and less**：心里的意思同"嘴上的话"（it）距离越来越远。

[7]

Although their *New York Times* came four days late, and although perhaps they were not in the thick of things, neither did their minds abide in Shangri-La. Visiting lecturers and vacationing friends were bound to admit that the insular community was remarkably *au courant* and that within it there was an exchange of ideas as brilliant and constant as the Colorado sun.

[注]

New York Times：纽约时报；知识分子爱读的报。因为地方偏僻，该报要迟来四天。**not in the thick of things**：置身世事之外。**thick**（名词）：浓密的部分。**abide**：居留。**Shangri-La**：英国小说家 James Hilton 所著小说 *The Lost Horizon* 中所描写的"世外桃源"。

visiting lecturers：从别处来讲学的人。**vacationing friends**：度假期的朋友。**were bound to**：不得不。**insular community**：与世隔绝的小社会（**insular**：孤岛似的）。*au courant*（法文）：适应潮流；跟得上时代，并不落后。

within it：在这个小社会之中，大家不断交换意见（所以说，那辈教授的心并不是在世外桃源里）。科罗拉多州的太阳，光华灿烂，四季永照（constant）；那辈教授在思想上的互相砥砺，也是四季不断，而且所讨论的内容也是非常精彩的。轻轻地一笔，就把那地方的天气，和那地方的学术空气连在一起，文势俯仰自如，令人佩服。

[8]

At first, when the Bohrmanns came, in 1912, they had no intention of lingering any longer than was absolutely necessary. But after little more than a year, neither of them could imagine living anywhere else; the immaculate air was deliciously inebriating and the sun, in those superlative heavens, fed them with the vibrancy of youth. They daily rejoiced in their physical existence, breathed deeply, and slept like children. They admired the turbulent colors of the sunsets, the profound snows of winter, the plangent thunderstorms of summer. There was, they said, some sort of spell upon the place that bound them to it; roving the tablelands, whence one could gaze for miles on miles upon the works of God, they paused in silence, their hands upon their quickened, infatuated hearts. And besides the land, they loved the people of it, both the autochthonous Town and the dislocated Gown; students thronged their house at the *gemütlich* coffee hour, and their coevals and their elders came at night to drink wine or beer and, endlessly, in witty, learned periods, to talk.

[注]

intention：意图。**lingering**：逗留。**the Bohrmanns**：他们一家人。这里仅指夫妇二人，他们没有孩子。他们此来，原为先生养病。病养了几年，也会好的，好了就可搬走。他们初来之时，无意在此地逗留：养病需要多少年，他们在此的居住期限，本不想超过养病所需要的日子。

imagine：想象。这里住了一年多，他们就不能想象在别的地方怎么能再住下去了。

immaculate：清净，不带丝毫尘垢。**inebriating**：有陶醉的力量。前面的一个副词用得也很妙：deliciously inebriating（空气醉人，又叫人舒服）。

the sun：这个词连动词 fed。本文作者善用逗号，前面已经说过。这里第一句就用了三个逗号。the sun 后面又插了一个说明短语 "in those superlative heavens"，目的无非要使句子内容丰富，句子进行缓慢。**superlative**：最高级的，特别好的。heaven 作"天空"解，常用复数形式。

fed them with：以……供养他们的心灵，使他们的心灵充满了……。**vibrancy of youth**：青春的颤动（？）。fed 与 vibrancy 二词，都是作者"炼字"的结果。fed 一词还不怎么难用，vibrancy 一词则很见功夫。此词如易以 vigor 或 vitality，似亦可通；但是这种词意思虽是"活力"，还是显得呆笨；唯有 vibrancy 最能表示"生命力之活跃"。这种"活跃"也不是激烈的活跃，只是轻轻的，自强不息的那种朝气。这个词，配以本句前半的 deliciously inebriating，最能表示高爽地区中的空气和阳光对人身心的良好作用。

physical existence：物质的生命。并不是指吃得好，穿得好，或是周围风景好。

只是觉得做人有意思。人有了这个身体，就觉得快乐。身体不复是累赘，而是直接可以给人快乐的工具。人的快乐有好几种：有理智的快乐，有灵魂的快乐；他们的快乐只是"身体的快乐"。

turbulent 这个词来形容夕阳的色彩，也是精炼所致。此词原义是"大动乱的"，试思日落之时，艳红火黄，金紫满目，好像是倒翻了染料缸。得此一词，情境如在目前。**profound**：深，而且附有"神秘"的联想。**snows**：积雪。**plangent**：惊心动魄的响。

spell：魔力。**that bound them to it**：把他们"拴"在这个地方，所以他们不想搬动了。

roving：漫步。此词在此处用作及物动词。**tablelands**：高原。从高原上望出去，重岭叠翠，嵯峨崔嵬，绵延数英里乃至数十英里，凡此皆上帝之杰作也，他们不得不停步瞻望，肃然无语，他们的手按在心上，那时候的心是着了迷了（infatuated），心跳也加速了。quickened, infatuated 两个形容词放在这个地方，文字经济。（若由庸手写来，为了这两个词，就得另外造一个句子。）他们不但爱这块地方，也爱这地方的人。**town and gown** 原为英文习语，作者拿它来活用，分前后两节来说。这个习语原来指牛津、剑桥等"大学城"的居民，town 是不属于大学的普通老百姓，gown（身穿学士服的）指大学的教员和学生。**autochthonous**：土生的（学生和教员可能是从别的地方来的）。**dislocated**：脱离了原来地方的。**thronged**：群集。**gemütlich**（德文）：欢愉的（教授原为德籍）。

their coevals：和他们年龄相仿的人。年轻教授和资深教授晚上到他们家里喝酒，不断地谈。in witty, learned periods 此一短语，按正常次序，应放在 talk 之后。但是作者在用了 endlessly 之后，故意让读者等候，隔了这四个词，才把 to talk 说出来。**periods**：句子，完整的句子。他们谈话中的句子，句句完整，有思想内容（learned），话又说得俏皮（witty）。这种谈话当然不会使人厌倦。

[9]

Sometimes Dr. Bohrmann and Hedda spoke of summering in Europe — in spite of their contentment, they were often grievously homesick for Freiburg — and occasionally they went so far as to book passage, but something always prevented them from going. One year, Wolfgang was engaged in writing a monograph on Maimonides for the *Hibbert Journal*, another year Hedda was bedridden for a long while after a miscarriage that doomed them, to their everlasting sorrow, to childlessness. After the Second World War, they no longer even spoke of going back, for the thought of how Freiburg now must look sickened them.

[注]

　　教授的名字叫作 Wolfgang，太太的名字叫作 Hedda，前面没有说明，现在在本段出现，读者也不难了解。**summering**：（在某某地方）过夏天（winter 也可以用作动词：过冬）。**contentment**：满足。美国山区生活虽好，他们也常常想念德国的老家。**grievously**：很厉害地。

　　book（动词）：订座（戏院等）。**book passage**：定船票（或飞机票，火车票）。**went so far as**：他们想家，常常说要回到欧洲去度暑假，他们不仅是说说而已，甚至于"做到订票准备动身的地步"，就差没有走。

　　engaged：特约。**monograph**：（专门性的）论文。**Maimonides**（1135—1204）：迈蒙尼德，12 世纪哲学家，西班牙的犹太教神学家、哲学家。*Hibbert Journal*：杂志名。**bedridden**：缠绵床笫，卧病。**miscarriage**：流产。**that doomed them to childlessness**：太太从此不能生育，此事判定他们这一辈子没有孩子的了。**to their everlasting sorrow**：使他们悲伤不已。to 常用以表示"产生某种情感"，如 to my surprise，to my astonishment 等。他们没有孩子，他们很悲伤——这是他们生命中的大事，可是作者把这件事放在一个从句里。本段所说的是，为什么他们这些年来从来没有回德国去一次，这是主要的意思，别的意思都只好称为附庸了。又，本文处处轻描淡写，表现一种闲情逸致；按照这种风格，这种语调（tone），本文是不容许有强烈情感出现的。但是强烈的情感有时非写不可，作者就极力把它压低，使它在文章中占不重要的地位。使情感受到风格的支配，做文章若能懂得这一点，大约也就算写"通"了。that doomed them … 这个定语从句含蓄的意思真不少，而它在语法结构上的地位又这样不重要，我在前文中曾说，"中国学生作文时，如能把定语从句任意活用，于文字通畅之道，已思过半矣。"这里再重复一遍。

　　第二次世界大战以后，德国疮痍满目，他们更不想回去了。这事也可以引起他们强烈的情感，但是作者又把它压低。**how Freiburg now must look**：他们故乡的现状（看来要成怎么样一个惨状，how 是中立性的词，不言"惨"而"惨"已在意中。**must**：表示猜测，想上去"一定"很惨）。**the thought of**：想起这件事（就使他们心里难受：sickened them）。

[10]

All in all, they had an uncommonly happy life and they so much enjoyed each other that when Hedda died, with no warning at all, of heart disease, Wolfgang's friends were afraid that he, too, might die, of grief. And, indeed, he asked for a semester's leave and spent the whole of it indoors, seldom answering his doorbell and never answering his telephone. But, at the end of that time, he merged as companionable and as exuberant as ever, as much at home with life.

[注]

all in all：总而言之。**enjoyed each other**：夫妻二人相亲相爱（两人在一起，日子过得很有趣），因此（so ... that）一个死了，另外一个恐怕也活不长了。**died of heart disease**：患心脏病而死。**with no warning at all**：事前一无征兆。he might die 之后跟一逗号，表示句子到 die 本可以结束："朋友怕他也会死掉的"，但是作者要补充说明：因什么而死呢？悲伤而死。

asked for leave：请了（一学期的）假。**the whole of it** = the whole of the semester。**answering the doorbell**：有人按门铃，主人出去开门（他难得去开的）。他杜门谢客，心中确乎悲伤到极点。

emerged：从隐居的生活中忽然"冒"出来。**companionable**：善与人交。**exuberant**：精力饱满的。**as ... as ever**：跟平常（太太死前）一样。as much at home with life 的后面也该有 as ever 二词，这里是省掉了。**at home**：并无落寞或陌生之感。**at home with life**：并不自视为遁世的人，正常地过日子。

A Writer's Life
作家甘苦

Catherine Drinker Bowen（1897—1973）

本文作者波文为美国著名传记作家，所著以 *Yankee from Olympus: A Bibliography of Oliver Wendell Holmes*（《奥利弗·温德尔·霍姆斯法官传》）最为世人传诵。本文原题 *Discipline and Reward: A Writer's Life*，刊于《大西洋月刊》1957年12月号。文中所述作家生活之甘苦，凡曾经用心写过文章的人，想必都有同感。本文风格近乎美国口语，很少经营刻画的痕迹。

[1]
In 1920, I sold my first piece to a magazine. I have been writing fairly steadily ever since. And fairly steadily I have been asked the same questions:

"Do you write at regular intervals, or do you wait for inspiration?"

"How do you manage with children, husband, household and find time to write?"

[注]
piece：一篇文章。**sold**：投稿录取。

steadily：不停地，不懈地。第二句的动词时态 have been writing 表示写作已有数十年历史，现在还是在写；这可以说是完成进行时的典型例子。

第三句把第二句的两个副词重复地用。所不同者：第二句中，副词放在动词之后，第三句中，副词放在主语之前。这样用法使前后两句连接得很稳。

at regular intervals：经常的间隔（如一天工作几小时，一星期工作几天等）。这句用现在时，表示习惯如此。

manage 在这里是不及物动词，《简明牛津词典》解作：succeed in one's aims（实现你写作的愿望，同时还得对付〈manage with〉家务）。

[2]

Now, in answering these questions I shall go beyond them to talk about discipline, about the rewards and sacrifices of a writer's life. I shall speak out of my own experience, though I have no way of knowing if my experience will prove of value to anyone besides myself.

[注]

go beyond them：超过这两个问题的范围。go 这个词应用很广，在这个场合，中国学生大致想不到用 go 这个词的。**discipline**：纪律，自律（想做的事不许做，不愿做的事偏该做）。**rewards and sacrifices**：报酬与牺牲，甘苦。about 重复地用，也是使语气通畅的一法。about 后面，如有三个宾语，读起来难免气急辞促之弊。这里 about discipline 两个词自成一段落，读文至此换一口气，换气之后再读 about the ...，岂不是语气就通畅了吗？

out of my own experience：从我自己的经验里面。**no way of knowing**：无法知道。**if** = whether。**of value**：有价值。

[3]

That is the risk I take: the risk of boring my audience, the risk of ridicule from overexposure of the person. This is the risk we all take when we walk on stage, or send our painting to be exhibited, our manuscript to a publisher: the risk of public exposure. It is no small thing, the incurrence of this risk, and it runs from beginning to end of a writer's life. After thirty-five years of writing for publication, I suffer from it more than I did in the beginning. As one gains in reputation, the risk becomes somehow larger, or one thinks it does. Consciousness of it generally strikes in the night when one wakes.

Actual physical sweating takes place, loud moans are rendered, and the question is put, "Why in God's name did one undertake such a venture, such a presumptuous, enormous, unlikely book? Why can't one be content to live an anonymous, respectable life?"

[注]

take the risk：冒险（I take 是定语从句）。risk 重复地用，也是使语气通畅之一法，本文原为一篇演讲稿，起稿时当把听众存在心头。risk 重复地用，节奏分明，容易唤起读者的注意。第一句说的是：我自己的经验，别人也许听了不感兴趣，我就冒了一个使听众生厌（boring）之险；我把自己的私人生活（或意见）过分在人前暴露（overexposure），也就冒了一个惹人嘲笑（**ridicule**：这里是名词）之险。

第二句把第一句的意思作更进一层的发挥。不但是我讨论自己的写作的经验，是冒了"抛头露面"（public exposure）之险，其他一切艺术活动如登台演戏，图画展览，投稿卖文又何独不然？

incurrence 的动词形式是 **incur**：招惹。这一句用了一个 expletive "it" 做主语，it 就是下面的 incurrence。所以如此说法，也是为了要语气通畅平易近人之故。如易成 The incurrence of this risk is no small thing，读起来就较为庄重，而且开头用了 incurrence 这种书卷气的词，后面 no small thing 这样平凡的词跟上去就有点不配了。照现在这样用法，主语是 it，incurrence 云云只是陪衬，读起来比较轻松。

runs：请参考前面我所说关于 go 的一点意见。人一做作家，就有这种危险，到停止创作搁笔不写时为止。

writing for publication：写文章不是为了自己怡情悦性之用，而是为了发表。
more than I did：初发表文章时，固然怕出丑露乖，现在比过去更怕了。

gains in reputation：声名日盛，这句主语改用 one（不用 I），表示是一般情形。
one thinks it does = one thinks the risk becomes larger。名作家出丑的危险不一定更大，但他自以为危险很大。盛名之累，不得不兢业从事。

consciousness：觉得（自己在冒出丑之险）。strikes 这个词可以易以别的动词（如 happens），但是 strikes 较有力量，充分表示：作者想到自己万一写糟了那时的惶恐情形。**in the night when one wakes**：午夜梦回之时。

sweating：出汗。吓得一身冷汗不是过甚其辞的说法，是实实在在身体上出汗。中国人说英文，很难做出 sweating takes place 这样的句子，我们很可能说 one sweats 这样的话。把动词 sweat 化成动名词 sweating，然后再找一个动词来配合成一个句子——这一点是和中国人思想习惯不合的。

rendered：发出。**the question is put**：自己问自己。

in God's name：只是为加重语气之用。**venture**：带点冒险性的尝试，成败难测的事情。**presumptuous**：自以为了不起的。**unlikely**：不可能写得好的。

anonymous：默默无闻的。**respectable**：令人尊敬的。这个词本来的含意是好的，但是现代英文中，这个词含有一点不好的意思，指的是不求真正的善，只是表面上的规规矩矩，奉公守法。

[4]

Well, I can't. And neither can anyone who intends to write. Perhaps this fear of the public is healthy. I think I like writers to be afraid. They can show their fear by a noble defiance in their work or by a beguiling charm and grace in seeking to win their public. At least fearful ones are not writing for themselves alone. They are seeking to communicate, and their fear is their proof of it.

[注]

can't：不能安分守己默默无闻地做人。**neither can**：重复 can't。

fear of the public：怕群众的指责。**healthy**：健康的。这种心理是有益的。

I like writers to be afraid：我喜欢作家有这种"畏人言"的心理。

noble defiance：昂然不顾的态度。故意标新立异，不投阿时好，抱这种态度的人，心里面明明有一个对象在。**beguiling**：讨人喜欢的。

at least 补充前面的 healthy 一词，至少这一点是有益的。**the fearful ones**：心存恐惧的作家们。

communicate：表达，有话说给人听。**proof**：证明作家不是在"自说自话"，写作确是有对象的。

[5]

Nevertheless this fear is something to wrestle with, especially in the beginning, at the outset of a career. Women writers are notably tender in this regard, possibly because women are trained, from the cradle, to please. It is the quite practical business of women to please. One way or another, most of us women get our living by it.

［注］

to wrestle with：与之搏斗，力求解决。**at the outset**：意即 in the beginning。

tender：温柔。**notably**：可以叫人特别注意的。**in this regard**：在这一点上。

from the cradle：从摇篮时开始。**to please**：此处用作不及物动词。妇女有讨人喜欢的习惯；女作家的文章也特别地要使读者读来感到舒服。

one way or another：方法不一。**by it**：使别人喜欢。

［6］

"Oh no, Mrs. Bowen," young women writers say to me. "Oh no! I mustn't write that scene. I couldn't put it on paper as I have just told it to you. I can't describe that child, that man, that mother, in such terms!"

The writer, I maintain, cannot afford such reservations, He must find a technique that will let him describe anybody, anything, any situation — a technique that will permit him to use all his experience of living, tragic, comic, embarrassing, cruel, beautiful.

［注］

scene：场景。剧本里的一个小段落称为场景（大段落是"幕"），通常借用作文章里写得生动的一节；有景物，有人物，有动作，有对白；其有声有色犹如舞台上的一个"场景"。

couldn't：此词含有轻微的假定语气：即使我要写，我也写不出来。平常说话中，I couldn't 是常听得到的。指的是这件事我非但不能做，而且也不"会"去做的。I can't 则单指：我没有这种能力。**told**：青年作家同前辈作家在讨论写作的问题。谈话的前一段是给作者省略了。我们可以想象：青年作家嘴里在讲一段事情给前辈作家听，前辈作家劝她写下来。

in such terms：用这种话。

maintain：主张。**reservations**：保留。我说"我什么都会"，这句话就是"没有保留"；我承认"我有些事情能做，有些事情不能做"，这就是"保留"。**can afford**：能够负担，而不致吃亏。**cannot afford such reservations**：作家假如有这种保留，他就不成其为作家了。

technique：技巧。这词重复地用，充分表示写作技巧的重要。在表达一方面，作家应该能够描写任何人物，任何事物，任何情境；在做人一方面，作家有了某种技巧，才能利用他所有的人生经验：悲剧的，喜剧的，令人窘迫的，残酷的，或是美丽的。

[7]

Few writers are born with this technique. They must search until they find it. The search, if it teaches nothing else, in the end will teach them to know themselves. Actually it is a little difficult to separate the techniques of writing from the techniques of living — which is another way of saying the style is the man. I have no patience with that view of writing — a quite prevalent view — which looks on style as a trick and on the great techniques of writing as a bag of tricks. I have heard people say to a writer, "Ah, but *you* could describe that man! I envy you. You could tell that incident as it really happened. You have the gift of words."

[注]

这种技巧，不是生而致之，而是学而致之。**few**：可以说是"绝无仅有"。

search：寻觅（即学习）。search 先用作动词，后用作名词。作家努力学习写作技巧，这种努力可使他很得益，别种得益且不必说（if it teaches nothing else），作家至少因此可以了解自己。写作技巧和做人有什么关系呢？这就是本文所要阐明的。

the style is the man：文如其人，这是法国批评家布丰（Buffon，1707—1788）的名言。本文作者说：作文技巧和生活技巧颇难分隔（二者颇有牵连），这就是布丰名言的另一种说法了。

have no patience with：不能忍受，听不入耳。**prevalent**：流行很广的。**trick**：小手法，雕虫小技。**a bag of tricks**：一大堆小玩意儿。

you 重读，表示一般人对于作家描写能力的羡慕。**describe that man**：作家所写书中的某一个人物。**that incident**：书中某一件事。

gift：天赋能力。

[8]

These people seldom tell a writer, "You have this gift of perception, this passionate concern with life and living, that enables you, or compels you, to watch and learn."

[注]

一般人只知道欣赏作家的天才，谁能了解作家的苦心孤诣呢？因此他们不会说出正确的赞美的话。

正确的赞美的话该怎么说呢？我们得承认作家有洞烛事物的能力（gift of perception），作家对于生活中的万事万物有强烈的关切（passionate concern），这种能力或关切使得作家观察人生，向人生学习。

说"使得"恐怕还太轻，我们应该说"迫使"（compels），作家所以肯细心观察学习，实在受本性所驱使，不得不然。**life and living**：life 是大事情，living 是小事情。人的生命全部是 life。他要做人（to live）就得做很多事情（如吃饭、穿衣、赚钱），这些事情就是 living。

[9]

Writing, I think, is not apart from living. Writing is a kind of double living. The writer experiences everything twice. Once in reality and once in that mirror which waits always before or behind him.

[注]

写作与生活不可分。**double living**：双重生活。作家和普通人不一样；普通人只生活一次，作家要生活两次。一次是真实的生活，一次是拿生活作为材料，从事回忆、考验、分析、综合、研究和写作。

作家的身前或身后，总有一面镜子在侍候着他。他在这面镜子里，把自己的生活再过一次。例如逃难，普通人逃难逃过就算了。作家要拿逃难的经验，仔细地思索，作为他写作的材料，充实他写作的（同时也是生命的）内容。

[10]

I maintain that this double living, these hours and scenes twice experienced, make up the inevitable sign of the natural-born writer. There is a compulsion to relive everything, repeat conversation to oneself, mimic a speaker's accent, tone of voice, gesture, as carefully as if one were rehearsing to do it before an audience. It is an odd practice and serves no immediate purpose, certainly. I sometimes think it derives from sheer love of life, or infatuation with life, even the parts of life that we hate and fear. The practice takes its toll, also, in fatigue, a peculiar exhaustion. A double life is a double burden.

[注]

these hours and scenes twice experienced 与 this double living 是同位语，人生中有些时刻，有些景象，人是要经验两次的（经验一次之后，还要加以玩味）。**make up**：造成（部分造成整体）。动词用复数形式，值得注意。很明显的，make 是跟靠近的 hours and scenes，而不是跟较远的 living 的。**inevitable**：不可避免的，非有不可的。**natural-born writer**：有写作天才的人。

a compulsion to relive everything：把任何东西生活两次的冲动。repeat 是和 relive 平行的，前面的 to 省掉了。mimic（模仿）也是和它平行的。把听来的谈话，在心里（然后在笔底下）重演一次，某一个人说话时候的（原文作：一个说话的人的）特殊的腔调、声调、姿势，私下细心模仿，好像练好了（**rehearsing**：排练）要演给人（audience）看似的。

如此做法（practice）无疑是很奇怪（odd）的，而且没有直接（immediate）的好处。

it derives from：如此做法的来源是，对于人生纯粹（sheer）的爱，或者说是，对于人生的着迷。

前面说过，人生的经验有 tragic，comic 等多种。天生的作家爱人生，迷恋人生，不单是人生中的可喜可爱的部分而已，人生中有令人憎恨害怕的部分，作家们对此也依恋不舍（如前举的逃难的例子；又如小时候给老师打手心）。

also：非但没有用处（serves no purpose），而且有害处。

takes its toll：叫人付出代价。这种代价是疲乏，一种特殊的心力交瘁（exhaustion）之感。人生本是负担，双重生活岂不是双重负担吗？

前面都用 double living，讲的是作家的"生活方式"，是动的。这里用 double life 是概括地讲一种生活，是静的（把流动的生命当作一个整体看），因此可以压在人的身上。

[11]

However, I happen to think a writer's life is the most privileged there is in our society. It is a life exciting, varied. If success comes, it is a life that lends itself to expansion both materially and spiritually. Expansion, surely, is what counts. Expansion is the prize of life. And, as with all of the best things in this world, the writer pays for that prize every inch of the way. Let us say he pays by the establishment and acceptance of certain disciplines, more rigorous than the disciplines that other people follow. I will try to describe them.

[注]

作家的忧患欢乐，都比人多一倍。作家的精力支出也比别人多。做作家该是苦差事了。可是我恰巧（happen to think）有一种想法：作家的生活是现实社会所有的各种生活之中，最为幸运的（**privileged**：享有特权的）。there is 前面省了个关系代词 that。

varied：多变化的，多彩多姿的。这两个形容词放在名词后面，重心就落在这两个形容词上，句子读起来有劲。如把形容词放在名词前面，这一句读起来便松。而且主语 It 就是 a writer's life，这个词和表语 a life，靠得很近，连接得很牢，好像成了 that life is a life 一般，这样句法自然紧凑。如在 a 与 life 之间，放了两个形容词，句子就松了。

if success comes：一旦写作成功。

it is a life 再出现一次，不过这里 life 后面跟的是定语从句。**lends itself to**：把自己出让，把自己交托给，使自己能够适合于扩张。**both materially and spiritually**：物质精神双方。

what counts（表语从句）：人生有价值的东西。count（不及物动词）：有价值，或能发生作用。

prize：奖品。（生命的）扩张是宝贵的。何谓生命的扩张，作者这里似乎交代得不够清楚。但是读者不妨想象一个成功的作家过的是什么样的生活。

as with all：就跟世界上一切（最好东西）一样，没有不劳而获的。**pays for**：得到这个奖品是付了代价的。**every inch of the way**：这五个词是副词短语（adverbial phrase），前面无需介词，和 every morning 之为副词短语一样；赛跑得奖，每一英寸都是用力跑出来的。

作家的生活，最后假如能够得到什么"扩张"的报酬，作家需付出的代价是：建立并接受某种纪律，这种纪律比别种人（并非作家）所守（follow）的纪律，更要严格。

作家要服从什么严格的纪律呢？且听我一一道来。

[12]

There is a channel down which your work pours. That channel must be kept clear, free-running. At all costs it must be so kept. Pain does not clog it, nor misfortune.

[注]

channel：水流之道。**pours**：如水一般地倾泻而下。本文作者并不主张文章应该"不加点窜，一气呵成"。一本大书，可能经年累月，始能竣工。可是在这许多年月之中，作家不可让杂务分心；宜专心一致，把全副精神放到写作里去。如此文思畅达，文章亦如长江大河，滔滔不绝，往前直流。**clear**：没有阻碍。不要让石块污泥来阻碍水的行进。

at all costs：不惜任何代价。so 即是 clear, free-running。

pain：人生的苦痛，甚至是写作过程中遭遇困境而产生的苦痛。**clog**：阻塞。人生有病痛，有不幸之事。但是作家能忍受，决不让这些事阻断他写作。孟子曰："源泉混混，不舍昼夜，盈科而后进，放乎四海。"这句话送给作家也是合适的。

[13]

What clogs the channel is laziness, inattention, timidity, the propensity to lie to oneself, to avoid looking straight at a situation — perhaps at the situation of your own work, the story or chapter you have just finished or thought you had finished. The most scrupulous honesty is necessary, in a writer. To know what one is doing, to ask oneself from time to time, Why am I writing this book? Whom am I trying to reach with my message, and have I a message? (You have, or you shouldn't be writing.) By a message I do not mean a moral. I mean a central idea which caused you to write your piece in the first place. Or your story, or your book, or any particular chapter in your book.

[注]

写作的阻碍是一、懒惰；二、注意力不够，不用心；三、胆怯（难写的怕写，不合一般趣味的不敢写），四、……。

propensity：倾向。**to lie**：说谎。作家对自己说谎，那么不真实地描写，不是由衷而发的意见都可以随随便便写出来了。

looking straight at a situation：正视某一情境。"正视"就是把一个情境仔细研究过，仔细想过，不歪曲，不掩饰，不畏惧，不加以美化。有些情境是你还没有写的，有些情境是你已经写过的。假如你草草了事，就算写好，那么你写作之"流"，就算给阻塞住了。

thought：你自以为已经写好（但事实上可以修改之处很多）。

scrupulous：多所顾忌，小心翼翼。**honesty**：随时责问自己，我有没有据实写下？我有没有敷衍塞责？假如能够"不自欺"，就是"诚实"。

to know：此系不完全句子。to know 与 to ask 恐系说明 honesty 者。**reach**：送达；说给谁听？**message**：使命，道理。括弧里面的话，是作者代你答复。你自己问自己，我有没有什么要紧的话要对人说呢？代答：有的；否则你也不会写作了。

be writing：问话的时候，你"正"在写作，故用进行时。

By A I mean B：我所说的 A，意思就是 B。这种句法，是常常可以看见的。这里 message 一词，意义欠明。作者作进一步的说明。她说她用这个词，并不是指的 moral。moral 在这里是名词,解作"寓意,教训"。《伊索寓言》于每则故事终了，必列一行 moral，说明本故事用意是劝人如何如何。近代人的写作，不可能有如此浅显之寓意，所以这里的 message 并不是指 moral。

可是你在写作之初，必有一中心思想；你一开头（in the first place）所以要写这篇东西（piece）或某篇故事，或某一本书，或书里的某一章就是受这个中心思想的驱使的。

[14]

I am trying to say that your central idea need not be noble. It can be frivolous or shabby. But it must be looked at honestly by the writer. There can be no cessation, during composition, of this honesty of purpose. No cessation of caring. No slacking of this high wire on which you have elected to dance. No turning to easier, less hazardous matters.

[注]

话愈说愈多了，我所想要说明的，就是你的中心思想不一定是要高贵的（不一定要冠冕堂皇）。

frivolous：没有什么了不起的（并不高明伟大）。**shabby**：陈旧的（并无新意）。可是作家一定要诚实地正视这个思想。

during composition：在写作的过程中。**no cessation of this honesty of purpose**：一心一意地把握住你的宗旨。**cessation**：停止。后面跟着 no 开头的三句，都是不完全的句子，句首 There can be 都省掉了。作者喜用不完全句子，大约是模仿口语之故。四句平行式的句子，也可以使语气通顺。

caring：用心。**slacking**：放松。**high wire**：高架钢丝。你既然选中了要在钢丝上跳舞，那么钢丝不可放松。写作之难，可以和走钢丝相比。因为钢丝既不可松，脚步尤其错乱不得也。**turning to**：改写。**less hazardous**：危险性较少的东西。文章往往写到中途写不下去了，那时一定要"不背初衷"，坚持写下去，不可马虎了事。至于写作之所以有危险性者，大约是因为有些东西很难写，不用心写就有"写坏"的危险。

[15]

The writer is in the position of a person who has accepted a grave responsibility, a task that is within his powers — his best powers — and which he has dedicated himself to accomplish. It means that the writer must live, during working hours, at the peak of his capacity. If one's best hours, best productive hours, are, say, four out of the twenty-four, it means that the other twenty hours must be ordered to this effect.

[注]

in the position of a person：作家所处的地位是同于这一种人的。他好像是担任下来一项重大的责任（简直可以和负守土卫民之责的军人相比；本文用 discipline 处很多，本来军人才有纪律，文人谈什么纪律呢），他的任务按照他的能力是可以完成的（within），但是他得把全身本事（his best powers）都拿出来。

dedicated himself：奉献自己，献身。

during working hours：在写作的时候。 **live … at the peak of his capacity**：（紧张

地）生活，把自己的能力发挥到最高点。

best productive hours：文思最灵敏，写作效率最高的时候。一天有二十四小时，但是真能用以写作的时间只有四小时。**say**：不妨如此假定。另外二十小时，就要好好安排（ordered），使得这四个小时可以发挥作用（如何安排，下文要说明）。

[16]

Such a discipline can be extremely irksome over a long period of time, the more so as it is self-imposed and can be so readily broken. Irksome is too weak a word, if the job is a long one — say, five or six years. *Painful* describes this discipline more exactly. Anxiety goes along with it, anxiety lest you break rhythm and the momentum be lost.

[注]

irksome：令人心烦的，伤脑筋的。**the more so as …**：因为如何如何，所以更是如此（令人心烦）。这一种句法是很常用的。**self-imposed**：这种纪律是自己约束自己的，随时（**so readily**：多么容易地）可以破坏。自找麻烦，所以更为难受。

一本书有时要五六年才写得完，那时的苦不是 irksome 所能表示，只好说是 painful 了。痛苦之外，更有 anxiety（忧虑，原文作：忧虑是跟着这种纪律一起来的）。**rhythm**：节奏。每天写三五百字，成了习惯，生活好像有了"拍子"。几天不写，拍子就断掉了。**momentum**：冲劲，势头。写文章有一股劲，隔了一个时不写，这股劲就没有了。作家一面以纪律约束自己，一面又担心文章脱了节，泄了气。**lest**（连词）：唯恐；所怕的是。break 和 be，都是虚拟式。你所担忧的事尚未发生，而且不一定发生，所以要用虚拟式。普通语法书里规定，lest 后面要用 should（即 should break），这里没有用。不用 should，单用虚拟动词也可以。

[17]

If you are a morning worker, with your best hours from, say, nine to one, your afternoons will have to be devoted to outdoor exercises, neglected housework if you are a wife, the tender loving care and feeding of family or whatever is necessary to make daily life go on, clearing the decks for tomorrow morning and keeping you in top health besides.

[注]

morning worker：早晨工作的人。前面说过 best productive hours。有些人适宜于早晨工作，有些人适宜于晚上工作，今以早晨工作的人为例。

will have to be：这里的 will 不含"将来"的意思。在条件从句里，前面的 if 从句假如用现在时，后面的主句通常用将来时。这是习惯用法，那个将来时仅是表示"猜测"，并不表示"将来"。**devoted to**：奉献给。下面跟五样东西：

（1）**outdoor exercises**：户外运动。作家为保持身心康健计，也该锻炼身体。

（2）受到忽略了的家务（假如你是个主妇）。

（3）照顾子女等等。

（4）这是个暗喻："整肃清理甲板"是海军作战前的准备，引申为"准备战斗"。作家为明天早晨的工作，此时亦可稍事准备，如买稿纸，墨水，整理书桌等。

（5）保持自己的康健。（睡个午觉亦自不妨）。**top**（形容词）：上好的；巅峰状态。

[18]

When five P. M. comes, if you are a biographer or historian you will have to stop what you are doing with fly screens or hemlines and begin reading for tomorrow's writing or for next week's or next month's writing, depending upon how you plan your research for a long book. With a pencil in hand, making notes or marking passages, you will read on and off until ten o'clock, when you go to bed. I myself usually climb in bed with my notes in hand for tomorrow's start, read them over casually, trying not to think, and turn out the light. I am a firm believer in the action of the subconscious during sleep. At supper or dinner that evening, you have not overeaten because it would disturb your sleep, and you know from experience that eight hours of sleep are necessary to put you through a morning's work, though you know also, from experience, that you can afford to miss one night's sleep occasionally. But not two nights, unless you are prepared to sacrifice your work on the third morning.

[注]

本段第一句的 will，意义同上段。**fly screen**：防苍蝇的纱窗。**hemline**：衣服的镶边。下午你本来在装纱窗，或者做各种家庭杂务。到五点钟，你应该开始读书（假如你所写的是传记或历史，其实写小说的人，暇时也该拿名著小说一读，读写并进，是有助于灵感的启发的）。**depending upon**：你所准备的是明天的，或是下星期的，或是下个月的写作，究竟是明天的还是下月的，就看（倚靠）你写这部长书的时候，如何计划你的研究工作了。

marking passages：在书中某几段文章上做记号。**read on and off**：断断续续地读。
when you go to bed："那个时候"，你上床睡觉了。这种补充用的定语从句（non-restrictive 从句），中国学生不大会用。文章如求松散自然，这一种的用法是值得模仿的。

climb in bed：前面刚说 go to bed，这里不好再说 go to bed 了。又，go to bed 并不含有多少"动作"的意义，climb in bed 才是真正的动作。**casually**：随随便便地。
the action of the subconscious：潜意识的作用。上床前不用脑筋思想，因为睡熟以后，潜意识也会替你"思想"。"灵感"之来，人莫能测。但是神经如果放松，优游自得，灵感可能不召自来。

disturb your sleep：晚饭多吃，有妨睡眠。睡眠不好，第二天写文章就没有精神。
miss one night's sleep：偶然一晚上失眠，也无大害。
but not two nights：这是不完全句子。全文是，you cannot afford to miss two nights' sleep.

[19]

Long ago, when I was in my twenties, I came across an awe-inspiring saying, in French: "If you abandon art for one day, she will abandon you for three."

[注]

in my twenties：我二十几岁的时候。**came across**：遇见；读到（这么一句使人肃然起敬的话，原文是法文）。

这句话是，你假如把艺术搁置一天，她就会把你丢弃三天,意思同中文格言"一曝十寒"，"拳不离手，曲不离口"相仿。art 这里是"人格化"了，故代词用 she。通常英文里是用 it 来代替 art 的。

[20]

It is true. It is all too lamentably true. Even with Friday's notes sitting on

A Writer's Life

your table staring you in the face — a map to guide you into Saturday's territory — even then, if you skip Saturday's work, on Sunday those selfsame notes will likely have gone dead. They will sit there, avoiding your eye. No message comes up; they are cold script. If Saturday's interruption has been forced from outside, something I could not help, like going to the oculist, I work every bit as well next day. Probably because I have sat in the oculist's office raging and impatient, with my chapter never out of mind. On the other hand if I succumb to invitation and go out to lunch, an interesting lunch on a working day, I am ruined. Or even an interesting dinner, which should not, practically speaking, interfere with morning working hours at all! But a dinner party means what shall one wear, or going to the hairdresser, or even looking in the shops for a new dress, and this is fatally distracting. Giving a party is the finish, in my judgment, to several days' work.

[注]

all too lamentably：太使人悲哀了。假如作家能够马马虎虎，高兴写就写，做人岂不是可以快乐得多？但是写作这个东西，是一天也不能耽搁的。前面一句格言既是真话，作家就苦了。

Friday：随便举一天。

notes：星期五下午所做的笔记，应该是供星期六早晨写作之用的。但是假如星期六你没有写（**skip**：跳过），星期天早晨再写，那些笔记可能对你就毫无意义了（**will have gone dead**：此处 will 同前文所用的意义一样）。那些笔记本来是带你进入"星期六的领土"的地图，但是你停了一天，现在（notes 这里是"人格化"了），它们只是坐在桌子上，对你发愣（**stare a person in the face** 是习语）。或者它们坐在那里，不来理你（**avoiding your eye**：避免你的眼睛，故意不来看你，这也是习语）。**selfsame** = precisely the same。

message：那些笔记可以激发你的思想，可以传"话"给你，但是现在"话"不来了，你写不出东西了。它们成了"冰冷的文字"，没有生命的东西。

写文章是耽搁不得的。但是耽搁的情形有两种：

假如外面有力量（from outside）打断了我的写作，假如我碰到了一件"无可奈何"（something I could not help）的事情（例如星期六我眼睛有病，要去瞧眼科大夫

oculist)，那么你星期天写作的时候，仍旧是文思通畅的（**every bit as well**：一点也不差）。原因可能是：我在眼科大夫那里，神魂不安，等得不耐烦，又很生气（**raging**：因为觉得光阴浪费可惜）。人虽在等大夫来给我治病，心中念念不忘的是我今天该写的那章书。

另一种情形：有人请我去吃午饭，我答应了。答应人家的邀请本来是件小事，但是这里的一个动词 succumb 分量很重。succumb 的意思是"屈服"，对不可抗力量的屈服，通常用于"战争失败"或"犯罪"等严重之事，用了这样一个严重之词，就是表示：人家的邀请可以使你分心，你上午写作时就不能专心，你假如答应了，就相当于"屈服于犯罪的诱惑"。**ruined**：这个词用得也很重，"我就毁了，完蛋了。"那天上午就不用想写什么好文章了。

dinner：美国通常是晚餐。晚上去赴宴，照理说不会影响你上午的写作的。

means：赴宴并不简单，它引起了许多别种考虑。对于女太太们说来，有人请客就"等于"（means）考虑这些事情：我要穿些什么（照语法书规定，这几个词的次序应排作 what one shall wear），去洗头烫发（替女人"做头发"的人是 hairdresser），或者到店里去，找一件新的晚礼服。

distracting：分心的。**fatally**：给你致命打击。作家之心不可旁骛，连宴会都不宜参加，这种生活多苦！

应召赴宴固然不可，自己请客（giving a party）更有大害。你有好几天静不下心来，工作也不能进行了。finish 这里是名词，连后面的 to："照我看来，你好几天的工作都要无法进行了。"

[21]

I dare not overwork. Let me write for too many hours, sit too long at the typewriter, and rubbish emerges on the page. When I am tired I write as a drunken man might write, deceived into spurious ecstasy. Spurious ecstasy is easy to achieve. But it is not communicable. I think the young writer should always remember that he is writing for strangers. And strangers require to be won. So when lunch time comes, I tamely stop and eat. After lunch I read over what I wrote in the morning, correct it, add marginal notes of things I have left out or facts that need checking historically. Also, if at lunch time I am still primed with ideas, I put them on slips of paper marked with the next day's date: "Raleigh's arrival for trial at Winchester. Horn at gate... Only 2 days between R. and his fate."

[注]

let me ... and ...：这种句法相当于假定句子，假如我如何如何，我就如何如何。

sit at the typewriter：中文大约应该说，坐在打字机的"前面"。

rubbish：不通的文字。**emerges**：出现。

我如疲倦，我的文章就像醉汉所写（might write 是虚拟式，我不一定知道醉汉的文章是怎么样的）。我糊里糊涂的笔底有一种狂热（ecstasy），但是这是假的（spurious）狂热。自以为文气很盛，其实是语无伦次（**deceived into**：受骗而做出某样事情）。这种假的狂热是不难写出来（**achieve**：达到）的。

communicable：可以使人看懂的。你自言自语，如醉语梦呓，别人是不能了解或欣赏的。青年作家该记住，写作是给别人看的，不是让你来自鸣得意的。读者你是不认得的（strangers），你该争取（won）他们，使他们喜欢你的作品。

tamely：乖乖地。上午写了四个钟头，到午饭时就停。

add marginal notes：上午所写的文章中，如有东西遗漏（left out），或者有些考据之事，一定要查书才能证实正误的，我就加"眉批"注明。但是补写是要等到明天再来，今天下午我只是休息或是处理杂务了。

primed：充满。有的时候文章欲罢不能，到午饭的时候，人虽疲倦，但是文思未尽，那时我还是停止工作，我把文思写在几张纸条上，注明明天的日期，等明天再来发挥。

举一个例子：作者曾写过一部英国文艺复兴时期的英雄 Sir Walter Raleigh 的传记。Raleigh 后来是判处死刑的，这几章文章可以写得很精彩。但是到该停的时候，她还是停下来。她只是记着，"Raleigh 到 Winchester，准备受审。门口号角声……他还有两天可活……。"这种笔记是不用脑筋的，写来不费力。今天先养精蓄锐，明天好好地来写。

We Need Humor
我们需要幽默

Malcolm Muggeridge（1903—1990）

本文原题"America Needs A Punch"，刊于 1958 年四月号 *Esquire* 杂志"英国专号"。作者曾任英国幽默杂志 *Punch* 之主编多年。这篇文章虽然讨论幽默，但是本身文字似颇严肃。此处所摘几段，大致可说明幽默对于人生之重要。

[1]

During the five years that I was responsible for bringing out the avowedly humorous publication, *Punch*, I brooded intermittently on the subject of humor. It was a somber, but by no means unrewarding endeavor.

[注]

bringing out：刊行。

Punch：英国幽默杂志，林语堂将它译为《笨拙》。按，Punch 原为英国木偶戏中的一个角色（好像中国木偶戏中的猪八戒），钩鼻红脸，圆睛长颏，*Punch* 杂志的标识就是这样的一个木头人。

avowedly：自认地、自称地。此词原为动词 avow（承认、自认），加 -ed 成形容词，再加 -ly 成副词。"笨拙"标榜幽默。

intermittently：断断续续。**brooded on**：思考。

it：思考幽默这个题目：这是件 somber（让人感到不愉快、不乐观）的工作，但是把这个问题想一想，也不是"划不来"的（by no means unrewarding）。

[2]

Humor, I have come to feel, is an expression in terms of the grotesque of the enormous disparity between human aspiration and human performance. Thus, self-importance is funny because everyone really knows in his heart that, whatever else is conceivable, it is quite outside the bounds of possibility that one mortal man should be inherently more important than another.

[注]

I have come to feel：我渐渐地有这个看法。这几个词一般中国学生用来，会把它们放在全句之首，成为主句，然后用连接词 that，再说 humor 如何如何，而以 humor is ... 为附属从句。在这里 I have come to feel 这五个词，只是临时插进去的（parenthetical），在全句文法结构上，几乎不占地位。按理说，这五个词本是可有可无，如把它们放在主句的地位，的确是太抬举它们了。中国学生对于这种"插入语句"（parenthetical expression）如能善加利用，英文句法可以活泼得多。照现在这样的用法，全句的重心在 humor 一词，I have come to feel 读起来很轻。这样读法，语气很顺。

human aspiration：人类的理想。**human performance**：人类的行为。人类的理想与"实际表演"之间有很大的差别（enormous disparity）。幽默就是以荒谬怪诞的方式（in terms of the grotesque），表现这种差别，例如，人人心中想做勇士、崇拜勇士；但是人实际上所表现的，却是以懦怯为多。西洋的滑稽电影，常常就由一个丑角（如 Danny Kaye），以奇怪的动作，配合荒谬的故事，演出一个"勇敢的懦夫"或"怯懦的勇士"。

grotesque：奇形怪状的。此词为形容词，此处和 the 连用，就当作名词用了。

self-importance：自以为了不起。everyone really knows 后面跟一个很长的名词从句，that ...，一直到全句之末。

whatever is conceivable：任何别的事情我们都可以想象（conceive），但是有一件事情我们是不能想象的（或者说：任何别的事情或者都是可能的，但是有一件事情是绝不可能的，是很难超过可能性的范围的——**quite outside the bounds of**

possibility)。此事为何？就是：大家都是人，谁都不是神（因此都是凡人 mortal），怎么会有一个人在本质上(inherently)比别人更重要呢？人人有超过别人的"理想"，但是他的表现却常常与别人无殊，有这么一点差别在，所以一个高视阔步，神气活现的人，也常常是个可笑的人。

it is quite ... 中的 it 代替后面的 that one ... 那个从句。

[3]

On a basis of this definition it can readily be seen why humor, in its social application, is normally distasteful to those set in authority over us. When the governed laugh, the governors cannot but have an uneasy feeling that they may well be laughing at them.

[注]

it 代替"why"从句。**readily**：这是很容易被看出来的,我们很容易了解这点道理。

in its social application：在它社会应用的一方面。在私人来往之间我们可以说笑话，做滑稽的动作；但是我们假如把幽默应用到社会上去，假如我们的幽默牵涉到的，不是我们自己，也不是我们的朋友，而是某种社会制度，或是社会上的知名之士，那么这种幽默就将为权威人士所不喜。

distasteful to：不对（某种人的）胃口。**normally**：通常说来。set 是过去分词。那种有权威，地位在我们之上的人。

the governed：被统治者。**the governors**：统治者。**cannot but**：不得不。统治者心里必有不安，以为人家很可能（may well）笑的就是他。laughing 用进行时使得前面 when the governed laugh 中的 laugh 更为生动。

[4]

Humor, in fact, is an aspect of freedom, without which it cannot exist at all. By its nature, humor implies, when it does not state, criticism of existing institutions, beliefs, and functionaries. Absolute power means absolute solemnity, and the degree to which a society is free, and therefore civilized, may be measured by the degree to which it permits ridicule.

[注]

aspect：方面。幽默是自由之一方面，没有自由（without which），也就没有幽默。

by its nature：就幽默的本质说来。幽默就包含着（implies）"批评"的意义：对于现有的制度，信仰和官吏（functionaries）的批评。**when it does not state**：这种批评有时候是明白说出来（state）的；即使在不明白说出来的时候，幽默也"暗含"着批评的意义。

absolute power：绝对的权力（没有限制、无可批评的权力）必须要配合着（means）绝对的庄重。一个社会自由到什么程度，（自由就是文明的表现，因此我们可以说，一个社会文明到什么程度）是有一样东西可以测量（measured）的：这个社会究竟许不许人家说笑话？许到什么程度？

[5]

All this is obvious enough, and we who inhabit what we like to call the "free world" complacently assume that, in contradistinction with the state of affairs across the Iron Curtain, with us humor is unrestricted and abundant. But is it? I have come to feel of late that in the United States, as well as in Britain, the area of life in which ridicule is permissible is steadily shrinking, and that a dangerous tendency is becoming manifest to take ourselves with undue seriousness. Irreverence is decidedly out of fashion, and the clown or satirist, if he is to continue in business, must keep a careful eye on his targets lest they frown unduly.

[注]

obvious：明显的。**we**：我们住在"自由世界"的人；作者认为这样说，意义尚未够精确，改为：我们这种居住于我们常称之为"自由世界"那地方的人。**complacently**：自鸣得意的。assume 作此假定。

state of affairs：情形。我们常自以为：和不自由地区的情形相比，我们这里(with us) 幽默是大行其道：丰富而不受限制。但是事实真是这样吗？（ **is it?** = is humor unrestricted and abundant?）

of late：最近。**I have come to feel**：在前面有一段是用作"插入语句"的，这里可是"主句"了。在前面那一段，作者要强调 humor 这个词，故把那五个词贬为"插入语句"。在本句中,作者要批评英美人,说他们的幽默逐渐丧失,这种话也许是不中听的,作者怕得罪人,乃吞吞吐吐,故意不把想说的话说出来。在这种情形之下,I have come to feel 就成了主句了。

此句的吞吞吐吐,可由其起句的缓慢见之。I have come to feel of late 非主要的话也(虽然文法上是主句);in the United States, as well as in Britain,亦非主要的话也,话说了这么多,说到主要的意思,仍旧用一种婉曲的说法:在英美两国,讥笑可以适用的范围是越来越小了;人生中可以容许讥笑的范围是不断地在缩小。英美两国,虽号称民主,但是碰到有些问题,也不敢出之玩笑口吻的。

I have to feel 后面跟两个从句。第二个从句,也是以 that 领头:我们可以渐渐看得见有一种危险的倾向(原文是:"有一种危险的倾向正成为明显"),那就是,我们把自己的生活弄得太严肃。**undue**:过度的。

irreverence:不敬,玩笑。**clown**:丑。**satirist**:讽刺家。

continue in business:假如他还想吃这一行饭的话。古之弄臣,可以谈笑之中进忠谏,今之滑稽明星,假如讥笑了社会上某种人士,他就可能不受欢迎。**targets**:(讽刺的)目标。丑角一定要时时看清楚他的目标,只怕(lest)受讽刺的人皱起眉头,脸色大为不悦。

[6]

In King Lear's misfortunes his only faithful and true counselor was the Fool. It might be so with us. The ultimate safeguard is perhaps not atomic weapons, larger and better bases, louder radio stations, but more fools. The foolishness of man, Blake wrote, is the wisdom of God; and it may well be that those who seek to suppress or limit laughter are more dangerous than all the subversive conspiracies which the F. B. I. ever has or will uncover. Laughter, in fact, is the most effective of all subversive conspiracies, and it operates on *our* side.

[注]

King Lear 是莎士比亚悲剧中的主人翁,他受不了女儿的虐待,无家可归,在暴风雨中彷徨,只有一个小丑(Fool)陪伴着他。小丑说些不着边际的话,其实都是针对着 Lear 的痛苦。**counselor**:顾问,谋士。在老王遭遇不幸的时候,唯一忠实而说真话的谋士，是那个小丑。我们现在也处在一个不幸的时代，我们可能也需要小丑来做朋友（It might be so with us）。

ultimate safeguard：（自由世界）终究的保障。

William Blake（1757—1827）：英国神秘主义诗人。

subversive conspiracies：颠覆（政府）的阴谋。

F. B. I.：美国联邦调查局（Federal Bureau of Investigation）。

uncover：揭发（阴谋）。联邦调查局历来揭发各种颠覆阴谋，将来这种工作还要继续下去，但是一切颠覆阴谋，要论危险，还比不上那种不许人家笑的人。事实可能是这样：那种设法（seek）要禁止人家笑，或是限制人家笑的人，是比那种种阴谋更为危险。这是一个 paradox。

事实上，笑才是最有效的颠覆活动。民主国家不怕老百姓笑口常开，极权国家才怕人笑。嘻嘻哈哈，而极权统治休矣。最后一句 *our* 重读，表示笑可颠覆极权的政府，是有利于我们自由世界的。

Skeffington's Decision to Run for Re-election
市长决心竞选

Edwin O'Connor (1918—1968)

下面几段选自长篇小说《最后一次欢呼》(*The Last Hurrah*) 之第一章。《最后一次欢呼》写一老年政客再度竞赛市长的故事，内容轻松幽默，作者态度于讽刺中带有同情，文笔有力。该书于 1956 年出版，即成畅销书，纽约时报评为"The best novel about American politics"。

该书虽是小说，但其主角乃影射波士顿某市长。今日之波士顿城，爱尔兰人势力甚大。本书作者奥康纳原籍爱尔兰，书中的市长也是原籍爱尔兰的。

[1]

It was early in August when Frank Skeffington decided — or rather, announced his decision, which actually had been arrived at some months before — to run for re-election as mayor of the city. This was a matter about which there had been public speculation for a good while: for, in fact, four years, ever since he had been inaugurated for what his opponents had fondly hoped was the last time. Since the beginning of the current year, however, the speculation had increased, not alone because the deadline was drawing nearer, but also because there was no other elections of importance coming up — the municipal elections took place in off years politically and so did not have to share the spotlight with national or state contests. Thus interest had mounted, and as it had, so had the hopes of Skeffington's opponents. For while he was admittedly among the most durable of politicians, he was just as admittedly getting older, and in recent speeches and press conferences he had expressed little interest in continuing his long political career. On one memorable occasion he had gone so far as to speak with a certain dreaminess of the joys of retirement, of the quiet time of withdrawal which would follow a lifetime spent in the service of the public.

[注]

从第一句可以看出来，英文意义之力求准确。此人是八月初决定竞选（to run）蝉联（re-election）市长的。话是这么说了，但是作者立刻自己修正。更正确（rather）的说法是：此人在八月初只是正式宣布决心竞选而已。那决心本身（which）是在几个月之前，就培养好了。英文说"达到"（arrived at）某种决心。此句的 decided，跟后面的 to run。横线中间的补充语句中的 decision 也是跟后面的 to run，这样的句法结构很紧凑。**mayor of the city**：注意 mayor 前面不用定冠词 the。

matter：决心竞选这件"事情"。

public speculation：公众的推测。市长任期快满了，他要不要再度竞选呢？大家纷纷猜测，如由中国学生写来，这一句中的"猜测"很可能用一个动词，不大可能用一个名词（speculation）的。大致说来，表示动作的词，如用名词来表示，全句的主要动词仅用一个平凡的 be（这里是 had been），这样一个句子，比较平稳而欠生动。现在作者只想平铺直叙地开头，这样平稳的句法，比较合宜。要看生动的场面，后面多得是。**for a good while**：猜测了好久。作者又加以补充说明，把 for 一字重复地用（for, in fact, four years），事实上是，猜测了四年，从（ever since）他上次当选就任时起，就有人猜想他会不会任满后竞选连任了。

inaugurated：就任。反对他的人希望那就是他的最后一任，for 连 the last time：最后一次。但是这样说法作者认为还不够严格，for 后面加了一个"what"从句：他们所希望的最后一次。**fondly hoped**：一厢情愿的希望。

the current year：本年度，今年。这一句用 speculation 做主语，呼应上一句的 speculation，句与句之间连接得很紧。**not alone** = not only。

deadline：限期。他是否想竞选连任，应该有所表示了。**drawing near**：移近。**municipal elections**：市区选举，选举市长等官员。**off years**：闲年，并非正式选举年。1952、1956、1960 等年是美国大选年。**politically**：就政治方面说来，市区选举并不在正式选举年举行，若是有更重要的选举（全国性或全州性的竞争，national or state contests），一般市民对于市长竞选一事，不会这么关心。现在所以推测增多，传说纷纭，就是为了这两个原因，一、他表明态度的日期日益迫近；二、此外别无重要选举事宜。**spotlight**：舞台或照相馆用的聚光灯。光集中一点，和 floodlight（光线遍照各处的强光灯）不同。聚光灯所照之处,必是使人最注目之处。现在只有这一样选举，市民只关心这么一件事，好像只有它一件事，为聚光灯所照射，它不必（did not have to）与别的选举去分享这盏聚光灯（或者说，去分占市民的注意力）。

mounted：增高。**and as it had** = and as interest had mounted。就在市民的兴趣增高的时候，Skeffington 的政敌的希望也增高了。**so had** = had mounted。

为什么他的政敌觉得有希望呢？因为他虽然公认（admittedly）是政海中的一个不倒翁（政客之中政治生命最长〈most durable〉的一个），可是同样也是公认的(just as admittedly) 春秋日高，恐怕将要退休。

press conference：记者招待会。**political career**：政治生涯。**with a certain dreaminess**：以梦想式的态度或语调。**had gone so far as to**：居然走得这样远，居然这样明白地表示。**speak ... of the joys of retirement**：说起退隐之乐。of the quiet time 的 of，也是连 speak 的。**withdrawal**：退出（政界）。**follow**：一生为公众服务之后，"继"之以退隐。

[2]

"Far from the madding crowd," he had said, gazing at the reporters expressionlessly. "The declining years spent in solitude and contemplation. Possibly in some rustic retreat."

This hint had not been received without a measure of cynicism; one reporter from the chief opposition paper had led the questioning which followed.

[注]

far from the madding crowd's ignoble strife：本是 Thomas Gray 诗中的句子。madding 即 mad，远离疯狂的人群。

he had said：此人在八月初公开表示要竞选，但是在此之前，他"曾经"暗示过要退休。他的再度竞选，既是"过去"的事，他一切关于退休的话，当然都是属于"过去的过去"。本文第一句用了 It was early in August，决定了时间先后的标准。在此以前所发生的事，该用过去完成时态。

declining years：晚年，衰落。**spent**：是过去分词。这是不完全句子。**some rustic retreat**：某处乡村偏僻的地方。retreat 也可解作"隐居的地方"，或"不受人打扰的地方"。如宿舍里太闹不能读书，一定要在图书馆里才读得成书，那么图书馆也就是你的 retreat。

hint：暗示。**received**：(被动语态) 领受，听到。那些记者听见此话，并不相信。**not ... without**：两重否定，即成肯定。**a measure of**：某些分量的。**cynicism**：此词很难译。《简明牛津词典》把 cynical 解作 incredulous of human goodness，不相信天下有好人好事；把 cynic 解作 sneering fault-finder，抱冷笑的态度专找别人错处的人。这样说法虽然简单一点，但还算能道出 cynicism 这一种态度的要义。普通英汉词典把它译成"犬儒主义"，这样非得大讲哲学史上这个词的来源不可了。

the chief opposition paper：反对党方面一家主要的报纸。**the questioning**：发问，发问是那个记者领导（led）的。**which followed** = which followed the hint。

[3]

"Tell us, Governor," he had said (for, as Skeffington had twice been governor of the state, the courtesy title lingered long after the office itself had been lost), "just how would you propose to adjust yourself to this rustic life? Wouldn't it be pretty quiet? What would you do?"

[注]

governor：州长。**the state**：这里指 Massachusetts。Skeffington 是市长，为什么人家称他做州长呢？

courtesy title：礼貌上的尊称。**lingered**：停留不走；继续被人使用。**the office**：州长那个职位。

just：用以加重 how 的语气。**propose**：建议，这里当然是自己向自己建议，想办法。**adjust yourself to**：调整改变，以求适应。

pretty（副词）= fairly。

[4]

"Read," Skeffington had replied promptly, "and reflect." At this his pale blue eyes had closed, and an expression of extraordinary benignity crossed the full, faintly veined and rather handsome face; the long, heavy head inclined perceptibly forward, and the reporters found themselves looking at the silver crown of his hair. It was almost as if, in anticipation, he were paying pious tribute to the time of ultimate retreat.

[注]

promptly：不假思索地。**reflect**：思想。

at this：说到这里。下面就是说明上面说过的 a certain dreaminess 了。

benignity：慈祥。**crossed the face**：掠过他的脸。他的脸是丰满的，青筋隐约可见（vein：静脉），相当清秀。**long, heavy head**：脑袋长而且厚实。**perceptibly**：可看得见地。眼睛闭了，头往前倾——正是像耽于冥想的样子。**the silver crown of his hair**：一头银发。

in anticipation：心里先行准备。**paying tribute**：致敬。**pious**：虔敬的。**ultimate**：最后的。

[5]

The reporter had coughed. "We know you've always been a great reader, Governor," he had said, a trifle sardonically. "Any idea of the kind of books you'd take with you?"

Skeffington's reply, made with eyes still closed, had been characteristically elusive. "The great books," he had said.

The reporter had been persistent, "Which great books, Governor?"

[注]

coughed：想必是假咳，干咳。

great reader：读书很多的人。**a trifle sardonically**：略带讥讽。

any idea：前面省略了 have you 等字样。**you'd** = you would。日常对话中，虚拟语气的用场是很大的。市长是否退隐，尚不得而知，故用虚拟式。

made 是过去分词。**characteristically**：这一点很能代表他说话的特色。**elusive**：闪烁其辞，使人捉摸不定。

persistent：坚持的，打破砂锅问到底。

[6]

Skeffington's eyes had opened, the silver head had lifted, and once more the reporters met the deadpan look. "I don't know whether you'd know them or not," he had said thoughtfully. "The Bible, which is a book composed of two parts, commonly called the Old and the New Testaments. The poems and plays of Shakespeare, an Englishman. And during the winter months I would also take the paper which you represent."

[注]

市长对新闻记者说，他要到乡间去隐居读书。敌党的报纸记者紧紧地追问他读什么书。他本来有点梦想的样子，现在他眼睛睁开，头抬起来了。记者们所看见的，又是他的板板的没有表情的脸了。

deadpan：无表情的；呼应前文 gazing at the reporters expressionlessly。

他的答复的话很简单，但是很刻薄。《圣经》和莎翁是为英语国家所家喻户晓的，他瞧不起那记者，故意替他解释，《圣经》是怎么样的一本书，莎士比亚是何国的人。

the paper which you represent：阁下所代表的那张报纸。

[7]

The reporter had said warily, "Thanks for the compliment, Governor. I suppose there's some special reason."

Skeffington had nodded. "During the long winter months a glowing fire might be welcome," he had said, "and I have found from long experience that your paper burns very well. Makes good kindling. I don't imagine, by the way, that most people are aware of that. If they were, your paper's very small circulation might be substantially increased. Any more questions, gentlemen?"

[注]

warily：小心翼翼地。这个老政客忽然赞美起敌党的报纸来了，恐怕话中有因。**compliment**：(隐含的) 赞美，捧场。

burns（不及物动词）**very well**：容易着火。

makes 的主语 it 省略。**kindling**：引火物。他之所以要订这份报纸原来是拿它来作生火之用。

by the way：顺便可以一提的。"我以为，很多人不知道贵报有这点长处。"原文作：我不以为很多人知道……。imagine 在这里的意思很轻，同 think，suppose 的用法相仿。

if they were：假如他们知道（were aware）。**very small circulation**：很小的销路。**substantially increased**：着实增加。大家都要来订你们的报纸来引火生炉子了。

[8]

It had been a typical enough interview, save for the suggestion of retirement. None of Skeffington's opponents quite believed in this, but on the other hand, neither could they afford to discount it. On the whole, any hint of this kind was felt to be encouraging rather than otherwise, especially when related to certain other signs. For example, there were the heartening rumors of Skeffington's ill health: among the true optimists it was confidently whispered that a mysterious disease was devouring his brain bit by bit, so that now there occurred intervals in every day during which he reverted to the habits of his childhood and expressed a desire to play marbles or hide-and-seek. The newspaper whose combustibility Skeffington had praised offered support of a more oblique kind. It began to run editorials reminding the voters that while the life span of man undoubtedly had been prolonged, the problem of senectitude had by no means been conquered, and that aged men in positions of public trust could constitute a definite hazard.

[注]

interview：访问。**typical enough**：有足够代表性的。他往常跟记者们的谈话，也是语带刻薄的。此次谈话若有什么与以前不同之处，那就是他提到了退休（retirement）。save 意即 except，但 save 较古雅。

discount it：对于此话半信半疑，把这句话打折扣。**neither could they afford**：如不相信此话，对他们自己也有害处。

any hint of this kind：任何这一类的暗示（关于他的退休）。**encouraging rather than otherwise**：他的政敌觉得有鼓励的作用，此种作用大于别种作用。related 是过去分词，形容 hint。他自己既暗示要退休，这种暗示同别种迹象（signs）联系起来时，政敌们更有跃跃欲试取而代之之意。

heartening 和前面的 encouraging 相仿，都是从他的政敌的立场说话的。optimists 也是政敌之中的乐观主义者。**rumors**：谣言。

it was confidently whispered 中的 it 是代替后面的 that a mysterious ... 这个从句。**devouring**：吞噬。

there occurred 中的 there 和普通 there is 中的 there 相仿，没有什么特别意义。**intervals**：短时期。**reverted to**：回复到。**play marbles**：玩（彩石或玻璃）弹子。**hide-and-seek**：捉迷藏。**combustibility**：易燃性。**oblique**：间接的。

run：连续发表。竞选也是 run，run 这个词的用处很大。

life span：生命的长度，寿命。**senectitude**：衰老。此词罕用，美国有些报纸的社论文章做得很古雅，这种罕用词、僻词、古词有时也会搬出来（此处没有用引号，但是这种句子很像有些报纸里社论的句子）。

that aged men 中的 that 是连接词，也是连前面 reminding the voters，使选民们勿忘此事。**aged men in positions of public trust**：老年人而居高位，身负万民重托。**constitute** = make up，形成。**hazard**：危险。（这种话无非要叫市长真的任满不干。）

[9]

But Skeffington smashed them all in a matter of minutes.

On his seventy-second birthday Frank Skeffington had lunch with his nephew, and over the meal told him of his plan to run again. That night, at a birthday dinner given him by the party leaders, he made the announcement public. It was substantially the same announcement that he had delivered in private that noon.

[注]

smashed：打碎。a matter of 有 about 之意：不消几分钟，把敌方的流言都打碎了。
announcement：呼应全文开头的 announced his decision。
delivered in private：私下表示的。

[10]

"My decision represents a submission to the will of the populace," he said, "and is against my very personal desire. I had hoped, at the end of my current term, to retire to a well-earned rest, but unfortunately one look at the names of those who have declared themselves as candidates for this office forced me to change my decisions. Why, the mind positively boggles at the presumption of these men! As one looks down this bold list one would think that the only qualification necessary to run for mayor of this great city was to be without any qualification whatever. This is a time for experience, for leadership; I cannot abandon this fine city to the care of such fumbling hands. And so, dutifully if reluctantly, I submit my name to you once again, realizing full well that while my own health and rest are important, it is far more important that this city of ours should not be allowed to revert to Government by Pygmies!"

[注]

这段话是市长在生日宴会上，对党内显要发表的谈话。市长年逾古稀，但是所说的话还是虎虎有生气，话里还骂了人。

submission to：屈服于（人民的意志）。
I had hoped：用过去完成时态，那是因为同本句的另一动词 forced 比较而得。forced 在后，hoped 在前，但是 forced 也是过去的事，所以一个用过去时，一个用过去完成时。**current term**：这一届任期。**a well-earned rest**：凭劳力挣来的休息，做了几十年公仆，老来也该享享清福。
one look：一看。这一看使我改变了主意。**boggles**：突然受惊，因此停止不前。**presumption**：胆大妄为。
as one looks down：和前面的 one look 不同。这里的 one 不是"一次"，而是"某个人"，即说话的人自己。**this bold list**：胆大的人的名单。

他们凭什么资格来竞选市长？我们将要以为，竞选市长的唯一资格就是没有什么资格，只有"一无所长，一无足取"的人才配来做这个大城市的市长。

for experience, for leadership：用了两个抽象名词；其实是我们需要有经验的"人"，有领导才干的"人"，英文于此地不用"人"这个概念，此乃中英文思想不同之处。**fumbling**：笨拙的，瞎摸的。**to the care of such fumbling hands**：交到这种人的手里去。

dutifully if reluctantly：心虽不愿，但是为了波士顿八十万市民计。**submit my name**：把我的名字提出来。**realizing full**（副词）**well**：同时我充分了解这点道理。后面随一"that"从句，此从句中又先出一"while"从句，后面又用 it 代替另一"that"从句（that this city ...）。

revert：此词前面已见过，是"返老还童"，这里也有"开倒车"之意。**Government by Pygmies**：林肯有 government by the people（由人民来做主的政府）的名言。这里是由 Pygmies（侏儒，小人物）来做主的政府。

[11]

This announcement had been carefully timed so that it would appear in the city edition of all morning papers; in this way, the maximum desirable effect would be achieved; the majority of his opponents would learn the bad news over their morning coffee. It was a thought which appeared to afford him a virtually limitless satisfaction.

[注]

timed：time 作动词用，解作"时间算准"。**city edition**：本市版。**the maximum desirable effect would be achieved**：可以达到希望中的最大效用。

it was a thought：（他的那些政敌一早起来，翻开报纸就看见他再度竞选的消息，不禁先则愕然，继则愤然，再则黯然）他一想到这点，心里就感到无限安慰。他事前封锁消息到那天晚上再公布，目的就要使他的敌人生一天气。**virtually limitless**：几乎是无限的。

Moon Shell
月形螺壳

Anne Morrow Lindbergh（1906—2001）

本文作者安·林德伯格是著名飞行家林德伯格（Charles A. Lindbergh）上校的夫人，她的父亲是外交官。林德伯格夫人写诗，也写小说；这篇文章选自她的散文集《海的礼物》(*Gift from the Sea*)。该书收文章 8 篇，大多是林德伯格夫人记录自己在海滨的各种思想，大多有关妇女问题和人生问题。她的思想大多又是海滨的各种贝壳所引起的，所以这本书名《海的礼物》。这种抒发个人感慨的散文，在中国是"散文正宗"，美国 19 世纪的散文也很多是这一种的，但是 20 世纪便很少见。林德伯格夫人此书出版后很受欢迎，列入畅销书。

[1]

This is a snail shell, round, full and glossy as a horse chestnut. Comfortable and compact, it sits curled up like a cat in the hollow of my hand. Milky and opaque, it has the pinkish bloom of the sky on a summer evening, ripening to rain. On its smooth symmetrical face is pencilled with precision a perfect spiral, winding inward to the pinpoint center of the shell, the tiny dark core of the apex, the pupil of the eye. It stares at me, this mysterious single eye — and I stare back.

[注]

snail：蜗牛。海滩上的贝壳，也有圆圆的像蜗牛壳的。**full**：丰满的。**glossy**：光泽鲜明的。**horse chestnut**："七叶树"所结的果子，据说以前是马的饲料。**compact**：满满的。comfortable 形容贝壳，似乎奇怪；但贝壳既比作为猫，此词也是妥当的。curled 是过去分词，作形容词用，形容主语 it。这两句的形容词，有些放在名词的前面，有些放在后面，其间颇有讲究。如第一句改成：This is a round snail shell，第二句改成：It sits comfortable, compact, and curled up，都比较差。

in the hollow of my hand：在我手心里面。

第三句又是以两个形容词开头。这种句法，至少可以省掉 verb to be；否则的话 it is comfortable and compact, it is milky and opaque，重复地说，句法很笨。现在把形容词放在一句之首，句子的主语还没出现，句子的重心不落在这几个形容词身上，句子里可以讲些更重要的事。

opaque：不透明的。**bloom**：红润之色。**ripening**：这个词来形容天空，很怪。原义是"成熟"，夏日黄昏，红云渐浓，乃作雨之兆。

symmetrical：对称的。**pencilled**：并不真是用铅笔画的；线条很细，好像是铅笔画的。**spiral**：螺旋线。此词乃本句之主语。

pinpoint：像针头那样细的。

core：核心。此词和 center 是"同位"。**pupil**：瞳孔，这个字也是同位语。圆形的螺壳，好像是只眼睛。**apex**：顶点。

[2]

Now it is the moon, solitary in the sky, full and round, replete with power. Now it is the eye of a cat that brushes noiselessly through long grass at night. Now it is an island, set in everwidening circles of waves, self-contained, serene.

[注]

作者看见这只螺壳，思潮大作，把它比作三件东西。now 连着用，表示"一下子这样，一下子那样"。

replete：充满了。**power**：把月亮看作是神，它有它的权力。通常以为月亮有一种 magical power，中国有僵尸拜月，狐狸拜月的传说，西洋人以为月亮能使人发狂。至少月亮有吸动潮水的力量。

a cat that 中的 that 代替 cat。**brushes through**：走过（身体跟外物摩擦的）。

set(过去分词)：放在。**self-contained**：自足的。**serene**：宁静的。这两个形容词，放到句子的结尾来了，形容 island。

[3]

How wonderful are islands! Islands in space, like this one I have come to, ringed about by miles of water, linked by no bridges, no cables, no telephones. An island from the world and the world's life. Islands in time, like this short vacation of mine. The past and the future are cut off: only the present remains. One lives like a child or a saint in the immediacy of here and now. Every day, every act, is an island, washed by time and space, and has an island's completion. People, too, become like islands in such an atmosphere, self-contained, whole and serene; respecting other people's solitude, not intruding on their shores, standing back in reverence before the miracle of another individual. "No man is an island," said John Donne. I feel we are all islands — in a common sea.

[注]

说到这个螺壳像一座岛，文章就转到"岛"上去了。岛的特性是隔绝的，在空间上隔绝的，或者是在时间上隔绝的。空间上的岛，像我在这里度假的那座岛。

ringed（过去分词）：围绕。**cables**：海底电缆。以前人所想家的岛是没有桥梁与其它陆地相联系的。但是现代人的想法不然，即使没有桥梁，有电报、电话，所谓孤岛也者还可以和外界联络。所以作者于 linked by no bridges 之后，再说 no cables，no telephones，这才表示彻底孤立。islands in space ... 是不完全的句子，后面两句也都是不完全的句子。

an island from 中的 from 有"隔绝"之意。英文的介词，往往有中文的动词之意义。如中文"民有、民治、民享"中间的"有、治、享"是三个动词，在英文里便成了 of the people，by the people，for the people 了。

另外一种岛屿是时间上的岛屿，如我这短短的假期。它和过去，和未来都是隔绝的（意思大约是说：我既不想过去，也不想将来）。

here and now（习语）：此时此地。immediacy 是 immediate 的名词形式，直接领略目前的情形。一个人要心无挂碍，无思无虑，才能做到这一地步。小孩子能，圣人亦能。

every day，every act 虽然是两件东西，动词还是用单数形式。

washed by time and space：把时间空间比作海水。**has an island's completion** = is complete in itself like an island：自身圆满具足。

在这种气氛之下，人也都像了一座一座的岛了，谁也不去管别人的闲事，"尊敬别人的孤独。"

既然把人比作岛，那么管人的闲事，就好像插足到别人的岛上去，闯入了别人的海岸（intruding on their shores）。

reverence 较之 respect 更多一层宗教上的"虔诚敬畏"之意。照基督教的看法，上帝创造人是一大奇迹（miracle），我身之外，另有他人，此他人者，既是奇迹，我观此奇迹，衷心敬之畏之，驻步不敢前(standing back)。人和人之间因此缺乏来往，这样，两个人就成了两座孤岛了。

John Donne（1572—1631）：约翰·多恩，英国名诗人，较莎士比亚晚生九年。他也是个有名的布道师。"No man is an island"是他的一篇讲道文中的名句，讲的是人人祸福相关，没有人可以孤立；海明威有一部小说的标题 *For Whom the Bell Tolls*，也出自同一篇文章：丧钟为谁而响呢？为你而响。——别人丧生，你也受到影响。

但是本文作者，从另外一个观点看来，以为人人都是孤岛。人是寂寞的，人和人之间沟通是困难的，所以一个人是一座岛。这和 Donne 人人祸福相关的看法不同。

[4]

We are all, in the last analysis, alone. And this basic state of solitude is not something we have any choice about. It is, as the poet Rilke says, "not something that one can take or leave. We *are* solitary. We may delude ourselves and act as though this were not so. That is all. But how much better it is to realize that we are so, yes, even to begin by assuming it. Naturally," he goes on to say, "we will turn giddy."

[注]

in the last analysis：分析到最后，归根结底。

basic state of solitude：人类的基本状态——寂寞。**we have any choice about** 是定语从句。对于人生之寂寞，我们并无选择之余地。人生而寂寞；如欲不寂寞，为不可能之事。只有寂寞的一条路，没有第二条路。

Rilke（1875—1926）：里尔克，奥地利诗人。**It is ... not something**：句法是上一句 this basic state of solitude is not something 的重复。**take or leave**（习语）：接受或不接受。人生有些东西（如非义之财），你可以取（take），也可以不取（leave），这就是所谓 choice，但是人生的寂寞，是无法避免的。

delude：哄骗。**act**：如此这般地做人。**as though this were not so**：好像是人生并不寂寞的。

that is all：仅此而已。假如有人以为人生并不寂寞，或者兴高采烈地和别人相聚为乐，这"无非"是自己骗自己，他忘记了这点基本事实而已。

how much better it is：it 代替 to realize "体会到"，领悟到我们确是寂寞（so 代替 solitary）。我们尽可自骗自，但是领悟到这一点，对于我们是有好处的。

yes = moreover, in addition。前面所说固然不错，我们还可以更进一步地说。**to begin by assuming it**：做人一开头就假定人生的寂寞，不要自骗自，这样更好。begin by + 动名词是习语，以某事开始，如 He began by scolding us, saying...（他对我们的说话是以责骂开头的；他一开头就责骂我们，说道……）。

we will：这里的 will 没有意志作用，只是表示将来。假如我们念念不忘人生的寂寞，无疑地我们将要头晕眼花（giddy），支持为难。

[5]

Naturally. How one hates to think of oneself as alone. How one avoids it. It seems to imply rejection or unpopularity. An early, wallflower panic still clings to the word. One will be left, one fears, sitting in a straight-backed chair *alone*, while the popular girls already chosen and spinning around the dance floor with their hot-palmed partners.

[注]

naturally：这是本文作者附和 Rilke 的话。Rilke 刚用过 naturally 这个词（原

文是德文），这里接着用一个。人领悟到人生的寂寞之后，当然是要头晕眼花的。

how one avoids it：it 可能是代替上一句 to think of oneself as alone。这两句以 how 开头，都是不完全句子。

imply：含有……之意。我们怕寂寞，因为寂寞含有不见容于人（rejection），或不受欢迎（unpopularity）之意。

early：早期所养成的。**panic**：恐慌心理。**wallflower**：舞会中无人邀舞的女子。西洋女子视舞会为正式社交场合，假如众人皆舞，我独向隅，这个味道是不好受的。她们很早就有这种心理，这种心理也就附着于（clings to）这个词上。**the word**：什么词？可能是 alone；较好的是 solitude。

one fears 是插入语句。怕的是什么呢？作者更具体地描写舞会中受冷落的情形。这样的寂寞确实可怕，但是人生的基本寂寞（basic state of solitude）和舞会里的寂寞不同。舞会里的寂寞只是 rejection，unpopularity 而已。

leave 这个词用处很大，前面刚刚见过 take or leave，leave 也有"不加理睬"之意，leave me alone（不要来惹我）是习语。这句话的结构，还是从这个习语脱胎而出，One will be left ... alone。**straight-backed chair**：靠背笔直的，强调不舒服的情形。人家跳舞，我在沙发上躺一回，也蛮舒服，偏偏坐在硬椅子上。

popular：受人欢迎，人见人爱。**spinning**：蛱蝶穿花似地转。这个动词很生动，目的也无非强调做 wallflower 的可怕。**hot-palmed**：掌心是热的，这个形容词也很生动。自己没有下场子跳，但是不难想象别人相依相偎的亲热情形，美国女人很早就有怕寂寞的心理，所以要逃避寂寞。

[6]

We seem so frightened today of being alone that we never let it happen. Even if family, friends, and movies should fail, there is still the radio or television to fill up the void. Women, who used to complain of loneliness, need never be alone any more. We can do our housework with soap-opera heroes at our side. Even day-dreaming was more creative than this; it demanded something of oneself and it fed the inner life. Now instead of planting our solitude with our dream blossoms, we choke the space with continuous music, chatter and companionship to which we do not even listen. It is simply there to fill the vacuum. When the noise stops there is no inner music to take its place.

We must relearn to be alone.

[注]

alone 是形容词，不可以做 of 的宾语，一定要加一个 being。**frightened of being alone**：我们畏惧寂寞。**never let it happen**：不让寂寞发生。想尽办法，消除寂寞。

fail：失败，不能帮我们消除寂寞。**fill up the void**：填补空虚。

need never be alone：need 用于否定句中，后面通常不用 to。alone 要和 be 连接着用，前面已经说过了。

soap-opera：肥皂剧，因电视连续剧集中多插播肥皂广告而得名。**at our side**：一面做家务工作，一面看电视，肥皂剧中的人物就在我们身旁，我们毋庸忧惧寂寞了。

这种消遣方法，本文作者是反对的。她认为看肥皂剧的时候，脑筋只是消极地接受，不能积极地创造。**day-dreaming**：白日梦。过去家里没有电视机，我们无聊的时候，只好胡思乱想。作者认为这样做白日梦反而多一点创造性。**was more creative**：注意时态。这是在收音机、电视机尚未普及之时。前面有一句 who used to complain 也用的是过去时。过去是那样，现在是这样。

it demanded something of oneself：做白日梦还需要自己动用脑筋。它向自己要求些什么。demand 和 of 是连用的，例如：he demanded a dollar of me。

fed：喂饲，滋养。做白日梦也可使精神生活内容更为充实。

使精神生活内容充实，作者在下一句换了一种说法：在我们的寂寞（的土地）上种上梦想的花朵。

the space：这块空地（即无聊的时候）。

choke：窒息。扼杀这块地皮的生机。我们非但不去(instead of)种花以培养生机，反而扼杀之。

continuous music, chatter and companionship：作者用这几个词代替广播或电视节目。不间断的音乐，不间断的聊天，不间断有人跟你作伴。我们虽说是在听广播看电视，其实也并不是在聚精会神地听或看。空闲的时候，本来可以用以思想的，现在让广播、电视节目占据住了，这些节目我们其实也不好好地收听收看的。

it is simply there 中的 it 代替 continuous music 等等。**fill the vacuum**：填补空虚。

人的奇思妙想，可以说是内心的音乐。但是近代人只依赖外面的杂声，以填补精神的空虚。外面的杂声停止之时，我们内心没有音乐去取代杂声的地位。

如何应付寂寞，也成了一种学问。古人是知道的，今人必须重新学习如何在寂寞之中，充实内心生活。

[7]

It is a difficult lesson to learn today — to leave one's friends and family and deliberately practice the art of solitude for an hour or a day or a week. I find there is a quality to being alone that is incredibly precious. Life rushes back into the void, richer, more vivid, fuller than before.

[注]

deliberately：故意地。**practice**：美国人将 practice 当动词用，英国人则用 practise。**practice the art of solitude**：实习独处之道。

being alone 两个词连起来，是一名词短语，前面已经说过了。介词 to 这样的用法，《简明牛津词典》里有一个例句：There is a moral to it.（这件事情里有一个教训，我们可以从这件事情得到一个教训。）这里是：我发现在寂寞里有一种性质，一种不可思议（令人难信）的宝贵的性质。

life：在寂寞之时，我们可以思想。我们想起各种问题，各种人物，好像生命又涌回到这段空虚里来。这时的生命，较之我们平日的生活更为丰富，更为生动，更为充实。

[8]

For a full day and two nights I have been alone. I lay on the beach under the stars at night alone. I made my breakfast alone. Alone I watched the gulls at the end of the pier, dip and wheel and dive for the scraps I threw them. A morning's work at my desk, and then, a late picnic lunch alone, on the beach. And it seemed to me, separated from my own species, that I was nearer to others: the sandpiper, running in little unfrightened steps down the shining beach ahead of me; the slowly-flapping pelicans over my head, coasting down wind; the old gull, hunched up, grouchy, surveying the horizon. I felt a kind of impersonal kinship with them and a joy in that kinship. Beauty of earth and sea and air meant more to me. I was in harmony with it, melted into the universe, lost in it, as one is lost in a canticle of praise, swelling from an unknown crowd in a cathedral. "Praise ye the Lord, all the fishes of the sea — all ye birds of the air — all ye children of men — Praise ye the Lord!"

[注]

这一段作者讲她自己 practice the art of solitude 的经验。前三句都用 alone 结尾，第四句用 alone 开头。这是造句变化之法。

pier：码头。**gulls**：海鸥。

dip：以身浸水。**wheel** 盘旋地飞。**dive**：俯冲。三个动词都是不定式。在 watched 后面的动词不定式是不要用 to 的。**scraps**：碎片（食物）。

a morning's work：这是不完全句子。**separated from my own species**：与我同类隔绝；离开人群。我因此和别种动物更为接近。

sandpiper：矶鹬。**unfrightened**：见人不畏。本是形容鸟的，但是作者用来形容 steps，鸟的动作（奔跑）因此更为传神。**shining**：此词乃是画龙点睛之笔。得此词而全景乃耀然光亮矣。

flapping：拍翅的。**pelican**：塘鹅。**coasting**：（乘风）滑翔（而下）。

hunched up：弓着背。**grouchy**：牢骚满腹的样子。**surveying the horizon**：仔细地看着天边。**kinship**："民胞物与"、"众生皆我类也"之感。

melted（过去分词）：融化消失（形容主语）。**canticle**：赞美歌。**swelling**：（乐声）扬起。

ye：古式的 you，所引歌词似出自《旧约·但以理书》第三章，但《旧约》的语句与此处所引略有不同。

[9]

Yes, I felt closer to my fellow men too, even in my solitude. For it is not physical solitude that actually separates one from other men, not physical isolation, but spiritual isolation. It is not the desert island nor the stony wilderness that cuts you from the people you love. It is the wilderness in the mind, the desert wastes in the heart through which one wanders lost and a stranger. When one is a stranger to oneself, then one is estranged from others too. If one in out of touch with oneself, then one cannot touch others. How often in a large city, shaking hand with my friends, I have felt the wilderness stretching between us. Both of us were wandering in arid wastes, having lost the springs that nourished us or having found them dry. Only when one is connected to one's own core is one connected to others, I am beginning to discover. And, for me, the core, the inner spring, can best be refound through solitude.

[注]

physical solitude：外表的 (物质的) 寂寞。下一句desert island, stony wilderness 即说明所谓physical solitude, physical isolation, 本段的两个desert都是形容词。

前面说 separates one from other men，接着说 cuts you from the people you love，这是用词的变化。

wastes：荒地。It is the wilderness in the mind ... 是不完全句子。后面省了that cuts you ... 等词。

lost 是过去分词，形容主语 one。a stranger 和主语 one 同位。

a stranger to oneself：自己不认识自己，不认识自己，焉能认识别人？这就是所谓 spiritual isolation。**estranged from**：（和别人）隔膜。

the wilderness stretching between us：在大都市里，我虽和朋友握手，但是我们精神上并无沟通，只是形式上的寒暄而已。我觉得我们之间有一块长长的荒地，把我们隔离。**stretching**：伸展。

both of us：此三词略有微疵。因为前面说的是 my friends；但是 both of us 应该是我和我的朋友（friend，单数）。代词所指不明。**arid**：干燥不毛的。**springs**：泉水，甘泉（即精神上的生机）。**nourished**：滋养。found them dry 的 them 代 springs。

connected to one's core：和自己的灵魂有联系；有自己的精神生活，不单是追逐声色货利。此句的主句中的动词 is 置于主语 one 之前。在前面有 only when 所引导的状语从句时，主句的倒装句法是很常见的。I am beginning to discover 是插入语句。

末句再说明 the core，那就是内心的甘泉，它是在寂寞之中最容易（best）被你重新发现的。

Invite

邀舞

John O'Hara（1905—1970）

约翰·奥哈拉生于美国宾夕法尼亚州的波茨维尔。他是写实派小说家，描写美国各阶层人物，甚为生动。电影《孽海长恨》(*Ten North Frederick*, Gary Cooper 主演)，就是根据他的一部得奖的长篇小说改编的。另一部电影《酒绿灯红》(*Pal Joey*, Frank Sinatra 主演)，也是根据他的若干篇小说改编的。

他的英文和前面所介绍的文章不同。他不走细腻婉约、精致典雅的一路，他最能模仿美国人的说话，因此文章里面俚语、俗话很多，句子也常常不合文法。但是他的文章读起来有一种自然粗犷之劲。

本文选自《奥哈拉短篇杰作集》(*The Great Short Stories of John O'Hara*)，是美国中西部的一个大学生写给东部一个女友的一封信，请她来参加舞会。里面略有故事，这里均删去。奥哈拉模仿美国大学生写作的笔调，值得一读；读者可以知道一般美国学生所写的是什么样的英文。再则，也可从里面约略知道美国大学生的生活。

[1]

Dear Betty:

I debated within myself a long time whether to call you Betty, not that I didn't call you Betty last summer and you me Harry, but as neither of us kept our promise to write I was not sure whether we should return to the formal basis.

[注]

中国人写这封信的时候,往往会在开头加这几个词:"当我提起笔来的时候。"这里没有用这几个词,可是意思已经包含在内了。

debated within myself:自己跟自己辩论,无法决定。**call you Betty**:叫人家的名字,而不称其姓(Miss so-and-so),这是熟朋友间的称呼法。写信的人和其女友已久无往来,也许应该客气一点,不直呼其名。

last summer:上一次的夏天。假如是秋季冬季写的,那就是今年夏天;假如是在春季夏季写的,那就是去年的夏天。这里恐怕是去年的夏天。去年夏天,我们一起玩得很好,那时我叫你Betty,你叫我Harry。我现在提起笔来,不能决定是否应该用客气的称呼,并不是因为过去我们没有好过,而是因为我们疏远已久了。

you me Harry 仿前面的 I didn't call you Betty。

kept our promise:我们分手之时,相约常常通信,但是我们都没有守约。

the formal basis:形式的(或客气的)基础(或原则)。因为我们疏远已久,我不知道我们应否回复到过去那种客气的来往的情形。

[2]

Well, how are you liking it at Smith? I hope better than you did freshman year. Remember I told last summer how you would like it better when you were a sophomore? Personally I did not mind freshman year so much. I made a lot of new acquaintances and friends freshman year and although some of them have not lasted, still some of them have, and now that I am an upperclassman I am satisfied to have my own circle of friends, some of them in the fraternity but some not, I am not narrow about fraternity stuff. Just because a fellow I like happened to go Phi Psi and I went Delt does not mean I have to hate him. That stuff went out years ago. In fact my father was not a Delt. When he was here he was a Tau Phi Alpha. When I came here he told me I could go anything I please."Any crowd that will have you, "he said humorously. I think that is the right attitude and if my son comes here he can go any fraternity he wants, preferably Delt because we have always had a good well-rounded house, not too many athletes and not too many honor students and not too many playboys. Three years ago we won the Heffelberger Cup, emblematic of having the highest scholastic average of any fraternity house on the campus, and last year we had captain of baseball, three Phi Betes, two guys that just missed Phi Bete, chairman of the junior Prom, and also were runners-up in inter fraternity tennis. So you see we have a well-rounded house with varied interests. We also have some wealthy alumni. At all our big football games you ought to see the Lincolns and Cadillacs parked in the driveway. One of the alumni from Lake Forest has a Rolls but he never brings it to the games.

[注]

Smith即Smith College,是美国东部的一所贵族化女子大学。男孩子是在美国中西部(芝加哥附近)一所大学里读书,看后文便知。like it中的it应该是代替life。

第二句话很简我希望你现在应该比你去年(读大学一年级的时候)多喜欢一点Smith的生活。去年夏天我们相聚的时候,你说过你不大喜欢那里的生活,那时我就说过,到你大学二年级(sophomore)的时候,你好感就会增加了。

did not mind：不在乎,不觉其生疏或枯燥。

freshman year应该是名词,但作者拿这两个词和last summer一样,当作副词用。第一处是better than you did (like it) freshman year,另一处是 made ... friends freshman year。

some of them：大学一年级所交的朋友,有几个不能保持友谊;有几个现在还是朋友。**lasted**：持续。

upperclassman：高年级学生。**fraternity**：兄弟会。兄弟会是美国多数大学生活中很重要的一部分。兄弟会自备宿舍,常常是一座漂亮的小洋房。会员住在里面,吃也在里面。兄弟会的名字大多是用希腊字母起名,希腊字母常常又是一句希腊文格言几个词开头的字母。各兄弟会之间在学业等方面竞争颇烈。

narrow：气量狭仄。**fraternity stuff**：兄弟会"那一套"。气量狭小的人不喜结交本会以外的朋友。

Phi Psi：两个希腊字母(i 读长音),是某一兄弟会。Delt 是希腊字母 Delta 的简称,是另一兄弟会。我的一个朋友 (a fellow I like) 恰巧加入了某会,而我入的是 Delta 会,我并不因此一定就要恨他,我们仍旧可以做朋友。

加入某某会,动词用 go：go Phi Psi, went Delt, 这是值得注意的。

that stuff：兄弟会之间互相仇视的那一套,好多年前就不存在了。

my father：美国习俗,父亲读什么大学,儿子也读什么大学,父亲加入某兄弟会,儿子也加入该兄弟会。

Delta 的会员,简捷当地称为 Delt；Tau Phi Alpha（另一个会）的会员,就是

a Tau Phi Alpha.

go anything I please：爱加入什么会，就加入什么会。go 的用法见前。

加入兄弟会，也不容易。兄弟会有拒绝申请者入会之权。父亲恐怕我在大学里不受人欢迎，因此幽默地说：哪一家会（any crowd）要收容你，你就去好了。你不一定要加入我的 Tau Phi Alpha 的。

我父亲既如此开明，我一旦有了孩子，我也将让他自由选择。最好（preferably）当然还是 Delta，因为几十年来（或一百多年来），我们这个会一直人才平均发展。**well-rounded**：面面都能顾到。**house**：指宿舍里所住的人。**athletes**：运动员。**honor students**：学业成绩卓异的学生。**playboys**：花花公子。

Heffelberger Cup：这个人所捐的银杯。**emblematic of**：（这只杯子）表示在全校（on the campus）各兄弟会中，我们这一会的会员学业成绩总平均最高。

Phi Bete：想是 Phi Beta Kappa 的简称。Phi Beta Kappa 是美国全国各大学间的优秀学生联谊会。大学高班生成绩优异的，得被选入会，会员得金钥匙一枚。金钥匙可以终身佩带，那就是说，在大学里得到好分数，这个荣誉是可以终身保持的。Phi Beta Kappa 似乎不备宿舍。因此各兄弟会之间也互相竞争，会员能被选入 Phi Beta Kappa，也是该兄弟会的光荣。Phi Beta Kappa 是一句希腊格言："哲学指导人生"三个词的起首的字母。

two guys：（美国俚语）：两个"家伙"。**just missed**：差一点拿到。**Prom**：（美国大学俚语）舞会。**Junior Prom**：大学三年级学生欢送大学四年级学生的盛大舞会，通常于暑期大考前举行。

runner-up：（运动会的）第二名。多数是 runners-up。**inter fraternity tennis**：各兄弟会之间的网球比赛。

varied interests：多方面的兴趣。

alumni：校友（复数）。单数是 alumnus。

Lincoln 和 Cadillac 都是美国高级汽车的牌子。**parked**：停放（汽车）。**driveway**：汽车道。

Rolls 即 Rolls Royce，是英国高级汽车的牌子，比 Lincoln, Cadillac 还要华贵，那个人不好意思坐下来看球赛。

这个兄弟会会员人才济济，校友中还有阔人。希望这位 Betty 小姐听见了心动，远道赶来参加舞会。

[3]

Well, I guess all this fraternity stuff doesn't mean very much to you, being an Eastern girl, but I just thought I would tell you a few things as I wanted to ask you if you could come out here for Junior Prom, as my guest. I know what you will think, too far. Well, it is pretty far but not if you come by plane. If you flew to Chicago I could meet you there in my car and it is only a pleasant drive from Chicago. We would be here in plenty of time for the tea dance Friday afternoon. (I hope your folks have no objection to flying.)

[注]

an Eastern girl：东部学校里的小姐。美国东部学校似乎不大注重兄弟会（或姊妹会）。例如哈佛和耶鲁两大学的本科学生，也像英国牛津、剑桥那样，住在不同的 colleges 里面，这个 college 不像中国的 College of Arts，College of Science 那样以学科来分；它主要是指一座宿舍，各 college 的学生在导师的训导之下，过有益身心的团体生活。

what you will think：我知道你有什么推托了——路太远了，怎么好来呢？

pretty far：路是很远（pretty 是副词）。但是你若坐飞机来，就不远了。

if you flew：此句为虚拟式。

tea dance：茶舞（非正式的）。

your folks：你家里人。

[4]

As to where you would stay while here you would stay at the Kappa house (Kappa Kappa Gamma). That is the best sorority on the campus and is just around the corner literally from our house. We and the Kappas have an arrangement that the men the Kappas bring to Prom stay at our house and the women we bring stay at the Kappa house. You would like the Kappas. A lot of them get their clothes in the East and have their own cars. Some of the other sororities call the Kappas a hi-hat crowd but I don't think that is fair. Several times during the year we have joint dances, informals, with the Kappas and you would not want to meet a nicer crowd.

[注]

while here：当你在这儿的时候。**would stay**（虚拟式）：女朋友来不来还没一定。

sorority：姊妹会，女学生所组织的。自备宿舍与兄弟会相仿。**Kappa Kappa Gamma**：三个希腊字母，是某一姊妹会之名。简称 Kappa，会员也叫 Kappa，复数是 Kappas。**around the corner**：在附近转角处。美国人说话中常说 just around the corner，表示"就在附近"。但是有时候言过其实，并不很近的地方也可以说它是 just around the corner。**literally**：照字面直解地，并不言过其实地。说是 just around the corner，我的意思就是"在附近转角处"。

arrangement：协定。**the women we bring**：women 这个词在美国大学里用得较广，女生常被称为 women。一个人只要不是 child（此词不分男女性），总可以说是 man 或 woman。

clothes in the East：东部的服饰趣味比较高雅。美国男人的西装也以东部八大学（所谓"常春藤联盟"〈Ivy League〉学生所穿的最为标准。

hi-hat：势利眼的。美国近来常有人把 high 写作 hi。**crowd**：此词不单是"群众"，亦有"团体"之意。本文前文有 Any crowd that will have you 之句。

joint dances：联合舞会（他的兄弟会和她们的姊妹会）。

informals 想是和 dances 同位；这种舞会是非正式的。

nicer：注意它的比较级。该姊妹会的人太好了，你不再想认识"更好"的人了。nice 除了"高贵讲究"之外，也有对人和蔼可亲之意。

[5]

Well, how's about it? You have plenty of time to think it over and I wish you would let me know the minute you decide. You could be back in Northampton Sunday night I believe. They are trying very hard to get Tommy Dorsey for Prom. It will be announced next week. The program is tea dances Friday afternoon and joint dinner at our house (Kappas and their guests and our guests and we). There be a basketball game that night but we can miss that as it is only a freshman game. There is also a Glee Club concert before Prom and that may be good. Then Prom until four and then breakfast party at the Kappa house. The next day (Saturday) there is nothing special doing till the tea dances when every house has open house and then Buffet supper at the Kappa house.

After that the 'varsity basketball game and after the game informal dancing at the gym. It has to be informal as there is a faculty rule that dancing has to end at 12 midnight Saturday night.

[注]

the minute you decide：一有决定，烦请即刻赐示。

Northampton：在马萨诸塞州，即该女生的 Smith College 所在地。

they：代名词所指不明（应该是舞会主办人）。语法学家认为是错误的，但这种说法很常听到。**Tommy Dorsey**：美国极有名的爵士乐队之领队。大学里的 Junior Prom 是件大事，他们不惜重金聘请有名乐队。

our guests and we：这里有四种人，自己（we）放在最后，这是习惯用法。

there be：be 的用法在这里很怪，恐怕不能以语法说明。我们只当它是 will be 或 is 可也。

miss that：不去看，大学一年级球队，无甚精彩。

Glee Club：歌咏团。**concert**：音乐会。

Prom until four：这是主要节目正式舞会，跳到天亮四点。

every house：指那些兄弟会，姊妹会。**open house**：欢迎来宾参加。那个 has 用得很怪。茶舞恐怕就在各兄弟会跳，Prom 悬在大地方举行的。

Buffet supper：自助餐（非正式的）。

'varsity basketball game：大学篮球比赛。'varsity 即 university，此词美国大学里很常用。**gym**：健身房。健身房是大地方，应该又是个大规模的舞会了，但是这还得是非正式的。原因是学校规则（faculty rule）不让他们跳通宵。**12 midnight**：午夜十二点。

[6]

You would only have to bring one evening dress that is for Prom. If you could stay over Sunday afternoon and evening there is a roadhouse about twenty miles from here that used to be a country club and is very nice. We usually go there Sunday afternoon when we have dates. It is just a pleasant drive and if you have never seen the farming country out here it might prove interesting to an Easterner.

[注]

would 还是虚拟式，因为她来不来还没有决定。

only have to：只要。**evening dress**：正式晚礼服。

roadhouse：公路旁的小酒店，也有舞厅设备。**country club**：乡下总会。那里除了饮食跳舞之外，还可打高尔夫、网球、骑马、游泳等。以前是俱乐部，现在改成酒店了。

dates：男女间的相约出游。

[7]

Well, I have sketched the Prom week-end for you and I hope it sounds interesting. If you would come it would be the first time one of our crowd has had a girl from so far East, and we would go to town showing you a good time.

So come on and let us show you that all the fun is not at Yale and Princeton and those places. I have a lot of things to talk about in person but that will have to wait.

[注]

sketched：简略描写。

one of our crowd：我们兄弟会里的人。**so far East**：从东方老远地请一个女朋友跳舞，我们兄弟会中还没有过呢。

town：学校之外，城里也可以去玩玩。

fun：热闹，有趣。all 这样用在英文里是普通的，但是和中国人想法不同。莎士比亚有句：

All that glitters is not gold. 此句之意是"璀璨者非皆黄金"，并不是说"凡是发金光的，都不是黄金"。

这里的 all 如放在稍后，fun is not all at Yale and ...（并不是只在 Yale 等等学校里，才有热闹好玩的事），意思较说得通。这里 all 放在前面，这是英文习惯用法，意思和 all 放到后面去是一样的。

in person：当面（谈）。

that：那件事（to talk）非得等你来了再说了。

Captain Carlsen

卡尔逊船长

Thomas Whiteside (1918—1997)

本文原载 1958 年 12 月 13 日 *The New Yorker*。*The New Yorker* 有一栏"人物小传",叫作 Profiles,所收的人物种类繁多,是很有兴趣的读物。*The New Yorker* 的文章大多写得都很工整典雅。前文也曾介绍过。本文作者怀特赛德所描写的卡尔逊船长是个航海英雄,他与暴风雨搏斗的事迹,可歌可泣。原文很长,这里只短短地节录了几段。因为文章篇幅长,原文的句子也都很长,这里也已缩短了很多,短文章里用长句子是很别扭的。

[1]

Of all the winter storms to sweep the North Atlantic in recent years, few are more sorely remembered by seafaring people and the inhabitants of many European coastal areas than the gales that prevailed over the eastern part of the ocean during the last few days of 1951. The area of disturbance extended from Scandinavia to the Iberian Peninsula, and even into North Africa, and the storms stretched westward into the ocean for several hundred miles.

[注]

sweep:吹过。这词隐含风的力量。**sorely remembered**:痛苦地记得。**seafaring people**:出海航行的人。**coastal areas**:海岸区域。**gales**:强风(速度约每小时 25

海里里至 75 海里）。**prevailed**：（在那个地方）发威。

首句的主要结构是 few are more sorely remembered ... than ...。历年冬季的暴风之中，很少有一次比得上那一年的。

area of disturbance：狂风所及之区。**Iberian Peninsula**：西班牙和葡萄牙所在之半岛。
stretched westward：狂风的影响范围往西伸展到大西洋中间去。

[2]

Of all the manifold adversities brought on by the storms, none attracted such intense interest here and throughout the world as the plight of a United States freighter named the *Flying Enterprise*. The American public began to hear about the *Flying Enterprise* on December 29th, when press dispatches from Europe reported that she was encountering severe hurricane conditions some three hundred and thirty miles southwest of Cape Clear, on the southern tip of Ireland, and that her situation was grave.

[注]

第一段第一句的句法是，of all the ... few are more ... than ...。现在第二段第一句的句法又是 of all the ... none attracted such ... as ...，这样似乎句法变化太少。但是原文的第一段很长，隔了很久，再出现一句结构相类似的句子，未足为病。

manifold adversities：多种的灾祸。**bring (brought) on**：引起。**intense interest**：强烈的兴趣。**here**：在美国。**plight**：（困难的）处境。**freighter**：货船。

press dispatches：新闻界的电讯。**she**：船用女性代名词。**hurricane**：比 gale 更强的风。此词的狭义是指从西印度群岛吹向美国东海岸的飓风。东大西洋的风实际上并不是 hurricane，但是情形已很类似。所以说这艘船"遭遇到类似飓风的情形"。**some**：大约。**tip**：尖端。

[3]

By the following day, the storms were at their worst over most of the eastern Atlantic, and it became apparent that the gravity of the freighter's position had deepened into desperation. While these events were dramatic, what really focused attention on the *Flying Enterprise* was the news that her captain had chosen to remain aboard after ordering everybody else off, and that he was sticking to his ship with the expressed determination to keep command of her as long as she remained afloat, or at least, a tug took her safely in tow. The name of the captain was Henrik Kurt Carlsen — a name that was to become familiar throughout the world over the next two weeks. The story of Carlsen's unremitting effort to save the *Flying Enterprise* relayed to the public in day-by-day installments in the press and over the air, was enough to excite anybody's imagination.

[注]

at their worst：凶恶到极点。这种习语很有用，如：he is at his best（表现得特别出色，正在最佳状态）。不用 best, worst, 而用其它形容词的最高级的形式亦可。

上段说 the situation was grave, 这是已经够严重的了。现在更进一步，于是说 the gravity ... had deepened into desperation。**desperation**：绝望。本来用形容词 grave, 现在改用抽象名词 gravity；此句最好的词是动词 deepen, 它把两个抽象名词连接得很稳。普通中国学生最觉得难用恐怕是抽象名词，因为一句的主语或宾语若是抽象名词，它前后的动词也非得慎加挑选不可。这句若改成 the situation had become desperate, 亦无不可。但是如把 grave 转化成为 gravity, 再使它 deepened into desperation, 这样读者也得到一种"思想条理清楚"之乐。

dramatic：戏剧性，紧张动人。原文所举的事情很多，故 these events 所指的很清楚。这里把那些事情都省略了，这两个词稍觉模糊。

focus attention on：使注意力集中于。**chosen**：自愿（善恶或勇怯间的选择）。**aboard**：在船上。**ordering ... off**：命令余人下船。

sticking to：坚守。

expressed determination：明白表示的决心。

remained：此词在本句中见了两次。remained aboard 与 remained afloat（还能浮在水面，不往下沉）。remain 和 be, become 等相仿，是系动词（linking verb），不过它所表示的是动词的"持续式"（durative aspect）——所说的情形要维持一个时候。**to keep command of the ship**：（继续指挥全船）也是表示"持续式"的。

tug：拖大船的小轮（马力甚大）。**take her in tow**：把这条船拖走。

unremitting effort：不懈的努力。**relayed**：传达。**installments**：一天报告一段的"段"。**over the air**：广播。

[4]

It was a drama that had all but pushed the war in Korea off the front pages for almost a fortnight, and public sympathy for Carlsen over the loss of his ship was exceeded only by the universally expressed admiration for his courage and resourcefulness in attempting to save her. New York gave him an enthusiastic ticker-tape reception, and medals and citations for bravery were pressed upon him by Congress and the governments of many other countries. All sorts of commercial offers were pressed upon him, too, and if he had accepted them, he would have become wealthy overnight. But Carlsen did not accept them; he refused to cash in on his popularity. "I only did my duty as a simple seaman," he explained. He seemed like a hero from another time.

[注]

all but = almost。**pushed ... off the front pages**：卡尔逊的事，占满了报纸第一版，反而把新闻几乎给"挤"走了。

两个抽象名词给一个动词连接起来，成一句子，前面已经说过，这里又是一个例子：public sympathy ... was exceeded by the ... admiration ...，此句的妙处也在动词（**exceeded**：超过）。卡尔逊船长的船终于沉海，全世界的人都对他同情得不得了。这种同情之大，似乎没有东西可以超过它了。但是有一样东西可以超过它，那就是举世所表示的对他的钦仰（admiration）。他努力救船，人们佩服他的勇气，也佩服他的智谋（resourcefulness）。

reception：欢迎。**ticker-tape**：电报纸带。英雄凯旋归来时，市民纷纷以彩色纸带向他抛掷。

citations for bravery：褒扬忠勇之辞，褒状。

pressed upon him：硬塞给他；他不要，也得要。

commercial offers：商业活动邀请，如请他代言宣传某种商品等。

pressed upon him 连用两次，第二次在后面加了一个 too。

overnight：一夜之间（顿成暴富）。

his popularity：他的"风头"。**cash in on**：利用之以赚钱。

a hero from another time：尽职而不求名利，实有"古风"。

Moscow, 1918
一九一八年的莫斯科

George F. Kennan（1904—2005）

本文作者凯南是美国的"俄国通"。他曾任美国驻苏联大使（1952—1953），卸任后曾在普林斯顿大学高级研究院及英国牛津大学任教。

这样一个兼具教授和外交家双重身份的特殊人才，同时还写得一手极漂亮的英文。下面所选的两段文章采自他的巨著《一九一七至一九二〇年间美苏关系考》(*American-Soviet Relations in 1917-1920*. Vol. II. *The Decision to Intervene*. 1958 年初版) 第二册的"前言"(Prologue)。读者将会发现：凯南教授对于炼字铸句，花了极大的苦心。他的目的——也是一切写描写文章的人的目的——是要使他所描写的东西，生动地出现在读者的耳目之前。凯南教授这部巨著共 3 厚册，所搜史料极为丰富，他于辛勤研究之余，竟有余力大写其文章。其人趣味之高雅、精力之充沛也自值得吾人钦佩的了。

[1]

In Moscow, by late March, all was confusion, heterogeny, and motion. The move of the government from Petrograd to Moscow was now in progress. Almost hourly the overloaded trains lumbered into the Moscow yards — strings of battered, befouled passenger cars, bursting with human bodies, or open freight cars piled high with filing cases and office equipment — and disgorged their loads into the prevailing chaos. The newspaper, carrying daily lists of the new Moscow addresses of government bureaus, gave a certain impression of order and purpose; but the reality was different: cavernous, unheated halls, full of the wrong packing cases, the unremoved belongings of the evicted last tenants, broken telephone wires, shattered windowpanes, litter, filth, and distracted people in fur coats and muddy boots, fumbling around in the confusion. Only slowly, with a million creaks and interruptions, did the governmental machinery of the Russian state install itself and come into some sort of ordered motion in the new capital.

[注]

首二句比较简短，只是用来引人入胜。第三句以后，才入文章的"胜境"。

第一句，连用三个抽象名词，亦足效法。照一般中国人思想习惯，这三个词应该是形容词的。形容词通常分量较名词为轻，因为形容词是依附名词而存在的。这里这三个抽象名词，站得很稳，好像大门上的柱子。进了大门，略走一步，便五花八门令人目不暇接了。

heterogeny 是 homogeneity 的反义词，意为"杂乱"。1918 年 3 月下旬，莫斯科的一切都是混乱、杂乱，一切都在动。

the move：俄国从圣彼得堡（俄国对德宣战后，改称 Petrograd，因为原来的名字，有点德文意味）迁都莫斯科。**in progress**：在进行中。

第三句只是说：火车不断地把人和家具搬运到莫斯科去。但是作者用了一种很不平凡的说法。

hourly：每小时（都有火车进站）。**overloaded**：装载过重的。这个形容词一用，trains 这个平凡的词就开始显出精神。**lumbered**：笨重东西的行动，这里指的是负荷过重的火车的行动。**yards**：火车站的火车停车处。

写到这里，作者的灵感忽被点燃。他用了 overloaded 和 lumbered 二词，把那火车的样子，已经略事描写了。但是他觉得不够，于是着手详写。

他说进站的火车有两种，一种是客车，一种是货车。客车怎么样呢？一串一串的（**strings**：按 train 之意义应该是"列车"）破旧的（battered）污秽的（befouled）的客车。battered 和 befouled 二词都是过去分词，不是纯粹形容词：这表示客车原来也完好洁净，后来给人打坏弄脏的。

open freight cars：敞篷货车。**piled**（过去分词）：堆得（高高的）。**filing cases**：

档案柜子。office equipment 办公室用具。有了这些东西，就像迁都了。

用了这几个词，辞藻已甚华丽，但是作者意兴未尽。前面只说"开进莫斯科车站"，这个说法似乎犹嫌平泛，不见精彩。这句主要动词有两个，一个是 lumbered；句子到了 office equipment 要结束本来也可以了，但是作者又想出了一个动词 **disgorged**。disgorged 的原意是"把吃进去的东西吐出来"。这些人和家具在圣彼得堡上车，到了莫斯科要下车；上了车，又下车，好像火车吃了东西再吐掉似的。所以此词用得很妙。

loads：所负荷之物，指那些人和家具。

吐，吐到哪儿去呢？当然是吐给莫斯科。莫斯科当时的情形，已见于第一句的三个词：confusion，heterogeny and motion。词汇量狭小或懒于思索的作者，想出了这么三个词，已经心满意足，再也想不出别的词来了。但是凯南教授又用了个新说辞 **prevailing chaos**：把车上的人物投入（当时莫斯科的）一片混乱之中。

daily lists：每天发表的名单。某政府衙门（government bureau）原址为圣彼得堡某地，新址为莫斯科某地。

gave a certain impression of：人们看来，似乎得到某种印象，做事有秩序（order）有目的（purpose）的印象。事实则不然。

本句的后半部是描写那些新迁衙门的混乱之状。那些新迁衙门的大厅，阴森如鬼域（cavernous），未装御寒设备（unheated），里面堆满了大件木箱（packing cases），这种木箱不是现成木箱，临时用木板钉成的），可是木箱还常常送错了地方，甲部的可能送到乙部，所以说是 wrong packing cases。原来住户（last tenants）虽已被逐出（evicted），但是他们的东西（belongings），也有尚未搬出（unremoved）的，那些东西就和新来的东西堆在一起。

新迁衙门的厅屋如此，其电话线则不通，其玻璃窗则破碎（shattered windowpanes），加上乱放的杂物（litter）和垃圾（filth），里面的人则形同疯狂（distracted），身上穿了皮大衣（莫斯科三月间还是冷，所以办公室如不 heated 是很可怕的），脚上是泥污的皮靴（大约和街上的冰雪有关）。乱七八糟地在里面乱扒乱摸（fumbling）。

秩序后来还是渐渐恢复了，但那是慢慢来的。出了一百万次的岔子（**creaks**：刺耳的声音），事情也曾经耽搁了（interruptions）一百万次，俄国（the Russian state）的政府机构（governmental machinery）方才建立起来（did ... install itself）。

既然政府比作一部机器（machinery），机器装置（install）了不够，还得要开动。所以后面说"... come into some sort of ordered motion."（能够相当有条有理地转动）。前面的 creaks 和 interruptions 都是和 machinery 有关的。机器转得顺利，不会发怪声，转动不会中辍。现在屡发怪声，屡次停转，其"政府机构"的进行情形可想。
the new capital = Moscow.

[2]

The cozy, comfortable, old-Russian city on the banks of the Moskva was not set up to absorb at once all the shocks of revolution and the invasion of new bodies and functions occasioned by the arrival of the government from Petrograd. Overcrowded and overwhelmed, it resembled a vast, disturbed ant hill. All day long the flood of brown-black garbed humanity — endless variations of khaki intermingled with the somber winter dress of the civilian — flowed through the premises and thoroughfares of the city, inundating the public places, spilling out from the narrow sidewalks into the streets where the snow had now been pressed into thick coatings of blackish ice. People clung in dense swaying masses, like clusters of insects, to the platforms and footrails of the battered streetcar trains, groaning and jangling their way through the confusion.

[注]

莫斯科本来是个闲适（cozy）舒服的旧城，本来容纳不下这许多衙门和人。这里没有用 Moscow，而用 old-Russian city on the banks（岸）of the Moskva（河名）。作者也没有说"容纳不下这许多衙门和人"，而说：莫斯科那样的城，不是一下子（at once）可以吸收（absorb）革命的震动，也不是一下子可以收 这么多新迁来的衙门机关。

invasion：侵入（某地）。body 此词有多种解释，这里的 bodies 指的是"机关"，functions 是机关的"公务"（公务员是 functionary）。新的机关和新的公务，侵入了莫斯科，所以致此者（occasioned by），是因为政府迁来了。

莫斯科人口大增（overcrowded），而且挤得喘不过气来（overwhelmed），它就像一只大蚂蚁巢（有几种蚂蚁聚土为城，犹如山状，其巢称为 ant hill），蚂蚁巢里虽然热闹，但不一定混乱。作者用了这个譬喻，觉得不十分妥帖，赶快加上一个形容词 disturbed 这一下这个譬喻就十全十美了。那是搅乱了的大蚂蚁巢。

下一句描写莫斯科的人。那些穿褐黑色衣服的"人类"（**brown-black garbed humanity**：颜色一经描写，人和蚂蚁之间的距离，似乎更形缩短了），像潮水似的 (flood)，流过了房屋（premises），流过了马路（thoroughfares）。作者既然把人比作了水，接着的一个动词，两个现在分词都是和水有关系的，动词 flowed 是水之流，inundating 是水之泛滥，spilling 是水之泼溅。人潮淹满了公共地区，从狭仄（作者处处不忘描写，这个 narrow 一用，读者对于当时的莫斯科可以有更清晰的印象）的人行道上"泼"到街道上来。

一说到街道，作者又要描写了。那时是三月下旬，积雪尚未全融，但是雪给人和车辆一压（pressed），压成了厚厚的暗黑色的冰层。**coatings**：表面的皮或"衣"（如药丸外面的"糖衣"）。冰层底下，恐怕还有雪，所以 coatings 此词用得很是妥贴。

这样描写，总算有声有色了。但是本句中两条横线之间，对于那些穿褐黑色衣服的人，还有进一步的描写。那些人穿的是卡其布（khaki），卡其布的种类无限（endless vacations），不胜枚举；这是军人和公务员的制服，制服又和平民百姓的深暗色的冬服混在一起（intermingled）。**the Russian civilian**：单数名词前面用冠词 the，可以代表"全体"，这在文法书上是讲到的。例如：The dog is a faithful animal.

莫斯科那时已有电车（**streetcar; streetcar trains**：电车附挂拖车的），电车本来也许还算宽敞舒适，但是现在也挤坏了。

末句结构主要关键是 clung ... to，这两个词给很多词分隔开来，乍一看也许不容易看出来。

clung 是"紧附"；照《简明牛津词典》的解释，不论是"黏住、吸住、抓住、抱住"，都是 cling。电车里太挤，乘客成为"紧紧地一团"(dense...masses)，而且站立不稳，摇摇摆摆的(swaying)，就像一簇一簇的昆虫似的。电车跟火车一样，是打瘪撞坏(battered)了的，那些人紧紧的贴住电车上月台（platform）司机所站之处和座位前放脚的栏杆（footrails），电车走的时候嗯嗯（groaning）地发声，好像不胜负载之苦，铃声叮当（jangling），在混乱的莫斯科市上行驶。

图书在版编目（CIP）数据

现代英文选评注 / 夏济安著. -- 北京：
北京联合出版公司, 2016.6（2019.11重印）
　　ISBN 978-7-5502-7752-6

　　Ⅰ.①现… Ⅱ.①夏… Ⅲ.①英语—语言读物
Ⅳ.① H319.4

中国版本图书馆CIP数据核字（2016）第107162号

现代英文选评注

著　　者：夏济安
修　　订：Stevens Powell
　　　　　陈　雨
封面题签：李爱华
特约编辑：刘智博
责任编辑：王　巍

北京联合出版公司出版
（北京市西城区德外大街83号楼9层　100088）
天津东辰丰彩印刷有限公司印刷　新华书店经销
字数522千字　720毫米×1030毫米　1/16　29印张
2016年8月第1版　2019年11月第2次印刷
ISBN 978-7-5502-7752-6
定价：42.80元

后浪出版咨询(北京)有限责任公司 常年法律顾问：北京大成律师事务所
周天晖 copyright@hinabook.com
未经许可，不得以任何方式复制或抄袭本书部分或全部内容
版权所有，侵权必究
本书若有印装质量问题，请与本公司图书销售中心联系调换。电话：010-64010019